human resource development

development

practice

human resource development

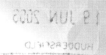

principles and practice

BRIAN L. DELAHAYE

WILEY

John Wiley & Sons Australia, Ltd

First published 2000 by
John Wiley & Sons Australia, Ltd
33 Park Road, Milton, Qld 4064

Offices also in Sydney and Melbourne

Typeset in 10.5/12 pt Berkeley

National Library of Australia
Cataloguing-in-Publication data

Delahaye, Brian L., 1946–
    Human resource development: principles and practice.

    Includes index.
    ISBN 0 471 34128 2

    1. Manpower planning. 2. Career development.
    3. Human capital — Management. I. Title.

658.3

Cover photograph: The Image Bank/Steven Hunt

Image of autumn leaves used throughout:
© 1994 PhotoDisc Inc.

Printed in Singapore by
Markono Print Media Pte Ltd

10 9 8 7 6 5 4

Every effort has been made to trace the ownership of
copyright material. Information that will enable the
publisher to rectify any error or omission in
subsequent editions will be welcome. In such cases
please contact the Permissions Section of
John Wiley & Sons Australia, Ltd who will
arrange for payment of the usual fee.

Dedication

Dedicated to my parents, Len and Evelyn
— true models of courage and caring

CONTENTS

PREFACE

My journey in writing this book had its genesis in two motivational influences. Firstly, I had been searching for a textbook in human resource development that combined both theory and practice. Adult learners with whom I had contact expressed frustration at available texts which described various theories but gave no indication of how those theories could be used in practice. The second influence came from my personal desire to move more fully into the 'newer' concepts of knowledge management. While I found these 'newer' concepts refreshing and exciting, I felt a need to record my 25-plus years of knowledge and experience with the conventional paradigms — not a very modest inspiration, but surprisingly strong just the same. So my journey started by concentrating solely on the four stages of HRD — the familiar 'investigate, design, implement and evaluate'. To my surprise, and undoubtedly designed by a higher being to bring me down from my immodest perch of self-importance, I found that I could not forget the 'newer' concepts nor divorce the conventional paradigms from them. So my journey became not so much a recording of my knowledge of conventional paradigms as yet another exciting, challenging and traumatic learning experience on my road to becoming a better adult educator. Having discussed the knowledge creation process of externalisation in the first chapter, time and again I had to acknowledge the irony of writing that externalisation is a difficult and energy-draining process while continually experiencing these challenges as I struggled to convert my tacit knowledge into its explicit form. So a lot of my experience in writing this book was about writing to adult learners while being an adult learner. This book, then, has been the marriage of two personal ideals — converting theory into practice and uniting the conventional paradigms of HRD with the new concepts of the management of knowledge.

An endeavour such as writing this book is not carried out in isolation. Firstly, my thanks go to all the adult learners who have entrusted me to help with their development. It has been a wonderful experience for me and I trust that I have the ability and humility to continue to learn what you teach me. I have also been fortunate to be surrounded by generous colleagues who willingly gave of their time and provided honest, accurate and fertile feedback. In particular, my thanks go to Dr Lisa Ehrich, Ms Erica French, Mr Malcolm Lewis, Dr Juanita Muller, Ms Ravinder Sidhu and especially to Dr Jennifer Pierce and Warrant Officer Neil Fisher. My thanks also to the unknown referees appointed by the publisher. Every author should be blessed with such a supportive, creative and professional publishing editor as Ms Judith Fox of John Wiley and Sons Australia, Ltd. Judith, I do not know what I would have done without you and the Editorial and Production team at Wiley Australia. Last but certainly not least, I acknowledge the quiet and enduring support of my loving life partner and wife, Yvonne — truly you are the wind beneath my wings.

While I have been given such constructive support and advice, I take full responsibility for any errors or misinterpretations that may occur in this book. I take some solace from Malcolm Knowles who advised, in his autobiography, that writers set down their words and ideas as they understand them at the moment. He also advised that, if future experience brings new understandings, writers should stand up for their right to change their minds. As my learning journey to become a better adult educator continues, I expect that my mind will be changed on a variety of issues.

Brian Delahaye, 2000

Introduction to HRD

CHAPTER OBJECTIVES

At the end of this chapter you should be able to:

1 describe the negative effects of management re-engineering on organisations

2 explain why knowledge is a unique resource

3 describe how the adult learning theories underpin human resource development

4 discuss the effects of the management of diversity and the functions of human resource management on HRD

5 explain how the theories of the creation of knowledge and the new management theories expand the definition of HRD.

This chapter begins by emphasising the rapid and continuous change that organisations now face. One response to this change has been **management re-engineering**. Management re-engineering has included such tactics as downsizing, outsourcing, creating flatter structures and cost cutting. Unfortunately, costs cannot be saved — they can only be transferred to another part of the system. Some of the negative effects of the cost-saving syndrome include loss of knowledge, ignoring critical processes and standards, forgetting that loyalty is a two-way street, succumbing to the 'everything is saved' mentality, the anorexic syndrome and the focus on the dollar.

With management re-engineering providing mainly false hopes, the attention of managers and academics is turning to the management of knowledge capital as a more positive response to the challenges of a fast-changing environment. **Knowledge** is a unique resource with three characteristics. Firstly, there is no law of diminishing returns, as the more knowledge is used the more knowledge results. Secondly, knowledge grows from sharing. Thirdly, there is a difference between information and knowledge. **Information** is itself inert but, when accessed and enacted on by an individual, information becomes knowledge. Therefore, organisations must maintain their current knowledge, disseminate specific knowledge to specific parts of the organisation, create new knowledge and 'unlearn' useless knowledge.

The HR developer has a robust role to play in the management of the organisation's knowledge capital. Central to the HR developer's role are the four stages of investigation (where needs are investigated and identified), design (where the aims, objectives and content are examined), implementation (where formal or informal learning activities occur) and evaluation (where the worth of the learning experience is judged). A variety of techniques have been developed to achieve the aims of these four stages. The four stages and their associated techniques are the main focus of this text.

The four stages of investigation, design, implementation and evaluation are informed and supported by a wider context. This context includes the adult learning theories, the management orientation of **diversity** and the human resource management (HRM) functions and the contemporary theories of the creation of knowledge and the new management theories. The adult learning theories are discussed in chapter 2 and concepts such as the principles of learning, instrumental learning, communicative learning and emancipatory learning are examined. The positive **management of diversity** is an important and dominant theme of modern organisations and is discussed in Chapter 3. The HR developer has a major role in mobilising and harnessing the energy of a diverse workforce. **Strategic human resource development planning** (SHRDP) is one of the central functions of HRM and has a significant impact on HRD. HRD is influenced by, and in turn should influence, the SHRDP of the organisation and this concept is discussed in chapter 4.

The four stages of HRD are then discussed in turn. Chapter 5 provides an overview of the **investigation stage**, commonly called the human resource development needs investigation (HRDNI). Specific techniques used in the HRDNI are discussed in the three following chapters. Chapter 6 examines the performance appraisal system which identifies the individual developmental needs of the staff. Chapter 7 discusses the information gathering techniques of interviewing and focus groups as well as approaches to analysing the resulting qualitative data. Chapter 8 then examines the design and use of questionnaires and the analysis of quantitative data. The attention of the text then focuses on the **design stage**.

Chapter 9 describes the two major variables in the design of adult learning experiences — the content to be learned and the learner. Chapter 10 examines other variables in the design process that the HR developer needs to consider. These variables include the strategic orientation of the organisation, organisational culture, key stakeholders and the designer's frame of reference. The chapter also overviews the whole design and discusses the HRD operational plans that need to be documented. The **implementation stage** is then discussed. Chapter 11 examines the structured learning strategies of the skill session, the theory session, the discussion, the case study, the role play and experiential learning. Chapter 12 describes the unstructured learning strategies of contract learning, action learning, change interventions and mentoring. The fourth stage, **evaluation**, is discussed in chapter 13. Ways of assessing learning, including Kirkpatrick's model and Brinkerhoff's model, are explained.

Two new theoretical concepts are examined initially in chapter 13 and then are discussed more fully in chapter 14. The **creation of knowledge** examines the four processes of generating new knowledge from the reflections and thoughts of individuals and groups: externalisation, combination, internalisation and socialisation. These processes differentiate between tacit and explicit knowledge. **Explicit knowledge** is knowledge that can be articulated. **Tacit knowledge** is in the subconscious mind of the individual but is so deep that the individual finds it very difficult to declare. However, it is felt that tacit knowledge plays a significant part in the decision processes of the individual. **Externalisation** occurs when an individual or group allows tacit knowledge to surface in the form of explicit knowledge, usually as part of a reflective activity. **Combination** occurs where the explicit knowledge of one person or group is merged with the explicit knowledge of another person or group. **Internalisation** takes this new explicit knowledge and transfers some of it to the subconscious mind. **Socialisation** is an osmotic process where complex information is transferred between the tacit level of two individuals.

The new management theories recognise that the older paradigms are based on the Newtonian assumptions of rationality and linear logic — any organism or machine can be broken down into its component parts, examined and then put back together, preferably so that it can operate in a more effective and efficient way. These older, conventional management theories — termed **ordinary management** — operate quite successfully under conditions close to certainty. Ordinary management uses negative feedback loops to dampen any variations from the planned standards or activities of the organisation. However, under conditions of far-from-certainty, the management is found wanting. **Extraordinary management**, based on **complexity theory** (a combination of chaos theory and quantum mechanics), is the preferred option for an organisation operating in an environment that is difficult to predict. Extraordinary management is based on values and creativity, relies heavily on the knowledge-creation skills and abilities of individuals, and uses **positive feedback loops** to enhance small variations, thus encouraging creativity. However, rather than an 'either/or' approach, modern organisations rely on both ordinary management and extraordinary management. An organisation can be depicted as consisting of two basic systems — the legitimate system and the shadow system. The **legitimate system** is responsible for the day-to-day activities of the organisation and concentrates on the near, and therefore relatively predictable, future. The legitimate system is best administered by ordinary management and is responsible for the maintenance of the organisation's current knowledge. The **shadow system** imports and creates new knowledge. This provides the organisation with a stockpile of options, based on this new knowledge, that can be used to defend the organisation against the surprises of the future and also to take advantage of any new opportunities that may arise.

This chapter, then, establishes the need for organisations to use the four stages of HRD constructively and sets these four stages within a theoretical context of adult learning, creation of knowledge and the new management theories as well as acknowledging the influence of the organisation's diverse staffing profile and its strategic planning process.

THE BUSINESS ENVIRONMENT

Managers are united on one front at least — they operate in an age of rapid and continuous change. Erudite observers point to many causes (see, for example, Field 1995; Pedler, Burgoyne and Boydell 1997) — the amount of information doubling every 10 years; the increasing impact of technology not just in manufacturing but also in communication and data analysis; the increasing pace of change; the need to improve quality; reduced time frames; a demand for integrated resources; and the need to improve the organisation's image. More recently there has been a new phenomenon — the globalisation of the economy, demanding efficiency as well as the ability to link customers' needs to tailor-made solutions. Where managers and academics alike are floundering is in identifying practical strategies that will predict a sustainable future. Unfortunately, employers as well as staff are paying a heavy price.

a closer look   1.1

Gas blast Esso's fault

by Rachel Hawes

ESSO's failure to train its workers to cope with emergencies left the multinational responsible for the Longford gas plant explosion that killed two of its workers and cut gas supplies to Victoria for a fortnight.

Esso's decision to blame its staff — including control room operator Jim Ward — backfired, with Longford royal commissioner and former High Court judge Daryl Dawson finding that the company's failure to equip workers with the "appropriate knowledge" was the ultimate cause of the explosion in September last year.

Sir Daryl said the tragedy could have been averted "had appropriate steps been taken" to deal with process upsets on the day.

In a 287-page report, Sir Daryl also criticised Esso's handling of safety issues at the plant, including incident reporting procedures and a decision to slash the number of supervisors ahead of the explosion.

The report said the causes of the blast — which killed maintenance supervisors Peter Wilson and John Lowery, and injured eight other staff — amounted to a breach of the Occupational Health and Safety Act by Esso, a subsidiary of US energy conglomerate Exxon.

"The ultimate cause of the accident on September 25 was the failure of Esso to equip its employees with appropriate knowledge to deal with the events which occurred," the report said.

"Not only did Esso fail to impart that knowledge to its employees, but it failed to make the necessary information available in the form of appropriate operating procedures."

The report found the explosion occurred when a heat exchange unit in gas plant one ruptured after workers attempted to pump hot oil through freezing equipment. Wilson, 51, and Lowery, 49, died instantly.

Gas supplies to Victorian homes and businesses were cut for almost two weeks at an estimated loss to industry of $1.3 billion.

Key recommendations by the royal commission include calls for stricter training obligations on Esso and the establishment of a State government body to specially administer safety procedures at "all major hazard facilities" within the State.

As the Government's safety watchdog, WorkCover, reopened its investigation to consider laying charges against Esso for safety breaches, the multinational, which is facing a $1 billion class action, refused to comment on the specific findings until after talks with the Government and regulators. "Esso's highest priority has always been the safety of our personnel and integrity of our operations, and we are deeply saddened by the accident," Esso chairman Robert Olsen said.

Premier Jeff Kennett also declined to comment, except to say the Government would "consider" recommendations for legislative action to extend safety case management to all major hazardous facilities, and the establishment of the specialist monitoring agency.

The main union at the site, the Australian Workers Union, claimed the report vindicated Longford workers, and it demanded an apology from Esso.

AWU State secretary Bill Shorten said union members were meeting to consider the recommendations and he called on the company to quickly implement them.

"Esso ignores the royal commission at their peril," he said.

After hearing 53 days of evidence, the commission found conditions at the plant on September 25 did not constitute a safe working environment.

Sir Daryl and commissioner Brian Brooks said operators and supervisors did not understand the dangers associated with a loss of lean oil flow, which was "directly attributable" to a deficiency in training.

"Not only was their training inadequate, but there were no current operating procedures to guide them in dealing with the problem which they encountered," the report said.

The commission found repeated delays to a safety audit known as a HAZOP, and the relocation of company engineers to Melbourne, were a result of "Esso's desire to control its operating costs" and may have been contributing factors to the explosion.

The report also said failure to report a cold temperature incident on August 28 last year "deprived Esso of an opportunity to alert its employees to the effect of loss of lean oil flow and to instruct them in the proper procedures to be adopted in the event of such a loss".

However, the commission found plant design shortcomings and maintenance policies were not to blame for the September blast.

Source: Australian,
29 June 1999, p. 1

MANAGEMENT RE-ENGINEERING

The initial reaction of organisations and managers to the turbulent and perplexing business environment of the 1990s has been to re-focus on the most familiar, easily observed and crucial resource — finance. This microscope on finance has generated a number of eagerly sought solutions based on rational economics, usually discussed under the term 're-engineering' — outsourcing, downsizing, creating flatter structures, cost cutting. The salutary goal of these options was the targeting of costly wastage and time delays that were still rampant within many organisations in the late 1980s. Quite rightly, organisations examined and reassessed core business efforts, staffing levels and organisational practices and procedures to ensure that resources were harnessed efficiently. Organisations had to be 'lean, mean fighting machines' to meet and surmount the challenges of the new millennium.

Unfortunately, this focus on dollar savings often became the sole justification for actions — even a fanatical belief system — in many organisations. Simplistic interpretations of management theory, combined with a blind faith that any action is positive action, led to untold damage and heartache in many organisations. This is because of the assumption that costs can be saved. In fact costs do not disappear magically; they can only be transferred. It is surprising the number of managers who forget that their organisation is comprised of a number of internal and dependent subsystems and, in the global view, their organisation is but a subsystem within a much larger interconnected system. Any costs saved in one part of the system re-surface in either another internal subsystem or in the external system.

A favourite ploy of the re-engineering aficionados is to close down a small section (or several positions) in the central office and deploy the work out to the strategic business units (SBUs) or operational sections — without transferring the resources for these units or sections to carry out the work. This is a cunning artifice. Each section or unit has to do only a small part of the original work and the strategy is successful provided not too much is transferred. Similar strategies are used to transfer the costs to an external system, for example to customers (longer waiting periods; messages on the telephone where the customer is expected to select a number to be put through to the desired contact point; fees for a variety of services) and to suppliers (charging for display areas).

There are two even more insidious schemes. The first is the flatter structures option — do away with middle management and establish teams. The assumption is that the energy generated by the empowerment and excitement of team work will more than offset the loss of the coordinating role and expertise of the middle managers. Unfortunately, this assumption is true only in highly specific situations where the type of work is very dependent on the group interacting and operating as one entity, i.e. as a team. The second scheme is the re-emergence of the techniques of management-by-objectives — usually under the new name of strategic management performance (SMP). The general strategy is to give a manager full responsibility for a SBU or operational section, increase the required performance objectives and decrease the amount of resources needed to run the unit or section. This forces the manager of the unit or section to make the re-engineering decisions just described — but at least upper management looks squeaky clean. The 'new' performance management strategies suffer from the same manipulative misuses that killed management-by-objectives. Management-by-objectives was designed originally to motivate and enrich management jobs. There were two very important assumptions — the manager would be fully involved in the setting of the objectives and would also have significant power over the resources needed. Only when these two assumptions are applied will SMP survive. These two insidious strategies of cutting middle management and SMP both suffer from the same terminal illness — they are simplistic interpretations of management theory and can be successful only in specific situations.

Such cost transference can turn into cost savings, provided the cost does not rebound. A cost saving, therefore, can be defined as a cost that is permanently transferred to another subsystem. Unfortunately, if the costs do rebound and return, they will do so with the multiplier effect. They will cost many times the original supposed 'savings'.

Some of the negative effects of the badly managed 'cost saving syndrome' are:

1. *loss of knowledge.* Evident particularly with the flatter structures option, loss of knowledge occurs when staff are retrenched. The retrenched staff's knowledge walks out the door with them. While some of their knowledge can be captured or documented, the big problem is the loss of tacit knowledge. As we will see later, tacit knowledge is the unarticulated, but critical, information that forms the important base for a large variety of decisions.

2. *ignoring traditional, but critical, processes and standards.* Re-engineering favours the new and, unfortunately, the old is often discarded without due thought. Some processes and standards have an essential and timeless quality. No matter what the changes, these critical processes and standards remain true. Machinery wears out in direct relationship to the usage time. Yet so many 'renewed' organisations ignore maintenance schedules to save costs. The fact that an event may have a low probability of occurring is immaterial if the cost of that event is extremely high. Some former government-run electricity generating and distribution organisations in Australia and New Zealand, now 'corporatised', are facing multi-million dollar payouts because they ignored this immutable fact of risk management. They have proved that a rebounding cost has a huge multiplier effect.

3. *forgetting that loyalty is a two-way street.* The re-engineering fad concentrates almost solely on the money resource. However, another highly valuable resource is the loyalty of staff, customers and suppliers. Staff in particular are usually extraordinarily forgiving, but only to a point. Once the pain threshold is overstepped, motivation drops very quickly and individual staff output decreases significantly. To make matters worse, recovering the situation takes anything from four to ten times the investment of the original 'saving'. This loss of loyalty is most common with the closing-down-and-transfer-of-tasks and the flatter structures options.

4. *the 'everything is saved' mentality.* This occurs particularly with the strategy of outsourcing. A function (such as catering in hospitals) is outsourced to an outside organisation. The justification is that the new service organisation, which specialises in the function (for example, catering), can produce the product or service much more efficiently. This is sometimes true. However, it must be remembered that it is in the outside organisation's best interest to provide service at the cheapest possible cost to maximise their own profits.

The host outsourcing organisation often errs in three areas. Firstly, by not using some of the money saved to institute an auditing process of the incoming produce or service, the risks of substandard or inappropriate incoming resources is increased dramatically. The new outside service organisation, which is often driven by the 'cost saving' mentality, will want to produce as close to the minimum standard as possible. A basic tenet of management is that responsibility is never delegated. However, the host organisation is still totally responsible for the quality of incoming resources. Managers of organisations which outsource functions must accept that not all the money salvaged by the outsourcing strategy is money saved. Some investment must be made in an auditing system. Even with an auditing system, the contractor often seeks only to meet the minimum standards of the contract, with little latitude given or discretion exercised, invariably leading to a drop in standards.

Secondly, by retrenching or re-deploying the staff of the original function outsourced, knowledge is lost. Unfortunately, it is this very knowledge that is needed to make the proposed auditing system operational and viable. Worse, as no staff are dedicated to the lost function, changes and new knowledge in that function are not imported by the host organisation.

Thirdly, the function no longer has a champion in the organisation. This means that the attention of the organisation is not drawn to the importance of the outsourced function. Because of the political nature of decision making, absolutely minimal resources are invested in the outsourced function.

These three losses — loss of current knowledge, no importation of new knowledge and the lack of a champion — means that the decision making in the organisation often ignores the impact of the lost function on the other systems in the organisation. Even when the lost function is considered in the decision making, the decision is usually founded on a sadly inadequate knowledge base.

5. *the anorexic syndrome.* Cost cutting, taken to the extreme, leaves no fat in the system — and all living organisms need some fat. In complexity theory, this fat is called 'redundancy' or 'exploratory energy'. The system makes two uses of this exploratory resource. Most obviously, the excess energy can be used in times of deficiency or stress — when new but temporary demands are placed on the organisation (for example, new government legislation requires additional reporting) or when resources are depleted for a short period (for example, influenza sweeps the human resource).

   The second use of the exploratory energy is more subtle, yet much more crucial. The additional resources allow the organisation to search the future for opportunities or threats, and to experiment with possible solutions. As we see later in the book, this is the important role of the shadow system. The closer to uncertainty the organisation operates, the more reliant on the shadow system (and hence the exploratory resources) the organisation is for its strategic planning.

6. *focus on the dollar.* Excess emphasis on cost reduction sends an unremitting message — save money at all costs. All staff should be efficiency conscious, but when attention on this theme becomes extreme, the entire focus of the staff shifts from the core business to cost reduction. Such a shift is as disastrous as it is insidious. Long-term solutions based on the future needs of the core business are sacrificed for the short-term benefits of cost saving. Staff interest, motivation and curiosity are no longer being stimulated by the core business. Staff satisfaction wanes as a focus on the satisfaction of a job well done comes a poor second to cold dollars.

By focusing on the dollar, management has ignored the basic premise of strategic planning — focus on the core business and the dollars will follow. This dictum assumes, of course, that the core business matches the appropriate market niche. If this is not so, no amount of cost saving will save the situation anyway. The only long-term solution in this case is in good strategic planning.

In times of external environment complexity and rapid change, this first reaction of focusing on saving costs is natural. If conducted in a reasoned, systemic and strategic manner, it is a vital first step. However, the cost saving strategy is good only for trimming excess fat. To survive an environment that is convoluted and changes rapidly, a much more complex, creative and impulsive resource must be brought to bear — the human resource.

During the late 1980s, the emphasis on strategic human resource management (SHRM) was heralded as the way to harness that most complex, creative and impulsive energy. To an extent SHRM did achieve this goal but still fell somewhat short. SHRM suffered the same deficiencies as conventional strategic planning, which was not surprising considering their close relationship. This was a frustrating time for managers. The conventional strategic management and operational theories were successful to a point but were found wanting when the organisation encountered unexpected and threatening events.

a closer look   1.2

Calls to stem staff cutbacks

By Shelley Thomas
industrial reporter

ONE in three Australian companies is struggling because staff lack critical skills.

A national study found 24 percent of companies were not competitive and a further 6 percent "inadequate" after a decade of corporate downsizing and a "slash and burn" mentality towards skilled staff.

Recruiting firm Drake surveyed 500 senior executives from all industries and found 70 percent of companies recognised downsizing and restructuring had passed the point of acceptability. Drake executive consulting national manager Chris Meddows-Taylor said the findings were disturbing and

warned Australia was at risk of lagging behind global markets.

Mr Meddows-Taylor said the study sent a strong warning to bosses to look at innovative ways to rebuild staff committment via training, family-friendly policies and communication.

He advised companies to share profits with all workers and offer greater job security.

"Companies have to move a lot quicker and go back to the basics," Mr Meddows-Taylor said.

"They need to loosen their belts and start rewarding staff more and build a win-win situation. Every employer should want to be an employer of choice."

Mr Meddows-Taylor also said the study found two-thirds of

rank-and-file workers were apathetic to company goals, with close to half of executives needing to lift their game.

He said corporate downsizing had created a class of mobile workers who had little workplace commitment or loyalty.

"The fallout from this activity (downsizing) is that we now have a workforce which is extremely mobile and one which has very little workplace commitment and loyalty. Any loyalty is to themselves," he said.

Mr Meddows-Taylor said staff who survived the "slash and burn" mentality of companies, mirroring labour market shifts in the United States, also felt a lack of direction due to a flattening out of middle management.

(continued)

(A closer look 1.2 cont'd)

They worked longer hours and often fell victim to stress and illness.

He said companies were recognising the backlash of staff-cutting and needed to act.

Labour market consultant Tom Dumbrell said it was worrying that the bulk of Australian companies did not take on-the-job training seriously.

Mr Dumbrell, author of the latest National Centre for Vocational Education Research industry survey, said most employers relied on external sources for training.

He said employees lacked the tools to do their jobs well.

Queensland Council of Unions assistant secretary Grace Grace said the Drake study echoed union movement warnings. Ms Grace said it was worrying it had taken managers so long to realise an organisation's competitive edge was determined by its workers.

She supported calls for more training and profit-sharing for workers at every level.

Queensland Chamber of Commerce and Industry workplace relations manager Judith

Himstedt said companies were addressing the issue of downsizing that had gone too far.

The Beattie Government, as part of its vision of Queensland as the "smart state", has encouraged all employers and trainers to take advantage of Skills Week 1999, running until Saturday.

Employment, Training and Industrial Relations Minister Paul Braddy will today open an international symposium on the mature-age workforce.

Source: Courier-Mail, 26 August 1999, p. 2

THE MANAGEMENT OF KNOWLEDGE CAPITAL

Managers looked elsewhere for a long-term solution. In 1990 Peter Senge, in his text *The Fifth Discipline*, popularised the concept of the **learning organisation** — to survive, an organisation had to continually learn and adjust to an ever changing environment. Chief executive officers (CEOs), academics and researchers eagerly grasped this concept as a viable alternative to rational economics. However, the concept proved to be vast in its complexity and the writings of the early 1990s, while providing important insights, had difficulty providing a sound, unifying and practical picture.

The situation was becoming very frustrating for both theoreticians and practioners. Concentrating on costs gave the organisation only the potential to become a lean, mean fighting machine. Overemphasis on costs led to highly undesirable, and possibly terminal, negative effects. SHRM gave some answers but raised more questions. As Gee, Hull and Lankshear (1996) commented, gone were the days when workers were hired from the neck down and simply told what to do. The Holy Grail of the learning organisation gave a glimpse into a powerful solution but the view was distorted and dim. What increased the frustration was that each of these potential solutions did provide some practical insights but an integrated resolution was still beyond their grasp.

Then in the mid-1990s, the focus concentrated on an intriguing concept — the management of knowledge capital. It was suggested that the knowledge of an organisation was a remarkable and critical resource.

> In this society, knowledge is *the* primary resource for individuals and for the economy overall. Land, labour, and capital — the economist's traditional factors of production — do not disappear, but they become secondary. They can be obtained, and obtained easily, provided there is specialized

knowledge. At the same time, however, specialized knowledge by itself produces nothing. It can become productive only when it is integrated into a task. And that is why the knowledge society is also a society of organizations: the purpose and function of every organization, business and non-business alike, is the integration of specialized knowledges into a common task. 🍂

(Drucker 1995, p. 76)

Sveiby (1997) suggests that knowledge is a unique resource because of three characteristics:

1. *There is no law of diminishing returns.* The law of diminishing returns states that, as long as output increases, there will come a time when the cost per unit will begin to rise — and this principle is valid in a world of limited physical resources. However, unlike coal or wool, knowledge is not intrinsically scarce. Knowledge can be conjured up by human minds from nothing.
2. *Knowledge grows from sharing.* Unlike physical resources, knowledge does not disappear from the 'giver' when shared or sold. The 'giver' retains the exact same level of knowledge. So, when knowledge is shared with someone else, it is doubled. In addition, the very act of dredging up knowledge from the unconscious mind brings new insights to the 'giver' through a process called externalisation. We will discuss this shortly.
3. *There is a difference between information and knowledge.* Information is what is printed on this page and is also contained in the data banks of computers. By and of itself, information is inert. When this information is accessed and enacted upon appropriately by an individual, this information then becomes knowledge.

So the gap of ignorance between theoreticians and practising managers was beginning to close. Yes, finance was one of the critical resources. No organisation can operate without income and no organisation will survive unless that income is wisely invested. However, on an equally crucial footing, no organisation will survive unless its knowledge capital provides a competitive edge in the market (see Drucker 1993; Reich 1991; Sveiby 1997). So two of the basic, critical resources of an organisation are finance and knowledge.

The notion that knowledge provides the competitive edge for most organisations raises several challenges for the CEO, among them:

- *Knowledge cannot be hoarded.* The competitive edge provided by knowledge is only temporary as competitors learn from each other and, if knowledge is created once, it can be created again.
- Unlike information, *knowledge is not subject to copyright or to patents.* No person or organisation can copyright or patent an idea; they can copyright only physical expressions of the idea.
- *Knowledge can be created by anyone* and this means that one organisation's competitive edge can be annihilated overnight.

Therefore, organisations have to be able to maintain their current knowledge, disseminate specific knowledge to specific parts of the organisation, create new knowledge and unlearn useless knowledge. Not only do the learning needs of the organisation and the learning needs of the individual have to be considered but the interaction between the two needs has to be fostered and nurtured. As Billett (1999) comments, never have enterprises and their workers needed each other more than they do now.

This, then, is the world of human resource development (HRD). HRD is a distinctive function within organisations. It is the only function that is at the interface between the organisation and that most complex, mobile, creative, frustrating yet critical asset — the human resource. All other management functions — whether planning, controlling or selecting — are at least one step removed from the interface. This is because most of the knowledge of an organisation resides within the minds of its people. Plans can be documented on paper, controls can be instituted mechanically and selection based on observation of the behaviour of the applicants for a job. But knowledge resides in the mind of each and every organisational staff member. It is the role of the HR developer to ensure that the appropriate processes are used so that the energy of the knowledge resource is harnessed productively.

THE HR DEVELOPER AND THE MANAGEMENT OF KNOWLEDGE

While the CEO and other senior managers have the most pervasive influence in the management of the knowledge capital of the organisation, the HRD function undoubtedly has one of the most significant roles to play. Strangely, given the erratic development of general management theory, quite robust and practical theories about HRD have evolved over the years.

Dewey (1938) championed the central tenet that meaningful learning design should be founded on the learner's needs and interests. Fifty years ago, Tyler (1949) and Knowles (1950) declared that the logical process of planned adult learning should follow the steps of determining the learner's needs, stating objectives, choosing the content, instructors and methods, and evaluating the outcomes — steps that were given a formalised imprimatur by London in 1960. In 1974, Goldstein collated these ideas and advocated a systems approach to HRD based on the three stages of needs assessment, training and development and evaluation. Brookfield (1987, p. 204) extended these three to four stages, commenting that there seems to be a great deal of consensus among the various process models as to the steps involved. These steps are:

1. an *investigation stage* where needs are investigated and identified;
2. a *design stage* where aims, objectives (or goals) and content are examined;
3. an *implementation stage* where formal or informal learning activities occur;
4. an *evaluation stage* where the worth of the learning experience is judged.

In the intervening years, a variety of techniques have been developed to achieve the aims of these four stages. These techniques have been documented in a variety of texts that usually concentrate on only one of the stages — on needs investigation or design or implementation or evaluation.

A number of these techniques have stood the test of time and have proven to be exceptionally useful tools in managing the knowledge capital in organisations. The question then arises: 'Why do organisations not use these techniques consistently and in the systematic manner that is recognised as best practice?' Part of the answer lies in the penchant for managers, under pressure to produce, to look for the quick-fix solution and in the concomitant increase in the number of fads that flooded the market in the 1980s in particular (for a fuller discussion, see Micklethwait and

Wooldridge 1996). Another somewhat related answer lies in the incredibly complex efforts and long lead times needed for effective HRD. Managers under pressure for quick solutions opted for the more immediate, if illusory, results promised by management re-engineering. Time showed that such ill-founded decisions increased staff frustrations while the underlying problems festered on. As Hilmer and Donaldson (1996) in their text *Management Redeemed* emphasise, there is nothing as successful as good, practical management techniques based on proven theory.

These four stages of HRD — needs investigation, design, implementation and evaluation — form the 'engine room' of the management of knowledge capital in organisations. The four stages produce the energy that drives the basic requirements so that the organisational knowledge is constantly identified, disseminated and reviewed. Accordingly, these four stages are the main focus of this text and as such occupy the central chapters.

ADULT LEARNING THEORIES

All four stages of HRD are underpinned by adult learning theories. These learning theories are so pervasive and instrumental to HRD that chapter 2, is devoted to an in-depth discussion of the concepts. While the basic types of learning, such as classical conditioning, behaviour modification and modelling, have provided some general principles of learning that apply to all humans, the andragogical concepts have suggested principles that are specific to adults. However, Mezirow (1990, 1991) has presented an encompassing theory of adult learning covering instrumental, communicative and emancipatory learning. This transformational learning, as it is called, provides a number of significant insights that must be considered when designing and implementing HRD. Further, critical thinking — comprising problem solving, creativity, evaluating, dialectic thinking and logical reflection — is often seen as a differentiating characteristic of adults and, as such, must be considered in any adult learning endeavour. Finally, these adult learning theories are discussed within the framework of organisational learning.

WITHIN A WIDER THEORETICAL CONTEXT

The four HRD stages of investigation, design, implementation and evaluation cannot be considered in isolation. The whole concept of HRD exists within a managerial orientation. Some important elements of this managerial orientation include the management of diversity and the functions of human resource management (HRM).

THE MANAGEMENT OF DIVERSITY

Australia is a multicultural society and this multiculturalism is reflected in the workforce of every organisation. Further, staff in an organisation represent every category of age, health and gender. Modern organisations cannot allow staff to be discriminated against or harassed. Firstly, legislation forbids such practices. Secondly, and more importantly, organisations need the variety of ideas, perceptions and knowledge that comes with a diverse workforce. This diversity is a form of energy that the modern organisation must mobilise and harness to ensure future viability. Because of its critical nature, chapter 3, 'Diversity and Globalisation', discusses the role of the HR developer in the management of diversity.

THE FUNCTIONS OF HRM

The functions of HRM define the roles that managers undertake as they manage the human resource of the organisation. Usually, these functions are listed as:

- *strategic human resource planning* (SHRP), which is linked directly to the organisational strategic plan. The organisational strategic plan identifies the market niche that the organisation will occupy and the strategies that the organisation will use to service its customers. SHRP identifies the type and number of staff the organisation will need to fulfill this servicing role.
- *recruitment*, where the community is advised that the organisation needs a certain number and type of staff. To recruit additional staff the organisation usually advertises in newspapers, professional journals and the Internet although, these days, professional recruitment consultants are also used quite extensively.
- *selection*, where the candidates who responded to the recruitment campaign are reviewed and assessed. Successful candidates are then selected for entry into the organisation.
- *induction*, where the successful candidates are introduced to the organisation. This induction may cover procedural or even technical training as well as socialising the selectees to the organisational culture.
- *human resource development*, where staff are continually developed so that their knowledge, skills and abilities are updated. This function is now seen as critical to the ongoing viability of the organisation and is often separated out from HRM. It is this function, of course, that is the topic of this book.
- *performance appraisal*, where the performance of staff is assessed and any improvements or developmental needs are identified.
- *career counselling*, where the long-term future of each staff member is planned for the good of the individual and the organisation.
- *discipline*, where aberrant behaviour is modified. The discipline function is directly affected by legal issues which proscribe both the type of behaviour that cannot be accepted by organisations and the process by which this behaviour can be encouraged to change.
- *separations*, where staff leave the organisation — either through retirement (age or ill-health), resignation or dismissal.

While it is common for HRD to be separated organisationally from the other functions of HRM, the strong interrelationships do continue. For example, when new staff are selected they often need specific development either to bring them up to an acceptable standard or to re-educate them to the unique skills or procedures required for that particular organisation.

There are two particular HRM functions that have significant overlaps with the role of HRD. The first is SHRP. The development of staff must be compatible with the strategic direction of the organisation. Further, quite often a change in strategic direction of an organisation requires a significant effort to re-develop the staff. Because of this critical link, chapter 4, 'Strategic human resource development', describes the process of planning strategically for the development of staff. The links with the organisational strategic plans are examined to show the very persuasive nature of the strategic orientation on the HRD process. The second HRM function that has a significant overlap with HRD is performance appraisal which is discussed in chapter 6.

THE FOUR STAGES OF HRD

Based on the adult learning theories and operating within a managerial orientation, then, are the four stages of HRD — investigation, design, implementation and evaluation.

An overview of HRD needs identification is provided in chapter 5. A definition of, and the purposes for, the human resource needs identification (HRDNI) are discussed. The two levels of awareness — surveillance and investigation — are examined and various techniques for data gathering and data analysis are discussed. The results of the investigation should be included in a report. Finally, suggestions are also made about selecting appropriate HRDNI methods and how to plan a HRDNI.

The HRDNI surveillance level method of performance appraisal is examined in chapter 6. Firstly, performance appraisal and performance management are discussed, concluding that performance appraisal is a subset of performance management. Performance appraisal is a natural and unique process in organisations although most managers do not realise that there are two basic types — administrative and developmental. Administrative performance appraisal is used for administrative decision making in the organisation, for example about promotions and salary increases. Developmental performance appraisal is used for identifying the developmental needs of individual staff members and, accordingly, is very useful for HRDNI. All performance appraisals should be based on a current job analysis before performance is observed and comparisons made with the key effectiveness areas and job specification. Feedback is then given with an appropriate interview before action plans for the development of the individual are instituted.

The next two chapters concentrate on the investigation stage of HRDNI. Chapter 7 discusses the two qualitative investigative methods of the interview and the focus group. Ways of appropriately structuring each of these interventions and the required skills needed to manage the processes of data gathering — questioning, listening, paraphrasing, probing and summarising — are examined. The differences between structured and unstructured interviews/focus groups are also explored. Finally, ways of analysing qualitative data are discussed.

Chapter 8 looks at the quantitative investigative method of questionnaires. After examining the four types of data — nominal, ordinal, interval and ratio — the chapter moves on to the design of questionnaires, including the instructions, factual and opinion items, response sets and sequencing. The need to pre-test the designed questionnaire is covered, along with issues such as face validity, content validity, construct validity and reliability. Finally, gathering and analysing the data using some common statistical techniques are examined.

The next two chapters move onto the design stage. Chapter 9 suggests that there are two main considerations when designing learning experiences for adults — the content and the learner. The content is the topics the learner will learn. This chapter puts forward a hierarchy of learning outcomes (HLO) that prioritises the content into an hierarchy. This hierarchy is divided into five major categories — programmed knowledge, task, relationships, critical thinking and meta-abilities — which move from the least complex (programmed knowledge) to the most complex (meta-abilities). These five major categories are further divided into subgroups of outcomes and each subgroup is broken further down into elements of outcomes. This HLO can then be associated with selecting appropriate learning strategies — with the structured learning strategies being most suited to programmed learning and the unstructured learning strategies being more suited to the meta-abilities category. This matching of learning outcomes to learning strategies is a relatively simple indicator of appropriateness. Any such initial decision would need to be reviewed and adjusted in the light of the second main indicator — the learner. Learners can differ on a variety of characteristics — including current knowledge, motivation, learning orientation and learning styles — and this variety of needs should be reflected in the final design of the learning experience. Chapter 10 examines other considerations that can be used to refine the design of the learning experience. These variables include the strategic orientation of the organisation, the organisational culture, the needs of the key stakeholders and the limiting effects of the resources available. As an overview, the whole design process is reviewed by examining the common curriculum design theories of the rational model, the interaction model and the platform model. Finally, it is emphasised that the design stage is not complete until all the HRD operational plans are documented. These operational plans include session plans, the program, the resource plan, the marketing plan, the budget and the evaluation plan.

The next two chapters move onto the implementation stage. Chapter 11 examines the structured learning strategies. The structured learning strategies discussed are the skill session, the theory session, the lecture, the discussion, the case study, the role play and experiential learning. However, where a learning strategy transforms from structured to unstructured is a moot point, as only the first three — the skill session, the theory session and the lecture — could be considered fully structured. In these three learning strategies the HR developer makes all the desisions on what will be learned, how it will be learned and how it will be assessed. In the other four learning strategies, starting with the discussion, the learner takes over more responsibility, with this responsibility increasing as the case study, then the role play, and then the experiential learning strategies are used. So these last four strategies become more unstructured. Chapter 12 examines the fully unstructured learning strategies of contract learning, action learning, change interventions and mentoring. The ways and means of managing the process, rather than directing the content, are examined in full as are the various skills required of the HR developer.

Chapter 13 explores the fourth of the HRD stages: evaluation. Ways of assessing learning are examined, including skills testing, objective tests, subjective written tests, performance tests, learning diaries and portfolio assessment. Kirkpatrick's four levels of evaluation are discussed. One disadvantage of Kirkpatrick's model is that the presage or input factors are not addressed and so the ways of evaluating the program design, the implementation and the implementing HR developer are also examined in this chapter. Two other approaches to evaluation — the scientific model and cost-benefit analysis — are then discussed. Finally, the need to develop an evaluation plan is emphasised.

Each of these nine chapters on the four stages of HRD have two consistent themes. Firstly, all the discussion is based on robust theories and principles. Secondly, these theories and principles are converted into practical explanations that provide the reader with pragmatic guides for application.

TWO NEW THEORETICAL CONCEPTS

As indicated in figure 1.1, HRD can be viewed as being embedded in HRM, although there is a tendency to recognise that HRD is an important entity in its own right. HRD is also significantly affected by diversity and, in turn, influences the organisation's positive management of diversity.

Figure 1.1 also indicates that HRD is crucially informed by two other concepts — the creation of knowledge and the new management theories — both of which are receiving burgeoning interest in the academic literature. These two concepts have provided a refreshing review of the role of HRD and explain why HRD has such a critical role in the management of an organisation. Further, the literature on the creation of knowledge and the new management theories present cogent explanations for the application of HRD techniques and also provide distinct guides for decision making within the HRD framework.

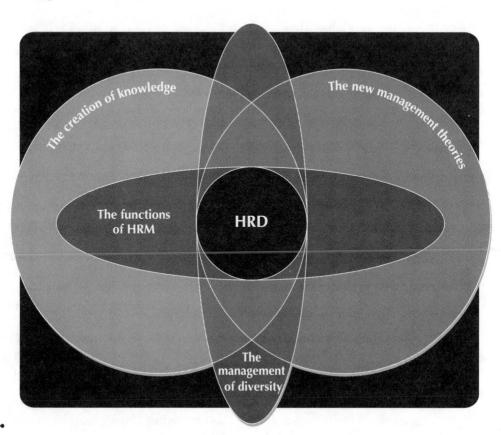

FIGURE 1.1
The wider theoretical context of HRD

The two concepts of the creation of knowledge and the new management theories are introduced in this chapter and are discussed during the remaining chapters to provide a rationale for certain actions or recommendations and to provide deeper examinations of the processes of HRD. While the two concepts are not the main focus of this book, they do have a fundamental influence on how HRD is viewed. Further in-depth discussion on the creation of knowledge and the new management theories and their relationship to HRD will be provided in the final chapter, chapter 14, 'The management of knowledge'.

CREATION OF KNOWLEDGE

Nonaka and others (Nonaka 1991; Nonaka and Takeuchi 1995; Nonaka, Takeuchi and Umemoto 1996, Nonaka and Konno 1998) have presented a model based on tacit and explicit knowledge that places the management of the organisation's knowledge capital firmly within the auspices of human resource development. Explicit knowledge is the knowledge that the individual can declare while tacit knowledge is in the mind of the individual but the individual is unaware of it or cannot declare it. Tacit and explicit knowledge are not totally separate but are mutually complementary entities and thus interact with, and change into, each other during the creative activities of human beings. Using tacit and explicit knowledge as a base, the authors have then proceeded to build a model that explains the four processes used to create or generate new knowledge.

1. *Externalisation (tacit to explicit)*. This process occurs when tacit knowledge is translated and expressed into forms that are comprehensible to the conscious mind of the individual and to others. Externalisation always occurs when an individual writes thoughts and ideas onto paper. While certain aspects of the conscious mind are transposed easily into the written word, the writer usually finds that some other ideas, embedded in the subconscious mind, also surface and give the original conscious thoughts a richer meaning and context. Reflection is one of the main forms of externalisation, through writing, discussions with others or contemplative thinking.

2. *Combination (explicit to explicit)*. One of the most common and obvious paths of knowledge creation, this process uses lectures, discussions, documents, meetings and electronic and computerised communications. Combination involves the conversion of explicit knowledge into more complex sets of explicit knowledge. Your reading of this book is a classical example of combination. The fact that the words have been expressed means that the ideas in this book are explicit knowledge. As you read this book, the explicit knowledge in the book is combined with your own explicit knowledge. Through a process of sorting, combining or categorising your current knowledge and the explicit knowledge of this book, you reconfigure your existing knowledge.

3. *Internalisation (explicit to tacit)*. The process of internalisation is seen most easily when an individual is 'learning by doing'. For example, there is a big difference between your reading about the techniques in this book and you doing them. In chapter 6, we discuss interviewing. When one reads about the interviewing skills they seem logical and straightforward. However, there is a difference when one tries to interview someone — and attempts to combine questioning, paraphrasing,

summarising and probing, to say nothing of taking notes. It is this whole body experience of 'learning by doing' that converts explicit knowledge into tacit knowledge. It is also suspected that internalisation can occur through re-experiencing another's experiences through methods such as oral stories or diagrams and models.

4. *Socialisation (tacit to tacit)*. This is an osmotic process where complex information is exchanged, and is often seen where a learner watches and interacts with an expert. While often accompanied by the combination process, socialisation is also a whole body experience where various nuances and nonverbal messages are received and synthesised into a complex appreciation of an intricate archetype.

This four-phase paradigm of knowledge creation — externalisation, combination, internalisation and socialisation — provides an interesting and detailed look at how new knowledge can be generated. Most organisations have used the combination process as the main, and often only, means of creating knowledge. One very strong message from the writings of Nonaka and others is that organisations must actively encourage the use of the other three knowledge-creating processes.

In addition, integral to the knowledge creation processes is the need for individuals, groups and organisations to interact with others who have different constructs of the world. So the concepts discussed in chapter 3 on the positive management of diversity also have a significant bearing on the creation of knowledge. To remain viable, organisations must be continually generating new knowledge. Interestingly, Nonaka originally saw that the creation of a knowledge model was applicable only to social systems (such as organisations). However, other writers such as Andrews and Delahaye (1998) have suggested that the model is equally applicable to individuals as well. This wider interpretation of the model will be used throughout this book.

THE NEW MANAGEMENT THEORIES

Traditional management theories can be divided into two broad classifications — conventional strategic management and operational management. Conventional strategic management recommends that the external environment should be analysed by identifying and assessing the factors that have a direct influence on the organisation — the customers, the competitors, specific government legislation and so on. From this analysis, the environment can be evaluated as on a scale ranging from predictable to relatively unpredictable. Based on this judgement, traditional management theories then allow the upper management of the organisation to create an appropriate organisational structure and to follow appropriate strategies. Once the strategies have been selected, they can be operationalised by using the operational management functions of plan, lead, organise and control (often called the PLOC model). These theories are based on what is called the **Newtonian paradigm**. Newton was a sixteenth-century mathematician and physicist who inspired significant original thought in science. The basis of his theories was the assumption that objects or matter could be broken down into their component parts, measured and then re-built. In the early nineteenth century, these assumptions were incorporated into the then new science of management, particularly by people such as Frederick Taylor (1911). Traditional management theories are heavily influenced by these values and, even today, there is a culture amongst so called 'hard-nosed' managers that if it cannot be measured then it does not matter. Now it is not so much that the Newtonian paradigm is wrong for management theory; it just does not go far enough — it only tells part of the story. (For an in-depth and critical analysis of the traditional management theories, see Mickelthwait and Wooldridge 1996.)

One of the most significant writers on the new management theories is Stacey (1996). He tagged the older, rationalistic approaches as 'ordinary management' and the new approaches as 'extraordinary management'. Further, he suggests that managers needed to combine the older rational skills and these newer ideas. He uses complexity theory — a combination of chaos theory and quantum mechanics — as the more logical and appropriate basis for management theory.

According to complexity theory, any system is drawn to two main attractors — equilibrium and inequilibrium. Now society has always assumed that inequilibrium is to be avoided, as the final outcome of that path is confusion, turmoil and anarchy. Hence, the Roman Empire, by staying firmly within the boundaries of equilibrium, remained a world force for centuries. Therefore, the assumption has always been that organisations need the stability of equilibrium — and it is in the state of equilibrium that the rationalist management theories of ordinary management operate to their fullest potential. However, it is now recognised that equilibrium also results in the death of the system — a slower death, but death just the same. In short, equilibrium does not guarantee success and longevity. An organisation in the state of equilibrium remains viable only while its external environment remains predictable and certain. The Roman Empire remained a vital force for so long because there were no dramatic changes in technology, climate or politics. When the external environment changes, the organisation that remains in a state of equilibrium will soon be by-passed — a slow death rather than the more spectacular demise by anarchy. It is just this very situation — a traumatic and uncertain external environment — that faces managers today.

If the states of equilibrium and inequilibrium are not the answer, what is? The initial part of the answer lies in the recognition that the solution will not be a simple 'either/or' option. Rather, Stacey (1996) suggests, organisations must operate in a state of **bounded instability**. In complexity theory, bounded instability is created by a 'strange attractor' — an attractor that is created by an outside force and which draws the system away from the two main attractors. In the case of organisations, the strange attractor of bounded instability is usually created by the CEO. Senge (1990), in discussing the new roles and skills of managers, describes some of the activities that a manager can take to operate in a state of balanced instability. These new roles are that of a designer, a teacher and a steward, and the new skills include building a shared vision, systems thinking, moving beyond blame and distinguishing detail complexity from dynamic complexity.

In the foreseeable future, managers must strive for bounded instability — a state where the organisation is partly in equilibrium and partly in inequilibrium. Under bounded instability, the organisation is seen as having two complementary and dependent systems — the legitimate system and the shadow system — that are continually in tension.

The legitimate system pulls the organisation towards equilibrium and is administered by the rationalist theories of ordinary management. The legitimate system has two important roles — to manage the day-to-day activities of the organisation and to audit the suggestions of survival that are generated by the shadow system. The legitimate system is best managed by the familiar management theory that is the basis of most management and business administration degrees, for example, the familiar circular PLOC model of the plan, lead, organise and control functions. In large part, these management theories derived from the engineering and military fields of practice and, as discussed earlier, are all based on the Newtonian paradigm. This paradigm assumes that cause and effect can be analysed by breaking the problem down into smaller and smaller components. Further, cohesion is achieved by basic laws. In organisations, these laws are called plans, policies and procedures. These laws operate on the principles of **negative feedback loops**. Negative feedback loops dampen any deviation from the 'norm' and bring such deviations back to the accepted or planned standard.

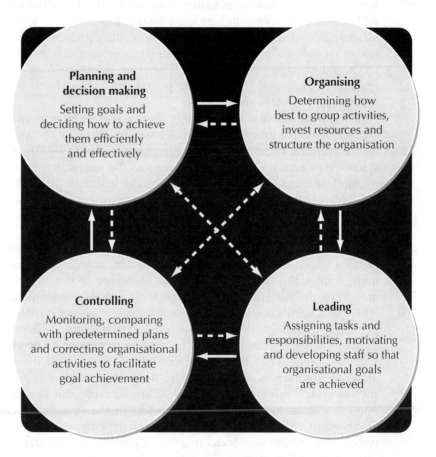

FIGURE 1.2
The management process: the four basic functions of planning, organising, leading and controlling

The role of the shadow system is to pull the organisation towards inequilibrium by continually testing the internal and external environment and to release the self-organising potential of the natural system so that future possible opportunities, challenges and threats are explored and analysed. The shadow system allows the organisation to continually evolve in a spontaneous, self-organising manner by exploring options and generating ingenious alternatives. The shadow system relies on extraordinary management — an approach that relies on chaos theory and uses the resources of redundancy, those resources that the system stores and invests in an effort to avoid stagnation and obsolescence. Creativity is valued above all else and its role may be seen as 'play without apparent purpose'. **Positive feedback** loops — feedback that enhances and amplifies — reign supreme. The ultimate aim of the shadow system is to produce a replacement for the current dominant schema, the legitimate system. Possible solutions to these future trends are promulgated and championed by the shadow system before being tested by the legitimate system for their robust potential to help the organisation survive.

It is interesting to note that the shadow system cannot operate unless there is a solid and secure legitimate system. Firstly, the shadow system depends on the legitimate system to provide sufficient resources to operate successfully. Secondly, the shadow system can only explore imaginatively and with complete freedom if it knows that the legitimate system is available to ultimately curb any ideas that are too outlandish. Yet the current legitimate system has to live with the knowledge that the ultimate aim of the shadow system is to identify and design new values and structures that will make the present legitimate system obsolete. This is the tension that CEOs and managers must manage. Therefore, managers have to learn to be flexible, embrace change and modify their policies and procedures as the shadow system introduces new ideas and concepts.

In terms of this new management theory, it is interesting to note that traditional management champions the legitimate system while the literature of the early 1990s on the learning organisation (see, for example, Senge 1990), advocates the shadow system. However, the current literature sees the interaction between the two systems — the legitimate and the shadow — as the hallmark of the learning organisation. The role of the modern manager is to manage both systems, and the interaction between them, simultaneously.

For HRD, this new management approach provides a greater understanding of the role needed to manage the knowledge capital of the organisation. In the first place, the four stages of HRD — investigation, design, implementation and evaluation — fit quite comfortably within the rational processes of the legitimate system. Indeed, most texts discuss HRD as if it is operating only in the legitimate system. However, HRD has a significant role to play in the shadow system. Firstly, as will be discussed in chapter 9, 'Design: the two main considerations' and in chapter 12, 'Implementing the unstructured strategies', staff have to be developed to be able to operate in the shadow system. They have to be very adept in using all the techniques described under the four stages of HRD and also need deeper and quite complex competencies, such as critical thinking and mental agility. Secondly, HR developers are often called upon to manage the process for the actors in the shadow system — skills that are discussed in chapter 11. Finally, HR developers are also asked to help the shadow system incorporate new ideas into the legitimate system and this also requires the skills discussed in chapter 12.

HOW TO USE THIS BOOK

Being in the written form, this book is based on a linear logic that assumes all readers will wish to start with the underpinning adult learning theories (chapter 2) and then go on to examine the managerial orientations of managing diversity (chapter 3) and strategic HRD planning (chapter 4) before working through the four functions in sequence — needs investigation (chapters 5 to 8), design (chapters 9 and 10), implementation (chapters 11 and 12) and evaluation (chapter 13). Chapter 14 examines the management of knowledge by exploring the concepts of knowledge creation and the new management theories, and the interaction of these with the four stages of HRD, to a deeper level.

However, two factors may make this assumption of linear logic unsuitable. Firstly, the needs of individual readers — perhaps those with more advanced knowledge of HRD or perhaps because of different learning styles — may indicate that a different order be followed. Secondly, the four stages of HRD are very closely interlinked and, indeed, overlap in some parts. Further, as already discussed, these four stages impact on, and are affected by, the functions of HRM and also the theories of knowledge creation and the new management theories. So some readers may prefer to examine first the four stages of HRD (chapters 5 to 13), as these four stages are the main theme of this book. Some readers may wish to start with one of the other stages — implementation, for example — rather than needs investigation. Other readers may be more intrigued by the creation of knowledge and the new management theories and prefer to go straight to chapter 14 before exploring the four stages of HRD. So, while a decision had to be made on the ordering of concepts in this book, readers may wish to take a different path.

GLOSSARY

bounded instability — keeping the organisation balanced between stability and chaos

combination — combining another's explicit knowledge with one's own explicit knowledge

complexity theory — a combination of chaos theory and quantum mechanics

creation of knowledge — using the knowledge-generation process of externalisation, combination, internalisation and socialisation to create new knowledge

design stage — the second of the HRD stages where aims, objectives and content are examined

diversity — the variation and differences between organisational staff members

evaluation stage — the fourth HRD stage where the worth of the learning experience is assessed

explicit knowledge — knowledge that can be articulated

externalisation — allowing tacit knowledge to surface so that it can be articulated as explicit knowledge

extraordinary management — the new management theories that are based on complexity theory

implementation stage — the third HRD stage where formal or informal learning activities occur

information — the inert data that are contained in books and computer data banks

internalisation — converting explicit knowledge into tacit knowledge

investigation stage — the first of the HRD stages where needs are investigated and identified

knowledge — a unique resource that does not adhere to the law of diminishing returns, grows from sharing and results from an individual accessing and enabling information

legitimate system — one of the two basic systems of the organisation, it is responsible for the day-to-day management of the organisation and its immediate future

learning organisation — using both the legitimate system and the shadow system to ensure that knowledge is adequately maintained and created so that the organisation will continue to survive

management of diversity — managing the energy of a diverse workforce in a positive manner

management re-engineering — the cost-saving approaches based on rational economics, designed to help the organisation to survive the rapidly changing environment

negative feedback loops — forces that dampen any deviation from the norm, used in ordinary management and the legitimate system

Newtonian paradigm — the assumption that all organisms can be analysed in a rational and linear manner

ordinary management — the conventional management theories that are based on the Newtonian paradigm

positive feedback loops — forces that enhance small variations, used in extraordinary management and the shadow system

shadow system — one of the two basic systems of the organisation, it is responsible for creating new knowledge and the distant future of the organisation

socialisation — exchanging tacit knowledge with another

strategic human resource development planning — the strategic plan for developing the staff in the organisation, derived from the corporate strategic plan

tacit knowledge — knowledge that is in the subconscious mind.

QUESTIONS

For review

1. List and explain the three errors caused by the 'everything is saved' mentality of management re-engineering.

2. Explain how knowledge is a unique resource and why this uniqueness raises challenges for the CEO or manager.

3. Briefly describe the four stages of HRD.

For analysis

4. What are the advantages and disadvantages of management re-engineering.

5. Compare and contrast the four knowledge-creation processes.

For application

6. Examine an organisation with which you are familiar and, by giving examples, describe how its legitimate system and its shadow system are managed.

REFERENCES

Andrews, K. and Delahaye, B. L. (1998). *Tacit Knowledge and Psychosocial Filters: The Knowledge Creation Process in Australia*. The Knowledge Creation Management in Asia Conference, Singapore, 6–7 March.

Billett, S. (1999). 'Guided learning at work.' In D. Boud and J. Garrick (Eds), *Understanding Learning at Work*. London: Routledge.

Brookfield, S. (1987). *Developing Critical Thinkers: Challenging Adults to Explore Alternative Ways of Thinking and Acting*. San Francisco: Jossey-Bass.

Dewey, J. (1938). *Experience and Education*. New York: Kappa Delta Pi.

Drucker, P. (1993). *Post-Capitalist Society*. London: Butterworth Heinemann.

Drucker. P. (1995). *Managing in a Time of Great Change*. New York: Truman Talley Books/Dutton.

Field, L. (1995). *Managing Organisational Learning: From Rhetoric to Reality*. Melbourne, Vic: Longman.

Gee, J. P., Hull, G. and Lankshear, C. (1996). *The New Work Order: Behind the Language of the New Capitalism*. Sydney: Allen and Unwin.

Goldstein, I. L. (1974). *Training: Program Development and Evaluation*. New York: Brooks/Cole.

Hilmer, F. G. and Donaldson, L. (1996). *Management Redeemed*. New York: The Free Press.

Knowles, M. S. (1950). *Informal Adult Education: A Guide for Administrators, Leaders, and Teachers*. New York: AAAE.

London, J. (1960). 'Program development in adult education'. In Knowles, M. S. (Ed.), *Handbook of Adult Education in the United States*. Chicago: AAAE

Mezirow, J. (1991). *Transformative Dimensions of Adult Learning*. San Francisco: Jossey-Bass.

Mezirow, J. and Associates. (1990). *Fostering Critical Reflection in Adulthood: A Guide to Transformative and Emancipatory Learning*. San Francisco: Jossey-Bass.

Micklethwait, J. and Wooldridge, A. (1996). *The Witch Doctors*. London: Heinemann.

Nonaka, I. (1991). 'The knowledge creating company.' *Harvard Business Review*, November–December, pp. 96–104.

Nonaka, I. and Konno, N. (1998). 'The concept of "Ba": Building a foundation for knowledge creation.' *California Management Review*, 40(3), Spring, pp. 1–15.

Nonaka, I. and Takeuchi, H. (1995). *The Knowledge Creating Company: How Japanese Companies Create the Dynamics of Innovation*. New York: Oxford.

Nonaka, I., Takeuchi, H. and Umemoto, K. (1996). 'A theory of organisational knowledge creation.' *International Journal of Technology Management*, 11(7/8), pp. 833–845.

Pedler, M., Burgoyne, J. and Boydell, T. (1997). *The Learning Company: A Strategy for Sustainable Development*. (2nd ed.). London: McGraw-Hill.

Reich, R. (1991). *The Work of Nations: Preparing Ourselves for Twenty-first Century Capitalism*. New York: Alfred A. Knopf.

Senge, P. (1990). *The Fifth Discipline: The Art and Practice of the Learning Organisation*. Milson's Point, NSW: Random House.

Stacey, R. (1996). *Strategic Human Resource Management and Organisational Dynamics*. London: Pitman.

Sveiby, K. E. (1997). *The New Organisational Wealth: Managing and Measuring Knowledge-Based Assets*. San Francisco: Berret Koehler.

Taylor, F. W. (1911). *The Principles of Scientific Management*. New York: Harper.

Tyler, R. (1949). *Basic Principles of Curriculum and Instruction*. Chicago: University of Chicago Press.

Adult learning

CHAPTER OBJECTIVES

At the end of this chapter you should be able to:

1 list the assumptions underpinning pedagogical and andragogical learning

2 discuss the basic types of learning — classical conditioning, behaviour modification and modelling

3 explain and distinguish the three levels of learning — instrumental, communicative and emancipatory

4 define the role of critical thinking in the process of adult learning

5 discuss the two models of unlearning

6 describe the holistic adult learning model

7 identify the role of the individual in organisational learning.

One constant theme that underpins any endeavour in human resource development is the body of knowledge that forms the theories, principles and approaches that describe our understandings of how adults learn. Historically, most learning efforts have been directed at children and youths. Interest in adult learning intensified in the nineteenth century, primarily because leading citizens felt a responsibility for the religious and moral salvation of uneducated adults, who formed the very large majority of the world's population at that time (Grattan 1955).

There has been quite some argument through the ages as to whether adults can learn. In these days of life-long learning, it may seem strange that such an issue could even be debated and we can thank Thorndike (1928) for laying the argument to rest. Adults can indeed learn!

This chapter looks briefly at the concept of learning before discussing the two schools of thought about learning that arose in the early decades of the twentieth century. The philosophies of these two schools of thought — Knowles (1990) calls them the scientific and artistic streams — hold sway even today. However, as is often the case, the tension between the defenders of each school has resulted in a deeper examination of learning and education providing us with important insights into the processes of adult learning. These important insights have resulted in a number of accepted learning theories and principles that form the very foundations of any learning experience.

The chapter begins by defining learning as a relatively permanent change in behaviour that results from one's experiences, and points out that having learning as their primary adaptive specialisation makes human beings unique among all living organisms. Malcolm Knowles has championed the belief that adult learners are a unique species. He originally proselytised the concept of **andragogy** — the art and science of teaching adults. Certainly, adult learners do have some unique characteristics which should always be taken into account. However, the basic types of learning — classical conditioning, behaviour modification and modelling — will always provide a foundation for any learning episode, whether for adults, children or animals.

Transformational learning is a formalised, comprehensive, idealised and, perhaps, ambitious model that explores adult learning. It is suggested that there are three levels — instrumental learning, communicative learning and emancipatory learning. **Instrumental learning** shows adult learners how to manipulate their environment. In a typical organisation, a lot of human resource development effort is directed towards instrumental learning as people are trained in the procedures of the organisation and the skills of operating equipment. Over the last century, psychological research has been directed at instrumental learning and this research has culminated in ten principles of learning that are generally agreed to be most useful to human resource development. **Communicative learning** involves, firstly, understanding the world of others by genuinely comprehending their values, ideals, feelings and even moral decisions and, secondly, validating one's personal beliefs. This deep understanding is shared by **rational discourse** where each party talks and listens respectfully to each other, even if personal views are diametrically different. **Emancipatory learning** is the deepest level of learning and examines an individual's **frames of reference**. Frames of reference are those deep-seated underlying values and beliefs that guide, shape and dictate an individual's everyday attitudes and behaviours. Emancipatory learning involves the individual transforming or changing certain frames of reference that are causing distress or are hindering the individual from achieving a satisfactory life. Changing frames of reference is a very difficult exercise and is usually accompanied by emotional experiences. Such changes are achieved using **critical reflection**.

When examining adult learning, there are two other important aspects that need to be discussed. The first is **critical thinking**. Whereas critical reflection entails the deep examination of the foundations and justifications of one's beliefs, critical thinking impinges on the logic one uses to add to or change personal knowledge of a topic. The knowledge generation process of externalisation and internalisation plays a significant part in critical thinking. Specifically, critical thinking uses five significant components — the problem-solving paradigms used by the individual; using creativity to devise novel responses; accurately evaluating a situation and oneself; using dialectic thinking, which accepts that an object or person may hold opposing values simultaneously; and logical reflection adds to the store of explicit and tacit knowledge. The final important aspect of adult learning that is examined is **unlearning**. In today's society, change is occurring so quickly that, for the first time in history, the natural process of forgetting is not fast enough. There are two models of unlearning suggested by the literature. The parenthetic model, where old knowledge is put to one side for later possible use, appears to hold the most promise for understanding the process of unlearning.

The chapter ends by presenting a **holistic** model of **adult learning** that combines the concepts of tacit and explicit knowledge, transformational learning and critical thinking and by comparing this individual adult learning model with the processes of organisational learning.

LEARNING

Learning is defined typically as a relatively permanent change in behaviour or behaviour potential that results from one's experiences (Sigelman and Shaffer 1995, p. 210). It is change — in thoughts, perceptions, or reactions to the environment — that is neither programmed by the genes nor due to maturation (Domjan 1993).

These usual definitions of learning may apply to most organisms. However, humans are a distinctive species on this earth. As Kolb comments:

> Human beings are unique among all living organisms in that their primary adaptive specialization lies not in some particular physical form or skill or fit in an ecological niche, but rather in identification with the process of adaption itself — in the process of learning. We are thus the learning species, and our survival depends on our ability to adapt not only in the reactive sense of fitting into the physical and social worlds, but in the proactive sense of creating and shaping those worlds.

(Kolb 1984, p. 1)

So Kolb (1984) defines learning not as fixed and immutable ideas where change can be measured, but as a process whereby concepts are derived from, and continuously modified by, experience. Further, to learn is not the specialised realm of one function, such as cognition or perception, but involves the integrated functioning of the total organism — thinking, feeling, perceiving and behaving. Brookfield (1990) goes further and points out that learning is not a rational, bloodless, ascetic phenomenon. He believes that learning is an activity invested with such significance by learners, and where their fragile egos face such potentially serious threats, that they must also experience it emotionally.

One could expect, therefore, the topic of adult learning to be complex and intriguing — and it is. While most organisms can adapt their behaviour, humans are unique in that learning is their primary adaptive mechanism and this learning is experienced emotionally as well as cognitively.

ADULTS AS LEARNERS

The scientific or traditional school of learning has had a very long history, dating back to the middle ages. Learning was then the sole prerogative of the upper class, the clergy and artisans. In the 1800s, when schooling became compulsory for children in a number of countries, the basic themes of control and imparting of a defined body of knowledge became imbedded in the educational system. Berte (1975) describes this as the Lancastrian system of mass producing students through a totally prescribed and regimented sequential curriculum. While the methods advocated by the traditional educators have been criticised over the years, there is no doubt that such schooling has provided a basic level of education across a wide section of the world's population. So the traditionalists were certainly doing something right. One of the leading lights of the traditionalist school was E. L. Thorndike. While he had a preoccupation for laboratory experimentation — he felt research in a classroom led to contamination — undoubtedly his contribution to education cannot be minimised. His Laws of Readiness, Exercise and Effect are still central tenets of adult education today.

The artistic stream, the members of which were sometimes referred to as the 'progressives', criticised the traditionalists for assuming that the learner was an empty vessel and the teacher the fount of all knowledge. Progressives felt that learning was a totality, a gestalt. They valued the expression of individuality, learning through experience, the importance of the learner's needs and the dynamism of active learning. John Dewey, the champion of the progressives, expressed the differences as follows:

> To imposition from above is opposed expression and cultivation of individuality; to external discipline is opposed free activity; to learning from tests and teachers, learning through experience; to acquisition of isolated skills and techniques by drill is opposed acquisition of them as a means of attaining ends which make direct vital appeal.

(Dewey 1938, pp. 19–20)

The progressive school of thought was the precursor of modern self-directed learning.

The proposition that adults may use learning processes different from those of children was launched in the English-speaking world by Edward C. Lindeman (1926). For the next 70 years this theme was championed by Malcolm Knowles, a writer and educator who is considered to be one of the leading thinkers and proponents of adult learning. Originally, Knowles believed that the pedagogical (from *peda* — a child) suppositions of learning were only relevant to children and that adults operated under a different set of assumptions, which he labelled 'andragogy'.

TABLE 2.1	CHARACTERISTIC	PEDAGOGY	ANDRAGOGY
Assumptions of the pedagogical and andragogical models	1. The need to know	Learners know only what the teacher teaches, if they want to pass and get promoted.	Adults need to know why they need to learn something before undertaking it.
	2. The learner's self-concept	The learner's self-concept eventually becomes that of a dependent personality.	Adults have a self-concept of being responsible for their own decisions.
	3. The role of experience	The learner's experience is of little worth as a resource for learning.	Adults come into an educational activity with both a greater volume and a different quality of experience from youths.
	4. Readiness to learn	Learners become ready to learn what the teacher tells then, when they want to pass and get promoted.	Adults become ready to learn those things they need to know and be able to do in order to cope effectively with their real-life situations.
	5. Orientation to learning	Learners have a subject-centred orientation to learning; they see learning as acquiring subject matter content.	Adults are life-centred. They must perceive that learning will help them perform tasks or deal with problems that they confront in real life situations.
	6. Motivation	Learners are motivated to learn by external motivations.	The most potent motivations are internal pressures.

Source: Based on work by Knowles (1980b, 1990)

This stance of the difference between learning for children and learning for adults was epitomised in the title of his 1970 text *The Modern Practice of Adult Education: Pedagogy versus Andragogy*. However, by 1980 this stance, and the subtitle of the book, had changed to *From Pedagogy to Andragogy*. Knowles recognised that, under certain situations, adults could learn best under the assumptions of pedagogy and at other times andragogical process would be more appropriate.

Accordingly, the pedagogical learning strategies used in HRD are often referred to as structured or other-directed or dependent and the andragogical approaches as unstructured or self-directed or independent. These descriptions indicate that in pedagogical learning a person other than the learner takes the responsibility for deciding what will be learned, how it will be learned and what will be assessed, while in andragogical learning the learner takes these responsibilities. Chapter 11 discusses the pedagogical or structured learning strategies used in HRD and chapter 12 explores the self-directed or andragogical learning strategies.

We will return to the effects of pedagogy and andragogy on HRD throughout the book. Knowles is correct — adults are different. Even though some of the theories, principles and approaches discussed later in this chapter are based on general considerations of teaching and learning, it should be recognised that some of the andragogical assumptions will always apply in adult learning. These include:

- The learning should be relevant to the real-life situations and problems. This enhances the motivation of the learner as well as embedding the new learnings into a context.
- The learning should incorporate the rich experiences of the adult learners, thus utilising that abundant resource, the tacit knowledge of the adult.
- The learning should involve the adult learner, at least to some extent, so that the individual's sense of self-responsibility ensures that the learning is transferred back to the operational site.

We now go on and examine some of the general theories and principles that apply to all human learning. However, bear in mind the three andragogical assumptions.

BASIC TYPES OF LEARNING

Writers, psychologists and researchers agree that there are three fundamental types of learning — classical conditioning, behaviour modification and modelling (or observational learning). Of the three, the last two — behaviour modification and modelling — are of significant interest in the development of the human resource in organisations.

CLASSICAL CONDITIONING

This is the world of Ivan Pavlov and his salivating dogs. Pavlov noticed that when dogs smelt food (the unconditioned stimulus) the dogs salivated (the unconditioned response). He then rang a bell (the conditioned stimulus) whenever the food was presented to the dogs. After a while, he did not present the food but just rang the bell — and the dogs salivated (the conditioned response).

In humans, classical conditioning is highly involved in the learning of emotional responses. Consider the individual who has just picked up his new car, with its distinctive 'new' smell of leather and upholstery — but who unfortunately has an accident, which causes anxiety and fear. In the future, the smell of a 'new' car may result in an increased heartbeat and sweating as the conditioned response of anxiety and fear returns. Such responses can be unlearned through counter conditioning. Accordingly, the area of classical conditioning is usually associated with counselling and psychotherapy rather than human resource development.

BEHAVIOUR MODIFICATION

Behaviour modification has its foundation in behaviourism (Watson 1925). Behaviourism presumed that any analysis about human development should be based on observations of overt behaviour rather than on unconscious motives or cognitive processes that remain unobservable. Further, learning was merely a matter of accumulating a series of stimulus-response (S-R) associations. Thorndike (1913, 1928), investigating ways that these S-R connections could be strengthened or weakened, identified the Law of Effect — if an experience is followed by a reward, the connection is strengthened.

Behaviour modification was explored more fully by Skinner (1953) in his concept of 'operant conditioning'. Skinner conducted a wide variety of experiments that showed that a behaviour can be magnified or modified by a reward. He suggested that there were two types of rewards (or reinforcements, as Skinner called them). Positive reinforcement occurs when a reward is added to the situation. A negative reinforcement occurs when something unpleasant or undesirable is removed from the situation. A classical example of negative reinforcement occurs when you feel the cold — you don a jumper or pullover, thus avoiding the unpleasant sensation of feeling cold. For a new behaviour to be developed, a new reward (either a positive or negative reinforcement) must follow. Hence the basic rule — to create a new behaviour first implement the reward. Initially, the reinforcement should occur every time the behaviour is exhibited. However, for long-term behaviour change, it is better to then switch to non-scheduled reinforcement — where rewards occur at intermittent and unpredictable intervals. The poker machines in the local club operate very effectively on this unpredictable, positive reinforcement schedule.

Managers frequently use operant conditioning to develop staff. If a staff member is new to a task, a significant part of the development plan should be to provide rewards by acknowledgement, words of praise and providing opportunities for more challenging and interesting work as the staff member exhibits appropriate behaviour and achieves expected levels of productivity. However, this example exposes one of the limitations of operant conditioning. Skinner basically believed that humans were passively shaped by the environment — in other words, only external or extrinsic rewards were valuable. This viewpoint shows the power of Watson's original exhortations to acknowledge only observable behaviour. These days we also acknowledge the power of intrinsic rewards — those motivations within a person that can also reward behaviour. So, in our example, the driving force of the manager's kind words is really the sense of pride or satisfaction within the staff member.

MODELLING

Bandura (1977) believed people have far more sophisticated cognitive abilities — they are cognitive beings whose active processing of information from the environment plays a major role in learning and human development. Sigelman and Shaffer

(1995) believed that nowhere is Bandura's cognitive emphasis more evident than in his highlighting of observational learning (modelling) as the most important mechanism through which human behaviour changes. Human beings (and other animals) attend to the behaviour of others of their kind and tend to imitate that behaviour (Gardner et al. 1981). This is learning to do new things by observing how particular models do them and then imitating the behaviour of those models. Indeed, people are more likely to model their behaviour on that of a significant other than to take notice of verbal counsel to behave in a certain manner.

Zimbardo (1988) suggests that a model's observed behaviour will be at its most influential when:

1. the model is perceived positively, i.e. seen to be of high status, liked, respected
2. the model's behaviour is visible and salient — stands out as a clear figure against the background of competing models
3. it is within the observer's range of competence to enact the behaviour
4. the model's behaviour is seen as having reinforcing consequences, i.e. there are appropriate rewards and punishments.

As Zimbardo (1988) points out, the advantage of modelling is that it enables us to acquire large, integrated patterns of behaviour without going through the tedious process of gradually eliminating wrong responses and building up the right ones through trial-and-error — to say nothing of profiting from the mistakes and successes of others.

So, behaviour modification and modelling provide some initial insights into how people learn. They are likely to perform a behaviour if that behaviour results in a reward. However, given the andragogical assumptions in table 2.1, adults are also likely to make individual assessments of the reward. Modelling is useful for acquiring large, integrated patterns of behaviour. Again, the andragogical assumptions may play a part in the adult's decision as to whether to follow the lead of the model. However, modelling does have some significant links to the knowledge creation process of socialisation. So, given the right conditions (i.e. andragogical assumptions), modelling can be a dynamic learning process for adults.

A THEORY OF ADULT LEARNING

Over the last decade or so, Jack Mezirow has formulated a 'comprehensive, idealized and universal' model of adult learning (1994, p. 222). While some of his concepts are not always easy to follow, and his ideas are not without their critics, Mezirow's contribution does have a lot of value. Mezirow (1990, 1991) has suggested that there are three levels of adult learning — instrumental, communicative and emancipatory.

INSTRUMENTAL LEARNING

Instrumental learning involves the process of learning to control and manipulate the environment or other people and is often task-orientated problem solving — how to do something or how to perform. This type of learning also allows us to establish the 'truth' by empirical tests and objective measurement — we can measure changes resulting from our learning in terms of productivity, performance or behaviour. In organisations, instrumental learning is evident in two spheres of activity:

1. *procedural training*, where all organisations have set procedures, for achieving outcomes. These procedures are important and, as pointed out by Sveiby (1997), such internal structures are a significant part of the organisation's knowledge capital. As discussed in chapter 1, the more fanatical followers of re-engineering have seen the opportunity for significant cost savings by reducing procedural training — with the resultant devaluation of the organisation's internal structures. Procedural training is the main contributor to the organisation's combination process of knowledge generation (Nonaka and Takeuchi 1995) and is a prime contributor to the organisation's well-being and survival. Organisations must continue to invest in procedural training to ensure the knowledge that forms the backbone of the organisation's competitive edge is widely disseminated.

2. *empirical research*, where, as well as the dissemination mechanisms, instrumental learning involves determining cause–effect relationships and learning through task-orientated problem solving. This frequently occurs during human resource needs investigations (see chapter 5) — for example, when determining the reasons for customer dissatisfaction or the skills needed to use a new piece of equipment.

Principles of learning

Our understanding of instrumental learning has been predominantly shaped by the assumptions of the traditional school of thought and the research of writers such as Thorndike (1913, 1928). From these assumptions and research come a number of **principles of learning** that are frequently cited in texts on human resource development (e.g. Delahaye and Smith 1998; Harris and DeSimone 1994; Goldstein 1993; Wexley and Latham 1991). These writers agree that these principles underpin the needs investigation, design, implementation and evaluation of learning experiences. A number of these principles have been recognised for over 100 years; some have come from the research of the traditionalist educators of the early 1900s; and some have been the result of more recent research, particularly in the area of human perception.

Some of the more important principles for adult learning are:

- *starting with the known*. In 1853, James Hole made the statement 'to raise the working man [sic] we must take hold of him where he is, not where he is not'. Lack of political correctness and indifferent grammar aside, this is a worthy maxim that all human resource developers should have engraved on their memory. Any learning episode must start at the learner's current level of knowledge or perspective and then gradually progress.

- *readiness to learn*. Thorndike's Law of Readiness (1913) emphasises what is, perhaps, the perfectly obvious — if the individual is ready to learn, he or she will find the experience more satisfying. While this tenet may be obvious, it is invariably honoured by its absence rather than its presence in most learning designs.

- *part learning*. Based on his experiments in the 1880s, Ebbinghause found that, in order to learn new material, it is more efficient to space practice than to mass it (see Grattan 1955). This has led to two themes. Firstly, any material for learning should be separated into reasonably sized pieces and then presented to the learner. Miller (1956) coined the term 'chunking' to describe this process. Typically, adult learners tend to store information that is given in smaller chunks. The usual 'rule of thumb' is 7 (+ or −2) — i.e., adults will remember information when it is divided into chunks of five to nine elements.

- *spaced learning*. The concept of chunking assumes that there is a space between the chunks. This has led to the second theme from Ebbinghause's experiments. The question then becomes: 'How should this space be constructed?' The most obvious answer is time — allow some time between the chunks, although not too much or the forgetting process kicks in. The second option is to use an activity that is associated with the information learnt.

- *active learning*. Delahaye and Smith (1998) suggest that using an activity to reinforce the previous chunk of information is called 'active learning'. The basic premise is that there is a difference between hearing about a concept and doing the concept. This idea has strong links with the knowledge-creation process of internalisation — where the 'whole body' experience becomes important. The saying 'I hear and I forget. I see and I remember. I do and I understand' encapsulates active learning quite well.

- *overlearning*. Another insight from Ebbinghause's work was that once something is learned, it is not forgotten at an even rate. Rather, most is lost very quickly and the rest is forgotten at a slow and fairly even rate. Thorndike (1913) established his Law of Exercise to combat this phenomenon — the more connections are used, the stronger they become. Hence, repetition increases retention. However, such repetition is often in conflict with an adult's power of self-responsibility — repetition can be quite boring. The design of any learning episode needs to incorporate repetition in a subtle, but effective, manner. McGehee and Thayer (1961) call such repetition 'overlearning' — practising beyond the point in time when the material or task is mastered.

- *multiple-sense learning*. Delahaye and Smith (1998) point out that humans are visual animals and it has been shown that we take in about 80% of our information through sight and about 10% through hearing. The use of multiple-sense learning means combining all the senses, although in reality educators are advised to concentrate on designing appropriate and effective visual aids — the talking side seems to come naturally!

- *feedback*. Feedback is critical to learning. Harris and DeSimone (1994) suggest that feedback has two dimensions. Informational feedback provides understanding on what has been done correctly and what needs improvement. Motivational feedback occurs when the recipient values the information. Both dimensions are important.

- *meaningful material*. The information being presented has to be acceptable and useful to the learner. McGehee and Thayer (1961) have shown that the more meaningful the material being presented, the more likely it will be learnt and remembered. Delahaye and Smith (1998) suggest that the material presented should be meaningful to the learner in two ways. Firstly, it should be linked to the learner's past and, secondly, it should be relevant to the learner's future.

- *transfer of learning*. Harris and DeSimone (1994) discuss a concept of Thorndike and Woodworth (1901) called identical elements. The more similar the learning and the performance situations, the more likely it is that the learning will be transferred back to the working situation. The human resource developer should always endeavour to 'bring the workplace into the training room' by using, as far as possible, the exact working materials and equipment during the learning episode.

While the traditional school has given us some important insights into adult learning, there is no doubt that some of the values of the school are at odds with the needs of adults. In particular, the assumptions that knowledge is a fairly fixed body of information (see Berte 1975), the impersonal and structured curriculum and the controlling nature of the expert (see Howe 1977) are the very opposite of the values of andragogy enunciated by Knowles. On the other hand, a significant amount of learning within organisations is instrumental learning — showing staff how to manipulate their workplace environment, whether it be using a machine, completing a form or entering information into a computer. Such procedural knowledge is the lifeblood of most organisations. The potential for conflict with the andragogical values, however, underlines the need for thoughtful and careful design of learning experiences for adults when using instrumental learning.

COMMUNICATIVE LEARNING

Communicative learning differs from instrumental learning on two counts. Firstly, rather than how to control or manipulate the external environment, communicative learning involves the dynamics of understanding others. In communicative learning, the approach is one in which the learner attempts to understand what is meant by another through speech, writing, drama, art or dance. You are involved in communicative learning as you are reading this text. However, such learning goes deeper than mere words. Communicative learning — trying to understand what someone means — often involves values, intentions, feelings, moral decisions, ideals and normative concepts which may be defined only by their contexts, like freedom, love, beauty and justice (Mezirow 1994).

Secondly, Mezirow (1994) contends that, instead of attempting to determine 'truth' (as occurs in instrumental learning), communicative learning seeks to establish the validity, or justification, for personal beliefs. It should also be noted that communicative learning is seldom amenable to empirical tests.

Debate

When considering a verbal interaction with another, the paradigm that most readily comes to mind is a debate. In a debate, one party attempts to convert the other to the 'true or correct' point of view. Argyris (1992, pp. 26–27) refers to this type of interaction as 'model I theory-in-use' and believes that there are four governing processes. The debater:
1. strives to be in unilateral control
2. minimises losing and maximises winning
3. minimises the expression of negative feelings
4. gives the appearance of being rational throughout the interaction.

In carrying out these processes, there are two underlying strategies. The communicator debates without encouraging enquiry. This strategy is designed to maintain control and eventually win. Secondly, to maximise the chance of winning, avoid upsetting and appearing to remain rational, the communicator tries to unilaterally save face — for both parties. A debate, then, has more to do with instrumental learning as the search is for 'truth'. However, once knowledge leaves the most basic level where 'truth' is indeed an identifiable entity (such as water is made up of two atoms of hydrogen and one atom of oxygen), then a debate becomes much less useful.

For communicative learning, an interaction called a rational discourse is much more useful.

Rational discourse

As espoused by Knowles (1990), one major defining feature of adult learners is the need to understand the meaning of what others communicate. This need to understand values, ideals, feelings and moral decisions can only be achieved through rational discourse.

> Discourse is used here to refer to that special kind of dialogue in which we focus on content and try to justify beliefs by giving and defending reasons and by examining the evidence for and against competing viewpoints. We search out those who we believe to be most informed, objective and rational to seek a consensus in the form of a best collective judgement. We settle for a best judgement, given careful assessment of reasons, arguments and evidence. ... [When new evidence is encountered], then the process of discourse continues, often in a series of one-to-one encounters, including authors of published texts.

(Mezirow 1994, p. 225)

Rational discourse, then, can be defined as a discussion that allows each party to understand the position of the other party and, in turn, to have his or her own position understood. Brookfield (1995) describes this process as 'democratic discourse' and defines it as the ability to talk and listen respectfully to those who hold views different from our own.

Rational discourse is more likely to be successful (Mezirow 1994) when the learners:
- have equal opportunity to participate
- are free from coercion and distorting self-deception
- are open to alternative points of view and care about the way others think and feel.

Argyris (1992, pp. 153–155) adds three more variables to these, when he discusses his model II theory-in-use. Model II is essentially a description of his double-loop learning, where an individual or organisation examines and/or changes the underlying governing variables or the master programs:
- The interaction is based on valid information.
- The participants have free and informed choice.
- The participants keep testing the validity of the choices, especially as the choices are being implemented.

Knowledge generation

Communicative learning can be seen in the knowledge-generating processes of Nonaka and Takeuchi (1995). When considered at the individual level, there are two major pathways for knowledge to be generated. Using pathway 1, person A selects some knowledge from his tacit level, perhaps using an analogy, and converts this to explicit knowledge (externalisation) which is then declared to person B. Person B adds this declared knowledge to her explicit knowledge (combination) and some elements of this new explicit knowledge may then progress into her tacit knowledge (internalisation). This may then trigger a previously unrelated thought in person B, which is then converted into her explicit knowledge (externalisation) and is declared to person A. Person A adds this to his explicit knowledge (combination) and, in turn, some of this explicit knowledge may progress to his tacit knowledge (internalisation) — and so rational discourse would continue.

Two points need to be acknowledged in this externalisation–combination–internalisation interaction. Firstly, it is difficult to be precise on the amount or type of knowledge that is internalised — as this knowledge is moving from the explicit (declarable) to the tacit (non-declarable) level, the individual concerned is most probably unaware of what has been transferred. Secondly, this externalisation–combination–internalisation path can be used in the debating method as well as rational discourse. However, in the debating method, internalisation is unlikely to occur as the listener is more concerned about defending a point of view rather than understanding the other's world of values and beliefs.

The second pathway connects the tacit levels of knowledge in the two individuals, via socialisation. Again, this will occur with debate and rational discourse. In debate, the tacit knowledge exchanged is more likely to be about power — attempting to sway the other to the 'true' point of view. In rational discourse, the two communicators pick up messages about feelings and emotions — they read nonverbals, for example — and this additional information enhances the level of knowledge of each of the communicators.

Using the two pathways in rational discourse provides what Nonaka and Takeuchi (1995) describe as 'total body communication' — shared experiences, not just mental experiences but at the bodily level as well so that the emotions and senses are involved also. They go on to point out that such learning is not only a forum for creative dialogue but also a medium for sharing experience and enhancing trust.

a closer look   2.1

Pathway 1 — Communicative learning using knowledge-generation processes

In a class on adult learning, I was discussing Mezirow's three levels of learning — instrumental, communicative and emancipatory. Some of my input had come directly from my explicit knowledge — by this time in my career, I know the basics of Mezirow off by heart! However, some had come from my tacit knowledge — for example, when I shared a long forgotten story about my abhorrence of some personal use of power. This explicit and tacit knowledge was declared to the class and was hopefully combined with their explicit knowledge to widen their explicit knowledge.

One of the class members, a principal of a primary school, commented that the three levels of instrumental–communicative–emancipatory most probably occurred in children as well. From my explicit knowledge I replied that there was certainly research in the area, usually indicating that, with children, it was felt that their emancipatory level was being developed while with adults the expectation was that the belief systems had already been developed and the emancipatory level was about change or transformation.

As I was declaring this explicit knowledge, I had a sudden memory of a TV documentary I had seen the previous week on siblings in the human race. The presenter had said that siblings were hardwired to compete and fight with each other but fortunately they were also hardwired not to kill each other. I could easily picture this segment of the documentary. I then related this picture to the class and went on to suggest that perhaps children were hardwired to learn at different levels depending on their age — instrumental learning between 1 and 5, communicative learning between 6 and 12 and emancipatory learning in their teens. Thus, with the interaction with the class member, my externalisation–combination–internalisation process created new knowledge.

I have since learned that this 'hardwiring' concept is not new in childhood education and is much more complicated than the interaction in my class suggested. As viewed from my own development, this is immaterial for two reasons. The interaction had generated new information for myself and the class members. Secondly, without this new insight, I would not have continued my queries with other professional colleagues at a later date, consequently increasing my (albeit limited) explicit and tacit knowledge of childhood learning.

The importance of communicative learning

Because of the difficulty in measuring objective outcomes of communicative learning, it is often sadly underestimated or even dismissed. A number of initiatives of the 1980s — such as industrial democracy, empowerment and total quality management — failed, or did not have the expected impact, because the techniques of instrumental learning were used instead of the principles of communicative learning. Communicative learning, a deeper and more complex process than instrumental learning, tends to have a more profound and long-term impact on the organisation's ability to survive. In addition, communicative learning, particularly through rational discourse, has a developmental effect on critical thinking and, as we shall see later, on critical reflection.

Communicative learning is involved in all the four steps of HRD. At the needs investigation stage, the researcher is attempting to uncover the deep, underlying values, beliefs and 'views of the world' of the information provider; during the design stage, the developer will need to make judgements on how knowledge that is more complex than facts (i.e. beliefs and values) can be presented; during implementation, the facilitator will be constantly looking for opportunities to use communicative learning; and at the evaluation stage, the evaluator will need to look beyond the simple facts and figures to gauge the level of complex learning that has occurred and its effect on the organisation.

EMANCIPATORY LEARNING

Mezirow (1996b) believes that emancipatory learning requires individuals to transform their basic frames of reference — hence the term 'transformational learning'.

Originally, Mezirow called these frames of reference 'meaning structures' and Argyris (1992) refers to them as 'master programs in the individual's head' that dictate the kind of meanings and behavioural strategies the individuals will or will not produce.

Frames of reference, then, are those deep-seated underlying values and belief systems that guide, shape and dictate our everyday attitudes and behaviours. We need these frames of reference. Every day we are bombarded with a variety of signals, cues and stimuli. If we tried to assess and judge each one of these inputs, we would become quickly overwhelmed. So, frames of reference provide us with a pre-disposition to act. Mezirow (1990) suggests that what we do and do not perceive, comprehend and remember is profoundly influenced by our frames of reference.

A hierarchy of assumptions

Mezirow (1990, 1991) suggests that there are two types of frames of reference — meaning perspectives and meaning schemes. While he has provided some fairly good descriptions of meaning perspectives over the years, the definition of meaning schemes is still somewhat unclear. However, Brookfield (1995) uses the term 'assumptions' and suggests that there is an hierarchy of three — paradynamic, prescriptive and causal.

Paradynamic assumptions

Paradynamic assumptions are the same as Mezirow's meaning perspectives (Mezirow 1990, 1991, 1994). These assumptions are the basic axioms we use to order the world into fundamental categories. Paradynamic assumptions are the broad sets of predis-positions and are the foundation for the prescriptive and causal assumptions. They provide us with criteria for judging right and wrong, bad and good, true and false, appropriate and inappropriate. Paradynamic assumptions are acquired uncritically in childhood through socialisation, often within a context of emotionally charged relationships with parents, teachers or other important adults. We may not recognise them as assumptions, even after they have been pointed out as such. Instead, we insist that they are objectively valid renderings of reality. When paradynamic assumptions are challenged and changed, the consequences for our lives are often explosive.

Mezirow (1990, 1994, 1996a) sees that there are three major sources of para-dynamic assumptions (or meaning perspectives):

1. *sociolinguistic* — such as ideologies, social norms, language codes. The first two — ideologies and social norms — imprint us with power perceptions and social relationships, especially those currently prevailing that are legitimised and enforced by institutions in our society. The way we address people, both verbally and nonverbally, as well as the accompanying emotions, come from this socio-linguistic foundation. Mezirow gives an illuminating example of language codes.

> A good example is the English language. The English language is a real problem in one specific way. We don't have any words between the polari-ties. Everything is big or little, fat or thin, rich or poor, beautiful or ugly. We don't have any intermediate words. A number of [other] languages have them. Certainly that's a severe limitation that forces us to think, and feel and see in certain ways.

(Mezirow 1996a, p. 9)

2. *psychological* — the way that neuroses and psychoses and personality tend to limit the individual's responses to the external environment. So, some people are extroverted and gain their energy from the external environment and interacting with others; other people are introverted and are happy to work with the images and thoughts within their mind (see Myers 1986).
3. *epistemic* — the individual preferences for taking in information. For example, people have different learning styles (whether one is a pragmatist, activist, theorist or reflector; see the discussion in chapter 9) and different sensory preferences for taking in information — print, visual, aural, interactive, tactile/manipulative, kinesthetic/manipulative, olfactory.

Prescriptive assumptions

These assumptions provide us with guidance on what ought to be happening in a particular situation, given that we all yearn to live in an ordered world. The **prescriptive assumptions** can be identified by the words 'ought' or 'should' in conversation.

Causal assumptions

Causal assumptions help us understand how different parts of the world work and the conditions under which processes can be changed. These assumptions are usually stated in predictive terms — 'If I smile when I look at a stranger, I will be accepted'.

THE ROLE OF FRAMES OF REFERENCE

These assumptions of frames of reference — paradynamic, prescriptive and causal — selectively order and delimit learning by defining our horizons of expectation which significantly affect the activities of perceiving, comprehending and remembering.

In addition to dictating how an individual acts, our frames of reference have three important qualities:
1. They filter information, accepting information that supports them and rejecting information that does not. This means they are rarely changed without some effort on the part of the individual. Argyris (1992, p. 10) points out that just because individuals experience inconsistency between their actions and their beliefs does not necessarily mean that they will change either the action or belief.
2. They are very well defended by the psyche of the individual so only particular change processes are likely to have any effect on them. This defence mechanism is quite sophisticated and complex and our understanding of the defence mechanisms is incomplete. Argyris (1992, pp. 12–25) has suggested that one such defence mechanism is the use of espoused values — values which an individual claims are his or her underlying master programs. However, there is a difference between an individual's espoused values and his or her theories-in-action. Theories-in-action can only be identified by observing behaviours. We have all heard of the boss who says 'My door is always open' but, when an employee tests this invitation, he or she receives significant negative nonverbal indicators that the boss is not really interested. In fact, this separation of espoused versus theory-in-action is so strong that individuals often use a paradynamic assumption (or, if you like, theory-in-action or master program) while simultaneously advising others not to do so (e.g. 'Your big problem is that you always criticise other people').

3. Any change to a meaning structure is usually accompanied by a high emotional reaction. The emotions may be of the more negative type, such as anger and fear, or more positive, such as wonder or excitement or satisfaction. More frequently, the emotions are a mixture of positive and negative. So an individual challenging a personal hegemonic assumption will experience fear of the unknown in letting go of a faithful servant (the paradynamic assumption or theory-in-action) but will experience also the sense of freedom and excited anticipation of a future unconstrained by the stultifying theory-in-action.

Changing frames of reference

For most people, the majority of their frames of reference operate as they should — guiding the individual, with relative safety, through the paths, traps and quagmires of everyday life. However, some of our frames of reference are what Brookfield (1995) calls hegemonic assumptions — assumptions and practices that seem to make our lives easier but actually work against our own best long-term interests. (Mezirow 1996a, p. 11) refers to these hegemonic assumptions as 'all libidinal, linguistic, epistemic, institutional or environmental forces that can limit an individual's options and rational control over one's life but have been taken for granted or seen as beyond human control'. So, for example, an adult learner may have a belief that he is hopeless at using a computer and this could be classified as a causal assumption. This causal assumption may be based on a paradynamic assumption that 'book learning is a waste of time'. However, if this adult learner wishes to succeed at further learning then he will have to challenge these hegemonic assumptions (both causal and paradynamic). Emancipatory learning is the liberation from these hegmonic assumptions.

There are two ways to change frames of reference. One is to gradually change an associated cluster of causal and prescriptive assumptions. This is often achieved through communicative learning and modelling. By exposure to others' values and belief systems, an individual can gradually change a series of causal and prescriptive assumptions and eventually an entire paradynamic assumption. For example, most new doctoral candidates are somewhat overawed by the various articles and texts they have to read. To them, the written word seems to take on the veracity of the Holy Grail, simply because it has been published in a journal or by a publishing company. So, what is written is copied automatically by the doctoral candidate, without due thought or consideration — an action called 'reporting the literature'. However, after watching their doctoral supervisor challenge several writings — commenting on both the worthy and inappropriate contributions to a particular theoretical stance — the candidate starts to recognise that published material is not necessarily the pure truth (a causal assumption). After several demonstrations, the candidate reads a journal article and identifies components that are supported by other literature and parts that are contrary to other literature. After doing this with several journal articles, the candidate then summons the courage to put these reasonings onto paper — a process called 'analysing the literature'. After several episodes of analysing the literature, the candidate suddenly realises that, when reading a journal article and not understanding it, her first response is not to castigate herself and assume that she is dimwitted. Rather, she firstly questions the writing ability of the author, then the quality of the content and finally cross-checks to see if, indeed, she has been mistaken. Thus the paradynamic assumption, that someone who has had a journal article published must be superior to a mere doctoral candidate, is broken.

The second way that frames of reference can be changed is by a **disorientating dilemma** — a divorce, death of a loved one, change in job status (Mezirow 1990). The individual is faced with an undeniable and significant fact or event that is at odds with the paradynamic assumption — a state of mental conflict called 'cognitive dissonance'. Under cognitive dissonance, given that the fact or event is indisputable, the individual experiences distress and is then motivated to reduce this distress by changing the paradynamic assumption. Mezirow (1994, p. 224) suggests that the individual passes through the following phases:

1. a disorientating dilemma
2. self-examination with feelings of guilt or shame, sometimes turning to religion for support
3. a critical assessment of assumptions
4. recognition that one's discontent and the process of transformation are shared and that others have negotiated a similar change
5. exploration of options for new roles, relationships and actions
6. planning a course of action
7. acquiring knowledge and skills for implementing one's plans
8. provisionally trying out new plans
9. renegotiating relationships
10. building competence and self-confidence in new roles and relationships
11. a reintegration into one's life on the basis of conditions dictated by one's new perspective.

CRITICAL REFLECTION

Whether the paradynamic assumptions are transformed by the sudden, and usually traumatic, occurrence of a disorientating dilemma or by the slower conversion of a cluster of causal and prescriptive assumptions, there is one common process that must transpire — critical reflection.

Critical reflection occurs when an individual discerningly examines the very foundations and justifications for his or her beliefs. The individual may ask such questions as 'What are these habits of thinking that I have fallen in to?', 'What are the frames of reference that support these habits?' and 'Where did these frames of reference come from?'. Brookfield (1995, p. 8) sees two elements that allow reflection to become critical. Firstly, when reflection is used to understand how considerations of power undergird, frame and distort processes and interactions. Secondly, when assumptions and practices that seem to make our lives easier but actually work against our own best long-term interests are questioned.

Mezirow (1990, p. 6) emphasises the differences of reflecting on the content, process and premises of problem solving and these can be linked to the three levels of assumptions:

- *content reflection*, which focuses on causal assumptions by examining the content of the problem
- *process reflection*, which focuses on prescriptive assumptions by examining the processes used to solve the problem
- *premise reflection*, which focuses on paradynamic assumptions by examining the basic premise of the problem.

An example of critical reflection

Managers often have difficulty in conducting a performance appraisal on one of their staff. If a manager wished to become critically reflective on the problem, he or she could examine each of the three levels:

1. *content reflection.* The manager would consider the various indicators he or she used — observations of behaviour, the quality of reports written, the number of errors. By looking closely at those indicators the manager would be critically reflecting at the content level.

2. *process reflection.* If the manager asks such questions as 'Have I seen enough of this staff member to make such judgements?' or 'Were all the errors directly attributable to that particular staff member?' then the manager is examining the process of problem solving and will analyse the prescriptive assumptions underlying these questions.

3. *premise reflection.* When the manager examines the very foundations of the decision

for any personal biases that may have occurred then he or she may ask a questions such as 'Why do I expect such precision in all that the staff do?'. This question strikes at the very heart of the decision. 'Are my expectations too high?', 'Do I always produce such perfect work?', 'Am I always error free?' These are confirmatory questions that could easily follow to check on the veracity of the paradynamic assumption.

Comment

Whether the manager then progresses through transformational learning and changes the paradynamic assumption depends on whether the disorientating dilemma was strong enough to challenge the paradynamic assumption or whether the content and process reflections changed a cluster of related causal and prescriptive assumptions.

For example, suppose the manager's judgement on the performance appraisal had been

overturned by a higher authority — the CEO or an appeals board (as they have in some public service organisations). Such a decision, contrary to the one that the manager made, may strike at the heart of the manager's paradynamic assumption and be so disorientating that the manager does proceed directly to the premise reflection stage. Or the contrary decision may be one of a series and the manager may reflect at the content and process stage over several cycles and gradually realise that the content and process reflections are identifying a common theme — 'Why do I not like a staff member to dress so casually?', 'Why should a report use headings and subheadings?', 'Can a staff member really be error free?' Then the manager could come to the conclusion that this common trend is really concerned with a deeply held belief about precision and that such an extreme belief no longer has a place in his or her work as a manager.

THE IMPORTANCE OF TRANSFORMATIONAL LEARNING

Emancipatory learning (or transformational learning as it is sometimes called) looks at changing frames of reference — paradynamic, prescriptive and causal — and is a very complex, value-laden and emotional process. At the heart of transformational learning is the process of critical reflection where the individual actively examines those assumptions or frames of reference to see if they still have a place in the individual's current life. Hegemonic assumptions — those assumptions that seem to make our life easier but in fact work against our long-term best interests — are usually recognised as worthy of change. However, in the modern management of organisations, managers often need to become aware of the 'mind maps' of staff for comparison with the strategic or legal imperatives faced by the organisation. Debilitating inconsistencies between the assumptions of the individual and the obligations of the organisation may demand the alteration of the individual's assumptions. For example, many public service departments have undergone significant change in recent years. Under the old bureaucratic model, a public service department made decisions based on the policies of the department, whether or not those policies made sense. Now the public service organisations are expected to operate a service to clients. Some public servants had great difficulty changing to this new way of making decisions and needed to go through transformational learning to make the adjustment.

If organisations are going to succeed in surviving the dynamic environments in which they now operate, staff will need to examine continually their own basic assumptions. Further, managers will be expected to become experts in the various strategies that facilitate the emancipatory learning process. Ironically, becoming adept at facilitating such change will mean that managers will need to work through transformational learning themselves.

CRITICAL THINKING

When discussing transformational learning, Mezirow concentrates on changing frames of reference. However, there is certainly more to individual higher level learning than this. One area of importance that is also discussed in the literature is critical thinking.

Critical thinking is different from critical reflection. Critical reflection involves the deep examination of the very foundations and justifications of one's beliefs. Critical thinking, however, impinges on our knowledge of a topic or the logic we use to change our knowledge of a topic. So, for example, during rational discourse, an individual may identify gaps in his or her knowledge or some dissonance between one concept and another. In closing the gap in the knowledge, the individual may simply add new knowledge. In challenging the dissonance between concepts the individual may work through a decision-making process that clarifies the situation.

The knowledge generation processes of externalisation and internalisation play a large part in the critical thinking process during rational discourse. As the two learners empathically disclose and listen, they are attempting to articulate tacit knowledge into explicit knowledge. The interaction helps the disclosing party to formulate and concretise the formerly undefined tacit knowledge. As this tacit knowledge becomes explicit the listener is trying to digest this new knowledge and create new, or change current, tacit knowledge. This process forms part of the individual's critical thinking ability.

Revans (1982) has suggested that 'Learning = Programmed Knowledge + Questioning Insight' (L = P + Q). He sees programmed information being available in the textbooks and journals in the library and being 'the stuff of traditional education'. He goes on to comment that traditional instruction prepares one for the treatment of puzzles or difficulties from which escapes are thought to be known, even though the escapes or solutions might be hard to discover, and calls for the skill of experts (Revans 1983, p. 11). The parallels of programmed knowledge with instrumental learning and explicit knowledge are obvious. However, the process of formulating questions and working logically through the various options, comparisons and alternatives is, to Revans, the real hallmark of learning. Therefore, this questioning insight deals with the resolution of problems, and the acceptance of the concomitant opportunities, about which no single course of action is to be justified by any code of programmed knowledge. This process of questioning is the basic foundation of critical thinking.

The literature gives surprisingly diverse views on the definitions and approaches of critical thinking. Typically, textbooks on the topic rely heavily on the technicalities of logic and provide detailed discussion of the anatomy of argument, inductive and deductive reasoning, the role of premise and fallacies of argument. These concepts throw little light on the processes of critical thinking. However, there is some agreement on what could be termed the components of critical thinking — problem solving, creativity, evaluation, dialectic thinking and logical reflection.

PROBLEM SOLVING

Problem solving tends to be seen as a major focus of critical thinking. In the learning literature, two processes — one by Dewey and one by Revans — provide some insight into the problem-solving component of critical thinking.

Scientific problem solving

As far back as 1910, Dewey suggested a robust problem-solving model that has stood the test of time. The model has been used extensively in textbooks over the years and generally follows seven steps — define the problem, identify possible solutions, evaluate each solution, select a solution, plan the implementation, implement, evaluate to see if the original problem has been solved.

It is surprising to see the number of people who define a problem as a possible solution — 'We need team building'. In fact team building is often just one possible solution — the problem is usually low productivity. There could in fact be a number of possible solutions to low productivity — improved communications, better control systems, lower staff turnover and so on. So the scientific problem-solving model helps the critical thinker to first identify the real goal. Another mistake that is often made is to analyse a possible solution as it is raised. Now, identifying possible solutions is a creative activity while evaluation is a logical, auditing exercise. To gain clarity of thinking, the two elements should not be mixed. Finally, the model ensures that the problem-solving activity results in an activity and that the outcome of this activity is compared against the original catalyst — the problem that needed solving.

System beta

In describing the way managers should solve problems, Revans (1982, 1983) believed that a five-step process, which he called 'System Beta', should be used. He saw System Beta as comprised of five steps:

1. *survey*, which is a stage of observation where the critical thinker collects data and finally admits that some dissonance or contradiction is occurring

2. *hypothesis*, which is a stage of theory, of conjecture, of testing. The critical thinker may make suppositions, or even guesses, at new relationships between the observed variables.
3. *experiment*, where practical tests are carried out to compare the new speculated relationships (or even guesses) with some standard. This standard may come from a reliable authority (a textbook or person) or even be some activity such as a rehearsal or a pilot study.
4. *audit*, where actual and desired results are compared. This may be highly objective with the comparison of measurements, or highly subjective, such as personal assessment of the outcomes or even a debate or discussion with another party.
5. *review*, where the speculated relationship between variables are retained or rejected.

This five-step process provides a simple yet vigorous paradigm that can be used to enhance critical thinking. While it does have similarities to the scientific problem-solving model, System Beta emphasises the role of observation and experimentation in critical thinking.

These two models — one by Dewey and the other by Revans — provide some insights into the critical thinking process. However, both are in the realms of explicit knowledge and there is a suspicion that professionals rely more on tacit knowledge for problem solving. Such tacit problem-solving knowledge can be built only by experience, often using the socialisation process with the novice professional working alongside the master.

CREATIVITY

Creativity is associated with novel responses. To act creatively, one brings previously unconnected elements together in new, unusual or adaptive ways. Creativity involves formulating possible solutions to a problem (note the link with problem solving here) or explanations for a phenomenon (Barry and Rudinow 1990, p. 6). Boden (1992, p. 47) believes that the goal of creativity is exploration — where the terrain explored is the mind itself. The individual draws on a wide reservoir of knowledge, a deep well of experience, and combines this with a vivid imagination and courageous intuition. Creativity is therefore a product of processing information in unique and imaginative ways.

EVALUATION

Evaluation in critical thinking is largely about testing for what is both relevant and significant — distinguishing the relevant from the irrelevant, the significant from the trivial, as Barry and Rudinow (1990, p. 4) remark. They go on to suggest that evaluation involves determining and assessing the reasons for a position, trying to find out whether a position is worth holding, thereby serving as a basis for further discussion and inquiry (p. 3).

Evaluation relies on a standard to provide a basis for comparison. Sometimes this standard comes from an individual's explicit knowledge, and the link between the standard, the issue being reviewed and the logic of the comparison being made can be readily articulated. However, the standard can also come from the individual's tacit knowledge or even from his or her frames of reference and in these cases the logical link is often more difficult to assert. This difficulty is not a reasonable justification for assuming that the evaluation is not valuable.

DIALECTIC THINKING

Sometimes referred to as relativistic thinking, dialectic thought allows the mind to accept that an entity has opposing attributes. For example, electricity can have both positive (provides warmth) and negative (causes fatalities) qualities. It is believed that dialectic thought is a characteristic of adults and is a trait that differentiates adults from youths (Labouvie-Vief 1985). Adults understand that all knowledge is relative and non-absolute and that thoughts, emotions, experiences, people and objects embody contradictory aspects (Perlmutter and Hall 1992). Recognising that an object or phenomenon may have more ephemeral qualities beyond the obvious and formal attributes allows an individual to imagine a wider variety of possibilities and options.

LOGICAL REFLECTION

Schon (1983, 1987) has commented on the importance of reflection in the learning of adults. Logical reflection is an important aspect of critical thinking as the adult learner reviews the problem solving and the results of being creative, and evaluates the issue under examination. It is through the logical reflection process that the adult adds to the store of explicit and tacit knowledge. Further, adult learners may conclude, through logical reflection in the critical thinking process, that critical reflection is needed to examine certain aspects of their frames of reference — thus creating a link between critical thinking and critical reflection.

THE AMALGAM OF CRITICAL THINKING

Critical thinking, then, is a higher order thought process that is complex and multi-faceted. Questioning is certainly a key activity in the process and the interaction between explicit and tacit knowledge often generates insights that appear magical. Critical thinking appears to be comprised of the components of problem solving, creativity, evaluation, dialectic thinking and logical reflection, at least. Further, it is apparent that these components mix and merge as the creative activity progresses. Finally, it is also suggested that critical thinking interacts vigorously with the frames of reference and the explicit and tacit knowledge of the individual.

UNLEARNING

Recently, there has been growing interest in the concept of 'unlearning'. Starbuck (1996, p. 727) suggests that people seem to have difficulty in discarding ineffective or obsolete methods and theories but that learning often cannot occur until after there has been unlearning.

It is interesting to reflect that the concept of unlearning only recently has become a phenomenon worthy of consideration in adult and organisational learning. Centuries ago, an individual's knowledge would last a lifetime, indeed knowledge would be passed down generations and still be highly useful. This has changed during this century until, as we pass into the new millennium, knowledge becomes rapidly obsolete — hence the need to consider the unlearning process. Surprisingly, there has been very little written on the topic.

Hedberg (1981) considers that obsolete knowledge is simply 'overwritten' — a process that is different to forgetting. With forgetting, the individual unconsciously loses knowledge, whether this knowledge is useful or not. Hedberg, however, suggests that the individual consciously erases obsolete knowledge in favour of knowledge that is more serviceable. Consider the situation where an individual is changing from a word processing package that uses keys for control instructions to the computer, to one that uses a mouse and a menu display. Hedberg's model assumes that the learner will overwrite the old knowledge on the key control with the new knowledge for the mouse control.

Klein (1989), however, believes that the new knowledge sits beside the old knowledge — hence the name of the 'parenthetic model'. He further suggests that the old knowledge can be dredged up if the individual returns to the original context. So, in our example, if the individual has to use an old word processing package that depends on keys for control of the computer, then the individual can happily revert to the old knowledge. Klein's model certainly seems closer to reality, although it does ignore the effect of Thorndike's Law of Exercise. If the old knowledge is not used for some time, certain elements of the old knowledge will be lost (i.e. forgotten). If you have ever tried to go back to a word processing package that uses keys for control rather than a computer mouse, you will know what this is like. There is usually a frantic hunt for an old instruction manual!

HOLISTIC ADULT LEARNING

Undoubtedly, organisations in the past have erred by viewing human resource development merely as instrumental learning. If an organisation's only competitive edge is the speed at which it can learn, then the individual staff member will need to be viewed as a learning entity — a holistic view of the human resource learning process is needed. Figure 2.1 provides an overview of the total entity of a learning adult.

Tacit knowledge and paradynamic assumptions are held in the subconscious mind of the individual. They are both unarticulated and therefore difficult to define and virtually impossible to measure. The two elements most probably overlap and interact but, with our present knowledge of adult learning, the exact nature of their relationship is not understood. What is now recognised is the power of both these elements of the subconscious mind in the life of the individual. As organisations come to rely more and more on the judgement, knowledge and commitment of people, the ability to provide opportunities for individuals to change, develop and adjust the tacit knowledge and paradynamic assumptions becomes critically important. The emphasis here is on the 'provide opportunities'. While there are definite moral dilemmas for organisations in attempting to manipulate tacit knowledge or paradynamic assumptions, the change processes are so subtle and difficult, it is doubtful that organisations could overtly force any change across a mass of staff.

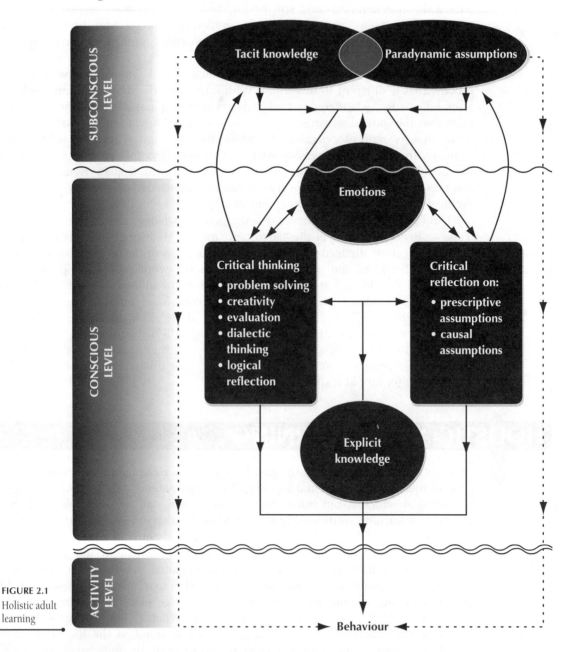

FIGURE 2.1
Holistic adult learning

Partly in the subconscious level and partly in the conscious, the emotions are an element of learning that the White Anglo-Saxon Protestant values would prefer to ignore. Yet emotions are a strong intervening variable in all but the most instrumental of learning events. Writers such as Brookfield (1990) recognise that it would be quite unnatural for learners not to experience learning emotionally. He goes on to compare teaching to the educational equivalent of white-water rafting (1990, p. 2) and learning as a gloriously messy pursuit in which surprise, shock and risk are endemic (1990, p. 1). The emotional energy of all stakeholders in a learning event is a powerfully pervasive force which, if ignored, will invariably lead to antipathy at the best or outright rebellion at the worst.

At the higher levels of the conscious mind are the processes of critical thinking and critical reflection. Critical thinking involves the problem-solving processes, creativity, evaluation, dialectic thinking and logical reflection. Critical reflection at the conscious level occurs on the prescriptive and causal assumptions. Critical reflection and critical thinking interact, most probably constantly and vigorously. For example, critical reflection on a prescriptive assumption would almost certainly require problem solving and creativity, and most probably would also involve evaluation and dialectic thinking as well. There could also be occasions, as an individual logically reflects on the critical thinking process, when the individual realises that a causal, prescriptive or even paradynamic assumption is the real barrier to progress. The individual would then have a choice of critically reflecting on these assumptions. Further, both of these critical thinking and critical reflection processes are influenced by the functions of tacit knowledge, paradynamic assumptions and the emotions. Critical thinking and critical reflection, in turn, affect explicit knowledge.

These functions and processes in the subconscious and conscious levels, of course, operate within the individual. To a second party, the only evidence of action is in the behaviour of the individual. This behaviour can be influenced by explicit knowledge, the prescriptive or causal assumptions or by the critical thinking processes — or even a combination of all three. Further, the behaviour of the individual can be directly influenced by his or her paradynamic assumptions and tacit knowledge.

Holistic adult learning, then, recognises the incredible complexities involved in the learning of adults. Appropriate learning experiences will depend on the nature of the change required and the emotional and motivational forces affecting the individual at the time. This totality of the human learning experience becomes a prime underlying metaprocess crucial to the four stages of needs investigation, design, implementation and evaluation.

ORGANISATIONAL LEARNING

Thus far we have concentrated on the learning at the individual level. Similar processes also occur at the organisational level and several authors discuss the organisational equivalent of emancipatory learning. Senge (1990, p. 113) believes that organisations must focus on both adaptive and generative learning. Adaptive learning is about coping while generative learning is about creativity as well as adaptive learning. Similarly, Argyris (1992, pp. 8–10) refers to double-loop learning and differentiates this from single-loop learning.

Single-loop learning occurs when an error is detected and corrected without questioning or altering the underlying values of the system. The emphasis on organisational single-loop learning may at least be partially due to the fact that most organisational activities are single-loop; that is, decomposing complex tasks into simpler tasks which produce the intended result when correctly carried out.

Double-loop learning occurs when the underlying values of the system are questioned or altered and eventuates when mismatches are corrected by first examining and altering governing variables and then the actions. These governing variables are not the underlying beliefs or values that the people in the organisation espouse; rather, they are the values that can be inferred from the actions and behaviours. Although single-loop activities are the most numerous in organisations, they are not necessarily the most powerful. Double-loop actions — the master programs — control long-range effectiveness, and, hence, the ultimate destiny of the system.

The organisational equivalent of individual hegemonic assumptions are **organisational defence mechanisms**. These defence mechanisms tend to keep an organisation in single-loop learning so that the underlying governing variables are not examined. Argyris (1992) suggests that two of these organisational defence mechanisms are:

1. *the undiscussables.* Certain issues in organisations cannot be discussed. The reasons why are often dimmed by history — but most people in the organisation know that the issue should not be discussed. New members are soon encultured into recognising the undiscussability by nonverbals or public 'put downs'. If the new member does not take the hint, then someone with higher power will be take on the responsibility to 'straighten him out'. Eerily, this enculturation into the world of undiscussables is quite overt, with the 'teacher' requiring no instruction to carry out the task. The process becomes even more bizarre, with the undiscussability of the issue becoming itself undiscussable.

   A classic example is the role of the 'assistant to' the CEO. We are not talking about a secretary or personal assistant here. The 'assistant to' is usually a professional (an engineer in an engineering company; an academic in a university). Now most research has found that the 'assistant to' tends to be involved in secondary or even tertiary tasks that the CEO does not wish to be bothered with. Often, these tasks now only exist because the CEO has not had the courage to say 'we will not be involved in this'. Any questioning of the role of the 'assistant to' is often met with a brusque comment from the CEO 'Don't talk to me about that' (indicating that the issue is undiscussable) or 'He does a very valuable job. I'm very disappointed that you would even raise it' (not only is the issue undiscussable but the undiscussable nature of the issue is also undiscussable).

2. *defensive routines.* Organisational defensive routines are highly protective and are designed to protect key members of the organisation from embarrassment, threat and surprises or to ensure that the organisation does not go in a direction that would cause discomfort to key members. Note that key members may not necessarily be at the higher levels of the organisation but are 'power centres' — people with a resource that gives them potency. This potency may come from a variety of sources, for example by being the reservoir of critical knowledge or by occupying a key indispensable position in the information flow of the organisation. Defensive routines used by organisations are many and varied and are often unique to a particular organisation. One common defensive routine is the meeting which identifies a series of issues but never decides on what must be done about those issues. Some defensive routines that use meetings are expert at proliferating other meetings and committees.

Defensive routines are very powerful and several attributes can be recognised:

- The organisation is avoiding double-loop learning.
- The organisation uses model I theory-in-action.
- Defensive mechanisms are invariably partnered with undiscussables.
- Defensive routines proliferate and grow in an underground manner.
- Instrumental learning may be used as a defensive routine as it does not challenge underlying values, but still gives the illusion of progress.
- Defensive routines are often used by the legitimate system to block the proposals of the shadow system.

As Nonaka and Takeuchi (1995, p. 59) comment, knowledge can be created only by individuals and therefore an organisation cannot create knowledge without individuals. However, an organisation can support creative individuals or provide contexts for them to create knowledge. To achieve this, an organisation must eliminate its defence mechanisms by becoming involved in double-loop or generative learning.

THE PRACTICAL APPLICATION OF ADULT LEARNING

Adult learning is indeed a complex and intriguing process. Historically, most organisations have viewed human resource development as merely instrumental learning — as procedural training and task-orientated problem solving. This view is based on the belief that learning in organisations is merely the transmission of explicit knowledge from one person to another, the knowledge generation process of combination. Such a stance presumes that the knowledge being transmitted has an indefinite life and will be suitable for any occasion. Now, this is partly true for some of the knowledge that is essential to the organisation's continual survival. Equipment that has an expected lengthy production life in a manufacturing company will be operated in a specific manner and needs to be serviced in a certain way at specific periods of time. As new staff are hired to work the equipment they will need to be trained in its safe operation. So, instrumental learning is an important component in organisational learning and in ensuring that the organisation's knowledge capital is passed on to those who can use it to produce income.

However, in today's complex business world, instrumental learning by itself is rarely enough. Teaching someone the safe operation of a piece of equipment is often only the start. The belief system of the individual — that safety is their responsibility — may also need to be changed and this can be achieved only through communicative and emancipatory learning. And such a change is only the start! Most organisations are trying to survive in very competitive and turbulent environments and they are becoming more dependent on staff who accept a wider responsibility — to identify new knowledge that will help the organisation survive. This challenges an even wider paradynamic assumption than 'safety is my business'. 'The future success of the organisation is also my business' is a paradynamic assumption that a majority of workers will look at in askance. Yet, if organisations are to survive the future, this is the very belief system that is needed.

The concepts of adult learning covered in this chapter should become a consistent underlying theme in the four stages of HRD:

1. *the investigation stage,* where the investigatory strategies and tools need to be selected and devised with the level of learning in mind. Survey questionnaires are ideal for instrumental learning but the interview and focus group are more likely to mine the rich context of communicative and emancipatory learning.

2. *the design stage,* where all aspects of adult learning — the basic learning types of behaviour modification and modelling; the principles of learning; rational discourse; and the considerations of challenging a paradynamic assumption — come together when designing the learning experience. Undergirding all these decisions are the deliberations of the contributions of the knowledge generation processes of externalisation, combination, internalisation and socialisation.

3. *the implementation stage,* where the human resource developers must have the skills to use the appropriate learning strategies. Instrumental, communicative and emancipatory learning all demand competence in specific skills and a thorough understanding of the values underpinning each approach.

4. *the evaluation stage,* where, in the legitimate system, evaluation completes the circle and so the issues raised in the investigation stage apply. The evaluation method used relies heavily on the level of learning. While instrumental learning is more susceptible to the mechanistic methods of cost–benefit analysis and facts and figures, such objective data merely provide gross indicators for communicative and emancipatory learning. For these two deeper levels a more active research strategy is required.

In the shadow system, that part of the organisation that explores the murky future, the adult learning theories, principles and approaches discussed in this chapter tend to operate in a most complex, even an apparently chaotic, manner. The organisational members in this system need to be very mature learners — able to apply and use all of the concepts, and more importantly, have the tacit knowledge that allows them to use the most appropriate approach at the most auspicious time.

GLOSSARY

andragogy — the art and science of teaching adults

causal assumptions — the lowest level of an individual's frames of reference

communicative learning — understanding the world of another person and establishing the validity for personal beliefs

critical reflection — where an individual discerningly examines the very foundations and justifications for personal frames of reference

critical thinking — the logical process of changing personal knowledge, by using problem solving, creativity, evaluation, dialectic thinking and logical reflection

disorientating dilemma — a significant, undeniable and usually traumatic fact or event that challenges a paradynamic assumption

emancipatory learning — transforming frames of reference, especially hegemonic assumptions

frames of reference — the deep-seated underlying values and belief systems that shape and dictate the everyday attitudes and behaviours of an individual

holistic adult learning — the total entity of a learning adult

instrumental learning — learning to control and manipulate the environment

organisational defence mechanisms — the organisational equivalent of hegemonic assumptions

paradynamic assumptions — the highest level of an individual's frames of reference

prescriptive assumptions — the second highest level of an individual's frames of reference

principles of learning — the 10 principles on which instrumental learning is based

rational discourse — used in communicative learning, meaning to talk and listen respectfully to others, even when they hold differing views

unlearning — the process of discarding obsolete or ineffective knowledge.

QUESTIONS

For review

1. Compare pedagogy and andragogy.
2. When is behaviour modification likely to be used in HRD?
3. Discuss the differences between instrumental, communicative and emancipatory learning.
4. How is rational discourse different from a debate?
5. Describe the three levels of assumptions that make up a frame of reference.
6. Describe the two ways of changing a frame of reference.
7. How does unlearning occur? Why is unlearning important in today's organisations?

For analysis

8. What is the difference between behaviour modification and modelling?
9. Describe at least one situation for each where instrumental learning, communicative learning and emancipatory learning will be most effective.
10. Think of a time when you were faced with a disorientating dilemma that changed part of your frame of reference. Did you experience the eleven steps suggested by Mezirow?
11. Compare and contrast critical reflection and critical thinking.

For application

12. Examine the model of holistic adult learning. Trace several personal learning experiences through this model. In the light of this analysis, how would you change the model?

REFERENCES

Argyris, C. (1992). *On Organizational Learning.* Cambridge, Mass.: Blackwell.

Bandura, A. (1977). *Social Learning Theory.* New Jersey: Prentice Hall.

Barry, V. E. and Rudinow, J. (1990). *Invitation to Critical Thinking.* Fort Worth: Harcourt Brace.

Berte, N. R. (Ed.). (1975). *New Directions for Higher Education.* San Francisco: Jossey-Bass.

Boden, M. A. (1992). *The Creative Mind: Myths and Mechanisms.* London: Cardinal.

Brookfield, S. D. (1990). *The Skilful Teacher.* San Francisco: Jossey-Bass.

Brookfield, S. D. (1995). *Becoming a Critically Reflective Teacher.* San Francisco: Jossey-Bass.

Delahaye, B. L. and Smith, B. J. (1998). *How to be an Effective Trainer.* New York: Wiley.

Dewey, J. (1910). *How We Think.* New York: D. C. Heath.

Dewey, J. (1938). *Experience and Education.* New York: Capricorn Books.

Domjan, M. J. (1993). *Principles of Learning and Behaviour.* (3rd ed.). Pacific Grove, CA.: Brooks/Cole.

Gardner, G., Innes, J. M., Forgas, J. P., O'Driscoll, M., Pearce, P. L. and Newton, J. W. (1981). *Social Psychology.* Sydney: Prentice Hall.

Goldstein, I. L. (1993). *Training in Organisations.* (3rd ed.). Pacific Grove, CA: Brooks/Cole.

Grattan, C. H. (1955). *In Quest of Knowledge: A Historical Perspective on Adult Education.* New York: Association Press.

Harris, D. M. and DeSimone, R. L. (1994). *Human Resource Development.* Fort Worth: Harcourt Brace.

Hedberg, B. (1981). 'How organisations learn and unlearn.' In W. H. Starbuck and P. C. Nystrom (Eds), *Handbook of Organisational Design Volume 1.* Oxford: Oxford University Press.

Howe, M. J. A. (1977). *Adult Learning: Psychological Research and Application.* Chichester: Wiley.

Klein, J. I. (1989). 'Parenthetic learning in organizations: Toward the unlearning of the unlearning model.' *Journal of Management Studies*, 26(3), 291–308.

Knowles, M. S. (1980a). 'My Farewell Address … Andragogy, no panacea, no idealogy.' *Training and Development Journal*, August, 48–50.

Knowles, M. S. (1980b). *The Modern Practice of Education: From Pedagogy to Andragogy.* (2nd ed.). New York: Cambridge Books.

Knowles, M. S. (1990). *The Adult Learner: A Neglected Species.* (4th ed.). Houston, Texas: Gulf.

Kolb, D. A. (1984). *Experiential Learning: Experience as the Source of Learning and Development.* Englewood Cliffs, NJ: Prentice Hall.

Labouvie-Vief, G. (1985). 'Intelligence and cognition.' In Birren, J. E. and Schaie, K. W. (Eds), *Handbook of the Psychology of Aging.* (2nd ed.). New York: Reinhold.

Lindeman, E. C. (1926). *The Meaning of Adult Education.* New York: New Republic.

McGehee, W. and Thayer, P. W. (1961). *Training in Business and Industry.* New York: Wiley.

Mezirow, J. (1990). *Fostering Critical Reflection in Adulthood: A Guide to Transformative and Emancipatory Learning.* San Francisco: Jossey-Bass.

Mezirow, J. (1991). *Transformative Dimensions of Adult Learning.* San Francisco: Jossey-Bass.

Mezirow, J. (1994). 'Understanding transformational theory.' *Adult Education Quarterly*, Summer, 44(4), 222–232.

Mezirow, J. (1996a). 'Transformational learning.' *Training and Development in Australia*, March, 23(1), 9–12.

Mezirow, J. (1996b). 'Contemporary paradigms of learning.' *Adult Education Quarterly*, 46(3), Spring, 158–173.

Miller, G. A. (1956). 'The magical number seven plus or minus two: Some limits on our capacity for processing information.' *Psychological Review*, 63, 81–97.

Myers, I. B. with Myers, P. B. (1986). *Gifts Differing.* Palo Alto, Ca.: Consulting Psychologists Press.

Nonaka, I. and Takeuchi, H. (1995). *The Knowledge Creating Company: How Japanese Companies Create the Dynamics of Innovation.* New York: Oxford University Press.

Perlmutter, M. and Hall, E. (1992). *Adult Development and Aging.* (2nd ed.). New York: Wiley.

Revans, R. W. (1982). *The Origins and Growth of Action Learning.* Sweden: Studentlitteratur.

Revans, R. W. (1983). *ABC of Action Learning.* Kent: Chartwell-Bratt.

Schon, D. A. (1983). *The Reflective Practitioner: How Professionals Think in Action*. New York: Basic Books.

Schon, D. A. (1987). *Educating the Reflective Practitioner: Toward a New Design for Teaching and Learning in the Professions*. San Francisco: Jossey-Bass.

Senge, P. M. (1990). 'The Leader's New Work: Building Learning Organisations.' *MIT Sloan Management Review*, Fall, 112–128.

Sigelman, C. K. and Shaffer, D. R. (1995). *Life-span Human Development*. (2nd ed.). Pacific Grove, CA: Brooks/Cole.

Skinner, B. F. (1953). *Science and Human Behavior*. New York: MacMillan.

Starbuck, W. H. (1996). 'Unlearning ineffective or obsolete technologies.' *International Journal of Technology Management*, 11(7/8), 725–737.

Sveiby, K. E. (1997). *The New Organizational Wealth: Managing and Measuring Knowledge-Based Assets*. San Francisco: Berret Koehler.

Thorndike, E. L. (1913). *The Psychology of Learning*. New York: Teacher's College.

Thorndike, E. L. (1928). *Adult Learning*. New York: MacMillan.

Watson, J. B. (1925). *Behaviorism*. New York: Norton.

Wexley, K. N. and Latham, G. P. (1991). *Developing and Training Human Resources in Organizations*. New York: Harper Collins.

Zimbardo, P. G. (1988). *Psychology and Life*. (12th ed.). Illinois: Scott, Foresman.

An ethical dilemma for a HRD manager

Susan Leong has been the human resource manager for Southern Ocean Finance for the last 8 years. Southern Ocean Finance, which can proudly trace its history back nearly 100 years, concentrates on merchant loans and affiliated insurance for customers throughout the southern Pacific Ocean and eastern Indian Ocean and has over 800 staff spread throughout the region. Customers come from the fishing industry, marine supply merchants and various yachting and fishing clubs throughout Australia. Indeed, for the last 10 years a majority of the company's new staff were recruited from the yachting and fishing clubs. It was believed that, with their background in these clubs, such recruits brought a deeper understanding of the needs of 'boating people', thereby giving the company a competitive advantage. Such recruits were given a 4-week induction program that heavily emphasised financial management and insurance assessing. Susan had conscientiously evaluated the induction programs over the last 8 years and was happily surprised to find that all trained staff maintained a very high level of skills and abilities on such important areas as risk analysis, cost–benefit analysis, investment evaluation, annuities and amortisation.

A recent strategic review of the company, however, has demonstrated that the yachting and fishing club market segment is extremely weak. Further, the company's market share in the fishing industry has fallen dramatically. Partly, this fall has been due to the increased volatility in the fishing industry — escalating costs, decreasing catches in the southern oceans and increasing surveillance by the various government and public environmental agencies. The customers in the fishing industry are looking for any cost advantage in all services provided to them — including insurance, banking and interest charges.

Enrita de Silva, the CEO of Southern Ocean Finance, analysed the income statements of the company for the last 3 years and came to the startling conclusion that over 80% of the staff recruited from the yachting and fishing clubs had not sold any products to any customers in the fishing industry.

Enrita made the decision that Southern Ocean Finance would no longer service the yachting and fishing clubs. The future of the company was to be with the fishing industry and the marine supply merchants. As she conveyed this decision to the management team, Enrita asked Susan to design a training package that would 'upskill the staff so that they can satisfactorily service the fishing industry especially'.

As it happened, Susan met a number of the staff in the company dining room the next day. She was pleased to see a number of the 'yachties and fishies', as they were known, with the group. She gave them a quick brief of the decision and asked them what should be in the training package. The responses from the 'yachties and fishies' quite astounded her. Comments that 'The yachts are where the big money is', 'Have you ever tried to talk to those professional fishermen? Every second word is the F word' and 'They work terrible hours. The only time you can talk to them is just before dawn' were the more polite complaints.

Susan realised that any training course for the 'yachties and fishies' would have to cover more than just skills. Indeed, there would have to be some significant changes to the personal values and beliefs for many of the individuals to survive in the new direction that the company was following. She thought to herself, 'How can I possibly put anyone through a development program that will force them to challenge such deep, personal beliefs?'

Discussion questions

1. What instrumental level learning has been carried out in the past?

2. To what extent has the training that concentrated on instrumental learning been successful?

3. Would you categorise the proposed training package to 'upskill the staff' as instrumental learning, communicative learning or emancipatory learning?

4. In the last paragraph of the case study, Susan is considering a development program that would ask the participants to challenge their values and beliefs. Such a program would involve emancipatory learning. Has Susan any right to force staff into such a program? What personal costs to the participants could result from such a program? What personal costs could result to either the participants or to other members of the staff, if such a program is not implemented?

Meeting organisational politics

John Henry was astounded. What did they mean, 'We don't need to go into that!'? It seemed to be such a sensible suggestion. To make it worse, after the meeting, no one seemed to want to talk to him or even be near him. Perhaps he had made a mistake in taking a promotion to this department.

Six months ago John had felt quite satisfied with himself. He had finally been promoted to the position of Internal HRD Consultant. True, he had to go to another department to win the promotion, but he was still in the Public Service. In the 6 months with his new department, he had conducted a number of successful training programs. The participants had provided good reviews of the programs and two of the section managers had made positive comments to him. However, especially when the training programs covered interpersonal skills, the participants were unanimous in their recommendations — the section managers all needed to attend these development programs. The general consensus of the participants was that their managers were grossly underskilled in interpersonal skills.

As part of his duties, John was minutes secretary to the departmental Training and Development Committee. This committee was made up of the HRD manager, all the other section managers and the assistant director of the department. John decided to raise the matter, of the need to develop all section managers in the area of interpersonal skills, at the next Training and Development Committee meeting. At the meeting he broached the matter under the agenda item 'Other matters'. There was silence in the room. The assistant director, who was chair of the committee, coughed, glanced around the room and then invited John to speak further.

John took a deep breath and then launched into a description of the feedback from the various programs he had conducted. He emphasised the constant theme from the participants that the section managers needed development in interpersonal relations, although he wisely kept the comment about 'grossly underskilled' to himself. When he finished speaking, there was again silence. Then one of the section managers rasped, 'Who has been saying that about me?' John felt flustered as he did not want to cause any trouble for the past participants of his programs. As he stuttered trying to enunciate some words, the assistant director broke in saying 'Now, now, we don't want to start a witch hunt' and then laughed. The other managers joined in the laughter. John could feel himself blushing furiously. Another manager asked if there were any other suggestions from the programs. Grasping this as a possible way of avoiding embarrassment, John replied that, yes, most participants were puzzled why this committee still had the antiquated name of training and development when human resource development was more modern.

Again, laughter met this suggestion. The assistant director called the meeting to order and commented that the last thing this committee wanted was to be seen as a bunch of dinosaurs. He then went on to say that perhaps a motion could be moved to change the committee name. This motion was quickly carried, although again accompanied with much hilarity and joking comments. John felt quite confused. The name change went through so quickly. 'But what about the development programs in interpersonal relations for the section managers?', he asked.

Again, the room was silent. John was conscious that all eyes were on him. 'We don't need to go into that!' the assistant director replied.

Discussion questions

1. What organisational defence mechanism has John encountered?
2. What is the frame of reference that is likely to be driving most of the section managers in this situation?
3. What would need to be done to change this frame of reference?

Diversity and globalisation

CHAPTER OBJECTIVES

At the end of this chapter you should be able to:

1 list the ways diversity contributes to organisational competitiveness

2 describe discrimination, stereotyping and harassment

3 describe the legal requirements for organisations in discrimination, equal employment and affirmative action

4 discuss how the HR developer should consider the adult learner characteristics of age, impairment, gender and culture

5 Explain the role of the HR developer in the globalisation of an organisation.

T he adult population in Australia outnumbers the children. Further, people are living longer and this has two results. Firstly, the adult population will continue to grow in numbers. Secondly, with differing experiences, each individual adult will refine and develop her or his personal frame of reference, thus expanding individual differences. In addition, Australia is a multicultural society and this multicultural society is reflected in all organisations in Australia. Multiculturalism can be defined as an acceptance, without prejudice or discrimination, of cultural differences within one nation (or even one organisation) with full equity for all. Davidson and Griffin (2000) suggest that the changing demographics of the contemporary labour market are affected by the broadening of gender roles, the strengthening profile of indigenous people, the higher profile of ethnicity issues and the growing population of people with disabilities. These influences of sheer numbers, individual differences and multiculturalism lead to diversity.

This chapter begins by pointing out that one of the biggest restraints on constructively mobilising the asset of diversity in organisations is ethnocentricity. **Ethnocentricity**, which is the belief in the intrinsic superiority of one's own cultural norms, leads to discrimination and stereotyping. There are three types of **discrimination** — **direct**, where an irrelevant criterion is used; **indirect**, where a seemingly neutral practice or decision disadvantages a minority group or individual; and **structural**, where discrimination becomes embedded in the system. **Harassment** is a particular form of discrimination designed to humiliate, offend, intimidate or otherwise make a person feel unwelcome. Discrimination and harassment are illegal. The federal government and all state governments have legislation prescribing fines and other punishments for individuals and organisations who transgress these laws.

However, organisations need more than the legislative equal opportunity approach. Managing the creative asset of diversity in organisations is essential. This approach includes emphasising the advantages to an organisation of managing positively the diversity among its employees. These advantages include cost savings, acquiring highly qualified staff, understanding the market better and being more creative and innovative, leading to better problem solving and systems flexibility.

There are four characteristics of adult learners that are particularly vulnerable to inappropriate decisions and behaviour. These characteristics are age, health, gender and the cultural backgrounds of the adult learners. Firstly, the HR developer should ensure that no adult learner is discriminated against on any of these characteristics. Secondly, the HR developer should identify ways in which these differences can be mobilised to enhance any learning endeavour for individuals and groups. The HR developer may consider at least two aspects of the adult learner's age. The stages of an adult's life cycle can provide the HR developer with some initial indications of the adult learner's motivation. For example, the married adult learner in her or his late twenties to mid-thirties often looks to education and learning for career security. The age of the learner may also provide some indications of **historical embeddedness** where a significant historical event, such as the Vietnam War, may affect an adult learner's predisposition towards certain responses or life-directing values. While good health is often taken for granted in Australia, the HR developer will need to consider the implications of health in various adult learners to ensure that no discrimination occurs and that learning experiences are fulfilling for all adult learners. The **gender** of the adult learner raises at least three issues. Firstly, for females the **liberatory models** highlight the need to examine all structures and systems that may oppress women in learning situations through inappropriate use of power and control. Secondly, the **gender models** emphasise the emancipatory process as women become free of hegemonic assumptions about the female role in learning. Thirdly, gender highlights the possibility of the learning needs of people with other sexual orientations such as homosexuality and bisexuality. Finally, the cultural backgrounds of the adult learners will certainly have considerable impact on the learning processes. The literature provides two useful frameworks for examining culture. Firstly, cultures can be considered as low context or high context in their styles of communication. In **low-context cultures**, the content of the message is the most important variable. In **high-context cultures**, the importance of the content is overshadowed by the context within which the message is communicated. Another useful paradigm is to compare **individualist cultures** (which value independence, creativity, solitude and equality) with **collectivist cultures** (which value reciprocity, humility, harmony and dependence on the group). Australia is a low-context, individualist culture. The HR developer must recognise that the values of such a culture may not be shared by learners with a different cultural background. To help the organisation manage its diversity positively, the HR developer should initiate **diversity training**, develop managers and supervisors in the skills and attitudes of harnessing diversity at the workfront, and develop and foster members of minority or disadvantaged groups.

For a number of organisations **globalisation** is an important strategic consideration. In such organisations, the HR developer will become heavily involved in developing the staff to interact naturally and comfortably with different cultures. Issues such as the different communication processes, male–female interactions, having a knowledge of the host culture and recognising the effect of speaking or not speaking, and even the impact of speaking with an accent, will need to be addressed. When conducting overseas learning interventions the HR developer will meet a number of challenges, including a variety of administrative issues in the host country, the different political environment and the distance of the overseas base from the organisational headquarters.

ETHNOCENTRICITY

One of the biggest restraints on constructively mobilising the asset of diversity in organisations is ethnocentricity. **Ethnocentricity** is the belief in the intrinsic superiority of one's own cultural norms. Unfortunately, this belief is often accompanied by feelings of paternalism, or even dislike and contempt, for other groups. A process that often accompanies ethnocentricism is stereotyping. **Stereotypes** are developed through generalisations which are often based on prejudice, and which often result in discrimination (Davidson and Griffin 2000). Stereotyping can be negative (for example, all males lack feelings) or positive (for example, all Africans are good at sports). All stereotypes lack accuracy and can impede learning. Both ethnocentricity and stereotyping may have been useful in ancient times when insecurity and local warfare were the norm, but neither has any place in a multicultural society such as Australia. In the organisational sphere, ethnocentricity and stereotyping are typified by discrimination and harassment.

Discrimination is the unfair treatment of an individual or a minority group based on some prejudice. In organisations there are three types of discrimination:

1. *direct discrimination,* where an irrelevant criterion is used to exclude a person or group from an opportunity — for example, not including a staff member in a wheel chair in a residential workshop because of the assumed difficulty of being able to travel to the location
2. *indirect discrimination,* where a seemingly neutral practice or decision advantages an individual or group over another individual or group — for example, commencing a developmental workshop on a Sunday, or at a certain time of the year, may discriminate against staff with certain religious beliefs and practices
3. *structural or systemic discrimination,* where the interaction of historical decisions, actions, policies and social attitudes allow discrimination to become embedded in the system — for example, sending a notice of a training course on computer hardware maintenance to men only, and considering it normal practice that does not need questioning.

Harassment is a particular form of discrimination designed to humiliate, offend, intimidate or otherwise make a person feel unwelcome or inadequate. Sexual harassment may be direct (for example, the expectation of performing a sexual behaviour to gain a benefit) or indirect (for example, using sexually explicit material or nudity on an overhead transparency). Harassment is a particularly insidious and nasty type of discrimination and is illegal in Australia and many other countries. It should also be noted that, in Australia, an employer will be held legally responsible if one employee harasses another employee.

The issues of discrimination and harassment are so serious that specific laws against the practices have been passed by governments.

THE LEGAL REQUIREMENTS

Federal anti-discrimination and equal employment opportunity legislation in Australia includes the *Racial Discrimination Act 1975,* the *Sex Discrimination Act 1984,* the *Human Rights and Equal Opportunity Commission Act 1986,* the *Affirmative Action Act 1986,* the *Equal Employment Opportunity (Commonwealth Authorities) Act 1987* and the *Disability Discrimination Act 1992.* All Australian states and territories also have anti-discrimination and equal opportunity legislation. This legislation makes it illegal to discriminate against people on such characteristics as age, sex, race, impairment, marital and parental status or religious beliefs. As Stone (1998) points out, this legislation clearly recognises that every person faces the possibility of being discriminated against although groups such as women and non-dominant racial or minority groups more often bear the brunt of such activities.

This legislation imposes specific legal requirements on HR developers so that involvement in learning opportunities is based on merit or individual needs rather than on irrelevant issues. Further, the design and implementation of learning experiences must be free of individual or systematic bias that could either directly or inadvertently discriminate against an individual or group. In addition, affirmative action legislation requires the organisation to consider equal outcomes, not just equal practices. Given that equal outcomes often require the different development of people so they can overcome past discrimination, then the HR developer will be the centre for such affirmative action undertakings within the organisation.

This legislative/legal approach to overcoming discrimination and harassment has been termed the equal opportunity (EO) approach. However, organisations need to be more pro-active than merely responding to legislative requirements if they wish to harness the full potential of their diverse staffing profile. As Stone (1998, p. 706) points out, organisations which ignore or d-value the potential of a diverse workforce miss out on a valuable source of new options. The devalued non-traditional workers often experience stress and expend considerable energy just trying to fit in. Organisations that are not inclusive waste precious human resources (Ewert, Rice and Lauderdale 1995). Further, in today's competitive environment, an organisation simply cannot afford the direct costs (for example, the fines and legal expenses under the discrimination laws) and hidden costs (for example, certain sections of the staff experiencing stress or high turnover) of discrimination and harassment.

While the EO approach has certainly produced a number of advances and provides judicial substance in combatting dehumanising practices, there are recent criticisms. Writers such as Wilson (1996) believe that the equal opportunity (EO) approach, with its reliance on external, legal forces, has not been as successful as originally envisioned. She comments that EO is more concerned with helping individuals fit in to the white, male, able-bodied norm, and people who are different are seen as problematical. In other words, the EO paradigm is trying to right a wrong for identified groups. Wilson (1996) suggests that a better approach is the management of diversity — which is about trying to get it right for everyone. The EO paradigm sees difference as a liability while the management of diversity perceives difference as an asset (Benest 1991). Further, the management of diversity sees discrimination and harassment as organisational defence mechanisms that need double-loop learning (see chapter 2).

THE ADVANTAGES OF DIVERSITY

Diversity must be celebrated within organisations. Diversity offers Australian organisations an unprecedented opportunity to ensure creativity and viability. This very diversity of backgrounds, cultures, ways of knowing and views of the world provides an almost limitless supply of options and perceptions. Organisations must ensure that the potential of this energy is harnessed so that every challenge and threat faced by the organisation will be fully examined and objectively analysed to ensure that the most feasible alternative actions are taken to ensure the organisation's future. As Stone (1998, p. 690) comments, such organisations can gain a competitive advantage whereby employee differences present opportunities to (a) improve staff management practices, (b) alter the workplace and work practices in ways which increase efficiency and safety, (c) make products and facilities more accessible to and appropriate for clients and customers, and (d) identify new products, services and markets. Davidson and Griffin (2000) present six arguments to demonstrate how diversity contributes to competitiveness. Organisations that manage diversity well:

- have higher levels of productivity and lower levels of turnover and absenteeism, thus leading to *cost advantages*
- become known among women and minority groups as good places to work and, therefore, attract qualified staff from these groups — this gives these organisations an advantage in *acquiring highly qualified staff*
- are better able to understand different market segments, providing a *marketing advantage*
- have multiple perspectives and ways of thinking, becoming more *creative and innovative*
- have an increased pool of information, giving a higher probability of realistic *problem-solving*
- have to become very flexible in managing a diverse workforce and this is then reflected in their *systems flexibility*. This systems flexibility allows organisations to respond more appropriately and quickly to environmental changes.

As Theophanous (1994) argues, social justice and economic growth can be complementary if both are pursued in such a way that the capacity to do both is maximised. For the HR developer, then, the first step in helping the organisation to manage its diversity asset, achieve social justice and economic growth is to acknowledge the differences between adult learners.

THE CHARACTERISTICS OF ADULT LEARNERS

Adult learners differ on a number of characteristics. Problems in learning and knowledge generation occur when social constructions of what is right and wrong are projected into learning episodes by those with power. This, of course, comes back to the personal frames of reference of those powerbrokers. Powerbrokers may be within the organisation (for example, managers) or outside the organisation (for example, union officials). So what is seen as 'true' learning by certain powerbrokers in an organisation may be contaminated by the very personal characteristics that those powerbrokers hold dear. The HR developer as *the designer* of the learning programs is one of the internal powerbrokers. In chapter 10, it is suggested that the designer of adult learning experiences becomes very familiar with his or her personal frame of reference and how this frame of reference may contaminate the design process. The HR developer as *the implementer* is another role where power can be used with undue influence (for example, ignoring certain learners during the learning episode).

For HRD, the literature identifies age, impairment, gender and cultural backgrounds as characteristics that are vulnerable, within adult and organisational learning, to social constructions and personal values. Basic hegemonic assumptions (see chapter 2) by powerbrokers about any of these characteristics — for example, younger people learn more quickly than older people or that people from certain racial backgrounds learn differently — can inhibit, interfere with or contaminate learning to an extraordinary degree.

AGE

Adult educators interact with learners of the widest age range. Generally, the literature tends to assume that adulthood commences at approximately 18 years and there are examples of adults still being educationally active into their eighties and nineties. This wide age range brings with it a variety of issues to be considered by the HR developer. There are two issues that are particularly worthy of understanding — the stages in an adult life cycle and the impact of historical events on an adult learner's expectations.

The stage models

Authors such as Levinson and Levinson (1996) and Sheehy (1995) suggest that adults move through a series of age-related stages in their life cycle. Each of these stages relates to particular needs and represents a transition in the adult's outlook and behaviours. In general, these stages start with the late teens and early twenties where young adults search for meaning in their lives. The mid-twenties to the mid-thirties are focused on raising a family and security. The mid-thirties to mid-forties are often seen as a time of crisis when the adult questions his or her life achievements thus far and perhaps opts for a different career direction. In the fifties the adult is coming to terms with personal mortality and the late sixties are seen as the years of contentment, or sorrow for lost opportunities.

While each of these **stage models** does appear to have some face validity, the research on which the concepts are based has been criticised for concentrating on white, male, middle-class subjects. Certainly, not every adult conforms to these sequences. Many adults meet life-changing circumstances — perhaps ill health or losing a life partner — which necessitate attention to other needs and wants. Further, the recent literature on the X-generation indicates that those in their early twenties may have different agendas than those suggested by the stage models (see, for example, Gozzi 1995; Howe and Strauss 1993).

However, a sufficient proportion of the adult population do conform to the suggested stages for the HR developer to make some initial, albeit gross, assumptions. Married staff are often searching for security and some find this security in accumulating career-related knowledge and skills. By their mid-thirties, a number of adults are looking at career changes and may need assistance in identifying possibilities and knowledge-based resources. Staff in their late fifties are often a wealth of knowledge and this knowledge should be accessed as an important knowledge silo (see chapter 14) for the management of knowledge capital.

Historical embeddedness

Baltes (1987) has suggested that the critical historical moments experienced by an individual may affect the perception of that individual. Historical moments are those events that were important to large societies at a particular time and are differentiated from those events that were more individual. An historical moment may have been the war in Vietnam or the sacking of the Whitlam government or the death of Princess Diana. As such, these momentous occasions have often affected significant proportions of the population of a particular age and influenced their outlook on certain organisationally initiated learning episodes. For example, the suspect actions of lending institutions in the 1980s may generalise into distrust of the concepts of financial management by some over-30-year-old staff.

The HR developer needs to consider these historical moments when interacting with adult learners. Firstly, the historical moment may have had an indelible effect on the frame of reference of the adult learner and this indelible effect may have been positive or negative. For example, a question relating to federal government decisions asked during a needs investigation may bring what appears to be an irrational, negative response from a Vietnam War veteran. This information needs to be treated with care and confidentiality. Secondly, those who have experienced an historical moment may have a wealth of knowledge that can be shared with other learners. When relevant, the HR developer should look for opportunities to tap into such a rich tapestry of information.

Learning and the older employee

Bennington and Tharenou (1998) have refuted a number of stereotypes about the older learner by finding that they do not have memory loss, declining intelligence, lower performance or less creativity. The older learner can keep abreast of change and new knowledge. Further, because of their rich experience and extensive backgrounds in the technical aspects of the tasks, they are valuable reservoirs of knowledge.

For further information on the development of the older staff members in the organisation see Plett and Lester (1991).

IMPAIRMENT

In Australia, with its well-developed health system, good health is usually taken for granted. Indeed, often good health is assumed to be a prerequisite for attendance at voluntary or paid employment. Such a utopian view is not, however, entirely correct. 'Impairment' is the term used in legislation to cover the variety of disabilities — either mental or physical — and health issues that can present a challenge to an individual in the working or learning environment.

As people age, certain biological changes occur and these changes can have an impact on health. Senses, particularly sight and hearing, often deteriorate in middle age. Reaction times on physical or motor skills may not be as fast as they once were. The incidence of other debilitating conditions, such as arthritis and cardiovascular disease, may increase with age. Of course, health impairments may become manifest at an earlier age. Loss of sight or hearing or mobility or other abilities may occur at birth or can be caused at any age by disease or accidents. Some refugees who have taken up residence in this country may have endured torture and abuse before coming to Australia and now experience debilitating anxiety and stress. Yet many people with these impairments or disabilities are still very active and productive members of the workforce.

While medical and technological advances have provided some corrective measures for these impairments, learning can still be a challenge because of health-related limitations. The HR developer must help the learner meet these challenges so that the important role of learning — important to the individuals and the organisation — can continue.

GENDER

It is hard to imagine that a little over 40 years ago married women were not allowed to work in the federal public service. In addition, women were paid less than their male counterparts for performing exactly the same jobs. A number of other large organisations of that time had similar policies. Such policies had negative emotional and financial effects on many individuals and families. One puzzling feature was that organisations with such discriminating policies did not recognise the extraordinary opportunities lost because they were essentially only tapping one half of the possible employment pool. These days, while there is still some distance to travel for complete equity, notable advances have been made. Women now have a significant presence in the professions and in higher educational institutions. However, there are still serious concerns over the limited representation of women in the upper levels of management in all industries (in Australia, 8% of top executive management and 15% of senior management — Elrich 1998) and other hidden forms of structural discrimination. Further, as Bem (1993) comments, males and male experiences are seen as the norm or standard and female and **other sexual orientations** are viewed as a sex-specific deviation from that norm — and this stance is still relatively common in organisations today.

Interest in feminist pedagogy has focused attention on the concerns of women in the teaching–learning interaction. Mirriam and Caffarella (1999) categorise the perspectives on oppression and empowerment of women in adult learning into two categories — liberatory models and gender models. The *liberatory models* highlight the structures and systems in society and organisations that oppress through power and control. Of particular concern is how these structures and systems are reflected in the learning episodes of the organisation and may consist of reproduction (for example, males dominating classroom discussions) or resistance (for example, females shunning developmental opportunities because of the psychological discomfort of operating in a male-dominant learning environment). The *gender models* emphasise the emancipatory process as the individual becomes free from hegemonic assumptions (see chapter 2) about the role of being a female learner. In this model, a connected approach to learning is advocated, where life experiences are valued, where a woman can have a voice and, hence, an identity (Mirriam and Caffarella (1999, p. 360). For an in-depth discussion of feminist pedagogy see Belenky, Clinchy, Goldberger and Tarule (1986), Hart (1992) and Tisdell (1995).

Knights (1995) proposes at least three points that should be of concern to HR developers when considering female learners in an organisation. Firstly, HR developers need to look beyond learning processes that accentuate competitive debate and 'objective' truth. Learning that features authentic understanding and relations and connectedness (see communicative learning in chapter 2) with others should also be emphasised. These learning processes that emphasise relations and connectedness are often referred to as the relational models (see Brown and Gilligan 1992). Secondly, the HR developers need to recognise that women who have been away from the workforce for a period of time (for example, being engaged in child rearing) may not have the technical qualifications or the confidence to engage in organisational development activities. Specific action is needed to support and develop women in these situations. Thirdly, with women still bearing the brunt of home management duties, difficulties can arise with attendance at organisational development activities, particularly at residential workshops or during after-school periods. Again, the HR developer needs to ensure that other developmental alternatives are available.

'Gender' was deliberately chosen as the heading for this section so that the debate on individual differences and diversity may include the other sexual orientations of homosexuality, bisexuality and transsexuality. That people with a different sexual orientation may view knowledge and learning from a different perspective than that advanced by the dominant male narrative has rarely been considered in human resource development or in adult education. As Hill (1995) has pointed out, the disenfranchisement of other sexual orientations that starts in preparatory schooling continues through all levels of adult education. There is very limited reported research on other sexual orientation learning preferences although D'Augelli (1994) provides a solid starting point for such research. The liberatory and gender models also provide a reasonable starting point for understanding the learning challenges and processes of adult learners with other sexual orientations.

As Weiler (1996) points out, there is no unitary, universal approach to women's learning experiences. However, the HR developer must analyse the gender roles within the learning environment, firstly to ensure that power — either from individuals or from organisational structures and systems — does not interfere in any way with the individual and organisational learning processes; and secondly, to question the nature and the construction of the knowledge being covered in both the formal and informal learning episodes that occur within the organisation. For further reading on gender issues see Hunter (1992), Smith and Hutchinson (1995) and Pierce and Delahaye (1998).

CULTURAL BACKGROUNDS

Any discussion of culture is vexed by differing definitions and by confusions with race, religion and ethnicity. In Australia, there has also been an increasing interest in cultural identity and a resurgence of cultural politics. While this resurgence has created a healthy awareness of multiculturalism, discussion of culture can also be confused by political agendas where varying groups push particular viewpoints to gain a political or economic advantage. In addition, culture should not be considered as only a national affair. In South-East Asia, for example, religion is taken very seriously and religious creeds become a way of life with beliefs transcending national boundaries. Culture, then, is a multifaceted construct and unidimensional interpretations should be avoided, particularly as culture is a changing and dynamic phenomenon (just compare the Australia of the 1950s with its current state).

However, despite these enigmas, the literature does provide some guidance through the maze. Gudykunst (1994) sees culture as a system of knowledge while Triandis (1994) suggests that culture imposes a set of lenses for seeing the world so that individuals select, interpret and process information to act in an established manner. This is a similar interpretation to Mezirow (1990) who includes culture as a construct of the individual's frame of reference (see chapter 2). As Hall (1976) points out, culture is not innate but is learned by the individual and, by being shared within a group, defines the boundaries of values and thus behaviours. To provide a more specific understanding, this text will concentrate on what Gudykunst and Kim (1984) refer to as an 'intercultural' interpretation — where a person from one culture is experiencing life in a different culture.

Gudykunst (1994) contends that the most useful frameworks of culture are those which examine the low-context/high-context styles of communication and the individualist–collectivist constructs. In *low-context cultures*, primacy is given to the content of the message in any communication (Hall 1976). Being direct and linear is valued so that 'what' is said is more important than 'how' it is said (i.e., being 'up front' and clear). The mass of information is explicit and purposeful. In *high-context cultures*, the content of the message is downgraded and the situational context — how the message is said, the non-verbals, what is not said, the overall theme of the communication episode and even the relationship between the participants — is most consequential (Hall 1976). In high-context communications, the relational interaction surmounts the actual wording, so literal interpretations of wording are of diminished importance. In high-context cultures, there is a greater distinction between insiders and outsiders. Further, low-context cultures tend to change faster than high-context cultures. Hofstede (1994) has suggested that cultures differ on an individualist–collectivist continuum. *Individualist cultures* prize self-reliance, creativity, independence, solitude and equality (Triandis 1994). The individual is encouraged to self-actualise and use her or his own judgement, even in contention with societal norms. In *collectivist cultures* individual goals defer to group goals. Characteristics of reciprocity (what one does for another, the other reciprocates), humility, harmony, dependence and proper action are honoured (Triandis 1994). Behaviour for pleasure is subordinated to social norms and duty defined by the group, and readiness to cooperate with the group is fundamental.

Australia has a low-context, individualist culture. This is not to say that there is a homogeneous entity in Australia but that there is a tendency for self-reliance, competitiveness, the attainment of individual goals, creativity, the high regard for action and the belief in the spoken word (for example, one's word is one's bond) to be valued highly. These values tend to be reflected in our educational systems and in the learning processes used within organisations. The challenge for the HR developer is to recognise the deep bearing and influence that a different culture may have on a specific learner or group of learners. For example, indigenous Australians have a profound respect for their elders, and learners from many South-East Asian countries have a prominent regard for authority. Also, in South-East Asia 'face communication' equates with the Western concept of self-esteem so that 'losing face' is the same as losing self-esteem, which can impede learning. Expectations that such learners will indulge in active debate with the trainer or teacher in front of class will ultimately cause confusion and disappointment for both parties.

As a starting point, HR developers should not automatically assume that learners will conform to the low-context–individualist behaviours and cues. Firstly, even within the individualist orientations of the Australian culture, there exist elements of collectivism. For example, individuals from certain rural locations, or from within industry groups, often have similar views on life. Secondly, if the learning episode to be designed or conducted will include learners from differing cultures, then the HR developer will need to investigate and understand the mores and ethics of those cultures before designing or implementing the learning experience. For further information see Brislin and Yoshida (1994), Hofstede (1994), Holton and Hedrick (1990) and Thorpe, Edwards and Hanson (1986). For specific insights into the education and learning of indigenous Australians see Bin-Sallik, Blomeley, Flowers, and Hughes (1994), Byrnes (1993) and Foley and Flowers (1990). For learning issues of adults with non-English-speaking backgrounds (NESB) see Federation of Ethnic Communities' Councils of Australia (FECCA) (1996).

THE IMPACT ON THE HR DEVELOPER

The HR developer is closely and deeply affected by diversity in at least two ways. Firstly, HRD is at the forefront in maximising the use of this most valuable asset. Whether this be in exploring options among learners when facilitating a learning episode or when encouraging actors in the shadow system to investigate new knowledge, the HR developer has to ensure that the advantages of a diverse work-force are allowed to exert a positive influence on the outcome. The second way diversity affects the HR developer is during the learning process itself. As Jarvis (1987) points out, learning rarely occurs in splendid isolation but is intimately related to the world in which the learner lives and is affected by it. The HR developer must 'start where the learner is at' (see chapter 2) as the history, culture and values of the learner are important components of the learner's world.

a closer look   3.1

Conflict in the classroom

... During a discussion on United States foreign policy, Ahmed, an Arab student, might shout out, "You Americans are imperialists who have never helped any country unless it was in your own interests! The only reason you went to Somalia was to establish military control in the Arab world."

John, an American student, becomes defensive and sees his classmate as "out of control". In an effort to calm things down, he resorts to objectivity and inductive logic. He lowers his voice and says in an unemotional, deliberate manner, "I don't support imperialism. And if you look at the facts, you'll find that we often help others for purely altruistic reasons. There's no strategic interest in being in Somalia."

The affective-intuitive or deductive style of rhetoric is common in the Middle East. Ahmed emotionally begins with his conclusion, which is supported by limited evidence. His classmate calmly suggests he consider "the facts", which causes this disagreement to become a conflict. From Ahmed's point of view, the student rejected his position and his sincerity.

John could acknowledge Ahmed's feelings and suggest other interpretations. He might say something like, "Ahmed, I know you believe that the U.S. government is imperialistic, but there are many Americans who think that the intention of the U.S. involvement in Somalia is altruistic — to prevent Somalis from starving."

... Ahmed becomes even more emotional to get across the affect and content of his position. "You Americans only put your arm around others to hold them still as you stab them in the back!"

... Mr. Smith, Ahmed's teacher, is pleased with the exchange of opinion. These are adults interacting in the classroom. He does not want to interfere, but things are getting a bit out of hand. With a broad smile, he says, "I'm sure you two can continue this lively discussion on U.S. foreign policy in the cafeteria."

Ahmed concludes that his teacher is quite irresponsible. Americans view the two disputants as directly responsible for the conflict and its resolution. The teacher wants to stay out of it. Ahmed expects a third-party intermediary to step in to prevent anyone from losing face. The teacher is the only person who can play this role. He is indirectly responsible for whatever happens between students in the classroom. And, if he does not assume his responsibility to intervene, he may be held accountable for perpetuating the conflict. ...

Source: Weaver, G. R., (1995) 'Communication and conflict in the multicultural classroom'. *Adult Learning*, 6(5), pp. 23–24

Hofstede (1994) has suggested that cultures differ on power distance as well as the individualist–collectivist continuum, and this concept can be very useful for the HR developer during interactions with learners. Power distance concerns the degree of deference that one individual (for example a learner) gives to another (for example a HR developer). Williams and Green (1994) believe that a learner from a high power distance culture would be more likely to see the HR developer as an expert and authority figure and prefer the more structured learning strategies (see chapter 11) while a learner from a low power distance culture (such as Australia) would prefer the more facilitative, unstructured learning strategies described in chapter 12. A brief comparison of the cultural variables is provided in table 3.1. However, the HR developer is cautioned against making any simple judgements based on this comparison. For example, a number of Australian learners are more comfortable with a high power distance relationship.

TABLE 3.1
A brief comparison of low-context and high-context cultures

LOW-CONTEXT CULTURES	HIGH-CONTEXT CULTURES
• Primacy given to the content of the message • Information is explicit and purposeful • Literal interpretation of the wording is important	• Primacy given to the context of the message • The relational activity between the parties surmounts the actual wording • Literal interpretation of the wording is not important
INDIVIDUALIST CULTURES	**COLLECTIVIST CULTURES**
• Prize self-reliance, creativity, independence, solitude and equity • Individual encouraged to self-actualise • Expected to use own judgement	• Honour obedience to authority, duty, harmony, dependence and 'proper' action • Deference of individual goals to group goals • Readiness to cooperate with group is fundamental
LOW POWER DISTANCE CULTURES	**HIGH POWER DISTANCE CULTURES**
• The HR developer is more of a colleague and friend • Preference for the more unstructured learning strategies	• The HR developer is an expert, authority figure • Preference for the structured learning strategies

Other than these considerations of low–high context, individualist–collectivist and low–high **power distance**, research has provided little information that provides the HR developer with specific advice on designing learning programs. Some thoughts that will provide a starting point are:
• Morrison (1992) found that some developmental interventions work in some organisations and not in others, and advises that any learning programs should be preceded by a human resource development needs investigation (HRDNI) to identify the precise needs of the staff.
• The HR developer should reflect on his or her own frames of reference (see chapter 2) about the characteristics discussed — age, impairments, gender and

cultural backgrounds. This reflection is likely to be more productive the more specific the behaviours that are considered — for example, how comfortable one is about accents or religious beliefs.

- When considering these so-called differences, it is often more productive to chart the common ground. For example, the characteristics of reciprocity, harmony, dependence and proper action are valued in the trade union movement as well as in collectivist cultures.
- Working with intercultural groups can result in very creative outcomes. However, some basic work at the begining of the learning episode by the HR developer can increase the probability of such a creative result. This initial work can be as simple as a 'getting to know you exercise' such as finding out one fact about another learner or can progress to a carefully facilitated (see chapter 12) value-sharing interaction.
- Making explicit, acknowledging and respecting differing communicative preferences. The Western world has an espoused belief (see chapter 2) in the benefits of quiet, logical discussion. As Weaver (1995) points out, in some Latino, Arab and African cultures, sincerity is demonstrated by stating a position with great emotion, hyperbole and overstatement, the use of metaphors and poetic phrases is considered an indication of sophisticated rhetoric and a calm, unemotional response is a sign of insincerity and lack of personal commitment.
- If the learning program is a residential workshop, or if food is to be provided, then ensure that suitable food (for example, kosher or halal or vegetarian) is available.

To help the organisation manage its diversity positively, Davidson and Griffin (2000) suggest specific strategies on which the HR developer should concentrate. These include:

- *diversity training* as a specific developmental activity designed to enable members of an organisation to function better in a diverse workplace. Cross-cultural training helps employees learn how they are both like and unlike others. Awareness training, as well as the organisational mission statement and policy, can identify legal obligations and ramifications. Both these types of training will depend on communicative learning rather than instrumental learning (see chapter 2). Wilson (1996) warns that stand-alone programs are unlikely to be successful and the development should have top management support, be open to all staff, not just specific groups, and include organisation-wide interventions.
- *developing managers and supervisors* in team building, conflict resolution and decision making to ensure that equity and diversity measures are addressed and biases are overcome at the workface. As Wilson (1996) points out, such communication and negotiation skills are really part of good management anyway, but managers need to be pro-active in using these skills in diversity management.
- *developing and fostering members of minority or disadvantaged groups* in leadership, conflict resolution and dispute resolution as well as providing literacy programs for those with English-as-a-second-language (see FECCA 1996). There is also a significant proportion of the English-as-a-first-language who have literacy and numeracy problems and who therefore need special consideration.
- *recognising prior learning and qualifications* gained elsewhere, as this offers flexibility in assessing organisational and individual needs and broadens opportunities for both individuals and the organisation.

For the HR developer, the EO approach tended to emphasise the development of staff in the areas of recruitment and selection (Wilson 1996). Thomas (1994) believes that the HR developer needs to firstly gain top management commitment, undertake a cultural audit as part of the HRDNI and ensure that any intervention has very clear objectives to provide a focused approach so that not too many issues are covered at once. With positive management of diversity, the HR developer anticipates ways in which differences between learners can be used as an empowering and emancipatory force and also looks at the different ways that knowledge is constructed and interpreted. Ewert, Rice and Lauderdale (1995) emphasise that, by promoting intercultural skills and studying non-Western world views, the organisation's ability to generate new knowledge is enhanced remarkably (see chapter 14).

GLOBALISATION

For a majority of Australian organisations, the world really has become a global village and globalisation has become an important strategic issue. Globalisation is not just the involvement in the economic and industrial activities of another country (for example, in erecting and managing a factory in another part of the world). It also includes interacting on a global scale with people from a variety of cultures in the normal course of one's job in Australia (for example, buying imported parts, exporting, being part of a foreign subsidiary or just competing with foreign imports). The advent of modern communications technology (for example, the Internet and e-mail) has broken the historic geographical isolation of Australia. Whether staff are operating from an Australian base or are expatriate staff in another country, simply selling the best product or the best service is not enough. Australian organisations must fully understand their clients, suppliers and peers, whatever culture they come from.

In helping the organisation deal with globalisation, the HR developer will have at least two major areas of interest. Firstly, staff — whether they are expatriates or interacting with other countries from an Australian base — need to be developed in the skills and attitudes appropriate to other countries. Secondly, the HR developer may be required to arrange and/or design and/or implement learning experiences in another country.

DEVELOPING STAFF

An increasingly important part of the HR developer's role is in developing staff so that they can operate in differing cultural contexts. Mamman (1994) suggests that, in order to improve intercultural effectiveness, several areas have to be addressed. These include:

- being aware of the *different communicative processes* that are used to acquire and use knowledge. Many countries operate on the high-context model of interactions and staff need to become adept at reading the context within which the message is delivered rather than concentrating on the content of the message.
- acquiring *knowledge of the host culture* and specifically being able to demonstrate culturally appropriate behaviours. For example, in many collectivist cultures, high

importance is attached to developing and fostering relationships before becoming involved in business transactions.

- recognising that sex role equality is often higher in an individualistic culture than in a collectivist society. This calls for careful consideration of *male–female interactions*, for both expatriate males and females. For expatriate females, dress codes may need to be accommodated to enhance intercultural effectiveness. For expatriate males, initial communication with females may need to be initiated through a male relative.
- full articulation in the *host country's language* may not be necessary as, in many countries, being able to speak English is seen as a socially desirable quality. However, some knowledge of the language can be of considerable assistance in developing business relationships. Being able to offer a greeting in the appropriate language is often looked upon with favour. Overall, though, the importance of linguistic ability will vary from country to country and the expatriate (or those living in Australia but interacting with people from another country) will need to understand not only the social implications of being able or not able to speak the language but also the implications of their accent when speaking the host language.

Developing staff to the levels of competency required to interact within the global village requires more than instrumental learning. Learning experiences based on communicative and, at times, emancipatory learning are needed. These deeper levels of learning use more energy, for both the organisation and the individual learner. For the organisation, the more unstructured learning strategies (see chapter 12) will have to be utilised and these strategies take more time and require the facilitative skills of an experienced HR developer. For the individual learner, achieving the desired level of learning outcomes demands commitment and a willingness to examine one's beliefs and values — activities that can be personally exhausting.

OVERSEAS LEARNING INTERVENTIONS

Marquardt and Engle (1993, pp. 10–13) contend that, for the HR developer, managing and conducting learning interventions outside one's home country differ on several factors. Firstly, there are likely to be learners from a *variety of nations* — from the local/host country, from the parent organisational country and from third countries (i.e., from countries other than the local or parent countries). Secondly, the overriding *dynamic of culture* will affect all aspects of the learning experience with intercultural (interaction of two or more cultures within a nation), cross-cultural (crossing cultures and national borders) and multicultural (involving many cultures) interactions. Thirdly, numerous *administrative issues* arise including transport, host government relations, language translation and housing. Fourthly, the *political environment* of the host country may need to be considered — whether the government is more democratic or more totalitarian; the skills and ability levels of the local labour and the wages paid to them; the likelihood of terrorism and kidnapping; the existence and quality of health facilities; and the weather. Fifthly, *the role of the HR developer* may differ in various cultures with some preferring a more laid-back and friendly approach and others expecting an authoritative, disciplined and even remote expert figure. Finally, the *distance* from the parent country can present challenges for communication with supervisors and for supply lines for equipment and materials.

The HR developer also needs to consider the impact of culture on the four stages of HRD. Marquardt and Engle (1993) provide an excellent discussion of specific issues the HR developer needs to consider. For example, during the human resource development needs investigation (HRDNI) it is difficult for respondents in some cultures to admit that there are problems or even become involved in such an investigation. In the Australian Aboriginal society, asking questions is often seen as bad manners (see Byrnes 1993). In collectivist cultures, even acknowledging that problems exist may cause the respondent or the respondent's manager to 'lose face'. Establishing learning objectives may be seen as presumptuous or threatening or even be against religious beliefs if the future is seen to be preordained and beyond the manipulation of humans. When designing programs, the HR developer needs to bear in mind that some cultures prefer a didactic, deductive and rote style of teaching and the Australian preference for independence, involvement (for example, using experiential learning) and generalising from specifics may not be acceptable. It is in the implementation stage that significant differences between cultures become most obvious. In some cultures the teacher/HR developer/facilitator is viewed as an omniscient fountain of knowledge and is expected to live up to this high ideal. The Australian casual and friendly attitude may run counter to this expectation. Apparently simple activities such as leaning on the desk (undignified) and asking questions (the teacher is the content expert and the learner should not have to help him/her) can lead to loss of credibility. Further, during implementation, the expatriate HR developer often works with a local HR developer. This does have advantages in overcoming language barriers and helps the expatriate HR developer to understand the local culture. However, the teacher/learner dichotomy may be exacerbated between the expatriate HR developer and the local HR developer in some cultures. Finally, there can be significant differences as to who evaluates, what is evaluated and how and when evaluation is carried out — particularly in cultures that value hiding feelings, not prying into the feelings and thoughts of others and where protecting the 'face' of an honoured person or guest is paramount.

The challenges for the HR developer managing and conducting a learning program in another country can be immense. Indeed, it can be argued that being an expatriate HR developer is a special and unique career move. The single, most important factor that emerges is that the HR developer concerned must become very knowledgable about the culture where the learning program is to be mounted. There are very few texts available for the global HR developer. Marquardt and Engle (1993) have provided a practical and detailed text with a number of sensible suggestions and specific tips for operating in various world cultures and this text is highly recommended. Iles (1996) provides an organisational view of HRD's role in an international/global organisation.

DIVERSITY AND THE ORGANISATION

Most organisations are going to continually confront, and will need to exist in, a changing and complex environment. One of the most valuable assets that will help the organisation to survive and prosper from such change and complexity is a sophisticated and diverse workforce. As Ewert, Rice and Lauderdale (1995) comment, those organisations that view diversity as a problem focus their developmental efforts on avoiding legal difficulties while those that hold the 'value-in-diversity' perspective define differences as opportunities to mobilise all of the organisation's human resources on behalf of the common good. Diversity provides a rich accumulation of perceptions and knowledge. By fostering and managing this diversity positively, the organisation handles uncertainty and challenge in a sophisticated manner that ensures success.

Adults differ on numerous qualities. This chapter has examined four — age, health, gender and culture — that are considered to be particularly pertinent to adult learning. Such differences have to be acknowledged, celebrated and mobilised. In addition, though, the HR developer must recognise that individual learners are a combination of many of these differences. A learner may be a young, female adult paraplegic or a male Aboriginal elder with an abundance of wisdom but limited formal educational qualifications. Acknowledging these differences and the variety of accumulated experiences and perceptions provides an inexhaustible source of knowledge and truth.

GLOSSARY

collectivist cultures — cultures that value obedience, duty, harmony, dependence and subordinate individual goals to group goals

direct discrimination — where an irrelevant criterion is used to exclude a person or group from an opportunity

discrimination — unfair treatment of a person or minority group based on prejudice, consisting of three types — direct, indirect and structural

diversity training — learning programs designed to enable staff to function better in a diverse workplace

ethnocentricity — the belief in the intrinsic superiority of one's own cultural norms

gender — a word that denotes the different sex or sexual orientation of a person

gender models — models in the literature that emphasise the emancipatory approach as the individual becomes free from hegemonic assumptions

globalisation — the involvement in the economic and industrial activities of another country and also interacting on a global scale with people from a variety of cultures in the normal course of one's job

harassment — a particular form of discrimination designed to humiliate, offend, intimidate or otherwise make a person feel unwelcome or inadequate

high-context cultures — where 'how' a message is said (the context) is more important that 'what' is said (the content)

historical embeddedness — historical moments experienced by an individual that affect the perception of that individual

indirect discrimination — where a seemingly neutral practice or decision advantages an individual or group over another individual or group

individualist cultures — a culture that values self-reliance, creativity, independence, solitude and equality

liberatory models — models in the literature that highlight the structures and systems that oppress women and other minority groups through power and control

low-context cultures — where 'what' is said (the content) is more important that 'how' the message is said (the context)

other sexual orientations — homosexuality, bisexuality and transsexuality

power distance — the degree of deference that one individual gives another

stage models — models of age categories in adults denoting transition periods and specific needs

stereotypes — categories of people developed through generalisations that are often based on prejudice

structural discrimination — sometimes called systems discrimination, occurs where the interaction of historical decisions, policies and social attitudes allow discrimination to become embedded in the system.

QUESTIONS

For review

1. List and explain at least four advantages to the organisation of managing a diverse workforce positively.

2. Define the difference between direct, indirect and structural discrimination. Why are these forms of discrimination illegal?

3. What age issues should a HR developer consider in adult learners?

For analysis

4. List at least two different profiles of adult learners based on age, health, gender and cultural background. Explain how the HR developer should allow for and use these differences in a learning program.

5. Explain how the characteristics of a high-context–collectivist culture could affect the design of a learning program.

For application

6. You have been asked to conduct a 4-day learning program in a town approximately 50 kilometres north of Lima, the capital city of Peru. There will be twenty participants from Peru, Argentina, Mexico and Japan. What issues would you consider in conducting this program?

Baltes, P. B. (1987). 'Theoretical propositions of life-span developmental psychology: On the dynamics between growth and decline.' *Developmental Psychology*, 23, 611–627.

Belenky, M. F., Clinchy, B. M., Goldberger, N. R. and Tarule, J. M. (1986). *Women's Ways of Knowing: The Development of Self, Voice and Mind*. New York: Basic Books.

Bem, S. L. (1993). *The Lenses of Gender: Transforming the Debate on Sexual Inequality*. New Haven, Con.: Yale University Press.

Benest, F. (1991). 'Marketing multiethnic communities.' *Public Management*, 75(12), 4–14.

Bennington, L. and Tharenou, P. (1998). 'Older workers: Myths, evidence and implications for Australian managers.' In R. J. Stone (Ed.), *Readings in Human Resource Management, Volume 3*. Brisbane: Wiley Australia.

Bin-Sallik, M., Blomeley, N., Flowers, R. and Hughes, P. (1994). *Review and Analysis of Literature Relating to Aboriginal and Torres Strait Islander Education*. Canberra: Department of Employment, Education and Training.

Brislin, R. and Yoshida, T. (1994). *Improving Intercultural Interactions: Modules for Cross Cultural Training Programs*. Thousand Oaks, Cal.: Sage.

Brown, L. M. and Gilligan, C. (1992). *Meeting at the Crossroads: Women's Psychology and Girl's Development*. Cambridge, Mass.: Harvard University Press.

Byrnes, J. (1993). 'Aboriginal learning styles and adult education: Is a synthesis possible?' *Australian Journal of Adult and Community Education*, 33(3), 157–171.

D'Augelli, A. R. (1994). 'Identity development and sexual orientation: Toward a model of lesbian, gay and bisexual development.' In E. J. Trickett, R. J. Watts and D. Birman (Eds), *Human Diversity: Perspectives on People in Context*. San Francisco: Jossey-Bass.

Davidson, P. and Griffin, R. (2000). *Management: Australia in a Global Context*. Brisbane: Wiley Australia.

Elrich, L. (1998). 'Women's under-representation in educational administration: Revisiting two solutions.' *Australian and New Zealand Journal of Law and Education*, 3(1), 49–71.

Ewert, M., Rice, J. K. and Lauderdale, E. (1995). 'Training for diversity: How organisations become more inclusive.' *Adult Learning*, May/June, 27–28.

Federation of Ethnic Communities' Councils of Australia (FECCA). (1996). *Life Long Learning for All: Adult and Community Education and People of Non-English Speaking Backgrounds*. Jamison Centre, ACT: Australian Association of Adult and Community Education.

Foley, G. and Flowers, R. (1990). *Strategies for Self-determination: Aboriginal Adult Education, Training and Community Development in NSW*. Sydney: University of Technology, Sydney.

Goodnow, J. J. (1990). 'Using sociology to extend psychological accounts of cognitive development.' *Human Development*, 33, 81–107.

Gozzi, R. (1995). 'The Generation X and Boomers metaphors.' *Et Cetera*, 52(3), 331–335.

Gudykunst, W. B. (1994). *Bridging Differences: Effective Intergroup Communication*. (2nd ed.). Newbury Park Cal.: Sage.

Gudykunst, W. B. and Kim, Y. Y. (1984). *Communicating with Strangers: An Approach to Intercultural Communication*. New York: Random House.

Hall, E. T. (1976). *Beyond Culture*. New York: Anchor Books.

Hart, M. (1992). *Working and Educating for Life: Feminist and International Perspectives on Adult Education*. London: Routledge.

Hill, R. J. (1995). 'Gay discourse in adult education: A critical review.' *Adult Education Quarterly*, 45(3), 142–158.

Hofstede, G. (1994). *Cultures and Organisations: Intercultural Cooperation and Its Importance for Survival*. London: Harper Collins.

Holton, R. and Hedrick, C. (Eds). (1990). *Cross Cultural Communication and Professional Education*. Adelaide: Centre for Multicultural Studies, Flinders University.

Howe, N. and Strauss, B. (1993). *13th Generation*. New York: Vintage Books.

Hunter, R. (1992). *Indirect Discrimination in the Workplace*. Sydney: Federation Press.

Iles, P. (1996). 'International HRD.' In J. Stewart and J. McGoldrick (Eds), *Human Resource Development: Perspectives, Strategies and Practices*. London: Pitman.

Jarvis, P. (1987). *Adult Learning in the Social Context*. London: Croom Helm.

Knights, S. (2000). 'Women and learning.' In G. Foley (Ed.), *Understanding Adult Education and Training* (2nd ed.). St. Leonards, NSW: Allen & Unwin.

Levinson, D. J. and Levinson, J. D. (1996). *The Seasons of a Woman's Life*. New York: Ballantine.

Mamman, A. (1994). 'Intercultural effectiveness: Implications for Australian expatriates and business people.' In R. J. Stone (Ed.), *Readings in Human Resource Management, Volume 2*. Brisbane: Wiley Australia.

Marquardt, M. J. and Engle, D. W. (1993). *Global Human Resource Development*. Upper Saddle River, NJ: Prentice Hall.

Mezirow, J. (1990). *Fostering Critical Reflection in Adulthood: A Guide to Transformative and Emancipatory Learning*. San Francisco: Jossey-Bass.

Mirriam, S. B. and Caffarella, R. S. (1999). *Learning in Adulthood: A Comprehensive Guide*. (2nd ed.). San Francisco: Jossey-Bass.

Morrison, A. (1992). Developing Diversity in Organisations. *Business Quarterly*, Summer, 42–48.

Pierce, J. and Delahaye, B. L. (1998). 'Human resource management implications of dual-career couples.' In R. J. Stone (Ed.), *Readings in Human Resource Management, Volume 3*. Brisbane: Wiley Australia.

Plett, P. C. and Lester, B. T. (1991). *Training for Older People: A Handbook*. Geneva: ILO Publications.

Sheehey, G. (1995). *New Passages: Mapping Your Life Across Time*. New York: Random House.

Smith, C. and Hutchinson, J. (1995). *Gender: A Strategic Management Issue*. Sydney: Business and Professional Publishing.

Stone, R. J. (1998). *Human Resource Management*. (3rd ed.). Brisbane: Wiley Australia.

Theophanous, A. C. (1994). *Understanding Social Justice: An Australian Perspective*. (2nd ed.). Carlton South, Vic: Elikia Books.

Thomas, V. (1994). 'The downside of diversity.' *Training and Development*, January, 60–62.

Thorpe, M., Edwards, R. and Hanson, A. (Eds) (1986). *Culture and Processes of Adult Education*. London: Open University.

Tisdell, E. J. (1995). *Creating Inclusive Adult Learning Environments: Insights from Multicultural Education and Feminist Pedagogy*. Information Series No. 361. Columbus, Ohio: ERIC Clearing House on Adult, Career and Vocational Education.

Triandis, H. (1994.) *Culture and Social Behaviour*. San Francisco: McGraw Hill.

Weaver, G. R. (1995). 'Communication and conflict in the multicultural classroom.' *Adult Learning*, 6(5), pp. 23–24.

Weiler, K. (1996). 'Freire and feminist pedagogy of difference.' In R. Edwards, A. Hanson and P. Raggart (Eds), *Boundaries of Adult Learning*. New York: Routledge.

Williams, T. and Green, A. (1994). *Dealing with Difference: How Trainers Can Take Account of Cultural Diversity*. Aldershot, Eng.: Gower.

Wilson, E. (1996). 'Managing diversity and HRD.' In J. Stewart and J. McGoldrick (Eds), *Human Resource Development: Perspectives, Strategies and Practices*. London: Pitman.

The truant adult learner

Shane sat in the public bar, his third beer in 20 minutes in his hand. Should he go back or shouldn't he? Would anyone know? Would they even miss him? It was all a waste of time anyway.

Shane was the Manager of Fine Printing at the Mid-Coast University. He supervised ten staff — five trade printers, three printers' assistants, a storeman and an administrative assistant. He had been in the printing industry for 40 years and a manager or supervisor in various printing works for the last 15. He took up the university job 5 years ago after running his own business for 14 years. Last week the Administrative Services manager had rung him up and said, 'Hey, Shane, you haven't been on any training for a while, have you? There is a 2-day Performance Review Workshop starting next Monday. You had better go'. No training for a while? Shane had not been in a classroom since being an apprentice. The thought of all those desks lined up in a room and the blackboard out the front and some smart young thing asking awkward questions brought back some horrible memories.

When he arrived on Monday morning it was not a 'smart young thing' out the front. It was a pimply faced boy younger than his son! Well, OK, in his late twenties. 'Still, seems rather young to be talking to old blokes like me,' thought Shane. Shane's limited enthusiasm dropped even further as he thought about the Monday morning. The young bloke kept switching the projector thing off and on, talking to the screen and telling them to look at the form in front of them. Shane had to keep taking his

reading glasses off and on and the bright light started giving him a headache. It was all talk, talk, talk. Why didn't he ask us for some examples? You would think 15 years as a supervisor would give some ideas. Performance review? It was just telling staff how they were going. And those bloody seats! They had sat on them all morning except for 10 minutes at morning tea. There could have at least been a bit of padding on them. That and not being able to walk around had started up the arthritis in his hip. It was all Shane could do to walk down to the pub when they were finally allowed to break at lunch time. At least the beer was starting to numb the pain in the hip.

'Well, should I go back or not? The smart little twerp. Standing out front there, spouting on. Reminds me of those useless, fresh faced, baby lieutenants over in Vietnam. Full of useless new ideas. Then they expected us to go out into the boonies and get shot at. Ah, bloody hell. I'll have another beer and then go back. With a bit of luck I'll fall asleep.'

Discussion questions

1. What should the HR developer have done when designing the course to cater for older learners such as Shane?

2. What should the HR developer conducting the program have done to cater for older learners such as Shane?

3. What should the HR developer conducting the program do when Shane returns from lunch?

Conflict in the classroom

Review 'A closer look 3.1: Conflict in the classroom'. Assume that you are the HR developer of an international company, with its headquarters in Australia, and are conducting an overseas learning workshop for supervisors in Mexico City, Mexico. The session topic has been on 'A country's foreign policy and our company'. The class is made up of twenty soon-to-be-promoted supervisors from Argentina, Australia, Brazil, India, Iran, Egypt, Nigeria, Singapore, Turkey and the United States of America.

Discussion question

How would you have managed this conflict situation?

Strategic human resource development

CHAPTER OBJECTIVES

At the end of this chapter you should be able to:

1 describe the conventional paradigm of strategic planning

2 list and describe the factors in the external environment that are examined by the strategic planning process

3 identify and describe the three major thrusts in the corporate strategic plan

4 explain how the strategic human resource development plan is influenced by the corporate strategic plan

5 explain how the micro-external environment and the internal subsystems influence the strategic human resource development plan

6 differentiate between the two types of operational plans and explain how they are influenced by the strategic human resource development plan

7 describe how the shadow system contributes to the strategic planning process of the organisation

8 discuss the critical nature of the strategic human resource development plan.

This chapter begins by examining the **conventional paradigm of strategic planning** and points out that this conventional paradigm is most appropriately used by the legitimate system of the organisation. Conventional strategic planning commences by examining the indirect and direct factors in the environment that impinge on the organisation. The **indirect factors** include economic conditions, socio-cultural issues, legal–political concerns, technology and the natural environment while the **direct factors** include the customers, competitors and suppliers. By analysing these factors, a critical judgement can be made on the volatility of the **external environment** (how quickly it is changing) and the appropriate **market niche** for the organisation can be identified. Based on this critical judgement, the **corporate strategic plan** is formulated.

The corporate strategic plan has three major thrusts. Firstly, the **mission statement** describes the customer need that is to be satisfied, the competitive edge that the organisation enjoys and the strategic objectives. Secondly, the **overall or general strategy** that the organisation will follow is articulated. There are seven general **strategies** that can be used — the entrepreneurial strategy, the dynamic growth strategy, the analyser strategy, the defender strategy, the rationalisation strategy, the liquidation strategy and the turnaround strategy. While smaller businesses tend to follow one of the general strategies, larger organisations commonly have combinations of strategies. Thirdly, the corporate strategic plan defines the structure of the organisation — often represented by a hierarchy chart. The selected structure is an indication of the way the organisation has decided to invest its resources.

The **strategic human resource development plan (SHRDP)** is one of the dependent strategic plans and flows from the corporate strategic plan. The SHRDP prescribes what development the people in the organisation need so that they can help the organisation achieve its strategic objectives. The type of general strategy chosen — entrepreneurial, dynamic growth, analyser, defender, rationalisation, liquidation, or turnaround — will have a significant impact on the type of developmental processes used for the people in the organisation. Because it is closer to the people of the organisation there are two other influences, other than the corporate plan, that affect the SHRDP. Firstly, the SHRDP has to be fine-tuned by considering factors in the **micro-external environment**, such as the local socio-economic conditions, local government regulations and laws, local employment conditions and the impact of local key external stakeholders. Secondly, **internal subsystems**, such as the information systems, the culture and key internal stakeholders, may have essential information or have some influence over what may or may not be done.

The strategic plans are converted into activities by two types of **operational plans**. **Standing plans** include policies, procedures and rules and provide guidance for common decisions and recurring situations. **Single-use plans** are used to achieve specific operational programs. In HRD, these programs are usually the workshops, training courses or interventions designed to help the people in the organisation develop particular expertise.

Through the corporate strategic plan, the SHRDP and the operational plan, the legitimate system ensures that the organisation has the skills and knowledge to survive the immediate future. However, the conventional strategic planning process can only provide answers in this close-to-certainty situation — i.e., the immediate future — and hence can be described as strategic programming. To ensure survival in the longer term, the organisation relies on its shadow system. The shadow system emphasises strategic thinking (rather than the strategic programming) by allowing the people in the organisation to explore the future and to learn. This means that the shadow system relies on an organisational culture of trust and loyalty. The strategic planning processes of the shadow system are explored more fully in chapter 14.

The chapter closes by examining the critical nature of the SHRDP process. Firstly, the conventional strategic planning carried out by the legitimate system is essential to the short-term survival of the organisation and also has a significant impact on the type of human resource developmental activities and also the content of those activities. Secondly, the strategic planning process is also a learning process — through knowledge generation, emancipatory learning and increasing knowledge capital.

CONVENTIONAL STRATEGIC PLANNING

Of all the concepts in management, strategic planning has had the most attention, certainly since the 1960s. Well-respected writers such as Chandler, Ansoff, Drucker, Sloan and Porter have provided thoughtful, structured and complex insights into the philosophical underpinnings, processes and techniques of strategic planning. As Mickelthwait and Wooldridge comment:

> For most of this century 'strategic planning' was regarded as the very kernel of management thought: indeed it often had a department devoted to it. Planning – a neat, definite, military concept – was adapted and refined into what seemed to be an evermore precise science.

(Micklethwait and Wooldridge 1996, pp. 159–160)

According to this conventional wisdom, the strategic orientation of the organisation (interpreted as its position in the marketplace) is identified and defined by the strategic planning process. In this process, strategic planners examine and analyse the organisation's external environment, assess the organisation's strengths and weaknesses and then plan the organisation's future activities and allocate its resources in such a way that will enhance the organisation's future viability.

Serious interest in strategic planning began with Chandler (1962) when he concluded that 'structure followed strategy'. It was from Chandler's writings that most organisations created large planning departments which examined and analysed data, recommended appropriate organisational structures and produced 5-year and 10-year plans. This innovation was followed by the SWOT analysis model from the Harvard

Business School — the organisation examined its strengths and weaknesses and then looked at the opportunities and threats in the external environment. This then allowed the organisation to define its strategic orientation by defining the market niche which allowed the most advantageous match of strengths and opportunities while weaknesses and threats were minimised. Various tools for identifying the most appropriate strategy-structure link were promulgated in the 1970s and 1980s, the most memorable being the BCG Matrix (Stars, Dogs, Cash Cows and Question Marks) and the Profit Impact of Marketing Strategies (PIMS). Then Porter (1985) suggested that there were four basic competitive positions that an organisation could follow — cost leadership, differentiation, cost focus and differentiation focus. This wisdom, accumulated for over 20 years, produced an accepted, conventional paradigm of strategic planning:

1. All organisations exist within an environment and need to assess the external environmental forces and conditions to ensure survival.
2. The organisation then identifies the market niche in which it can most successfully operate.
3. This market niche is described in the mission statement. The mission statement enunciates the customer need that will be satisfied and what competitive advantage the organisation enjoys over competitors.
4. The competitive advantage is maintained by deploying resources appropriately by using a suitable organisational structure.

This rational, although prescriptive, paradigm appears to be very useful and has a certain academic elegance. The study of botany and zoology tells us that organisms exploit a specific niche in the environment to survive. Thus a giraffe has a long neck which allows it to feed off young leaves on the top of trees. There is very little competition for this food source so the giraffe has matched a strength with an opportunity. Notice, however, that with the strength comes a weakness. The giraffe is very vulnerable when drinking water. Yet, despite this vulnerability, the giraffe survives as a species showing that the strength–opportunity match far outweighs the weakness–threat combination. In a similar way, it was believed, organisations should flourish, provided the conventional strategic planning process was followed.

UNCERTAINTY AND DOUBT

As some wit once said, 'Prediction is difficult, particularly of the future'. With the demise of a number of well-known national and international organisations in the late 1980s, it became obvious that the conventional strategic planning paradigm did not tell the full story. There were at least two major flaws in the application of conventional strategic planning. Firstly, there was the unchallenged assumption that, while the external environment did become more volatile in the 1980s, all that was needed to uncover its convoluted complexity was more analysis. The second major flaw was the simplistic view that the whole organisation faced the same external environment. In reality, the organisation faces multiple external environments with, for example, the production department facing a relatively predictable environment while the marketing department may exist in a more changeable environment. In addition, it is usual for the higher levels of the organisation to face a more unpredictable environment than the lower levels. While certainly not dead, strategic planning has long since fallen from its pedestal (Mintzberg 1994, p. 107). Mintzberg went on to suggest that strategic planning, in reality, was the result of a stream of decisions by managers and therefore more of an emergent phenomenon. And in this he is partly right.

In fact, if we think of the complexity concepts of an organisation consisting of a **legitimate system** and a **shadow system**, then both points of view are correct. The shadow system, on the one hand, wrestles with the challenges of the long term and this will be discussed more fully in the final chapter. The rational, prescriptive paradigm of conventional strategic planning, however, is suitable for the legitimate system.

The one fact that has remained unchallenged in the attacks on conventional strategic planning wisdom is that the external environment has a significant influence on the ongoing longevity of any organisation. What has been challenged is the ability of planners to make long-term predictions of the convolutions and changes in that external environment. The closer to the state of certainty that the predictors are operating, then the more likely the assumptions on which the planning is based will be correct. So conventional strategic planning techniques can be quite useful in the short term. The time duration of this 'short term' will vary from industry to industry and from organisation to organisation within an industry. However, in today's erratic climate one could not expect to foresee much more than 2 years at the most and, quite often, only a few months. Given this short time horizon, conventional strategic planning is critical to the operation of the legitimate system in two ways:

1. The identification of the organisation's mission and strategies allows the legitimate system to keep the organisation moving in the right direction for the immediate future by designing and maintaining the appropriate organisational structure and investing the appropriate type and correct amount of resources in the relevant area of the organisation. The legitimate system can also instigate and maintain the correct processes, procedures and techniques to ensure that the organisation is managed efficiently and effectively.

2. The legitimate system can use the accumulated wisdom from the strategic planning process to assist with the process of auditing the ideas emanating from the shadow system about the future direction of the organisation. As we will see in the final chapter, the auditing process of the shadow system's recommendations, conducted by the legitimate system, is a struggle that is partly logical and analytical and partly political.

The legitimate system, then, is responsible for the *intended or deliberate strategy* of the organisation while the shadow system searches for, and tries to have implemented, the *emergent strategy* (see Mintzberg, Quinn and Voyer 1995). The combination of the intended and emergent strategy is the *realised strategy* that the organisation actually follows and is the result of the bounded instability created by the tension between the legitimate system and the shadow system.

This chapter, then, will examine first the rational-prescriptive strategic planning processes used by the legitimate system to manage the close-to-certainty situations that occupy a large proportion of the time in most organisations. In particular, we will see how the conventional strategic planning processes impinge on the development of the human resource endeavour. Figure 4.1 gives an overview of the strategic planning process used by the legitimate system. At the end of the chapter, we discuss the contribution of the shadow system to the strategic planning process although this discussion will be continued more fully in chapter 14.

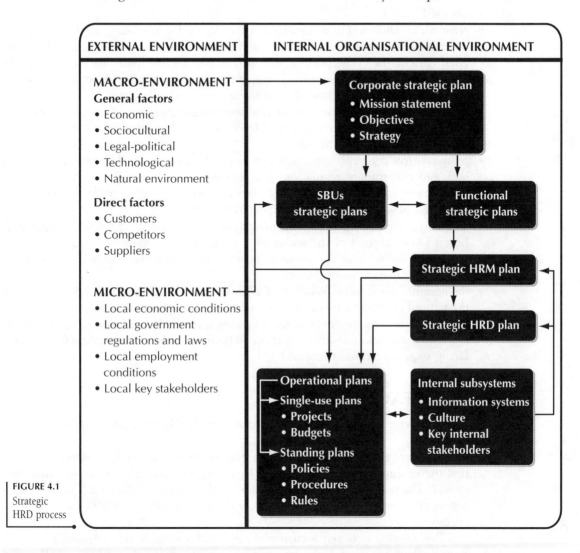

FIGURE 4.1
Strategic
HRD process

THE EXTERNAL ENVIRONMENT

Scanning the external environment allows the legitimate system to scrutinise various factors that may have an impact on the operations and survival of the organisation. As Robbins and Barnwell (1998) point out, to the extent that this scanning can lead to accurate forecasts of environmental fluctuations, it can reduce uncertainty and allow management to anticipate changes and make internal adjustments rather than react after the fact. The environmental factors to be scanned are usually divided into indirect and direct factors.

INDIRECT FACTORS

Schermerhorn (1996, pp. 58, 60–63) suggests that the indirect factors commonly scrutinised include:

- *economic conditions.* Organisations must compete for advantage in times of economic decline as well as economic growth. Further, in today's tempestuous business environment, the cycles of economic growth and decline follow each other rapidly. Organisations need to scrutinise and interrogate indicators of economic health such as gross domestic product, unemployment and inflation.
- *sociocultural issues.* In the age of multiculturalism, organisations must not only respect alternative cultures and workforce diversity but embrace the differences to create a competitive advantage.
- *legal–political concerns.* Organisations not only have to work within the various laws and government regulations but also understand and deal with a variety of government agencies. Businesses are expected to meet high standards of corporate social responsibility and ethical expectations.
- *technology.* Technological advancements occur at exponential rates. Organisations have to keep abreast of the technological changes that impinge directly on their product or service and also on more general advancements, especially those in the area of information management.
- *the natural environment.* While part of corporate social responsibility, respect for the natural environment is a significant theme throughout present society. Indeed, these expectations for environmentalism are quite wide, with the belief that businesses should take an active role in helping to solve environmental problems facing societies around the world.

DIRECT FACTORS

The direct factors can be examined under three headings: customers, competitors and suppliers.

1. *customers* are the raison d'être for the organisation. The catchcry is not so much that the customer is always right as 'How can we make the life of the customer easier?' The reason a customer approaches a business, whether for a product or a service, is to solve a problem or to allow them to operate more efficiently or more effectively.

   Differentiating between a customer need and a want is also important. A need occurs when a person feels deprived of something (food, clothing, shelter and so on) while a want is a need that is shaped by a person's knowledge, culture and personality (McColl-Kennedy, Kiel, Lusch and Lusch (1994, p. 10). So, a person may feel hungry and need food; the choice of food would reflect a want. Importantly, a need is purchased by non-discretionary expenditure while a want is a reflection of discretionary expenditure. In other words, we must spend money on food to survive. The purchase of basic food items (bread, vegetables, meat, milk) involves no choice or discretion while spending money on treats such as chocolate or alcohol is a choice and we can elect to make the purchase from the money we have left over after the non-discretionary expenditure is completed.

2. While we may prefer to operate as a monopoly, the reality for most organisations is that *competitors* are also vying for a share of the same market niche. The question then becomes 'How do we satisfy the customer need better than the competitors do?' Answering this question helps to identify the competitive edge that the organisation has over other operators in the same industry. When analysing competitors, Kotler and Armstrong (1991) believe that the organisation needs to focus on three levels of the product or service:
   - *The formal product or service.* This is the item or action that the customer actually sees and comprises the tangible items. This may be a car or a training course. By itself, the physical representation of the product or service is inert and has little effect on the customer.
   - *The core benefit.* Delahaye and Smith (1998) suggest that this level answers the question 'What is the customer really buying?' When buying a car, we are not purchasing metal, vinyl, leather and paint. Rather we are purchasing a means of transporting ourselves and our families from one place to another. This basic need may be specialised further by the addition of other needs — for example, safety and comfort. The issue may then be complicated further by the addition of wants — a particular look (sporty; expensive; conservative); high power; an even more comfortable ride.
   - *The augmented advantages.* These are the intangibles that may make the product or service just that little bit better — a warranty, credit facilities, customer service, after-sales service. Augmented advantages tend to satisfy the little worries and niggles that the customer may experience.

   Two issues should be noted. Firstly, the more that the product or service demanded is a mixture of needs and wants in the core benefits, the more complex the customer environment becomes. Secondly, depending on augmented advantages for a competitive advantage over competitors leads to a very volatile, and therefore more unpredictable, external environment.
3. *Suppliers* are the providers of specific raw resources that the organisation needs. The more specialised, or the more the organisation depends on the particular type of raw resource, the more critical the supplier becomes — and the more volatile, and therefore the more unpredictable the external environment.

THE CRITICAL JUDGEMENTS

From the analysis of all this environmental scanning, conventional strategic planning makes two critical judgements — on the volatility of the environment and about the specific market that should be occupied.
1. The *volatility of the environment* is an estimate of the degree and speed of change that the organisation faces. The less volatile the environment, the more confident the organisation can be about its predictions of the future. This, in turn, means that the legitimate system can rely on more mechanistic management processes such as policies and rules in decision making. These mechanistic procedures concentrate on the behaviours of staff, dictating how they should behave in a particular situation. However, when facing a more volatile environment, an organisation will concentrate on the outputs. To do this, the judgement of the staff becomes paramount and the legitimate system has to rely on importing staff with

the required abilities or developing those abilities in the current staff or a combination of the two. If the external environment becomes too volatile then the organisation leaves the close-to-certainty arena and the strategic planning becomes largely dependent on the shadow system.

2. The *market niche* of the organisation is described by the mission statement and is ultimately defined by the analysis of two key factors:
   - The needs of the customer become the central theme of any strategic planning as the organisation will survive only if it satisfies the needs of its customers. The more basic the customer need being satisfied, the more long-term predictions about customer behaviour can be made. Basic customer needs tend to revolve around the sustenance requirements or what the economists call the non-discretionary expenditure — food, simple clothing, basic household goods. Where customers prefer to make more exotic choices, the needs being satisfied are more likely to be more complex and this leads to a more volatile environment that gives the organisation less lead time — in other words the time horizon for predictions shrinks rapidly.
   - The more vigorous the competition for customers, the more volatile the external environment will be. Usually, this means that there is less room for error in satisfying the customer need and a higher requirement for flexibility in satisfying the minute variations in the needs of individual customers. If the customer need is more basic then the external environment only becomes somewhat more unpredictable. The shadow system may be called on in an episodic fashion but generally the organisation can rely on the legitimate system to reorganise the operational processes and the staff (again by either employing new staff or developing current staff or a combination of these approaches). However, if the customer need is quite complex and there is high competition, then the organisation is most probably operating far from certainty and will thus rely more on the shadow system for continued viability.

These critical judgements then form the basis for the organisation's conventional strategic plan.

THE CORPORATE STRATEGIC PLAN

The corporate strategic plan has three major thrusts — the mission statement, the overall strategy and the structure of the organisation.

THE MISSION STATEMENT

The mission statement describes the market niche that the organisation has decided to service. Traditionally, mission statements need three components:
1. the customer need that is to be satisfied
2. the competitive advantage that the organisation enjoys
3. the strategic objectives that will indicate that the organisation is satisfying the customer need sufficiently to survive.

Table 4.1 shows a comparison of the mission statement and strategic objectives of two organisations. Such mission statements provide an overall direction for decision making. So, the mission for Organisation No. 1 ('no frills' and a high turnover for a relatively less profit) indicates that costs have to be carefully considered when designing and implementing a learning experience.

TABLE 4.1

Comparison of two organisations

	ORGANISATION No. 1	ORGANISATION No. 2
Mission	Provide basic personal and household goods at the lowest possible price with a 'no frills service'	Provide personal service so that customer choice of quality personal and household goods is maximised
Strategic objective	Turnover of $15M per year with an after tax profit of $1.5M	Turnover of $7.5M per year with an after-tax profit of $1.5M
	Staff turnover of no more than 30%	Staff turnover of no more than 10%
		At least 1.5% of income spent on staff development

Ideally, of course, the mission statement should become a *governing variable* (see chapter 2). Where this is not the case, the mission statement becomes espoused theory rather than theory-in-action (see chapter 2). Embedding a mission statement as a governing variable requires a complex learning process based on the unstructured learning strategies (see chapter 12).

THE OVERALL STRATEGY

Two of the most commonly used typologies for the overall strategy to be followed by an organisation are those suggested by Miles and Snow (1984) and Schuler (1988). Another that has similarities to the Miles and Snow (1984) approach is that of Sonnenfeld and Pieperl (1988). There are some overlaps and some differences between the two typologies but when combined they give us a reasonable picture of the options available to the legitimate system as it tries to navigate the organisation through the fair winds, squalls and reefs of survival:

- An *entrepreneurial strategy* is implemented when the organisation decides to establish new ventures and initiatives. Current products or services are consistently audited and resources are quickly redeployed from ailing activities to enhance the development and viability of new ones. Risk taking and creativity are seen as worthy virtues. This strategy runs very closely to the role of the shadow system. However, under the entrepreneurial strategy, competition between staff members is often fostered and failure results in the ultimate penalty — loss of status or even job.

- A *dynamic growth strategy* is used when the concern is to build capabilities for the future. Some of the income from currently successful investments are diverted to explore opportunities of possible growth in areas outside the organisation's level of expertise and knowledge. While some unifying factor is needed (for example, good financial planning and control techniques; or a culture valuing staff and the ability to manage human resources well), the organisation will take very calculated risks.
- An *analyser strategy* is used where the organisation chooses to grow, but uses a more cautious approach, with a preference to seek expansion in markets where the organisation has a growing understanding. Within their own market niches, these organisations continually search for specific and specialised nooks where they can use their current strengths to advantage. The growth may come from doing more of the same through increasing current market share at the expense of competitors; by widening the geographic catchment area; by diversifying distribution paths; or by adding more augmented advantages.
- A *defender strategy* is used where the preference is to defend current markets and market share by concentrating on high volumes and low unit costs. These organisations can operate only in environments of high predictability and compete by efficiently controlling costs and maintaining a level of quality that is just above customer expectations.
- A *rationalisation strategy* is used when the organisation finds it must maintain profits through streamlining and cost cutting. When an organisation finds that it has debilitating inefficiencies or that competitors have overtaken them with innovative advances, it turns to rationalisation. Either situation usually means that the shadow system has been starved, or has barely been operational, for some considerable time and that the legitimate system has become moribund and negligent in its duties. SBUs that have not shown a return on investment are cut and costs are reduced. The problem with the rationalisation is that it often falls into the errors of management re-engineering discussed in chapter 1. Costs to be transferred have to be closely examined to ensure that they will not boomerang and the decision makers have to be constantly aware of the effects on staff morale.
- A *liquidation strategy* is used when the organisation finds that profits are declining so severely that entire parts of the organisation must be divested. This strategy usually indicates that the organisation has been caught by surprise, either by the external environment changing rapidly or the organisation making incorrect assumptions about how close to certainty it has been operating. This strategy is very close to rationalisation, except that it is not just low performing SBUs that are eradicated. Assets, including the staff, are purposely selected for divestment in order to bring in cash that can be used to rejuvenate other areas that show more promise of survival.
- A *turnaround strategy* is used where the organisation is in such dire straights that radical short-term restructuring is needed in an attempt to achieve long-term viability. This is a combination of liquidation and rationalisation — and often a hint of entrepreneurialism, with a search for new direction.

As presented, the strategies form somewhat of a hierarchy. The entrepreneurial strategy is the most aggressive one of growth with this aggression diminishing as the strategies move through dynamic growth, analyser and defender. The last three — rationalisation, liquidation and turnaround — are associated with negative growth.

Smaller businesses will tend to adhere to one type of strategy. On the other hand, it is common for most large organisations, particularly those with a large number of strategic business units, to follow one main strategy, with components of other strategies being used for parts of the organisation that face different external environments. For example, large national firms will usually have a major theme in their national outlook but this may be fine-tuned across states as different external factors impinge. However, such a hybrid approach must be viewed carefully, as one reaction of the legitimate system to the organisation rapidly approaching conditions of uncertainty is to attempt to use multiple strategies or, worse, try to rapidly switch from one overall strategy to another. Such reactions were very evident in companies during the late 1980s and are a sure sign that the shadow system has been inappropriately managed — usually for quite some period of time.

THE ORGANISATIONAL STRUCTURE

Once an organisation has decided on its overall strategy, or mix of overall strategies, and identified its appropriate mission statement and strategic objectives, it must then harness its resources in order to capitalise on its market niche appropriately. The major indication of the way in which an organisation has decided to invest its resources is the way it structures itself.

Burns and Stalker (1961) were the first to suggest a direct link between the external environment and the most appropriate internal structure of an organisation. They found that a stable environment suited 'mechanistic organisations' and that 'organic organisations' were more suitable when the external environment was rapidly changing and uncertain. In table 4.1, Organisation No. 1 is representative of a mechanistic organisation and Organisation No. 2 is typical of a more organic organisation.

Organisation No. 1 is expecting to work in a market niche that satisfies customer needs of basic personal and household goods. The organisation is looking at high turnover with low profit margins. Both of these factors — basic needs and low profit margins — suggest a market niche with high competition. However, the organisation appears to have decided that it will not allow any flexibility in meeting customer preference, hence the 'no frills service'. The acceptance of high staff turnover suggests that the organisation is unwilling to invest in staff development or other staff services. Both the 'no frills service' and the limited investment in staff considerations suggest that the organisation has a high priority in cost savings. This organisation sees its competitive advantage as satisfying basic needs (i.e., simple but necessary needs) at the lowest possible cost.

Organisation No. 2, on the other hand, is looking to satisfy more complex needs. To achieve this aim, the organisation requires staff who have well-developed skills in customer service, good knowledge of the product and a willingness to be helpful. Hence, the organisation is willing to invest in staff development and other staff services to keep staff turnover low. The organisation needs to keep staff as these skills and knowledge take some time to develop. The profit margin on articles sold has to be larger to cover these extra costs.

When examining these two examples, notice the connection between the overall strategy, the mission statement and the strategic objective. Organisation No. 1 has chosen a defender strategy, a mission statement that emphasises basic customer needs at a low price and a strategic objective that predicts high turnover and a lower percentage of profit margins. Organisation No. 2, on the other hand, is following the path of a more analyser strategy to fully exploit the current market, represented by complex customer needs, has a lower turnover but imposes higher costs as customers are more willing to use non-discretionary expenditure to satisfy needs that are more a matter of choice. However, satisfying such complex needs requires a well-trained staff and so there is also a recognition in the strategic objectives that good staff must be kept and that staff must be continually developed. It should also be recognised that Organisation No. 2 could not be considered fully organic as it has chosen the analyser path. Organic organisations tend to follow the dynamic growth or entrepreneurial options.

THE STRATEGIC HUMAN RESOURCE DEVELOPMENT PLAN (SHRDP)

As well as giving the direction for the investment of resources of the organisation, the themes of the corporate strategic plan flow down to the dependent strategic plans. As shown in figure 4.1, there are two levels of strategic plans — those for the strategic business units and the functional strategic plans.

Most large organisations are divided into *strategic business units* (SBUs). These units are defined as strategic because they encompass a critical process of the organisation. They may interact directly with the customer (for example, as a major store of one of the national retail companies) or be in a support role (for example, as the state warehouse for the goods that the retail company sells). Each of these SBUs will have a strategic plan, derived from the corporate strategic plan, that guides the decisions of the unit. The strategies usually incorporate a mission statement and strategic objectives at least, the overall strategy often being provided by the corporate strategic plan. However, if a SBU's strategy is different from the corporate strategy, this alternate strategy has to be documented.

Each of the functions that support the SBUs — for example, marketing, finance, vehicles and equipment, buildings acquisition and maintenance, and human resource management — also has strategic plans, called *functional strategic plans*. It should be noted that some of these supporting functions become actual departments in some organisations, but not all of them. Who delivers the support depends on how the organisation decides to marshal its resources. Sometimes staff and other resources are dedicated to a function which is then given an appropriate name — for example, the Human Resources Department or Section. Other times the role is given to a more general area, such as the Administrative Department, or may even be outsourced. However the role is operationalised, each function should have a strategic plan.

As can be seen in figure 4.1, the strategic human resource development plan (SHRDP) comes directly from the strategic human resource management plan (SHRMP) — indeed, in some organisations, the SHRDP is part of the SHRMP. Either way, the conventional strategic planning paradigm assumes that the HRD strategies will be heavily influenced by the corporate strategic plan and the type of structure chosen. While concentrating mainly on human resource management, the original thoughts of Miles and Snow (1984) and Schuler (1988), together with interpretations of such writers as Forster and Browne (1996) and Greer (1995), give us some insights on the likely impact of the chosen corporate strategies on the SHRDP.

ENTREPRENEURIAL STRATEGY

The extent to which staff need to be selected rather than developed is a serious consideration for an organisation following the entrepreneurial path. Some of the desired characteristics, such as risk taking and creativity, may be more natural than nurtured. However, the developmental process can be one of uncovering or freeing such abilities. Attributes such as willingness to accept responsibility can certainly be developed and are often a product of experience. There are also some complexities in the development of staff. The entrepreneurial strategy is marked by conflicting requirements in staff — for example, the need to be cooperative on the one hand, but the underlying need for a competitive spirit. While this aggressiveness ideally should be retained for competitors, or in achieving self-established standards, it is difficult for the energy not to spill over into competition with colleagues. Finally, there is a critical need for key employees to remain in the organisation so that hard-won knowledge is not lost. Unfortunately, in such a 'pressure-cooker' environment, staff burn out quickly or become the victims of a succeed-or-out culture within the firm.

Developmental activities have to be more emancipatory in nature, often informally and spontaneously. These activities have to be closely related to the job problems and challenges and usually occur within the job. They need high participation and are marked by high levels of self-direction.

DYNAMIC GROWTH STRATEGY

Organisational identity and the loyalty of staff are critical with the dynamic growth strategy — not only in key staff, but also in staff supporting those principal members who need to be retained. Deeper attributes of analytic ability, controlled innovation, flexibility, and willingness to accept ambiguity are paramount. High levels of task orientation are also required.

There is some emphasis on emancipatory learning, although this is usually focused on accepting organisational values. Therefore, communicative learning is frequently used to share and create a deeper understanding of those values. Developmental activities tend to concentrate on critical thinking abilities such as logical analysis, on identifying with the 'company way of doing things', financial analysis and developing flexibility and a tolerance of ambiguity. With the need for self-sustaining, semipermanent groups, team-building interventions are reasonably frequent. One challenge for human resource developers is to keep such team-building exercises relevant, task-orientated yet novel.

The more aware organisations following the dynamic growth strategy will invest in development and educational activities that may not appear to be useful immediately. Gaining college and university degrees and attendance at various conferences are used frequently to achieve this end.

ANALYSER STRATEGY

Technical knowledge is valued highly in this strategy so that information can be gathered carefully and analysed skilfully. Allied with this is the need for extensive product or service knowledge. The combination of these two knowledge bases allows the organisation to progress prudently within the carefully defined parameters of the mission statement. Some creativity is encouraged although such energy is tolerated only within specified constraints.

Instrumental learning is predominant although communicative learning is used to further the understanding of the more complex aspects of the products or service.

DEFENDER STRATEGY

Instrumental learning is the hero of the day. Staff, especially those at the lower levels, are not encouraged to think too creatively. Rather, the best way to operate has already been identified and staff need to manipulate their environment in the manner ordained by the organisation. Above all, management needs to be confident that the operational processes will function in the manner expected. These operational processes have been analysed and planned so that maximum efficiency can be achieved. In addition, surprises or different approaches result in higher expenditure.

RATIONALISATION, LIQUIDATION AND TURNAROUND STRATEGIES

For human resource development, each of these strategies has one challenging theme — knowledgeable staff are critical but developing, and keeping, them is expensive. All three levels of learning — emancipatory, communicative and instrumental — are needed as the organisation strives to change direction and values to take advantage of new markets. With such tight cost restraints, the learning experiences have to be carefully and especially targeted to ensure maximum effect. These complex decisions, of course, are being undertaken at a time of maximum turmoil when time is at a premium. Is it any wonder that so many organisations, faced with these strategies, simply consign human resource development to the 'too hard basket'? Unfortunately, such a reaction merely hastens the downfall, unless the organisation is remarkably lucky.

In summary, then, the SHRDP is influenced by the corporate strategic plan in that certain types of learning are likely to be indicated. For example, the defender strategy prefers instrumental learning while the dynamic growth strategy needs more communicative learning to achieve its goals.

TWO OTHER INFLUENCES

While being a dependent strategic plan — its content and themes flowing down from the corporate strategic plan through the functional strategic plan of the SHRMP — the SHRDP deals with people, and the people of the organisation are the ultimate catalyst for any action in the organisation. Therefore, there are two other influences that affect the SHRDP. Of all the strategic plans, these two influences — the micro-external environment created by local conditions and the internal subsystems of the organisation itself — are unique to the SHRDP (see figure 4.1). It is only the human resource that can make the complex and often minute adjustments to the gross strategic directions dictated by the corporate strategic plan.

MICRO-EXTERNAL ENVIRONMENT

The corporate strategic plan is based on a wide vision of the external environment. Closer to the source of action, there are a number of smaller yet forceful factors that impinge on the operations of the various SBUs and functional departments. The SHRDP has to be fine-tuned to recognise these local factors, such as the following:

- *Local socioeconomic conditions*, such as the sociological profile, cultural mores and community economic well-being, all impinge on human resource development decisions. The ability of the employees to travel to and from work sites, standards of dress, approaches to learning and community values can all affect the types of learning experiences that need to be designed.
- *Local government regulations and laws* can cover a wide variety of organisational activities. These regulations and laws can have two effects. Firstly, staff may have to be aware of activities that they can or cannot do — such as building require-ments or the proper disposal of refuse and waste. Secondly, staff may have to be trained in particular actions to comply with local government requirements, as is often demanded under health by-laws with food preparation.
- *Local employment conditions*, encompass two significant issues — the level of unemployment and the level of skills and knowledge present in the community. If unemployment is low, then the organisation may need to provide additional career-enhancing development activities for staff. If certain skills and knowledge are not available in the local employment pool the organisation may have to con-duct special courses and workshops before employment of new staff can com-mence. Jupiters Casino on the Gold Coast in Queensland has provided a classical example of this. Before the casino could be opened, the organisation realised that there was a dearth of qualified dealers in the catchment area, so workshops were conducted before the casino opened. This not only created a pool of skilled labour, but also provided an excellent initial selection process.
- In most localities, there a some *local key external stakeholders* — people or organ-isations who influence the endeavours within the community. This may be a flam-boyant town mayor or the editor of a local newspaper or a large industrial enterprise that provides most of the employment in the local area. Such key stakeholders may provide opportunities or challenges that the organisation may need to meet.

INTERNAL SUBSYSTEMS

The second influence on the SHRDP is created by the various subsystems within the organisation, including the following:

- The workplace educator must tap into the various *information systems* of the organisation. These systems may be part of the computer system or may be con-trol systems in the operational departments. These are two types of information to which the workplace educator needs access. The first type provides insights into the health of the organisation — what problems are occurring? What new opportunities can the organisation capitalise on? Where can new efficiencies be achieved? What is the morale of the employees? Information systems that provide indicators for these types of questions — such as financial controls and quality assurance systems — can give the workplace educator a longer lead time to plan appropriate developmental activities. The second type of information is that which deals directly with the developmental needs of the individual. The most practical and valuable of these is the performance appraisal system. However, other worthwhile information can be gleaned from the selection programs, from the evaluations of development activities and from career planning.

- The *culture* of the organisation can be defined as the values, beliefs and rituals that guide an organisation, often unconsciously, to act in certain manner. This culture may be divergent from the direction ordained by the corporate strategic plan — and this usually leads to disaster. In addition, the culture of an organisation is notoriously difficult to change. Large organisations tend to have dominant or core cultures with subcultures developing to reflect the common problems, situations or experiences that various organisational subgroups face (Robbins and Barnwell 1998).

- *Key internal stakeholders* are frequently members of senior management but may be other power centres, such a union shop stewards or staff with particularly important organisational knowledge. These key organisational members often exert disproportionate power on the decision-making process in the design and implementation of learning activities. Personal preferences of these key stakeholders can dictate the nature of the learning strategies. For example, in one Australian national retail organisation, one state manager had previously experienced a very negative outcome from a role play. The Training and Development Department in that state was forbidden to use role plays in any of their developmental workshops — despite the proven efficacy of role plays in developing competence in customer interactions.

The SHRD Plan, therefore, is an amalgam of influences — directly from the SHRMP and indirectly from the corporate strategic plan; from the micro-external environment; and from the internal subsystems of the information systems, the culture and key stakeholders (see figure 4.1).

OPERATIONAL PLANS

The SHRD plans are turned into activities through the HRD operational plans. There are two types of operational plans — standing plans and single-use plans (Schermerhorn 1996; Stoner, Yetton, Craig and Johnston 1994).

STANDING PLANS

Standing plans are written instructions that provide guidance for common decisions and recurring situations. Standing plans are created by a hierarchy of three elements — policies, procedures and rules — and serve organisations by giving staff a framework for acting in common ways over time (Schermerhorn 1996, pp. 143–144).

- *Policies* communicate broad guidelines for taking action. They should focus attention on matters of special organisational importance and guide people on how they are expected to behave in respect to them.
- *Procedures* provide the step-by-step actions that are to be taken to ensure that the policy is carried out appropriately.
- *Rules* define what must or must not be done.

Each policy is usually supported by a series of procedures and rules and these standing plans are usually documented in handbooks or manuals often called 'Manual of Procedures' or 'Standard Operating Procedures' (MOPs or SOPs). The manager of the human resources development section or department is responsible for ensuring that appropriate standing plans are promulgated in the MOPs or SOPs so that the appropriate HRD policies that are needed to support the corporate strategic plan are widely disseminated. Further, particularly when new policies are created because of a shift in the corporate strategy, the manager of the HRD section will often arrange for training programs to be designed and implemented.

a closer look   4.1

An example of an HRD standing plan

Policy
All supervisors and managers will be competent trainers.

Procedure
1. When promoted to supervisor level or beyond, staff will attend a Train-the-Trainer Workshop.

2. Supervisors must attain the Australian Workplace Trainer Competencies Category I.
3. Managers must attain the Australian Workplace Trainer Competencies Category II.
4. These competencies must be achieved within 6 months of promotion.

Rule
Any supervisor or manager who does not achieve the required competency level within 6 months of promotion will revert to his or her original position.

There are five issues that must be emphasised with regard to HRD standing plans:
1. They are derived from the hierarchy of strategic plans so that they support the strategic direction of the organisation.
2. Standing plans dictate the appropriate behaviour that should occur in particular situations and are expected to be in operation for a reasonable period. This means that they operate under the assumption that the situation and conditions will not change. Therefore, they can operate only under conditions of certainty. So the actions that standing plans control must be affecting only that part of an external environment that is close to certainty.
3. Because of the turbulent environment that most businesses operate within, standing plans can become obsolete quite quickly. This presents some managers with a conundrum — standing plans are needed for the efficient operation of an organisation; but they can become dated very quickly. One option that some organisations have chosen is to do away with standing plans altogether. Unfortunately, this choice is correct only if the organisation is facing a very volatile external environment — and is therefore highly reliant on the shadow system.

In situations where the legitimate system still has a role, and this covers the majority of situations, then standing plans are essential. The challenge is to formulate them correctly, have them influencing only decisions that need a common direction and that emanate from a stable environment, and to ensure that they are audited regularly.

4. Organisations using a defender, and to a certain extent an analyser, strategy tend to have a higher dependence on standing plans. Those operating under the other strategies tend to have a lesser dependence — although very few organisations can do without them altogether.

5. Standing plans form an important part of the knowledge capital of the organisation.

So standing plans are an important part of the everyday management of the legitimate system. However, they need to be relevant and up-to-date and, thus, should be reviewed regularly.

SINGLE-USE PLANS

Single-use plans are designed to achieve the objectives of a particular project. For HRD, single-use plans are most commonly seen as the learning programs that are designed and implemented. As we will see when discussing the needs investigation stage, the demand for learning programs may come from the corporate plan (for example, the company is to invest in new equipment and therefore staff will need to be trained in its operation) or from one of the internal information systems (for example, the quality control system indicates that the high number of product rejections is caused by a lack of skill amongst staff). As discussed in chapter 10, the HRD single-use plan usually comprises of at least four subplans — the learning program (including session plans), the marketing plan, the evaluation plan and a budget. The HRD section would plan and implement a series of single-use plans throughout the year.

THE LEGITIMATE SYSTEM

Conventional strategic planning is conducted by the legitimate system to ensure that the organisation runs effectively and efficiently in the short term — perhaps a couple of months or even up to 2 years. As such, the conventional process identifies the deliberate strategy the organisation should follow. Now, just because this deliberate strategy may be relevant only for the period in which the organisation can operate close to certainty does not mean that such deliberate strategic planning is trivial. The conventional strategic planning process may indicate a change in strategy (for example, from a dynamic growth to an analyser strategy) or even the takeover of a competitor or conquering a new market. However, any such change will remain within the mission and the current values that the legitimate system is bound to uphold.

The corporate strategic plan impinges on the HRD function in several ways:

• The mission of the organisation provides a simple yet robust indicator of the market niche the organisation is to service. This mission statement then becomes the initial benchmark for any decision making.

- The corporate strategy selected (for example, defender or analyser) tends to dictate the type of learning that will be most appropriate (for example, instrumental learning in the defender strategy).
- The content or topic of learning programs (the common HRD single-use plan) often comes from the strategic planning process. This can occur in several ways — when one strategy is changed for another (for example, going from a dynamic growth to an analyser strategy); when new equipment or a new market means new knowledge has to be disseminated through the organisation; or when a new policy is promulgated and staff have to be trained in new procedures.
- The whole organisational planning process, from the corporate strategic plan to the standing plans, provides the standards for the auditing process of the legitimate system for the ideas that emanate from the shadow system.

THE SHADOW SYSTEM

Mintzberg (1994) criticises conventional strategic planning as being, in reality, strategic programming. He sees strategic programming as being a mechanistic process based on the manipulation of figures and rote behaviour. Indeed, conventional strategic planning can descend to this level if it is not viewed for what it is — a short time horizon activity to ensure that the organisation runs efficiently and effectively. Accordingly, conventional strategic planning is quite appropriate for the legitimate system which is operating in an environment that is close to certainty.

However, Mintzberg is quite right when he claims that strategic programming can interfere with strategic thinking. Because of this, strategic thinking should be the role of the shadow system.

> Strategic thinking, by contrast, is about *synthesis*. It involves intuition and creativity. The outcome of strategic thinking is an integrated perspective of the enterprise, a not-too-precise articulation of direction ... Such strategies often cannot be developed on schedule and immaculately conceived.

(Mintzberg 1994, p. 108)

He goes on to point out that such emergent strategies must be free to appear at any time and at any place in the organisation, typically through the messy process of informal learning that must be necessarily carried out by people at various levels who are deeply involved with the specific issues at hand.

Such strategic thinking and emergent strategies, then, are the main goals of the shadow system. Further, Mintzberg's ideas indicate two critical aspects of the shadow system:

1. The staff in the shadow system come from various levels throughout the organisation. However, they must be involved, committed and motivated by the specific strategic issues at hand. Such staff may not be occupied all of their time in the shadow system. Of course, this may occur — for example, specific staff are selected for a project which examines the strategic future of the organisation. However, the more frequent scenario is that staff members operate most of their time in the legitimate system (in their usual role) but, perhaps once or twice a day

or even a week, they think strategically about an issue that has come to their attention. Some of the biggest breakthroughs in science have come from such serendipitous events. Penicillin was found because a window was left open in a laboratory one night. Velcro was created by an engineer who, following his hobby of photography, was walking through the countryside. Intrigued by the burrs that stuck to his pants, he examined them under a microscope and saw the hooks on the end of the spikes on the burrs. The thought came that this may make a good connection device.

2. The shadow system is all about learning. This learning occurs on two levels. Firstly, it occurs at the level of the individual in the shadow system. She or he must be mature enough to be willing to learn and to have redeveloped the required levels of curiosity. The second is the organisational level. The learning of the individual must be shared with others — using the knowledge-creating processes of externalisation, combination, internalisation and socialisation.

Such activities cannot be accomplished by a mechanistic system, only by a motivated and committed human resource. So, while the processes of conventional strategic planning can be documented (as has been done in this chapter), the processes of the shadow system are partly about management of the human resource and partly about learning. Therefore, in the first part, the development of emergent strategies is achieved by the skilful and wise management of the chief executive officer (CEO) with the assistance of the upper management of the organisation. Above all, a culture of trust and loyalty has to be engendered to provide the safe and caring environment in which the delicate organism of learning can grow. This topic is addressed more fully in chapter 14.

The informal learning processes that are so critical to emergent strategies, however, are in the realm of the HRD function. The management of these learning processes is discussed in chapter 12. Briefly, HRD function takes a much more proactive role as the shadow system develops the emergent strategies. The HRD function helps to manage the various processes — learning, exploring the unknown and introducing the changes to the legitimate system. This can be compared to the reactive role in conventional strategic management, where the HRD function is affected by the results of the corporate strategic plan.

THE CRITICAL NATURE OF THE SHRDP

The strategic planning process, on an initial inspection, may appear to be a fairly dry and unimportant activity from the human resource development perspective. Such a reaction is fallacious. Strategic planning is critical to human resource development on two counts — its impact on development approaches and the learning process involved in conducting strategic planning.

IMPACT

The legitimate system has to ensure that the operational activities of an organisation are conducted in the most efficient manner possible. It also has to ensure that the activities will produce an effective outcome — an outcome that will be attractive to its customers. To make such judgements the legitimate system relies on standards — some overt, others covert. Some of the covert standards are preserved in the organisational culture, are often subjective in nature and subject to the whims of key or powerful people. To offset this sometimes insidious influence, the legitimate system must have a healthy strategic planning process to provide a more objective standard.

Within the legitimate system, then, the influence of the strategic planning process cascades down the dependent strategic plans to the strategic human resource development plan (SHRDP). While this influence is somewhat sweeping, the corporate strategic plan does establish certain parameters that delimit the type of developmental activities that are more likely to be successful. So the defender strategy tends to predetermine more structured learning experiences that rely on instrumental learning while the analyser strategy depends on communicative learning to surface and pass on certain guiding values and beliefs.

Within the shadow system, the HRD function becomes actively involved in the process itself, helping the actors in the system to learn and to discover. It is this role in the shadow system that has made the HRD function such an exciting and dynamic operational arena — although the extent to which this will continue depends on the vision of wise and skilful CEOs and managers.

THE LEARNING PROCESS

The strategic planning process, in itself, can be a learning process. To achieve this exalted status, however, the strategic planning process must raise itself above the mechanical, procedural level — what Mintzberg calls strategic programming. He goes on to admonish that strategic planning must be about strategic thinking.

> [T]he strategy-making process should be [about] capturing what the manager learns from all sources (both soft insights from his or her personal experiences and the experiences of others throughout the organization and the hard data from market research and the like) and then synthesizing that learning into a vision of the direction that the business should pursue.

(Mintzberg 1994, p. 107)

From our understanding of organisational and adult learning, we can view this learning process as:

- one of *knowledge generation*. As the decision makers wrestle with the soft and hard data, they externalise knowledge by allowing previously unarticulated insights to surface. As the substance from the corporate strategic plan cascades down to the strategic plans of the SBUs and the functions, a combination of generating processes occur as differing foci and technical knowledge are brought to bear on the extraction of the relevant themes. Finally, the individual actors in the decision making will internalise insights to add to or re-form their tacit knowledge, knowledge that will be used in the ongoing strategic thinking process.
- One of *emancipatory learning* as the organisation struggles with new data which may indicate a change in fundamental organisational values. This struggle is what Senge (1990) refers to as organisational generative learning and Argyris (1992) as double-loop learning. The more power that the shadow system is given in this

emancipatory learning, the more it is likely that fundamental values will be changed.

- One of *increasing the knowledge capital* of the organisation. The more staff are involved in the strategic planning, the more the increase of individual explicit and tacit knowledge. In addition, the knowledge capital in such material locations as the computer system and MOPs or SOPs will be increased and changed.
- One in which the *culture* of the organisation also gradually changes. This is partly a result of the changes accrued from double-loop learning and partly because of the changes in individual tacit knowledge. The culture is also more likely to undergo fundamental change the more the organisational defence mechanisms are challenged. The ultimate culture change is one that allows, indeed encourages, the organisation to constantly challenge fundamental precepts and values — for this is the culture of a learning organisation.

MORE THAN WORDS

So the SHRDP is more than words on paper. The strategic endeavours and decisions must be seen as thinking processes, not simply programming. Above all, it must be seen as an essential and crucial activity that holds the future of the organisation in its hands.

By importing and analysing data, the organisation is exposing itself to new interpretations. The knowledge-generating process of externalisation, if astutely managed, can be successfully incorporated into the planning process to allow new knowledge for the organisation to surface. Once the planning process moves from the corporate strategic plan to the dependent plans, the knowledge-generating process of combination can occur — provided that the planning process is not degraded to a mechanical procedure of simple transposition.

GLOSSARY

conventional paradigm of strategic planning — a process of conducting the strategic planning process that has evolved over the last three decades, used mainly by the legitimate system

corporate strategic plan — the organisation's over-riding strategic plan

direct factors — the forces and variables in the external environment that impinge directly on the organisation

external environment — anything that is outside of the organisation

indirect factors — the forces and variables in the external environment that impinge indirectly on the organisation

internal subsystems — the subsystems within the organisation that may impinge on the SHRDP

legitimate system — the part of the organisation that is involved in the day-to-day activities

market niche — the segment of the market that the organisation decides to service

micro-external environment — the local conditions in the external environment that may impinge on the SHRDP

mission statement — a description of the market niche that includes the customer need being serviced and the organisation's competitive edge

operational plans — the plans used to convert the strategic plans into actions

overall or general strategy — one of seven strategies (entrepreneurial, dynamic growth, analyser, defender, rationalisation, liquidation, turnaround) that can be used by the organisation in its corporate strategic plan

shadow system — the part of the organisation that looks ahead to the future

single-use plan — one type of operational plan

standing plan — another type of operational plan

strategic human resource development plan (SHRDP) — the strategic plan for developing the staff in the organisation, derived from the corporate strategic plan

strategy — the way the organisation chooses to invest its resources to best service the chosen customer needs.

QUESTIONS

For review

1. Briefly describe the four elements of the conventional strategic planning paradigm and explain why this paradigm is most suitable for the legitimate system.

2. List and describe the indirect and direct factors that need to be analysed in the external environment so that the organisation's market niche can be defined.

3. Describe at least four strategic options that are available to the legitimate system.

4. What is the difference between standing plans and single-use plans?

For analysis

5. Compare and contrast how the SHRDP will be influenced by the dynamic growth strategy and the defender strategy.

6. Discuss, using examples from your own experience, how the micro-environment could affect the SHRDP.

7. By referring to the seven general strategies — entrepreneurial, dynamic growth, analyser, defender, rationalisation, liquidation and turnaround — explain how human resource development can contribute to the competitive advantage of an organisation.

For application

8. Using an organisation that you know, explain the impact of the internal information systems, the organisational culture and key internal stakeholders on the SHRDP.

9. By comparing two organisations in a particular industry (for example, Woolworths and David Jones in the retail industry), explain how the SHRDP is critical to the success of each company.

REFERENCES

Argyris, C. (1992). *On Organisational Learning*. Cambridge, Mass.: Blackwell.

Burns, T. and Stalker, G. M. (1961). *The Management of Innovation*. London: Tavistock.

Chandler, A. D. (1962). *Strategy and Structure: Chapters in the History of Industrial Enterprise*. Cambridge, Mass.: MIT Press.

Delahaye, B. L. and Smith, B. J. (1998). *How to be an Effective Trainer*. New York: Wiley.

Forster, J. and Browne, M. (1996). *Principles of Strategic Management*. South Melbourne, Vic: MacMillan.

Greer, C. R. (1995). *Strategy and Human Resources: a General Management Perspective*. Englewood Cliffs, NJ: Prentice Hall.

Kotler, P. and Armstrong, G. (1991). *Principles of Marketing*. (5th ed.). Sydney, NSW: Prentice Hall.

McColl-Kennedy, J. R., Keil, G. F., Lusch, R. F. and Lusch, V. N. (1994). *Marketing: Concepts and Strategies*. (2nd ed.). South Melbourne, Vic: Nelson.

Micklethwait, J. and Wooldridge, A. (1996). *The Witch Doctors*. London: Heinemann.

Miles, R. and Snow, C. (1984). 'Designing strategic human resources systems.' *Organizational Dynamics*, 13.

Mintzberg, H. (1994). 'The fall and rise of strategic planning.' *Harvard Business Review*, January–February, 107–114.

Mintzberg, H., Quinn, J. B. and Voyer, J. (1995). *The Strategy Process*. Englewood Cliffs, NJ: Prentice Hall.

Porter, M. E. (1985). *Competitive Advantage: Creating and Sustaining Superior Performance*. New York: Free Press.

Robbins, S. P. and Barnwell, N. (1998). *Organisation Theory: Concepts and Cases*. Sydney: Prentice Hall.

Schermerhorn, J. R. (1996). *Management*. New York: Wiley.

Schuler, R. S. (1988). 'Personnel and human resource management choices and organisational strategy.' *Human Resource Management Australia*, February, 81–99.

Senge, P. (1990). *The Fifth Discipline: The Art and Practice of the Learning Organisation*. Milson's Point: Random House.

Sonnenfeld, J. A. and Peiperl, M. (1988). 'Staffing policy as a strategic response: a typology of Career Systems.' *Academy of Management Review*, 13(4), 591–594.

Stoner, J. A. F., Yetton, P. W., Craig, J. F. and Johnston, K. D. (1994). *Management*. (2nd ed.). Sydney: Prentice Hall.

A choice of strategy

Southbank Advertising and Graphics is a relatively small marketing company based in an industrial complex in the northern suburbs of Melbourne, Victoria. They target smaller industries and communities by publishing journals that contain news and information of special interest to that particular industry or community. For example *The Ceramics and Pottery Quarterly* is published every 3 months and contains such stories as successful new businesses in the industry, descriptions of new technology and an analysis of new trends overseas. While the readers pay a delivery fee of 10 dollars annually, the main income comes from the advertising in the journal. They also publish newspapers for community groups ranging from tourist destinations (multiple copies are sent to hotels and motels) and self-help groups such as the Australian Asthma and Arthritis Support Group. Again, while these newspapers contain articles of interest to these community groups, the main source of income for Southbank Advertising and Graphics comes from the advertising. In total, they have fifty-eight different journals and newspapers.

The company has a staff of eighteen, including the two founding partners. Ten of the staff maintain very close and personal contacts with the main clients in the industries and community groups. For example, one staff member is very well known in the horse-racing industry. The journal targeting this industry, *Turf News*, has a client base of over 5000 including breeders, trainers and horse equipment stores and is a very successful publication. While these 10 staff members gather the news and information, the writing of the articles is left with two journalists. Four other staff members concentrate solely on advertising and public relations. Two staff look after administration.

The mission statement of Southbank Advertising and Graphics is 'Top quality publications

through personal contact'. Their current structure, with over 60% of the staff directly linked with the target industries and community groups, certainly supports this mission statement. However, while the company has been highly successful since its start 7 years ago, the partners would like to keep expanding 'slowly but surely' as one of the partners keeps saying. There are other specialist industries that they are considering, for example the timber industry and some of the sporting arenas.

One area of robust debate for expansion has been the production of film for the advertisements. Currently, the company can complete the digital printing and artwork but has to use outside sources to produce film proofs and film suitable for printing. This is quite time consuming, often holding up production for over a week, as the proofs are firstly produced by the outside source, returned to Southbank Advertising and Graphics, sent to the advertising customer for approval and, on receipt of approval, returned to the outside source for a film template for printing. One partner knows of a film producing company, Interlink Photographics, that could be purchased. The purchase cost is well within the budget of Southbank Advertising and Graphics.

Discussion questions

1. What type of strategy is Southbank Advertising and Graphics following? Justify your choice.
2. If Interlink Photographics is purchased, what structural and staffing issues will the partners have to think of?
3. What aspects of instrumental, communicative and emancipatory learning will have to be considered?

CASE STUDY 4.2

Now the rubber hits the road

Jak Patel, Senior Workplace Educator for the Tableland Bay Shire Council, contemplated the Shire Strategic Plan (SSP) for the next calendar year. In particular, he focused on the OneStopShop schedule. The OneStopShop concept had been the idea — some staff called it a 'hobby horse' — of the shire clerk for a number of years. The OneStopShop consisted of three new purpose-designed buildings where the ratepayers of the shire could pay any fees or rates and also purchase any shire licences. No longer would ratepayers be shunted from one department to another.

There was quite a lot for the Learning and Development Department to consider. As the manager of the Learning and Development Department said to Jak, 'This is where the rubber hits the road. Strategy is alright, but we have to make it work'. Firstly, all staff of the OneStopShop would have to be thoroughly familiar with all the various

fees, rates and licence payments that the council collected. Then there was the new computer system for the three shops. Not only did this computer system record all transactions but any information on council operations could be accessed so that the ratepayers could be given advice. The shire clerk was adamant that the OneStopShop would be user friendly, where ratepayers could find assistance on any council matter. Further, to establish pride in staff, the shire clerk insisted on all staff in the OneStopShop wearing a newly designed uniform. 'Thank goodness', thought Jak, 'he at least had the sense to involve the staff in the design of the new uniform'.

Discussion questions

1. What operational plans will Jak Patel have to institute?

2. Provide a brief description or an example of these operational plans.

An overview of HRD needs identification

CHAPTER OBJECTIVES

At the end of this chapter you should be able to:

1 describe the four categories of a human resource development needs investigation (HRDNI)

2 discuss the purpose of an HRDNI

3 explain how the surveillance stage of an HRDNI can give early indicators of HRD requirements

4 describe the two parts of the investigation stage of the HRDNI

5 discuss the issues to be considered when creating a realistic action plan for an HRDNI

6 explain how to select appropriate HRDNI methods

7 identify the three forces that may impede an HRDNI

8 list the elements of an HRDNI report.

The chapter opens by emphasising the importance of **human resource development needs investigation (HRDNI)**. There are four categories of HRDNI — a performance deficiency, a diagnostic audit, a democratic preference and a proactive analysis. Whatever the type of HRDNI, a strong word of caution is raised. A HRDNI should be conducted only after a general needs investigation to avoid the common mistake of assuming that human resource development can overcome any problem in the organisation.

There are two stages to an HRDNI. The **surveillance stage** is a continuous monitoring process that provides early warning indicators of HRD requirements. The **investigation stage** occurs once an early warning has been received. An investigation has two phases. First, data has to be gathered by examining organisational records, observation, assessment centres and the critical incident technique. Secondly, the data has to be analysed impartially and objectively. The results of this analysis are the **learning objectives** or **competencies** or **learning outcomes** to be achieved and prioritising these outputs. The learning objectives/competencies/learning outcomes play a pivotal role in the three later stages of HRD — design, implementation and evaluation.

An **investigation plan** needs to be developed and issues such as the authority base, the key role players, the appropriate investigation methods and establishing time frames for the investigation need to be considered. When selecting an appropriate HRDNI method, the HR developer should consider the strategic orientation of the organisation and the advantages and disadvantages of each method. As part of this planning activity, the HR developer should acknowledge that there are at least three forces that may impede the progress of the investigation — organisational politics, espoused theories and organisational defence mechanisms.

The end result of this investigative effort is the **HRDNI report**. The report should cover such matters as the reason for conducting the investigation, the investigative processes used and the learning objectives/competencies/learning outcomes, and provide information that will assist with the later design of a learning episode. This information would include curriculum matters, the type of HR developers needed and the resources needed to conduct the learning episode. In addition, the HRDNI report should include a basic plan for the later evaluation of the learning episode.

The chapter ends by emphasising the importance of HRDNI. HRDNI is a dynamic and continuous process that ensures the wise and relevant allocation of resources. A well-conducted HRDNI not only contributes to an increase in efficiency and effectiveness, but also decreases the risk that inappropriate action will be taken.

THE IMPORTANCE OF HRDNI

Human resource development needs identification (HRDNI) often goes by other names — HRD needs analysis or HRD needs assessment are quite common. Yet HRDNI is much more than these alternative names suggest. Certainly analysis and assessment are involved but other processes such as data gathering, description, verification, classification and interrelationships are also present. In the HRDNI, the HR developer becomes an investigator who carries out all these activities.

In these days of change and pressure, it is easy to dismiss HRDNI as an unnecessary and time-consuming impost. Such a stance is fraught with danger. As Goldstein (1993) comments, while there is a temptation to begin human resource development without a thorough HRDNI, learning programs are designed to achieve goals that meet certain learning outcomes. As is common in today's turbulent climate, yes–no decisions are rarely suitable and are usually an indication of lazy management.

The conventional HRDNI, as discussed in this chapter, is the prerogative of the legitimate system. Remember that the legitimate system has two main functions — to manage the day-to-day activities of the organisation and to audit the new ideas discovered by the shadow system. HRDNI is heavily involved in both of these roles — ensuring that appropriate training is conducted so that the day-to-day activities are carried out effectively and efficiently; and to assimilate and integrate the new ideas. However, the methods, techniques and skills discussed under HRDNI are critical to the shadow system. The actors in the shadow system need to be highly adept in these methods, techniques and skills as they are using them constantly in their search for new knowledge that will help the organisation survive.

HRDNI DEFINED

At its most basic, an HRDNI is a process that identifies the gap between what is currently happening and what should be occurring. Rothwell and Kazanas (1989, p. 81) suggest that, traditionally, 'what is' and 'what should be' are considered. Dalzeil (1994) concurs, believing that a developmental need exists in an organisation when there is a gap between the present skills and knowledge of its employees and the skills and knowledge they require or will require for an effective performance.

However, this traditional stance on HRDNI — sometimes called a gap analysis — focuses too much on performance deficiencies. An HRDNI process also should be future orientated, pro-active and positive rather than being reactive and negative. Accordingly, writers such a Brinkerhoff (1986) suggest that there are four categories of HRDNI:

- *a performance deficiency*, which concentrates on the measurable difference between what the organisation expects and what is actually occurring — the gap analysis. So, a construction supervisor may expect that a carpenter gang would take 3 days to erect a house frame, but sees that one gang is averaging four and a half days.
- *a diagnostic audit*, which focuses on the future rather than on existing problems or issues by searching for ways that will lead to more effective performance or prevent performance problems. For example, an organisation should always be searching for new technological advancements that will maintain the organisation's competitive edge. This category of HRDNI would emphasise the impact of the strategic planning process of the organisation discussed in chapter 4.
- *a democratic preference*, in which staff and managers may become aware of programs that they perceive will meet their unique needs. Such options have the

advantage of having high acceptability when staff are involved fully in the decisions. The democratic preference category empowers staff to consider their own developmental needs. Opportunities for democratic preference often surface in the developmental performance appraisal which will be discussed in chapter 6.

- *a pro-active analysis*, where the emphasis of the search is for future problems and challenges, before such issues are evident. As such, this category is firmly in the arena of the shadow system as the organisation operates close to the edge of uncertainty and pro-actively searches for new knowledge.

So, the concept of HRDNI can have multiple meanings. It may refer to a one-off investigation, as in the performance deficiency category. It may also refer to an ongoing surveillance of the knowledge levels within the organisation. It may also refer to a scanning of future problems and challenges that may confront the organisation.

a word of
CAUTION!

However, a strong warning must be raised. Too often there is an automatic assumption that organisational problems are caused, and can be subsequently fixed, by the training and development of staff. Organisational problems have many potential causes. Therefore, it is more accurate to depict HRDNI as part of a general needs analysis. Further, the general needs analysis must be conducted first. If the general needs analysis indicates that lack of staff development may be the cause, or if the solution will eventually involve staff development (for example, if new equipment is to be installed), *then* an HRDNI can be carried out.

THE PURPOSE OF HRDNI

HRDNI is based on the powerful premise that diagnosis should come before action. This prior emphasis on diagnosis is common to all professions — engineers survey the building site and then draw construction plans; doctors ask questions, conduct a physical examination and take tests before making a decision. Diagnosis is a two-part process — the gathering of accurate and relevant data and the impartial analysis of that data. Such a careful diagnosis ensures that the aim of the development is well defined and understood and that the subsequent developmental effort will be both effective and efficient.

An HRDNI, then, is a process that identifies and defines an organisation's HRD needs. DeSimone and Harris (1998, p. 97) suggest that an HRDNI is a study that can be used to identify:

- an organisation's goals and its effectiveness in reaching these goals
- discrepancies between employees' skills and the skills required for effective job performance
- discrepancies between current skills and the skills needed to perform the job successfully in the future
- the conditions under which the HRD activity will occur.

The HRDNI seeks answers to such underlying questions as:

- What is going well? What needs improvement? What content needs to be covered? What examples are there of good practice? What examples are there of bad practice? How can this content be categorised — is it explicit or tacit knowledge; is it to do with the frames of reference of the learners? Are we seeing cause-and-effect or do the variables under investigation merely have a correlational relationship?

- Who needs to be developed? What are their levels of knowledge, skills and abilities? Are there groups of potential learners or is the issue more individually based? How motivated are they? How do they prefer to learn?
- What resources are needed to conduct the learning experience? What resources are available? What is the overall time frame within which the development should be achieved? What has to occur first, what second and so on?
- What are the organisational political ramifications of this issue under investigation? Who is likely to support it? Who besides the learner will benefit? Who is likely to feel threatened by the outcomes of the learning? What are the opinions of the key stakeholders? What are the levels of outcome that are likely to be accepted by the key stakeholders — do they want the learners to be highly proficient or will a coping level be accepted? What level and type of resources are the key decision makers willing to invest in the learning outcomes?

ORGANISATIONAL AWARENESS

Organisations are continually being exhorted to be pro-active and, in the arena of HRD, the imperative is no less. Delahaye and Smith (1998) suggest that organisations need to be at two levels of awareness — surveillance and investigation.

THE SURVEILLANCE STAGE

The manager of the HRD department or section, as well as individual HR developers, need to ensure that the external and internal environments of the organisation are constantly surveyed.

The *external environment* is mainly monitored via the strategic plan and the HR developer must be guided by the themes in the organisation's strategy. Goldstein (1993, p. 30) believes that HR developers must understand clearly the strategic direction of their organisation because designing developmental systems that do not fit into the organisation's goals and plans would not make sense. In addition, as pointed out in chapter 4, the HR developer as an HRDNI investigator frequently has to scrutinise the local external environment so that any minor adjustments can be made. For example, the local supply of a particular type of employee may be limited and this can mean that specific training workshops have to be planned and conducted.

The *internal environment* of an organisation is monitored by tapping into the various organisational information systems (see chapter 4). Some of the more important information systems are:

- the *quality control system*, which is an important indicator of the effectiveness of the organisation. If the quality standards are not being maintained then customer needs are not being met and resources are being wasted. Now the cause may or may not be a human resource problem but monitoring of the quality control system will give the HRD needs analyst an early warning of possible issues.
- the *financial system*, which provides a measure of the basic health of the organisation. If cost budgets are being exceeded or if cash flows are too low then the organisation is in serious trouble. Again, early warnings of such basic troubles give the HRD needs analyst some lead time in which to carry out further investigations.

- *staff turnover and sick leave figures*, which frequently reflect the state of staff morale. Again, there may be other causes of high staff turnover (for example, not paying high enough wages) but high staff turnover and high levels of sick leave may be indicators of serious staffing problems such as bad management practices, low conflict resolution abilities and lack of skills leading to feelings of ineptitude. Some of these problems may be resolved through appropriate human resource development strategies.
- *safety reports*, which can signify the extent of a safety problem (by the number of reports) and the type of safety problem (by the content of the reports). Safety is a serious issue, not simply because of the grave legal consequences, but also because of the potential cost in human suffering.
- the *performance appraisal system*, which comes under a number of different headings these days — performance review, performance management, performance counselling and staff development system. Whatever the name, they all have one thing in common — they compare the performance of the individual or the team to requirements of the job. The performance appraisal system is one of the most critical surveillance processes available to the organisation. It provides an early warning system of problems and opportunities in the human resources and also furnishes complex details of individual staff development needs. Yet performance appraisal systems frequently become one of the worst designed, badly managed and demotivating practices in the organisation. Because of its critical nature, the performance appraisal system will be discussed in detail in chapter 6.

Keeping a constant surveillance of such organisational information systems can give the HR developer early indicators of human resource development requirements. Once prewarned, the HR developer can then proceed to the specific investigation — the stage on which most writers concentrate when addressing HRDNI.

THE INVESTIGATION STAGE

Once an early warning of an opportunity (for example, from the strategic plan or from the shadow system) or a problem (for example, from safety reports) is received, the HR developer then commences a specific investigation. The investigation stage is in two parts — the **data gathering** and the **data analysis**.

Data gathering

There are a number of data gathering methods. Three of the most common are the qualitative approaches of the interview and focus group and the quantitative technique of the survey questionnaire. These methods will be discussed fully in chapters 7 and 8. Other data collection methods include those discussed below.

Organisational records

This is usually an automatic extension of the surveillance stage. The organisational system that has alerted the analyst in the first place is examined in deeper detail. So if customer complaints indicate that the incidence of grievances has risen above the acceptable standard, the investigator will examine all the complaints recorded over an extended period of time. The analyst may also be alerted to other organisational records. For example, in an hotel the original complaints may have been about room service but the investigator may need to look at the rosters at the reception office as the guests' telephone calls are often re-routed through the reception desk when the room service area is busy or unattended.

Observation

The analyst may observe a staff member completing some task to gain a deeper insight into the complexity of the skills needed. This observation may involve a listing of the sequence of the steps taken to complete the task or even a time measurement of particular parts of the job. A particular problem with this technique is ensuring that the act of observing does not contaminate the outcome. It is sometimes difficult for the person observed to act naturally when being observed. This can be particularly so, for example, when a safety issue is being examined and the person being observed is afraid of making a mistake.

Assessment centres

Assessment centres are used by other HRM functions — such as selection and performance appraisal — as well as for HRDNI. Assessment centres are special locations where employees are observed carrying out tasks by specially trained people. Often, senior line managers of the organisation are trained as assessors and are teamed with psychologists as observers. The assessments can be made on individuals or on groups. Rothwell and Kazanas (1989) describe the process as one where individuals are interviewed, tested, and asked to participate in various individual and group exercises (the exercises are based on the activities of a job, as identified through a job analysis) and the performance of the individuals is assessed by trained evaluators.

The expense of the procedures usually confines their use to highly paid employees so that the return on investment is higher. However, Byham (1983, p. 222) reports that, for the management level, assesment centres are superior to any other technique in identifying management potential and, at the same time, taking part in a centre is a powerful management training experience for both the participants and their higher management assessors.

Critical incident technique

The critical incident technique (CIT) was first described by Flanagan (1954). The essence of CIT is to discover the tasks and skills that are critical to good performance. As such the CIT often compares good operators and mediocre operators. One of the challenges is that the critical skills are often based on tacit knowledge and so the analyst is often involved in the externalisation process of knowledge creation by trying to surface the tacit knowledge. CIT usually relies on interviewing and, during this interaction, the analyst is often involved in concretisation — helping the interviewee to make more concrete definitions of generalised responses.

Data analysis

Once the data has been gathered it must be analysed. The analytic techniques depend on the type of data collected — either qualitative or quantitative. These types of analytic techniques are discussed further in chapters 7 and 8. The key outcome of the HRDNI is to define what the learners should be able to achieve after completing the designed learning experiences. These key outcomes have been called, variously, the learning objectives, competencies and learning outcomes.

Learning objectives

The term 'learning objectives' (sometimes called 'training objectives') has been used commonly in training and development since at least the early 1950s. Delahaye and Smith (1998) suggest that a learning objective should have three components:

- a *terminal behaviour statement*, which defines the observable behaviour that the learner should demonstrate at the end of the learning experience (for example, repair a Barthon-Lewis drill press)
- *standards*, which define how well the learner should perform the behaviour (for example, in 20 minutes)
- *conditions*, which describe the physical environment under which the learner is expected to perform the terminal behaviour (for example, using only hand tools).

Each of these components of a learning objective have some influence on the design and implementation of the learning program. The terminal behaviour statement indicates the content or topics to be learned. The standards dictate the length of time that the learning program may take. For example, the learners would need more time to practise the skills if the standard was 10 minutes rather than 20 minutes. The conditions can affect both the length of the learning program and the content covered. In example above, if the conditions allowed the use of power tools, the practice may be shortened (as the learners could complete the task quicker) but there would need to be additional content input about using the power tools. To add to the decision making required of the HR developer (both for conducting the HRDNI and also for designing the program), sometimes the need for conditions in the learning objectives becomes superfluous. For example, if the terminal statement is 'to list all the moving components of a steam railway engine, without error', the conditions would be 'using a pen and paper'. However, most tests in a classroom assume that a pen and paper would be available, so quite often that phrase is omitted.

Learning objectives came under severe criticism during the 1970s, mainly in the school education system rather than in workplace education, for being too reductionist — they reduced the results of learning to trivialities. In some cases, this was certainly the case, especially when basic motor skills (for example, pick up the screw driver) were included in the list of objectives. Generally, however, learning objectives as defined by Delahaye and Smith (1998) continue to serve very well in the delivery of adult and workplace education.

Competencies

The concept of competencies has become more popular in workplace education over the last decade. Table 5.1 provides an example of two elements from one of the competencies in the 'Certificate IV in Assessment and Workplace Training'. This sample of elements covers just two of eight elements for the competency 'Conduct assessment'. A competency statement was originally intended to cover a combination of skills, knowledge, abilities and attitudes. Further, competencies were intended to be observed in the workplace and the person being observed was expected to demonstrate the competencies several times in this workplace situation.

Writers such as Hager and Gonczi (1991) and Lovat and Smith (1995) have listed a number of concerns about competencies, among them being:

- Competence does not necessarily equate with performance.

- While the approach claims to be objective, in reality, it is no more objective than any other approach.
- The utility of the process can be outweighed by the time investment needed to establish it. Further, on-the-job tasks often change (for example, because of new technology) and the time-consuming process of developing competencies cannot always mirror this speed of change.
- Competencies deny the pluralism in society and are overly instrumentalist and highly bureaucratised.

TABLE 5.1

Competency, elements and performance criteria — from the Certificate IV in Assessment and Workplace Training (Unit number: BSZ402A; Competency: Conduct assessment)

NUMBER	ELEMENT	PERFORMANCE CRITERIA
BSZ402A/01	Identify and explain the context of assessment.	The context and purpose of assessment are discussed and confirmed with the person(s) being assessed.
		The relevant performance standards to be used in the assessment (e.g. current endorsed competency standards for the specific industry) are clearly explained to the person being assessed.
		The assessment procedure is clarified and expectations of assessor and candidate are agreed.
		Any legal and ethical responsibilities associated with the assessment are explained to the person(s) being assessed.
		The needs of the person being assessed are determined to establish any allowable adjustments in the assessment procedure.
		Information is conveyed using language and interactive strategies and techniques to communicate effectively with the person(s) being assessed.
BSZ402A/02	Plan evidence gathering opportunities.	Opportunities to gather evidence of competency, which occurs as part of workplace or training activities, are identified, covering the dimensions of competency.
		The need to gather additional evidence which may not occur as part of the workplace or training activities are identified.
		Evidence-gathering activities are planned to provide sufficient, reliable, valid and fair evidence of competency in accordance with assessment procedure.

Source: Courtesy National Training Information Service

In addition to these concerns is the practical reality of how competencies are now presented. Competencies are invariably broken down into 'elements' and further broken down into 'performance criteria'. In a high number of instances, these performance criteria now invoke the same criticism as was aimed at learning objectives in that they are often too reductionist — or, as Wolf (1993) comments, are a never-ending spiral of specification.

However, the competency movement has been quite useful to HRD. Firstly, as Delahaye and Smith (1998) comment, competencies have raised the awareness of HR developers that the outcome of a learning experience must be exported to the workplace. Secondly, various jobs and positions within industry, which were previously accorded only informal acknowledgement (for example, administrative positions and workplace trainer positions) now have official recognition through qualifications. Thirdly, the official recognition of competencies in the Australian Qualifications Framework has meant that qualifications can be transported from organisation to organisation and from state to state. In addition, qualifications based on competencies can be used for recognition of prior learning (RPL) and for articulation to higher level qualifications.

HR developers tend to prefer to use learning objectives when designing and implementing learning experiences, rather than using competencies. Firstly, the competency–elements–performance criteria hierarchy is sometimes too reductionist to be useful. Secondly, standards and conditions invariably are not present in competencies, thereby providing only a limited picture of the desired learning achievements. Thirdly, there is the requirement that competencies be tested in the workplace several times. Such a requirement usually places too much of a demand on the limited time of the HR developer. Of course, when a qualification is based on competencies, then the HR developer has no choice but to ensure that the competencies are assessed appropriately.

For an in-depth discussion of competencies see Harris et al. (1995).

Learning outcomes

The overall problem with both learning objectives and competencies is that they are suitable only for instrumental learning. Both learning objectives and competencies describe ways that the learner can manipulate or cope with their working environment. As Lovat and Smith (1995) comment, some of the most important knowledge, skills, and materials — for example, any creative and problem-solving activity — cannot be reduced to such specific terms. Therefore, it is very difficult to compose learning objectives or competencies for communicative or emancipatory learning.

Accordingly, when communicative and emancipatory learning are involved, it has become customary to describe the intended results of the learning experience as learning outcomes. Learning outcomes (for example, positively handle conflict situations in the workplace) subsume a number of highly interactive and complex skills, knowledge and abilities. Gonczi (1999) calls learning outcomes 'integrated competencies'. He suggests (Gonczi 1999, p. 183) that integrated competencies are, firstly, combinations of attributes that are linked with tasks. Secondly, any competency is invariably linked with other competencies. For example, while the HRDNI investigator is gathering facts from a staff member, she or he is also building a relationship with that staff member. Thirdly, integrative competencies (or learning outcomes) are normative and evolving as professional practitioners constantly ask the question, 'How ought I to act in this situation?'

The problem is, of course, that learning outcomes (or integrative competencies) are a relatively generalised statement compared to learning objectives. So, HR developers, when they are involved in designing or implementing learning experiences based on learning outcomes, often also formulate tentative learning objectives to represent the skills, knowledge and abilities subsumed under the learning outcome. Such learning objectives are recognised as being only representative of the rich mix that makes up a learning outcome. However, these tentative learning objectives do provide the HR developer, whether in the designing or implementing role, with a more explicit goal on which to focus.

Prioritising the outputs

Recognising the various constraints on using learning objectives and learning outcomes, the HR developer conducting the HRDNI usually prioritises the expected learning achievements. If the expected learning achievements involve communicative or emancipatory learning, then learning outcomes are used. If instrumental learning is involved, then learning objectives are used. Further, to assist the designer, the HRDNI investigator will often include a hierarchy of tentative learning objectives under any learning outcomes listed.

A pivotal role

The learning objectives and learning outcomes play a pivotal role in the other three stages of HRD. As discussed in chapter 9, they are one of the two main considerations when the HR developer is designing a learning experience. Learning objectives and outcomes also provide the HR developer with a focus during the implementation. When conducting learning sessions, the HR developer is always assessing the learners to judge the extent that they are progressing towards the designated terminal behaviour. Finally, the learning objectives and outcomes provide the evaluation plan with its basic comparison — were the intended learning objectives and outcomes achieved?

Other components

As well as analysing the data for learning objectives and learning outcomes, the investigator will examine the data for answers on other components — indicators of the appropriate curriculum to be used, the target population of learners, the type of HR developers who should be involved in the implementation of the learning experience, the possible locations where the learning episodes could take place and the possible resources that will be needed to design and implement the learning episodes. These other components are discussed more fully later in the chapter under the HRDNI report.

THE INVESTIGATION PLAN

The investigation stage of the HRDNI, as with any activity, should be based on a realistic action plan. The following need to be considered for such a plan.

1. *An operational base.* The HR developer who is the investigator will require a physical location from which to conduct the investigation. A desk, filing space and a telephone are the usual basic requirements. However, these days a personal computer with appropriate word processing, statistical and qualitative analytic packages are also high on the list of essentials.
2. *An authority base.* The investigator is usually an 'interloper', even when an internal consultant. Therefore, some official authority is needed to allow the investigator access to records and to use the time of the staff. Often this authority base comes in the form of an official letter from someone with appropriate power in the organisation.

   The support needed to undertake an HRDNI should not be underestimated and, at this planning stage, the investigator should carefully consider the ramifications. As Goldstein (193, p. 32) comments, an intervention, such as an HRDNI, is a procedure that interrupts organisational members' daily routines and patterns of work behaviour and therefore the success of an HRDNI largely depends on the extent of support offered by the organisation and its members towards the investigatory process.
3. *Identification of the key role players in the investigation.* The more obvious role players will be the staff who do the actual work and other people who may have specific information germane to the investigation. However, you may need to consider:
   - *the initiator.* This is the person or group who first called attention to the HRD need. While this person (or group) can give valuable indicators of the problem, it is also essential not to be biased by this person's perceptions or opinions.
   - *the decider.* This is the person who has the power to decide whether the investigation, and even the eventual developmental episode, will go ahead. It is essential to anticipate the rationale of this person's involvement.
   - *the loose connections.* These are the people who, initially, may seem to have nothing to offer the investigation but who can provide valuable and unusual insights — for example, non-customers.
4. *Identification of other sources of information.* Sources worth investigating include company records, business plans, minutes of meetings and control systems.
5. *Review of the appropriate investigation methods.* There are a variety of investigation methods available, each of which has strengths and weaknesses (see table 5.2). The investigator usually selects a multi-method combination, bearing in mind the objectives of the HRDNI and ensuring that the advantages and disadvantages of those methods selected offset each other.
6. *Establishment of appropriate time frames for the investigation.* Often, it is better to start at the end (the date when the investigation should be finished) and work backwards, listing all the key actions that have to be taken and allow for the amount of time investment that each action needs.
7. *Allowing time for the analysis of the data and writing up the report.*

SELECTING AN HRDNI METHOD

Selecting a suitable investigatory method is a complex decision often owing more to art than science. However, there are two parameters that can impose some logic onto the decision.

THE STRATEGIC ORIENTATION

As discussed in chapter 4, organisations have a specific strategic orientation which defines the market niche that they will capitalise on. This strategic orientation can provide a crude, initial indicator of the type of HRDNI method that may be most useful. For example, an organisation facing a predicable environment will tend to be more interested in trends rather than cause-and-solution. Such an organisation also has a preference for less costly interventions — lower cost is how they usually differentiate their product. Therefore, low cost, fact-providing methods such as the survey questionnaire and organisational records analysis tend to more appropriate. An organisation facing an unpredictable environment will need methods that provide rich and complex material — the interview and focus groups.

ADVANTAGES AND DISADVANTAGES OF HRDNI METHODS

Several writers (for example, Steadman 1980; Smith, Delahaye and Gates 1986; Goldstein 1993) describe the advantages and disadvantages of the various HRDNI methods. These writers recommend that the investigator tries to maximise the advantages and minimise the disadvantages of the various HRDNI methods according to the situation being faced by the investigator. Table 5.2 provides a list of advantages and disadvantages.

TABLE 5.2
Advantages and disadvantages of HRDNI investigatory methods

METHOD	ADVANTAGE	DISADVANTAGE
Interviewing	• Involves and hooks the individual giving information. • Provides complex information including feelings and opinions. • Encourages the knowledge-generation process of externalisation. • Allows deeper probing of issues because of the face-to-face nature. • People more willing to disclose controversial information. • Can flexibly investigate a variety of issues. • Good for identifying relationships, causes and problems.	• Can be quite time consuming. • Some people find the personal approach intrusive. • Relies on a skilled interviewer. • Subjective analysis of data.
Focus groups	• More time efficient than an interview. • Individuals can creatively bounce off the ideas of others. • Encourages the knowledge-generating process of externalisation. • Permits on-the-spot synthesis of different viewpoints. • Can flexibly investigate a variety of issues.	• Arranging logistics can be difficult — facilitator, information givers, room, equipment. • The views of one person can predominate. • People less willing to disclose controversial information. • Subjective analysis of data.

(continued)

TABLE 5.2 (cont'd)	METHOD	ADVANTAGE	DISADVANTAGE
	Survey questionnaires	• Can gather information from large groups of people. • The data can be analysed objectively. • Issues to be investigated can be targeted very specifically. • Data can be easily summarised and reported. • Some decision makers feel more at home with hard data. • Relatively inexpensive.	• Does not allow flexibility of investigation into other issues. • Has a built-in bias because the issues are decided upon by the investigator. • Low involvement of staff. • Needs return rates high enough to allow confident predictions. • Analysis depends on special skills, data recording, use of computers and analytic tools • Are of limited utility in identifying cause and solutions.
	Organisational records	• Can provide an excellent, guiding overview. • Identify the historical context of the issue. • Can provide measurable evidence of problems. • Can indicate possible trouble-spots. • Information can usually be gathered quite easily.	• Do not indicate cause and effect. • Tend to reflect only the past history. • No indications of the complexity of the issue.
	Observation	• Direct gathering of data by the investigator — no interpretation of others' perceptions. • Highly relevant data on the issue. • Good for cross-checking data gathered by other methods.	• The very presence of the observer can contaminate the outcome (for example, the observee acting unnaturally). • Requires a highly skilled investigator with both process and content knowledge. • Can depend on 'serendipity' — sometimes something occurs and sometimes it doesn't.

METHOD	ADVANTAGE	DISADVANTAGE
Assessment centres	• Very appropriate for upper level and management positions. • Gathers very complex data.	• Very expensive. • Can result in 'psychological' casualties when some individuals are confronted with unacceptable weaknesses.
Critical incident technique	• Gathers very useful, rich and appropriate data. • Individuals tend to relate to the information because of its relevance.	• Questions over the validity and relevance of the data are often raised. • The data has to be representative over time.

FACE VALUE?

When investigating problems in, or future challenges for, organisations, the investigator must always bear in mind that initial impressions may not always be accurate. There are three forces to be aware of — organisational politics, espoused theory and organisational defence mechanisms.

ORGANISATIONAL POLITICS

Politics are a normal part of business life. Emphasising certain points while obfuscating other points to bring about a preferred outcome is, in many ways, human nature. This may be an unconscious process, for example driven by individual frames of reference, or may be quite overt because an individual sees particular personal or group benefits if facts are interpreted in a particular way.

ESPOUSED THEORY VS THEORY-IN-ACTION

These have been discussed in more detail in chapter 2. Argyris (1992) has suggested that the way people say they will behave and the way they actually behave often differ in reality. He calls the way that people say they will behave 'espoused theory' and the manner in which they actually behave as 'theory-in-action'.

ORGANISATIONAL DEFENCE MECHANISMS

Again, this was discussed in chapter 2 but needs to be kept in mind while investigating issues for a needs identification. Argyris (1992) has identified a hegemonic process he calls organisational defence mechanisms. These mechanisms are designed to protect powerful members of the organisation. In practical terms, certain events surrounding, or behaviours of, powerful people (or even those under the protection of powerful people) become 'undiscussable' — no one is allowed to talk about the events or behaviours. Any attempt to investigate these protected issues will result, initially, in all types of avoidance actions. If the investigator attempts to pry further, then some organisational proscription will ensue. The ultimate in organisational defence behaviours is where the undiscussable becomes undiscussable — the very act of talking about the undiscussability of an event or behaviour cannot be discussed. Any proscription or punishment from contravening the 'undiscussability of the undiscussable' is amplified accordingly.

BETWEEN A ROCK AND A HARD PLACE

These three forces — organisational politics, espoused theory and organisational defence mechanisms — cannot be dismissed lightly as they place the investigator 'between a rock and a hard place'. On the one hand they cannot be ignored but on the other 'bravely treading where angels fear to tread' can lead to disastrous results — no information, incorrect information, forfeited credibility and even a lost career. In these situations, the analyst needs good judgement — a quality that can be gained only by experience — and excellent investigative skills. These investigative skills are discussed under interviewing, focus groups and questionnaire design.

The life of a needs investigator is not always easy and perhaps we can borrow from the experienced air pilots' adage — there are old investigators and there are bold investigators but there are no old, bold investigators!

THE HRDNI REPORT

The end result of all this investigative effort — gathering data and analysing it — is the HRDNI report. The HRDNI report should cover the following issues, at least:

- *Explain the reason for conducting the HRDNI.* This section describes how the need came to the attention of the investigator, perhaps through the strategic plan or because of an indicator from one of the information systems being monitored in the surveillance stage. If someone higher in the management hierarchy ordered the investigation, then this is usually noted as well.
- *Describe the investigator's position in the organisation, qualifications and experience.* This gives the reader some background on how the information and analysis is likely to be interpreted and should also bring credibility to the report.
- *Describe the investigative processes used.* This would cover the methods used to gather and analyse the data, the people contacted and the organisational records accessed. This section allows the reader to make judgements on the accuracy of the conclusions drawn and also allows the investigation to be replicated. As we see in chapter 7, accuracy and replicability are two important and basic foundations of scientific research. Further, this description provides valuable information for the planning of the evaluation stage (see chapter 13).
- *Define the learner population.* The target population of learners needs to be described accurately — what sections or departments they come from, what levels in the organisation they belong to, what professional/technical positions they occupy, the salary levels as well as the total number of learners in the target population.

- *Define the learning outcomes and learning objectives.* As discussed earlier, these are the key result of the HRDNI and need to be documented carefully and fully. Preferably, they should also be presented in a hierarchy of outcomes and associated objectives to provide the HR developer, who will later design the learning experience, with as much assistance as possible. If qualifications based on competencies are needed, they should be fully described and linked to the Australian Qualifications Framework.

- *Justify the design of a learning experience to achieve the learning outcomes and objectives.* The HRDNI report is not just a device to communicate information; it is also a persuasive document. The need for the learning has to be sold to key stakeholders. These key stakeholders may be the chief executive officer (CEO), upper management or the managers whose staff are to be developed. Sometimes key stakeholders outside the organisation, such as union officials, also have to be convinced of the need for the development. Persuasive arguments based on needs identified in the strategic planning process or on logic or on decision support mechanisms such as cost benefit analysis (see chapter 13) are often used.

- *Note information to assist with the later design of the learning experiences.* Such information would cover:
  - the curriculum, which describes the content to be taught and the methods to be used. During the needs investigation, information is gathered on the content that needs to be covered. Further, practical examples of best practice can be gathered, as well as examples of not so good practice, that can then be used as examples during the course (see the principle of learning, 'transfer of learning', in chapter 2). The possible learning strategies that may be the most appropriate are also canvassed during the needs investigation. The design of learning experiences is discussed in chapters 9 and 10 and, as we shall see, the appropriate learning strategy depends on a number of variables. However, at this stage of the HRDNI, the needs investigator will be interested in the preferences of the potential learners, perhaps gathering information on learning styles, for example. There may also be indicators of the type of strategies that are not acceptable by individuals or by the organisational culture. Certainly the investigator will be trying to assess whether the learning should be instrumental, communicative or emancipatory.
  - The HR developers and facilitators need not only the content knowledge but also the ability to conduct the appropriate developmental activity. Developers and facilitators provide a focal point for the learning experience and must be selected carefully.
  - The learning can occur in a variety of locations from on-the-job to in-house classroom to live-away courses. Recommendations on the preferred choices of location should be given.
  - A variety of resources are required to conduct a developmental activity — from HR developers to classrooms or workshops to visual aids to guest speakers, to name a few. In addition, a financial budget will be needed.

- *Plan the evaluation* prior to the implementation of the developmental activities to ensure that the expected outcomes are achieved. Quite often the later evaluation of the learning experience uses the same methods as that used for the HRDNI. Therefore, it is often helpful, when planning the evaluation, to know the methods and processes used in the HRDNI so that they can be duplicated.

So, the HRDNI report is an important document that has multiple goals. It needs to communicate information that will provide significant assistance to the later design stage. In addition, it needs to persuade key stakeholders to support the later stages of design, implementation and evaluation.

THE NEED FOR HRDNI

The HR developer needs to be aware of a pragmatic reality — not everyone embraces HRDNI with a passion. DeSimone and Harris (1998, p. 98) comment that, despite its importance, many organisations do not perform a needs analysis as frequently or as thoroughly as they might. They go on to suggest a number of reasons:

1. A HRDNI can be a difficult, time-consuming process.
2. Action is valued over research.
3. Fads, demands from senior management and the temptation to copy the HRD programs of widely admired organisations or competitors appear to be a more attractive option.
4. There is a lack of support for needs assessment as decision makers often think in terms of bottom-line, or monetary, justification. The problems with this viewpoint were canvassed in chapter 1 under management re-engineering.

HR developers need to sell the importance of HRDNI to key decision makers in the organisation. There are several important precepts that underlie HRDNI:

1. HRDNI is a dynamic and continuous process. It is not a one-off event nor does it occur just at the lower levels of the organisation. In reality, it is incorrect to refer to 'a' HRDNI as the process should be ever present and ongoing, covering the whole organisation and its environment.
2. The investigation stage is a means to an end. It is established to satisfy a demand, whether that demand is to surmount a challenge, take advantage of an opportunity or to overcome a weakness in the organisation.
3. The whole HRDNI process is an investment of resources — usually time and money — to ensure that the subsequent action is more efficient and effective. In other words, the cost of the learning experience and the result of the learning outcome will be outweighed by the savings in costs of solving the problem or the increased earnings of taking advantage of the opportunity.
4. The overall aim of the HRDNI is to ensure that not only is there an increase in efficiency and effectiveness, but there is a decrease in the risk that inappropriate action will be taken.

The key to organisational survival is the knowledge capital of the organisation. One of the most basic processes that ensure this knowledge capital is utilised efficiently and effectively is the HRDNI. Successful organisations recognise this and regard HRDNI as an important investment in the future survival of the organisation.

GLOSSARY

competencies — similar to learning objectives, but intended to cover skills, knowledge, abilities and attitudes and also to be assessed by observation several times in the work environment, used mainly for instrumental learning (see also learning objectives and learning outcomes)

data analysis — the process of examining the gathered data to identify trends or conclusions

data gathering — the collection of information that may define, explain or describe the opportunity or problem being investigated

HRDNI report — the written document that describes the process used and the results of the investigation

human resource development needs investigation (HRDNI) — the diagnostic process where data is gathered and then analysed to ensure the effective and efficient development of staff

investigation plan — the action plan that describes how the investigation will be conducted

investigation stage — a specific investigation of an opportunity or problem identified by the surveillance stage, consists of two phases — data gathering and data analysis

learning objectives — identified by the HRDNI, learning objectives describe the expected results of the learning experience to be designed, used mainly for instrumental learning (see also competencies and learning outcomes)

learning outcomes — the expected outcome when the learning experience is based on communicative or emancipatory learning (see learning objectives and competencies)

surveillance stage — the first stage of the HRDNI where the organisation constantly surveys its external and internal environment

QUESTIONS

For review

1. Identify and describe the four categories of HRDNI.
2. Can all organisational problems be solved by HRD? Explain your reasons.
3. Why should an HRDNI be conducted and what should an HRDNI look for?
4. Discuss the role of the surveillance of HRDNI and explain how the surveillance stage is conducted.
5. Briefly describe three data-gathering methods that can be used during the investigation stage of the HRDNI.
6. Describe the pivotal role of learning objectives/competencies/learning outcomes.
7. What issues need to be considered when planning the investigation stage of an HRDNI?
8. Identify and briefly discuss the issues you would expect to cover in an HRDNI report.

For analysis

9. Compare and contrast learning objectives, competencies and learning outcomes.
10. Discuss at least four reasons for conducting an HRDNI.
11. Identify five important questions that you would ask during an HRDNI and explain why these questions are so important.

For application

12. Visit a large retail store and identify a possible deficiency in their operations (for example, poor customer service in a particular area or the untidy layout of products). Assuming that the possible solution is an HRD intervention, select the HRDNI method you would use. Justify this selection.

13. Consider an organisation with which you are familiar. What organisational politics and organisational defence mechanisms might you encounter if you conducted an HRDNI?

REFERENCES

Argyris, C. (1992). *On Organizational Learning.* Cambridge, Mass.: Blackwell.Brinkerhoff, R. O. (1986). 'Expanding needs analysis.' *Training and Development Journal*, 40, 64–65.

Byham, W. C. (1983). 'The use of assessment centres in management development.' In B. Taylor and G. Lippitt (Eds), *Management Development and Training Handbook.* London: McGraw-Hill.

Dalzeil, S. (1994). 'Planning and managing training and development.' In J. Prior, (Ed.), *Gower Handbook of Training and Development.* (2nd ed.). Hampshire, England: Gower.

Delahaye, B. L. and Smith, B. J. (1998). *How to be an Effective Trainer.* New York: Wiley.

DeSimone, R. L. and Harris, D. M. (1998). *Human Resource Development.* (2nd ed.). Fort Worth: Dryden.

Flanagan, J. C. (1954). 'The Critical Incident Technique.' *The Psychological Bulletin*, 51(4).

Goldstein, I. L. (1993). *Training in Organizations.* Belmont, Cal.: Brooks/Cole.

Gonczi, A. (1999). 'Competency-based learning: a dubious past — an assured future?' In D. Boud and

J. Garrick (Eds) *Understanding Learning at Work.* London: Routledge.

Hager, P. and Gonczi, A. (1991). 'Competency-based standards: A boon for continuing professional education?' *Studies in Continuing Education*, 13(1), 24–29.

Harris, R., Guthrie, H., Hobart, B. and Lundberg, D. (1995). *Competency-based Education and Training: Between a Rock and A Whirlpool.* South Melbourne, Vic: MacMillan.

Lovat, T. J. and Smith, D. L. (1995). *Curriculum: Action of Reflection Revisited.* Wentworth Falls, NSW: Social Science Press.

Rothwell, W. J. and Kazanas, H. C. (1989). *Strategic Human Resource Development.* Englewood Cliffs, NJ: Prentice Hall.

Smith, B. J., Delahaye, B. L. and Gates, P. (1986). 'Some observations on TNA.' *Training and Developmental Journal*, (August), 63–68.

Steadman, G. T. (1980). *The Basics of Organisations.* Sydney, NSW: Butterworths.

Wolf, A. (1993). *Assessment Issues and Problems in a Criterion-based System.* London: Further Education Unit.

The quick and efficient HRDNI

Nathan McPherson contemplated the safety record for the retail division of his company. While the figures were not too far above the average for the company, the increase of 17% in lost time hours over the last 3 months was concerning. 'And the retail area is not really a dangerous place', thought Nathan to himself, 'especially when compared to the production division. I know, I'll ring John up, he'll give me some answers'. John's telephone rang for some time before it was answered by Shirley, one of the customer service assistants.

'No, he's off sick', said Shirley. Nathan asked for one of the supervisors. 'Well, Amelia is the only one on, but she is tied up with two customer complaints at the moment', she replied. Nathan thanked her and hung up. John was the assistant manager and having him away as well as two of the supervisors was quite unusual. With a flash of intuition, Nathan used his computer to call up the sick leave records for the retail division. A quick analysis of the data showed that the sick leave in the retail division had increased over 20% in that last 6 months. Looking at the Daily Sick Leave Report, Nathan was amazed to see that Fridays and Mondays were the most 'popular' days for sick leave with one memorable Friday having 42% of the staff in the division away. 'That's a staff morale problem', he thought, remembering his studies in human resource management. He mused on, 'Well, I had better do something about that. Perhaps a re-vamped version of the Induction Workshop would do. That would raise their awareness of the importance of high sales to the company. Aw, hang on, I had better do a bit of a training needs investigation I suppose'.

Thinking about his options, Nathan thought that some interviews would be the best approach. They would allow him to sense any complex issues and he could also probe deeper into issues if needed. He didn't think that focus groups would be much good as people may not wish to disclose information in front of each other. And questionnaires at this stage would be useless. Now, he needed someone else to help him. Perhaps Jennifer. She did not have much experience with interviewing but she would soon pick it up. Yes, that would be the way. In quickly, interview about six or seven — about 12% of the staff in the retail division, check to see if the Induction Workshop material would cover the concerns, and then start the program off.

'Right, I had better see who is around to interview', he thought. 'Oh, I had better see if Jennifer can come down with me first.'

Discussion questions

1. As a HRDNI investigator, what did Nathan do well?

2. What errors did Nathan make?

3. What else should have Nathan thought of, before rushing out to do the investigation?

The plan

Tammie Nelle left the HR manager's office, her mind swirling with a variety of thoughts. She told herself to calm down and took several deep breaths. Entering her office, she sat for a moment gazing sightlessly at the desktop for a moment before re-reading the letter from the HR manager authorising her to talk to any of the staff at the downtown registry. She then picked up a pen, pulled the writing pad towards her and wrote at the top in capital letters 'PLAN FOR THE DOWNTOWN REGISTRY HRDNI'. She contemplated the heading for a moment, feeling a deep sense of pride that the HR manager had given her the project — her first needs investigation. She then wrote the following notes:

1. Ring Registry manager. Refer to her conversation with the HR manager about the registry staff's communication skills. (NB — also ask about the informal leaders in the registry). Make date to see her. Also about parking as will need to drive over there.

2. Need to talk to other managers who use registry's services. Pick three or four out of internal phone book.

3. Talk to couriers? — see HR manager.

4. Look at minutes of Managers' Forum for the last 6 months — supposed to be several complaints. Look for source, topic, number.

5. When got above info, decide on methods. Interviews — yes, staff; registry customers; suppliers; will need to look out for underlying issues.

Perhaps questionnaire based on data from the interviews. Any other org. records?

6. Do time frame — have to finish analysis by Friday 2 weeks — 2 days enough? Report to HR manager by following Tuesday. Monday enough time to write up? Need to list key actions. Make up a Gantt chart.

7. Need somewhere to work at Downtown. That office out the back? Has desk, chair, computer already there. Check with Registry manager to see if OK.

Based on these notes Tammie drew up a comprehensive HRDNI plan. The Gantt chart showing the start and finish times for each key action was a bit fancy, but Tammie was determined not to make any mistakes with her first investigation.

Finally, the day arrived. As she parked the car at the downtown registry, Tammie felt a little apprehensive but also a flutter of excitement. She walked confidently through the entrance doors, down the corridor and into the back office. 'A bit small but it will do', she thought. Then she drew a sharp breath — there was no telephone!

Discussion questions

1. Referring to Tammie's notes, what were the issues she covered for her HRDNI plan?

2. Did Tammie omit anything else beside the telephone? Justify your answer.

Performance appraisal

CHAPTER OBJECTIVES

At the end of this chapter you should be able to:

1 explain performance management and describe the relationship of performance appraisal to performance management

2 discuss how performance appraisal is a natural and unique process

3 identify the ways that HR developers are involved in performance appraisal

4 differentiate between the two types of performance appraisal

5 describe the job analysis process

6 describe the observation process in performance appraisal

7 describe the comparison process of performance with job expectations

8 differentiate between the types of feedback

9 describe the role of action plans.

The chapter commences by positioning performance appraisal as a subsystem of **performance management** and as having, through performance management, strong connections with the strategic planning and other organisational subsystems of the organisation. Performance appraisal is a natural process, in that we make hundreds of judgements on a variety of variables each day. However, within organisations, performance appraisal is a unique process that engenders personal communication and trust. It should also be noted that performance appraisal has a pivotal role in HRD in that it is used in HRDNI, is a developmental tool in its own right and is a highly valid and practical evaluation process. Therefore, the HR developer needs to be fully involved in the organisational performance appraisal system.

There are two types of performance appraisals — administrative and developmental. **Administrative performance appraisal** concentrates on making decisions for salary increments, promotions, retrenchments and succession plans. **Developmental performance appraisal** identifies the developmental needs of an individual for present and future performance. While these two types of performance appraisal involve the same people — usually the supervisor and the appraisee — they are separate systems. This duality is often of concern to supervisors and managers, but is a natural and necessary part of life.

There are five phases to a performance appraisal, whatever the type — the job analysis, observation, comparison, feedback and the **action plan**. Before a performance appraisal can be conducted, a **job analysis** has to be carried out. There are two parts to a job analysis — gathering and recording information about the job and converting this data into the two basic job documents, the **job description** and the **job specification**. Once the job description and the job specification have been established, the performance of the staff member is observed. This observation is usually carried out by the supervisor or manager, but more recently the concept of the 360 degree appraisal has become more popular. The information gathered during this observation phase is then compared to the requirements established in the job description and the job specification and decisions on either administrative or developmental issues are made. This information is then conveyed to the appraisee using the feedback process of the **tell-and-sell**, **tell-and-listen** or the **problem-solving interview**. Finally, an action plan is formulated to help the appraisee achieve the desired developmental outcomes.

A good performance appraisal system is a key component of the HRDNI surveillance stage. By tapping into the organisational performance appraisal system, the HR developer can identify trends and pro-actively anticipate future developmental needs. Further, a good performance appraisal system assists the organisation with the creation and maintenance of knowledge by increasing trust between staff and by emphasising the importance of each staff member's individual development.

THE IMPORTANCE OF PERFORMANCE APPRAISAL

Performance appraisal provides the most direct and dynamic link between on-the-job performance and human resource development. Performance appraisal is not only the prime organisational system for HRDNI but a good performance appraisal system provides an automatic and highly valid basis for the evaluation of all learning and developmental endeavours.

Yet performance appraisal is one of the most misunderstood functions of human resource management. It is frequently and inappropriately used as a replacement for psychological counselling and as a discipline process. Such improper application of this critical human resource management function has led to an almost inherent swirl of persisting mistrust as a constant companion to performance appraisal. In attempts to make performance appraisal more palatable, it has been given a variety of new names — performance evaluation, performance assessment, staff development, performance counselling, to name a few. It is as if managers believe that, by anointing the process with a new name, they will be allowed to avoid the effort and energy that are essential to make a performance appraisal system a success. While certain performance appraisal activities must take place for an organisation to flourish — for example, staff need to be assessed for salary increments — these activities are often forced underground, or given only cursory attention, by its undeserved threatening reputation. Worse, the most positive and helpful features of performance appraisal are lost.

Partly as a result of this negative reaction, and also because of the perceived need that a results orientation is essential to survival, a new term has entered the lexicon of management theory — performance management.

PERFORMANCE APPRAISAL WITHIN PERFORMANCE MANAGEMENT

Performance management concentrates on the overall achievements of the organisation and ensures that all actions are linked strongly and directly to the strategic direction of the organisation. Stone (1998, p. 265) sees the key elements of performance management as:
- being the creation of a shared vision of the organisation's strategic objectives
- having performance objectives for each strategic business unit, function, team and individual
- using a formal review process of progress towards these objectives
- linking performance evaluation with employee development and rewards to motivate and reinforce desired behaviour.

Armstrong (1994, pp. 21–22) sees performance management as bringing new, integrating features:
- It is regarded as a normal interactive process between managers, individuals and teams, not an administrative chore imposed from above.
- It is based on agreements on accountables, expectations and development plans — it measures and reviews performance by reference to both input/process factors and output/outcome factors.

- It is a continuous process, not relying on a once-a-year formal review.
- It treats the performance review as a joint process which is concerned primarily with looking constructively towards the future.
- It can provide the basis for a performance-related pay decisions.
- It attaches much more importance to the 'processes' of forming agreements, managing performance throughout the year and monitoring and reviewing results.

If texts such as Cummings and Schwab (1973) and Henderson (1984) are examined, we see that a number of these 'new' features have always been viewed as part of an ideal performance appraisal system — in particular, the strong connection between performance appraisal and strategic planning. Further, there is no doubt that performance management does take a wider organisational view in its appraisal process and, therefore, performance appraisal is usually seen as a subsystem of performance management. Performance management, therefore, unites performance appraisal with the other organisational subsystems and strategies. Performance appraisal does, though, concentrate on the individual and provides a unique set of information for HRDNI. Accordingly, this text will use the familiar term 'performance appraisal' to differentiate the challenging, frustrating and exciting process that concentrates on the human resources from the performance management of the other systems in the organisation.

A NATURAL PROCESS

A dictionary definition of appraisal usually includes the words 'measure' and 'value', so when appraising something we are measuring the extent that we may value it. In fact, appraisal is a natural process. We make hundreds of judgements on a variety of events each day. Deciding what to eat is an appraisal process, albeit made largely unconsciously.

Any appraisal has four stages — having some predetermined standard, observing some event or object, comparing this observation against the predetermined standard, and taking some action. With the decision on food, we usually have some predetermined standard in our unconscious mind about what will satisfy our hunger. If, for example, we are in a cafeteria, we observe the options that are on offer; we then compare them with our predetermined unconscious standard and make a purchase decision. So, making appraisals is a quite normal process in our everyday lives.

A UNIQUE PROCESS

Human interactions are complex events and, in organisations, these interactions need to be ongoing and constant. One important component that helps to ensure that these interactions continue, in a positive manner, is trust — but trust is such a delicate organism. Performance appraisal can play a unique role in engendering or destroying trust (see figure 6.1).

Figure 6.1 shows that communication is the key. The greater the communication between the manager and the staff member, the more there is trust. The more there is trust, the higher are the levels of communication. Conversely the less trust, the more conflict will ensue; the less communication, the more conflict; the more conflict, the less trust and communication. So, an intensively negative relationship develops. The only way that trust can be increased is by increased communication — and performance appraisal can provide an excellent vehicle for meaningful communication between manager and staff member.

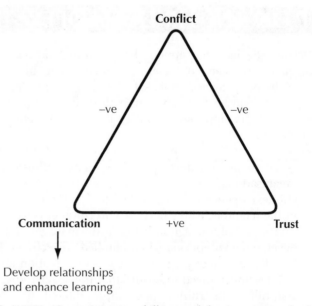

Based on Dick, R. (1979). 'Communication skills: non-defensive communication for improved relationships and problem solving.' Paper No. 2. Brisbane: Organisational Studies Unit, University of Queensland.

Performance appraisal is also unique because of its pivotal role in HRD. It is not just a dynamic tool for HRDNI. By its very nature, it can also be a powerful and continuing developmental event. The communicative engagement between manager and staff member can be escalated to true communicative learning for both parties. By interacting with the appraiser, the staff member is involved in the knowledge creation process of externalisation (as the staff member uncovers ideas and thoughts) and of internalisation (as the staff member integrates the suggestions made by the appraiser). Finally, the performance appraisal system becomes a eclectic agent for the evaluation of the investment of developmental activities. After the implementation stage, the appraiser and the learner should be involved in another performance appraisal to see if the developmental needs, identified in the original performance appraisal, have been achieved. Therefore, it is a moot point on where to position the topic of performance appraisal in a textbook — with the needs investigation or the implementation stage or the evaluation. This text has chosen to discuss performance appraisal at the HRDNI stage because of the rich and complex material that a performance appraisal can uncover for the HRDNI. However, reference will be made to the various aspects of performance appraisal throughout the book.

It could also be said that these two unique elements — trust and its pivotal nature in HRD — provide some insight into the reasons some managers shy away from performance appraisal. Trust is so delicate and the thought that a mistake in the communication episode may damage it can become overwhelming. The very complexity that its pivotal nature in HRD denotes only adds to the stress. Conversely, the two elements also explain why so many managers continually hope that a new name for the appraisal will make life easier!

IMPACT ON THE HR DEVELOPER

Despite the fact that appraisal is a normal process, the difficulties managers and organisations seem to encounter demand that the HR developer be totally familiar with the performance appraisal as a unique and high-impact system. HR developers will find themselves involved in performance appraisal in a number of ways:

- It is a very important input to both the surveillance and investigatory stages of HRDNI.
- Because of their distinctive position and knowledge, HR developers are often asked to design, develop and instigate performance-appraisal systems into the organisation.
- HR developers are usually asked to develop both the managers and the appraisees in the reciprocal skills necessary to conduct performance appraisals.
- The appraisal interaction between the manager and the staff member is a dynamic developmental episode when handled correctly — but an absolute disaster when handled incorrectly. As stewards of the creation and maintenance of knowledge, HR developers need to ensure that the special interaction between managers and staff fulfills the fruitful opportunities offered.
- The results of performance appraisals provide specific and indispensable information for the evaluation stage.

The key to successful performance appraisal is a system that is based on sound principles, open communication and the involvement of the appraisee. There are seven principles for a successful performance appraisal system:

1. the recognition that there are two types of performance appraisal systems — administrative and developmental
2. the need to base performance appraisal on a current job analysis (to establish the pre-determined standard)
3. the use of appropriate observation methods (observing the events)
4. the use of realistic comparisons between the observed data and the predetermined standard
5. the use of appropriate feedback methods (taking action)
6. the creation of action plans
7. the recognition that the action plans must become the inputs for a developmental program.

TYPES OF PERFORMANCE APPRAISAL

Writers have suggested for some time that there are two basic purposes for performance appraisal — administrative and developmental (see, for example, Cummings and Schwab 1973; Fisher, Schoenfeldt and Shaw 1999). Some of the administrative reasons for performance appraisal include making decisions for salary increments, promotions, retrenchments and succession plans. Developmental performance appraisals concentrate on identifying, honestly and accurately, the developmental needs of an individual for successful present and future performance in an organisation.

These two reasons — administrative and developmental — are conflicting in nature and this leads to the need for two performance appraisal systems if an organisation is going to perform successfully in today's highly competitive and tumultuous environment. In administrative performance appraisal, the appraiser has the final responsibility for all the decisions on salary increments, promotions or retrenchments. In other words, the appraiser is judge and jury. Under developmental performance appraisal, however, the appraiser undertakes the role of helper and ally — a role that becomes very difficult with administrative performance appraisal. One of the most common mistakes occurs when organisations try to make one performance appraisal system cover both administrative and developmental processes.

This is not to say that no developmental outcomes can emanate from an administrative performance appraisal. If someone is assessed for promotion and found to be limited in some area, then a manager would be negligent not to organise some developmental experience for that individual. Whether an administrative outcome can originate from a developmental performance appraisal is a matter of debate. The main variable is trust. If a trusting relationship exists between the appraiser and appraisee then the information volunteered by the appraisee during the performance appraisal may be used, without negative effect, for some administrative purpose. If the trust factor is not high, and the appraisee believes that the information may be used for future administrative decisions, then the appraisee is more likely to filter the information to ensure that the best picture is painted of him or her.

Many managers have difficulty in accepting that there are two types of performance appraisal. They are often confused at the expectation that they conduct both but, at the same time, keep them separate. However, many of our life roles expect this duality. As a parent, we have a nurturing and a disciplinarian side. Teachers and university lecturers are expected to be both advisor and assessor. In chapter 2, we discussed dialectic thinking — the ability to recognise that an entity has opposing attributes. These opposing attributes apply to performance appraisal, which can be both evaluative and developmental. One way to split the two types of appraisal, of course, is to conduct them at different times and this works quite well for most managers. However, keeping the basic schism between them is not always easy as both processes have commonalities. The first of these commonalities is the job analysis.

JOB ANALYSIS — CONSTRUCTING THE PREDETERMINED STANDARD

Stone (1998) believes that a job analysis is a basic HR activity because it focuses attention on what employees are expected to do. Figure 6.2 shows the wide variety of purposes for a job analysis and this list serves to underline the importance of the activity. Three of the purposes for the job analysis relate to those for performance appraisal — identifying the developmental needs (1), the administrative prerogatives of decisions on pay and pay equity (2) and promotional processes (5).

1. To identify the developmental need
2. To maintain external and internal pay equity
3. To identify the working conditions (such as levels of temperature or noise)
4. To identify the machinery or equipment to be used
5. For selection and promotion processes
6. To ensure that health and safety legislation is not violated
7. To ensure that discrimination laws are adhered to
8. To ensure that award provisions are adhered to
9. As a basic input to the human resource planning process and to determine recruiting needs
10. To ensure all jobs contribute to the strategic direction of the organisation

FIGURE 6.2
Purposes of
job analysis

There are two stages for conducting a job analysis – gathering and recording information on a job and creating the two basic job documents of the job description and the job specification. Gathering data for a job analysis is carried out using many of the same methods as used for an HRDNI analysis — for example, interviewing, focus groups and questionnaires. In addition, sometimes the engineering approaches of time and motion studies, ergonomic analysis and micro-motion studies are carried out. There are even questionnaires designed to analyse a wide variety of jobs (for example, the Position Analysis Questionnaire by E. J. McCormick and the Management Position Description Questionnaire by W. W. Tornow and P. R. Pinto).

Whatever the procedures used, the data gathering process of job analysis is designed to answer two questions in particular: 'What are the tasks and duties of the occupant of this particular position?' and 'What are the expected outputs/outcomes of these tasks and duties?' In addition, the context of the job — for example, the relationship to other positions, the conditions under which work is performed — will also be of interest to the job analyst.

THE TWO BASIC JOB DOCUMENTS

Once the data has been gathered it is analysed to create the two basic job documents — the job description and the job specification (these are sometimes called 'position description' and 'position specification'). These two documents then become the predetermined standard for the performance appraisal as a comparison point for the occupant's behaviours and abilities.

The job description

A typical job description contains a lot of information about the position (see the example in figure 6.3). The initial information in the job description identifies the position by title, department and position number. The second segment of information defines the relationship of the position to other positions — who the person reports to, the subordinate staff and other internal and external contacts. These two segments provide the contextual or background information of the position.

Position title: **Department**:
Administrative Selection Officer   Human Resources Directorate

Salary scale: Level 6 Administrative   **Position no.**:   HR00411

Supervisor: Manager, Staff Selection   **Subordinate staff**: Nil

Internal contacts: **External contacts**:
              Manager, Strategic Planning   Recruitment Consultants
              Manager, Payroll   Advertising Agencies
              Line Managers

Position summary
Select staff for Administrative positions throughout the company.

Duties
1. Conduct job analyses using quantitative and qualitative methods.
2. Arrange selection of applicants for administrative positions.
3. As chair of the Selection Panel, conduct selection processes of administrative applicants.
4. Write legally defensible reports on the selection decisions.
5. Arrange the commencement of the selected applicant.
6. Advise unsuccessful applicants.

Performance indicators
1. 90% of selected staff remain with the company for at least 6 months.
2. 98% of selected staff are assessed as satisfactory by their line manager at the 3-month probation performance appraisal.

FIGURE 6.3
A job description

The third segment, and usually the largest, shows the job duties (Fisher et al. 1999) or domains (Schuler et al. 1992). As can be seen by the example in figure 6.3, the job duties list the activities that are carried out by the position occupant. This list defines the role of the position.

Finally, the outputs/outcomes expected of the position are listed. Stone (1998, p. 128) refers to these outputs/outcomes as **performance indicators**. The importance of performance indicators was originally recognised in the early 1960s, when they were called 'key effectiveness areas' and were the total focus of an approach called 'management by objectives' (MBO) — see a closer look 6.1. The performance indicators for the position of Administrative Selection Officer (figure 6.3) have been defined quite explicitly. They pass the two basic tests of performance indicators — they are observable and measurable. This is not always possible in all jobs as some have outputs that are difficult to measure. For example, the performance indicators for a HR developer are usually more generally described because the successful outcomes are about the extent to which people have been developed. The results of such development are often not evident until some time after the learning episode that the HR developer has facilitated — and this is particularly so when the learning episode was based on communicative or emancipatory learning. In these cases, the manager and the HR developer would need to meet and agree to more specific indicators.

a closer look   6.1

Management by objectives

First used in the 1960s, management by objectives (MBO) was seen as an exciting management tool that freed staff from the strictures of bureaucratic control, bequeathed self-control, unleashed their creativity and allowed their dynamic energy to be focused on the task at hand. This management nirvana was to be accomplished quite simply. In a consultative process between the manager and staff member, goals or objectives were to be defined — in an observable and measurable form — and the staff member then proceeded to meet the objectives. These observable and measurable objectives were called 'key effectiveness areas' (see Reddin 1971).

The basic tenet of MBO made some simple assumptions. Firstly, that the staff member would be highly motivated by being involved in the mutual objective-setting process. Secondly, that the staff member's goals and the organisational goals would be unilaterally common. Thirdly, that the resources needed by the staff member to achieve the set objectives would be unfettered and easily available. Fourthly, that the staff member had all the skills required, for the present and in the future, to meet the objectives.

MBO programs gradually fell into disfavour during the 1970s because the results were very limited. Programs floundered for a number of reasons but largely because they did not adhere to the basic assumptions. Some of the assumptions were quite naive — who could expect every staff member's personal objectives to coincide with those of the organisation? Others were impossible to achieve — no staff member has total control over the resources needed. Yet others felt manipulated — what staff member would disagree with a manager's stated expectation of the objectives? In addition, Armstrong (1994, p. 19) saw MBO schemes failing because:

- they became a largely top-down process with insufficient dialogue between managers and the staff member;
- they became bureaucratic and centralised;
- there was an over-emphasis on the quantifiable at the expense of the qualitative factors and behavioural aspects of performance.

While the pure concept of MBO has left us, the legacy of key effectiveness areas is still an essential and powerful ingredient in managing the performance of staff. These days we see that the key effectiveness areas (or performance indicators as they are called in this book) are but part of the story for performance appraisal. The other part is supplied by the characteristics of the job specification. Together, these two parts give the appraiser a more holistic view of the individual's performance and what can be done to improve performance. Secondly, as Drucker (1974) recognised some time ago, performance indicators not only provide a focus for an individual's job but also define the contribution of that job to the immediate work unit, the contribution the immediate work unit makes in assisting other work units achieve their objectives (and, reciprocally, how those units contribute to the immediate work unit's objectives) and how all these contributions help the organisation achieve its strategic objectives. 'Right from the start, in other words, emphasis should be on teamwork and team results' (Drucker 1974, p. 436).

For performance appraisal, then, the two main outcomes of the job analysis are the job duties and the performance indicators.

The job specification

The job specification lists the characteristics (sometimes referred to as knowledge, skills and abilities) that the position occupant needs to carry out the duties and successfully achieve the performance indicators. The job analyst interprets and extrapolates the job specifications directly from the list of duties. Figure 6.4 shows a possible job specification for the position of Administrative Selection Officer described in figure 6.3. As you can see, characteristic numbers 1, 2, 3 and 4 come from the duty number 1 listed in the job description. If you go down each of the characteristics, you will be able to relate each to one of the duties in the job description. The job specification is the third major outcome of the job analysis.

Position title: **Position no.:**
Administrative Selection Officer   HR00411

Characteristics of position holder:
1. Knowledge and ability to design and administer survey questionnaires.
2. Knowledge and ability to analyse quantitative data using parametric and non-parametric statistics.
3. Knowledge and ability to design and conduct interviews and focus groups.
4. Knowledge and ability to analyse qualitative data.
5. Ability to write reports that are clear, concise and legally defensible.
6. Ability to organise selection panels and schedule selection interviews.
7. Knowledge and ability to administer personality inventories.
8. Knowledge and ability to conduct selection interviews.
9. Experience in chairing committees.
10. Knowledge of, and experience in administering, discrimination and EEO laws and regulations.
11. Knowledge of company forms and procedures for the commencement of staff.
12. Ability to counsel and handle mild conflict situations.

FIGURE 6.4
A job
specification

If you think of the job specification and the list of duties and the performance indicators in the job description, they represent three of the characteristics of an open system (von Bertalanffy 1956) — an input stage (the job specification), a throughput stage (the duties) and an output stage (the performance indicators). This is a very handy way to view the three major components of a job analysis. The job specification defines the characteristics that the individual puts into the job; the job description describes how the individual's inputs combine with the other energy inputs (for example, materials, machinery, plans) to produce the observable and measurable outputs of that endeavour.

THE PREDETERMINED STANDARD

Earlier, it was suggested that appraisal was a natural process and an example of selecting food in a cafeteria was given. However, most of us do not give the process of making a decision over food much conscious thought and the identity of the pre-determined standard on what food we like is usually implanted deeply in our sub-conscious. The problem with performance appraisal of individuals in organisations is that the process is often just as unconscious. Unfortunately, and similar to our food example, the predetermined standard is often hidden in the appraiser's unconscious mind and may have no validity. The role of the job analysis is to ensure that the predetermined standard for performance appraisal is valid, open, and indisputable. This is achieved through the job analysis and, from this process, the performance indicators and the job specification become the predetermined standards.

OBSERVING THE PERFORMANCE

If performance is to be assessed it must be observed, which raises two questions: 'What is observed?' and 'Who does the observing?'

THE WHAT

What is observed is defined by the performance indicators and the job specification of the position. The information on the performance indicators is usually quanti-tative — because performance indicators are observable and measurable. This means that whoever is conducting the appraisal needs to physically gather the measure-ments over the period of time that is being used as the appraisal period. In our example in figure 6.3, the appraiser would need to ensure that the information on the staff selected by the administrative selection officer — who has stayed and who has left; the opinions of the managers on the selected staff — is readily available or can be gathered before the appraisal is conducted.

The judgements on the characteristics within the job specification are often largely subjective. For example, with the characteristic 'Ability to write reports that are clear, concise and legally defensible' there is the opportunity to count the number of spelling and grammar mistakes but this quantitative data does not give a full rep-resentation of the quality of the report writing. Someone needs to make a judgement on the descriptors 'clear', 'concise' and 'legally defensible'. This judgement, even when professional and tenable, is still subjective. However, to make this judgement the appraiser still needs to gather information over the period in question. So, the manager may read samples of the administrative selection officer's reports — say, two each week for 6 months — and make notes on the strengths and weaknesses of the report writing style and content. Based on this information, the appraiser can then make a more informed judgement.

An additional option used in the gathering of data to ensure that the comparison stage is fully representative is to use the critical incident technique. For performance appraisal, the critical incident technique is a means of eliciting data about effective or less effective behaviour which is related to examples about actual events — critical incidents (Armstrong 1994, p. 71). By keeping a record of these highs and lows over the entire appraisal period, the appraiser can draw realistic trends and conclusions.

In summary, then, the information gathered for the performance indicators is usually quantitative while that for the job specification is generally qualitative. This differing emphasis — quantitative for the performance indicators and qualitative for the job specification — is an important dichotomy, particularly for the administrative performance appraisal. In making the critical, but potentially contestable, decision in administrative performance appraisal on another's career, the appraiser will need more than the subjective opinion of the judgement on the job specifications.

The support of quantitative evidence on the performance indicators is a safety net that cannot be ignored. The performance indicators are also useful for developmental performance appraisal but they tend to play a more informing, rather than a confirming, role.

THE WHO

The most obvious person to do the observing is the supervisor of the appraisee and, indeed, this is the case in most organisations. Certainly for the administrative performance appraisal the supervisor has the legal and professional responsibility.

For the developmental appraisal, the net is sometimes thrown wider and the opinions of other people are sought. This wider net most frequently occurs with managers and the term '360 degree appraisal' has become popular over the last few years. The principal behind 360 degree appraisal is based on the concept of 'role theory' (for a full discussion see Katz and Khan 1978). Role theory assumes that the tasks a person carries out as part of their job (or role) do not happen capriciously. Nor is the role defined solely by the supervisor. Each role occupant receives messages from role senders. These messages are called 'expectations'. Based on a number of decision processes — possible rewards; the power of the role sender to cause problems; the charismatic power of the role sender; personal preferences and values — the role occupant accepts or rejects specific expectations in the stream of messages and thus constructs the most preferred role. Of course, various role senders are always attempting to sway the judgement of the role occupant and so the dynamics of organisational life continue. However, out of the tensions, a relatively stable role is created and maintained. The 360 degree appraisal selects representatives from the various role senders and formalises the process of message sending. So, the appraisee may receive information not only from the supervisor but also subordinates, peers, clients and suppliers.

THE FULL PERIOD

The final point to be emphasised is that the information must be representative of the full period over which the appraisee is being assessed. For a 6- or 12-monthly appraisal, there is not much point in using data from only the last month. There could be all types of reasons why this one month of data is biased, from personal traumas to problems that are organisationally wide. This means that the appraisers and role senders — whether for administrative or developmental appraisal — need to keep records of the observed behaviours for the entire period of the appraisal. As suggested earlier, the critical incident technique is a useful approach.

Once the data and information has been gathered, attention then turns to the comparison of the occupant's performance with that expected when looking at the performance indicators and the job specifications.

This comparison is best achieved by using some permanent or semipermanent visual record. One of the more practical approaches is to create a 'form' with two basic sections — one for the performance indicators and one for the job specifications.

THE VISUAL RECORD

For the performance indicators, a simple list with space for the quantitative figures usually suffices. For the position of Administrative Selection Officer (figure 6.3) this would simply mean having the two indicators — 'selected staff remaining' and 'assessed as satisfactory' — together with the appropriate figures. Some organisations include a history of the figures so that the performance indicators can be compared across a number of assessments (see figure 6.5).

Position title: Administrative Selection Officer

Position no.: HR00411

PERFORMANCE INDICATOR		March	June	September	December
Selected staff remaining	Total selected	22	15	28	30
	Total remaining	20	10	25	27
	% Remaining	91%	67%	89%	90%
PERFORMANCE INDICATOR		March	June	September	December
Assessed as satisfactory	Total assessed	20	10	25	27
	% Satisfactory	100%	100%	98%	93%

FIGURE 6.5
Performance
Indicators

Making decisions at this comparison stage on the characteristic of the job specification is often a complex and difficult task. In response to this perceived threat, a plethora of processes have been recommended over the years — forced choice, forced distribution, ranking, paired comparisons, behavioural observation scales to name a few. However, these particular processes have limited practical use in modern performance appraisal, so they will not be discussed further in this book. If you are interested in them, Rudman (1995, pp. 67–93) provides an in-depth discussion.

Two approaches that provide some reasonable levels of objectivity are the graphic rating scales and the **behaviourally anchored rating scales** (see a closer look 6.2). The comparison for the job specification segment is usually handled differently for the administrative than for the developmental appraisal. For the administrative process, each characteristic in the job specification is assessed on a 'satisfactory/not satisfactory' basis. However, as indicated in the 'a closer look' segment, organisations may have to consider the use of BARS for administrative performance appraisal in the near future.

a closer look   6.2

Graphic rating scales and BARS

Graphic rating scales are very similar to Likert scales, except the requirements that the scale have an uneven number of points and that the mid-point be either neutral or passing are waived. In reality, most graphic rating scales conform to the Likert scale requirements. For a performance appraisal episode, the graphic rating scale is simply placed after each characteristic of the job specification. The appraiser then reads each characteristic and circles the rating that he or she believes best represents the appraisee's level of competence.

Behaviourally anchored rating scales (BARS) are a more complex form of a graphic rating scale. Rather than having a generic word such as 'Good' or 'Fair' to describe each point, a description of the behaviour that is represented by that point is provided. The same is done for each point on the scale. If there are five points on the scale, then five behavioural descriptors are given. This process is followed for each characteristic in the job specification. For a full description of the development of BARS see Schneier and Beatty (1979a, 1979b).

For the first characteristic of the job description for the Administrative Selection Officer (*Knowledge and ability to design and administer survey questionnaires*), the behavioural descriptors for a BARS may be:

1 (Poor) Can write understandable question items but has no concept of reliability and does not understand the basics of statistical analysis.

2 (Fair) Can write understandable question items that have content validity and can calculate descriptive statistics.

3 (Satisfactory) Designs question items that are valid, understands the concepts of validity and reliability and can give basic instructions on the requirements for statistical analysis of results.

4 (Good) Designs valid and reliable questionnaires and has a good knowledge of multivariate statistics.

5 (Excellent) Proves validity and reliability of question-naires, chooses samples appropriately and analyses results using appropriate computer packages.

The process for designing BARS is quite time consuming, expensive and complex. Swan (1991) suggests that there are usually several groups involved. One group of job-knowledgeable individuals identifies specific sets of effective and ineffective behaviours (or incidents) for the job, a second job-knowledgeable group assigns these incidents to the job specification characteristic that best describes it, a third job-knowledgeable group rates the collection of incidents, within each characteristic, on a scale (1 to 5 or 1 to 8, whatever is chosen). A fourth group may then be charged with validating the BARS for each characteristic. The BARS is then often pilot-tested.

Because of the cost and complexity, BARS is not often used. However, with the legal climate surrounding human resource management, organisations may be forced to consider the process in the near future, as a viable option for administrative performance appraisal schemes.

For the developmental process a more detailed comparison than the 'satisfactory/ not satisfactory' is needed to provide data that is rich enough for an HRDNI. Unfortunately, the use of BARS is usually too expensive. Basically, the appraiser needs answers to questions such as 'To what extent does the job occupant have the skill, knowledge or ability?' and 'What does the job occupant need to do to become better at the job specification?' To answer these questions each characteristic in the job specification can be assessed using two different decision mechanisms:

1. A judgement on each characteristic in the job specification can be made using a graphic rating scale. A graphic rating scale forces the assessor to make a clear decision on the extent to which the appraisee is satisfactory or not satisfactory on that characteristic. For developmental performance appraisals, graphic rating scales have the advantage of being easily and inexpensively created, gives the appraiser a reasonably objective measure and, most importantly, provides a sound starting point for meaningful discussions.

2. The appraiser provides some qualitative information by answering the question, 'Why is the appraisee not a 5?' (if using a five-point Likert scale). If the '5' has been circled (the staff member is rated as excellent on that characteristic), then the appraiser should justify that decision by writing reasons in the space provided.

One of the advantages of these justifying statements is that they can be translated into learning objectives very easily.

Figure 6.6 shows an example of a form for this dual judgement mechanism for three of the characteristics of the job specification for the administrative selection officer.

Position title: **Position no.:**
Administrative Selection Officer   HR00411

Characteristics of position holder:
1. Knowledge and ability to design and administer survey questionnaires
   (a) _____

1	2	3	4	5
Poor	Fair	Satisfactory	Good	Excellent

   (b) Why not a 5? _____
   _____

2. Knowledge and ability to analyse quantitative data using parametric and non-parametric statistics
   (a) _____

1	2	3	4	5
Poor	Fair	Satisfactory	Good	Excellent

   (b) Why not a 5? _____
   _____

3. Knowledge and ability to design and conduct interviews and focus groups
   (a) _____

1	2	3	4	5
Poor	Fair	Satisfactory	Good	Excellent

   (b) Why not a 5? _____
   _____
   _____

[and so on for each specification]

FIGURE 6.6
Making a decision on the job specifications

This visual record or 'form' should not be confused with a bureaucratic form. Firstly, it is merely there to assist making the comparison between the staff member's actual performance and the expected performance. Secondly, it provides a focal point and catalyst for the discussion between the appraiser and appraisee. Thirdly, the 'form' is not a permanent entity, as a new 'form' should be constructed for each performance appraisal and be based on the results of a recent job analysis.

TWO ADDITIONAL POINTS

Two points should be noted. Firstly, the performance indicators and the job specification are linked in this judgement mechanism. If the job occupant is achieving satisfactory results for the performance indicators then it would be difficult to judge any of the job specification characteristics as 'unsatisfactory'. However, if a performance indicator is below standard then the cause may be traced to some problem in one or more of the job specification characteristics. Secondly, while it has been suggested that the judgement on the job specification for the administrative appraisal should be on a 'satisfactory/not satisfactory' basis, the appraiser can use graphic rating scales. However, this is riskier in the administrative process as the appraiser will need to justify the decision (for example, 'Why a 3 and not a 4?'). For an in-depth discussion of rating and appraisal see DeNisi (1996).

THE WHO AGAIN

The final issue to be decided is who should do the comparisons. In the administrative appraisal the manager or supervisor really has the final responsibility. While the appraisee sometimes is given the opportunity for some input, the manager or supervisor is the one who has to make the final decisions. However, with the developmental process, the appraisee is commonly involved to a marked degree. This involvement has two benefits. First, the appraisee is more likely to own the outcome. Secondly, the appraisee can provide some unique insights into the various judgements to be made. Further, as discussed previously, the 360 degree appraisal can also be used to great benefit in the developmental appraisal as the additional information provided allows more informed decisions.

FEEDBACK

Over the years, the feedback process has been referred to under a variety of names, with 'performance appraisal interview' being most common although 'performance review discussion' (see, for example, Stone 1998) is becoming more popular.

Whatever the name, a number of managers find the interpersonal, face-to-face nature of the performance appraisal interview a difficult and distressing task. However, there is little point in conducting the comparisons unless the appraisee is going to be advised of the outcome. There are several reasons for this apparent reluctance. Firstly, many managers believe that they do not have the interpersonal skills needed for such a complex and possibly emotionally charged interaction as a performance appraisal review. The interviewing skills discussed in chapter 7 are of critical relevance in this regard. Another reason for the reluctance of managers is that they do not perceive that there are appropriate feedback models for particular situations.

Maier (1976) has proposed three different performance appraisal interviews — tell-and-sell, tell-and-listen and problem solving. These three approaches are still seen as the basic options today (see, for example, Fisher et al. 1999, Schuler et al. 1992) In the tell-and-sell interview the appraiser has already pre-judged the situation and simply tells the appraisee of the decision. This type of interview assumes that there is a power differential between the appraiser and the appraisee — i.e. the appraiser has a great deal more power than the appraisee. This power differential comes from either having a higher position in the organisation or because the appraiser has a broader and more relevant knowledge base. The tell-and-listen interview allows some appraisee involvement in the interaction. The appraiser advises the appraisee of the decision and the reasons for the decision and then invites comments from the appraisee. At the very least, it is assumed that this involvement will encourage the appraisee to accept the decision and, at the best, that the appraisee will provide new and unique information that will enhance the decision. In the problem-solving interview, the appraiser and the appraisee have equal power with the assumption that each comes to the interaction with valuable and unique information. The aim is to combine this information for the most beneficial result.

Generally, the tell-and-sell and the tell-and-listen are most suitable for the administrative appraisal. The base line is that, in this administrative process, the appraiser (who is usually the manager or supervisor) has the responsibility to make the final decision. The responsibility cannot be fobbed off onto the appraisee. Indeed, the appraiser will often lose credibility if he or she attempts to transfer this obligation. The problem-solving interview is most appropriate for the developmental appraisal. It is crucial for the appraisee to have ownership of the final recommendations if meaningful development is to occur. In addition, the complexities of designing appropriate learning experiences means that the appraisee's personal preferences and insights are just as paramount as the expert judgement of the appraiser.

As with any general rule, there are exceptions to having the tell-and-sell and the tell-and-listen for the administrative appraisal and the problem-solving for the developmental appraisal. The decision pivots on the job maturity of the appraisee. If the appraisee has a good knowledge of, and a deep interest in, the job then it is more likely that the administrative process will be based predominantly on the common problem-solving approach. An appraisee with very high job maturity will already know how he or she compares with the job specification. The appraiser still has the responsibility for the final decision but, with a high job maturity, the appraisee's and the appraiser's assessments are very likely to agree. On the other hand, an appraisee of low job maturity (perhaps he or she has recently commenced in the position) is unlikely to have sufficient knowledge to make worthwhile comments on his or her performance even in the developmental performance appraisal. In this situation, the tell-and-listen interview would be more efficient and effective.

ACTION PLANS

An interview is ephemeral in nature — the spoken words disappear into thin air and the only history is in the memories of the participants. Unfortunately, memories are not as infallible as we would like to believe. A more permanent and reliable record is needed.

For the administrative appraisal, the usual record is a report — either especially written for the occasion, as in a promotion, or as a pre-printed form, as is common with a salary increment. The report, in whatever form, is then forwarded to the appropriate department — the Human Resource Department in the case of the promotion report or the Salary and Wages Department in the case of the salary increment.

The more informal nature of the developmental appraisal does not negate the need for a permanent record of the decisions. In fact, a permanent record is vital if future development is to eventuate and should be in the form of an action plan. An action plan covers the what, who and how of the decision. What are the learning objectives? Who will be responsible for carrying out the activities? By when should the activities be completed? An example of an action plan is included in figure 6.7.

Position title: Administrative Selection Officer   **Position no.:** HR00411

LEARNING OBJECTIVES	HOW TO BE ACHIEVED	WHO IS RESPONSIBLE?	BY WHEN?
1. Analyse a questionnaire using descriptive statistics.	Attend the Basic Statistics Course.	Manager, HRM Department	20 December
2. Improve ability in chairing committees.	Sit on five committees over the next month and write a reflective journal on the experiences.	Administrative Selection Officer	15 November
3. List the major components of the EEO laws.	Read the state EEO laws and regulations and compile a list of the major components.	Administrative Selection Officer	30 October
4. Effectively counsel applicants who are not selected.	Attend the Interviewing and Counselling Workshop.	Manager, HRM Department	10 October
	Have developmental discussions with Manager, HRM after each counselling session.	Administrative Selection Officer	Commencing on 15 October

FIGURE 6.7
Action plan

INPUT INTO THE DEVELOPMENTAL SYSTEM

One of the characteristics of an open system (von Bertalanffy 1956) is that, to avoid the entopic process (i.e. dying), the outputs of the system must become the inputs of another system. The results of the deliberations in the administrative performance appraisal system are always forwarded to another system — the Payroll Section in the case of salary increments or to the Selection Section in the case of promotion appraisals.

However, the action plan from the developmental appraisal is still in danger of becoming a non-event. It is quite easy for the plan to be filed away and forgotten. A procedure needs to be instituted to ensure that all action plans from developmental performance appraisals become the inputs to the organisational human resource development plan. There are a variety of ways that this can occur but usually the process becomes one of accumulation — the actions plans from a section are collated, these are then coalesced into departmental requirements and this information then becomes the basis of the organisational human resource developmental plan.

SURVEILLANCE SYSTEM

The developmental performance appraisal process is the key surveillance system for any HRDNI. While each action plan classifies the needs of each individual, the collation of section and departmental action plans can disclose trends which can foreshadow possible problems or challenges for the organisation. Therefore, the information on the action plans is used for two purposes. The first use is to design learning programs for individuals. Secondly, the trends that are identified from the collation of several individual action plans have to be investigated for further hidden needs. The means of investigation are discussed in the following three chapters.

The information from the administrative performance appraisal can be of use for HRDNI but the degree of this usefulness is hampered by the fact that the outputs of the administrative process (i.e. the reports) are usually confidential. In practical terms, the analyst is usually dependent on the appraisers to forward 'censored' information — material on identified needs that is not tied to individual identities.

While this chapter has concentrated on the performance appraisal system as a surveillance mechanism, other systems should also be monitored. Any of the control systems — quality control, bench marks, production figures, absentee figures — must be scrutinised for trends and these trends contrasted and compared with the trends of the performance appraisal system. An HRDNI is a pro-active role with the qualities of curiosity and detection high among the desirable characteristics.

KNOWLEDGE CREATION AND MAINTENANCE

A well-designed developmental performance appraisal system forms the basic building block for the creation and maintenance of knowledge. The critical feature of a learning organisation is a culture that sets high values on learning. The fundamental expectation is that learning will occur. The developmental performance appraisal establishes this expectation by, firstly, bringing together key people to focus on the development of one person. Secondly, this close interaction increases the trust between the players. The more communication that occurs, the less conflict ensues and higher levels of trust result. Conflict has a great deal of difficulty existing where there are high levels of trust and communication. Thirdly, the constant interaction regularly emphasises the importance of an individual's development and this regular emphasis eventually becomes a permanent custom. Fourthly, the performance appraisal system encourages the knowledge generation process of converting tacit knowledge to explicit knowledge. The frequent scrutiny of an individual's development, and the open discussion with another, forces the thought mechanism to constantly cover the circle of tacit to explicit to explicit to tacit. The subsequent learning experiences that come out of the resultant action plans only reinforce this knowledge creation process ten-fold.

In this chapter, we have consistently referred to the performance appraisal *system*. The emphasis on the word 'system' conveys the wider perspective and recognition that the performance appraisal system is part of performance management. This means that the performance appraisal system is in constant and direct interaction with the other systems in performance management. In addition, the performance appraisal system must contribute, significantly and overtly, to the strategic objectives of the organisation.

Above all, though, performance appraisal systems are about people. As Cousens and Cousens (1994, p. 70) comment, performance appraisal schemes that work are geared for continuous improvement. They seek to empower people and are necessarily based on respect for people.

GLOSSARY

action plans — the permanent record of the intended activities decided on in the developmental performance appraisal

administrative performance appraisal — one of the two types of performance appraisal, concentrates on administrative decisions such as salary increments and promotions

behaviourally anchored rating scales — a method of judging an individual's characteristics in the job specification

developmental performance appraisal — one of the two types of performance appraisal, concentrates on the developmental needs of the individual

job analysis — the process of gathering and analysing data on a job, so that the two basic job documents, the job description and the job specification, can be formulated

job description — one of the two basic job documents, lists the job title and other contextual information, the job duties and the performance indicators

job specification — lists the characteristics (knowledge, skills and abilities) required by the job holder

performance indicators — the observable and measurable outputs of the job

performance management — the management of all systems that affect individual and organisational performance to ensure a strong strategic direction

problem-solving interview — where the appraiser and the appraisee have equal power and approach the appraisal process as a common problem-solving event

tell-and-listen interview — where the appraiser informs the appraisee of the decision but is also willing to listen to the responses from the appraisee

tell-and-sell interview — where the appraiser simply informs the appraisee of the decision

QUESTIONS

For review

1. Discuss the relationship between performance appraisal and performance management.

2. Explain why performance appraisal is a unique and natural process.

3. List and discuss at least three ways in which HR developers become involved in the organisational performance appraisal system.

4. Describe the role of job analysis in performance appraisal.

5. Discuss the difference between the data gathered for performance indicators and the data gathered for the job specification.

For analysis

6. Compare and contrast the two purposes of performance appraisal.

7. Compare and contrast the job description and the job specification.

8. Explain how performance appraisal helps the organisation to create and maintain its knowledge capital.

For application

9. Give at least two examples of each for when you would use the tell-and-sell interview, the tell-and-listen interview and the problem-solving interview.

10. Explain how you would identify the people who should be involved in the performance appraisal of a position, using examples to justify your decisions.

11. Using at least four different characteristics of the job specification, develop a basic behaviourally anchored rating scale for a position with which you are familiar.

REFERENCES

Armstrong, M. (1994). *Performance Management*. London: Kogan Page.

Cousens, L. and Cousens, T. (1994). *Performance Appraisal: Making It Work*. Springwood, NSW: Australian Education Network.

Cummings, L. L. and Schwab, D. P. (1973). *Performance in Organizations: Determinants and Appraisal*. Glenview, Ill.: Scott, Foresman and Co.

DeNisi, A. S. (1996). *Cognitive Approach to Performance Appraisal*. London: Routledge.

Dick, R. (1979). 'Communication skills: non-defensive communication for improved relationships and problem solving.' Paper No. 2, Brisbane: Organisational Studies Unit, University of Queensland.

Drucker, P. F. (1974). *Management: Tasks, Responsibilities, Practices*. London: Heinemann.

Fisher, C. D., Schoenfeldt, L. F. and Shaw, J. B. (1999). *Human Resource Management*. (4th ed.). Dallas: Houghton Mifflin.

Henderson, R. I. (1984). *Performance Appraisal*. Reston, Va.: Reston.

Katz, D. and Kahn, R. L. (1978). *The Social Psychology of Organizations*. (2nd ed.). New York: Wiley.

Maier, N. R. F. (1976). *The Appraisal Interview*. California: University Associates.

Reddin, W. T. (1971). *Effective MBO: the 3-D Method of MBO*. New York: McGraw-Hill.

Rudman, R. (1995). *Performance Planning and Review: Making Employee Appraisals Work*. Melbourne, Vic: Pitman.

Schneier, C. E. and Beatty, R. W. (1979a). 'Performance appraisal revisited, part I.' *Personnel Administrator*, July.

Schneier, C. E. and Beatty, R. W. (1979b). 'Performance appraisal revisited, part II.' *Personnel Administrator*, August.

Schuler, R. S., Dowling, P. J., Smart, J. P. and Huber, V. L. (1992). *Human Resource Management in Australia*. Artamon, NSW: Harper Collins.

Stone, R. J. (1998). *Human Resource Management*. (3rd ed.). Brisbane: Wiley Australia.

Swan, W. S. (1991). *How to do a Superior Performance Appraisal*. New York: Wiley.

von Bertalanffy, L. (1956). 'General systems theory.' *General Systems. Yearbook of the Society of General Systems Theory*, 1, 1–10.

The critical incident

John Bartlett was the supervising education officer for the Community Learning and Development Unit (CLDU). He was one of five staff members, the others being the community and general manager and three education officers. CLDU was a partly government-funded community education organisation. The government funding provided a 3-year budget for the development of disadvantaged youth in the community area. The remaining income for CLDU came from adult learning classes, a very popular pastime in this fairly large seaside and farming district.

John was about to conduct a developmental performance appraisal with Clark Vosper, one of the most experienced education officers. John believed that he ran a 'tight ship' and, conscious of the limited budget of CLDU, aimed to be efficient in all his duties. He had reviewed the Education Officer job description and job specification and determined that these were up to date and contributed to the CLDU Three Year Strategic Plan. John had used a simple graphic rating scale for judging the characteristics on the job specification and was quite pleased with the clarity of his analysis. Having been in the job for 4 years, Clark was a good education officer so his performance on most of the job specifications had been rated as high or very high. Conscious that no one was perfect, he had marked two of the characteristics as satisfactory.

John had given Clark 2 days' notice of the interview which was to be held in the interview room. John commenced the interview by asking Clark about the latest program he had been teaching and, after a few minutes, said, 'Ah, yes, that's good. Now let's do this appraisal'. John then spent 20 minutes giving Clark feedback on his assessment and ended with a recommended list of development activities for Clark. Clark

was silent for a while and then John butted in and said, 'So you're happy with that then?' John was rather pleased that the interview had gone so well and, looking at the clock, was even more pleased that the whole episode had only taken a little under 25 minutes.

John was startled when Clark suddenly said, 'I don't understand why you have given me only a satisfactory on client relations. All you have to do is look at the Client Satisfaction figures we agreed to collect after each course. Remember, you called them a performance indicator and said we should collect them for the last 6 months'. John's heart dropped as he suddenly realised that he had not looked at the performance indicators each education officer had been sending him at the end of each month. Looking at his notes, John said, 'Well, there was that incident where you were shouting at that older student. Remember, about 3 weeks ago?' 'Oh, come on', said Clark, 'That was Bill, he had turned his hearing aid off again and was about to walk out in the rain. I was just trying to warn him'.

John looked back at his notes again but could find no answers there. Clark rescued him by saying, 'Look, I can see that you have put a lot of work into your assessment and I do appreciate it. But I need time to think about what you said. I've also got some ideas about what I would like to develop. How about we meet again this afternoon to see if we can come up with something we both like?'

Discussion questions

1. What did John do right?
2. Where does John need to improve? Justify your answers.

The job specification

Lenore Mottram was to conduct her first performance appraisal. David Delmau, one of her administrative assistants, had applied for promotion to Training Officer Level 1. Her supervisor, the manager of the Learning and Development Section had given her the following job description for the position. When Lenore asked for the job specification she was told that it had not been completed yet and that she should construct one herself.

Discussion questions

1. What improvements would you make to the job description?

2. Construct a job specification for Lenore.

Position title:
Training Officer Level 1

Department:
Learning and Development Section

Position no.:   2710

Supervisor: Manager, Staff Selection

Position summary
Conduct the Induction Workshop and basic courses in report writing and basic communication.

Duties
1. In conjunction with the departmental selection officer, identify new staff who should attend the monthly Induction Workshop.
2. Undertake all the logistical arrangements for the Induction Workshop.
3. Conduct the Induction Workshop.
4. Conduct report writing and basic communication as required.
5. Arrange appropriate training rooms and equipment for the other staff in the Learning and Development Section.
6. Complete monthly returns on trainee attendance and forward to Head Office.

Performance indicators
1. All new staff attend the Induction Workshop within 3 months of commencement date.
2. All courses and workshops are rated by the trainees as satisfactory or above.
3. All returns are received by Head Office by the due date.

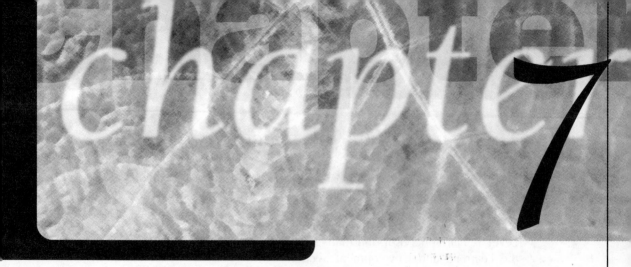

Interviewing and focus groups

CHAPTER OBJECTIVES

At the end of this chapter you should be able to:

1 define qualitative research

2 discuss the types of sampling designs

3 explain the pattern of a good interview

4 describe the questioning, paraphrasing, probing and summarising and listening processes

5 differentiate between structured and unstructured interviews

6 identify the six factors that a focus group process has in common with an interview

7 describe the process of conducting a focus group

8 explain how qualitative data can be analysed.

As discussed in chapter 5, an HRDNI consists of two phases — data gathering and data analysis. Two of the most common methods of gathering qualitative data are the interview and the focus group. This chapter firstly examines HRDNI as qualitative research before discussing the interview and the focus group. It then discusses the methods of analysing the resultant qualitative data.

Because interviewing and focus groups come under the auspices of qualitative research, HR developers who use these qualitative methods in HRDNI should strive to achieve accuracy and replicability. **Accuracy** means that the research tools and analytic processes used are as precise and correct as possible. **Replicability** means that the research should be able to be repeated with the same results. In interviewing and focus groups, HR developers use a number of options to achieve accuracy and replicability — **trustworthiness**, **verification**, acknowledging subjectivity and bias, reporting the sequence of events, limiting **interpretation**, ensuring **referential adequacy** and faithfully describing the research path followed.

As gathering data from the full population (for example, the entire workforce of an organisation) is usually too costly, researchers often use **sampling** to reduce costs and reduce time. There are several useful types of sampling and these can be categorised on a continuum from probability to non-probability sampling — simple random sampling, systematic sampling, stratified random sampling, convenience sampling, purposive sampling, convergence sampling and snow ball sampling.

Interviewing provides the HRDNI investigator with an opportunity to gather rich and complex information from the individual. Good interviewing skills enhance the likelihood that this rich and complex information will be disclosed. There are six foundation interviewing skills. Using an appropriate **pattern of an interview** — working through the stages of **entrance investment time** to bring the interviewee into the **rapport zone**, gathering the data from the **interviewee**, entering the **intimacy** level if deep and personal information is being investigated, and **exit investment time** — establishes the overall progression of the interview. Appropriate **questioning**, particularly the use of open questions with a stem-plus-query design and the funnel sequence, allows the HR developer as the investigator to control the direction of the interview. **Paraphrasing** provides the interviewee with the feedback necessary to establish security, trust and the motivation to continue answering. By **probing** — the combination of questioning, listening, paraphrasing and further questioning — the **interviewer** can explore specific issues or ideas. **Summarising** should occur at the end of each major questioning sequence (for example, at the end of a funnel sequence) as this gives both parties a chance to review the information disclosed to that point. Finally, the interviewer should be aware of the non-verbal behaviour of both the interviewee and the interviewer. The interviewer's **nonverbal behaviour** can affect the responses of the interviewee and the interviewee's nonverbal behaviour provides an insight into the extent that the interviewee has entered the rapport zone.

Interviews can be considered as being on a continuum, structured at one end and unstructured at the other. In a **structured interview**, the interviewer uses pre-prepared, standardised questions that are asked in the same sequence. This does, however, limit the opportunities for the interviewee to provide additional information. **Unstructured interviews** commence with a broad, open question and then rely on the interviewer's skills to probe deeper. The disadvantage of the unstructured interviews is that they can be very time consuming and can cover ground not germane to the research question.

Whereas the **interview** concentrates on the individual, the **focus group** collects data using group interaction. As a data-gathering medium, the focus group has a number of similarities with the interview — the same pattern to manage the overall progression, listening, questioning, paraphrasing, probing and observing nonverbal behaviour. Focus groups can also be unstructured or structured.

However, the **facilitator** needs to consider other issues. There is the *logistical challenge* of bringing together a number of people at a common place at a common time. The **group composition** needs to be evaluated — homogeneity, representation, whether it is better to have a group of strangers or a group of acquaintances, and the size of the group. When conducting the focus group, decisions have to be made about who will be on the facilitation team, how the data will be recorded, the use of visual aids, allowing the respondents thinking time and the effect of **group dynamics**.

Once the interviews or focus groups have been completed, the qualitative data needs to be analysed. In the structured or semistructured interviews or focus groups, the preplanned questions provide an automatic formation for analysis. The HR developer as the analyst simply needs to list the responses under each pre-planned question. For the more unstructured interviews and focus groups, the analyst uses **content analysis** to identify, code and categorise the primary trends in the data. HR developers have to accept that the analysis of qualitative data is a rich, messy and complex process.

Finally, HR developer need to recognise that being involved in interviews and focus groups for HRDNI purposes is actually the beginning of the learning process, as both the investigator and the respondents are learning as the investigation continues.

QUALITATIVE RESEARCH

Interviews and focus groups are qualitative research methods. As such, both approaches come under the heading of scientific research. Scientific research is based on the twin pillars of accuracy and replicability. The data gathered have to be an accurate representation of the phenomenon being investigated (if you are investigating the type of skills needed to operate a new machine, there is little point in conducting interviews on customer complaints); the cues or instruments used to gather the data have to be appropriate and accurate tools; the data have to be accurately recorded; the data have to be accurately interpreted; and the results have to be accurately reported. In addition, if someone else conducts the same investigation then that second investigation should come up with the same results, i.e. the research should be able to be replicated. It must be acknowledged, however, that these twin pillars of accuracy and replicability are ideals, as no research method entirely achieves the high standards thus envisioned. The good investigator, though, always tries to achieve these utopian ideals.

ACHIEVING THE UTOPIAN IDEALS

Qualitative research is open to criticism for being subjective and biased. Its advantage, however, is the ability to amass rich and highly useful data. Qualitative researchers, therefore, respond to the demands of accuracy and replicability in a number of ways. Writers such as Burns (1994, pp. 270–273) and Neuman (1997, pp. 332–335) list a number of options.

Trustworthiness

To a qualitative researcher integrity is everything. A qualitative researcher always endeavours to observe, report and interpret the complex field experience as accurately and as faithfully as possible.

Verification

A basic tenet of qualitative research is not to accept anything at face value. Qualitative researchers try to ensure that their research accurately reflects the evidence and have checks on their evidence and interpretations.

As an aid to verification, triangulation is a common theme in qualitative research and Cohen and Manion (1989) suggest three types. Researcher–subject corroboration involves cross-checking the meaning of data between the researcher and the respondents. This cross-checking may occur during data gathering or after interpretations of the raw data have been made, for confirmation of accurate reporting. Secondly, confirmation from other sources, about specific issues or events identified, is always paramount. Thirdly, two or more methods of data collection should be used and the resultant interpretations should be compared. A final triangulation option is called researcher convergence (Huberman and Miles 1998) — using another researcher to analyse the raw data and then comparing the two analyses.

Acknowledging subjectivity and bias

Qualitative researchers assume that it is impossible to eliminate the effects of the bias and subjectivity of the researcher and suggest that quantitative researchers sometimes hide behind supposed 'objective' techniques. A qualitative researcher takes advantage of personal insights, feelings and values but uses two techniques to limit the contamination. Firstly, the researcher overtly takes measures to guard against inappropriate personal influences by being aware of his or her frames of reference that may contaminate any analysis of the topic under investigation. Secondly, it is common for a brief description of the researcher to be incorporated in the final report. This brief description includes any relevant personal history of the researcher that may effect the interpretations — either by providing a unique insight, or by possibly causing subjectivity and bias, to the interpretation. Frequently, research assumptions and biases are also shared with the reader.

Process and sequence

The passage of time is an integral part of qualitative research. The sequence of events and what happened first, second, third and so on, provides confirmational evidence for the qualitative researcher.

Interpretation

Interpreting the complex behaviours, messages, forces and conditions of an event is the central theme of qualitative research. As a safeguard to accuracy, the qualitative researcher uses two techniques. The first is to report 'in the voice of the source' by using the actual words of the respondent — either in the phrasing of a sentence or verbatim as an example of an opinion or fact. As Burns (1994, p. 12) comments, the task of the qualitative methodologist is to capture what people say and do as a product of how they interpret the complexity of their world, to understand events from the viewpoints of the participants. The second technique is to report the logic of interpretation used to come to a particular conclusion.

Referential adequacy

The comments and descriptions in the report should be of sufficient detail and richness so that the reader has no difficulty in imagining the context, situations and thematics discussed (Eisner 1991). Thus citations of the raw data collected in qualitative research should be frequent enough to give the reader confidence that the raw data has been reported accurately and that the themes extracted are valid.

Paint the path

It is impossible to exactly replicate a qualitative study — there are too many complex variables involved. For example, just having a different researcher introduces an immediate variant to qualitative research, as the researcher is such an central part of qualitative research.

However, to help the reader of the report understand the source and theme of the interpretations, the qualitative researcher provides quite a detailed description of the research process in the final report. Huberman and Miles (1998) call this 'transparency' and suggest that description should be provided of the sampling decisions, data collection operations, database summary (size, how produced), software used (if any), an overview of the analytic strategies used and the inclusion of key data displays supporting the main conclusions. To this list could be added the timing and timeliness of observations, spatial arrangements of interviews, relationships with subjects, categories developed for analysis and protocols of analysis.

Summary

When involved in qualitative research, the HR developer as an investigator in an HRDNI needs to ensure that triangulation is built into the research design. At the very least, two methods of data gathering should be used, and preferably more. Frequently, this means the use of either interviews or focus groups and survey questionnaires, but need not be limited to this qualitative/quantitative combination. During the report writing stage, referential adequacy and providing support for interpretations are prime requirements. Describing the data gathering and analysis choices — painting the path — needs to be adequate but sufficiently detailed.

SAMPLING

Gathering data from entire populations of respondents is usually too costly and time consuming. The usual solution to this dilemma is to gather data from a sample of the population. The problem then arises of ensuring that the sample is representative of the entire population at which the research objective is aimed. There are various types of sampling designs, but writers such as Dick (1990), Minichiello, Aroni, Timewell and Alexander (1990) and Sekaran (1992) discuss several useful types.

Simple random sampling

Similar to being in a lottery, every population member has an equal chance of being selected. Some random sampling process (names in a hat; a table of random numbers) is used to identify the chosen research subjects. The simple random sampling process is totally unbiased but can become cumbersome and expensive.

Systematic sampling

Every *n*th person in the population is chosen. While this is a cheaper option, systematic bias can creep in. For example, every *n*th member of the organisation may share some common characteristic — unlikely, but it can occur.

Stratified random sampling

Some subgroups of people in the organisation may be expected to have different opinions or experiences (e.g. upper managers, supervisors, front-line operators). Each stratification or subgroup is identified and then some random sampling process is used for selection. This is one of the most efficient designs but care has to be taken to ensure that the stratifications are meaningful and are appropriate to the research objective. One specific method used in HRDNI is called the 'slice group'— slice the organisation from top to bottom and have representatives from each level.

Convenience sampling

The first of the non-probability designs, this sampling design collects data from those in the target population who happen to be most conveniently accessible. The opportunity for systematic bias is high but it is a very cheap option.

Purposive sampling

Purposive sampling involves specifying the types of people who should be targeted, based on predetermined parameters. So, the investigation may target organisational members within certain salary brackets. Specific and rich information can be gained from this method but it is wide open to researcher bias.

Convergence sampling

Another option is to use the convergence technique. In this technique, the investigator starts by finding two people from the target population who are significantly different on some important parameter — for example, an engineer and a social worker (i.e. different professions). The selection process continues until the variations on the parameter converge to having no expected effect on the data to be provided.

Snowball sampling

This type of sampling involves using an initial group of informants and asking them to recommend further informants and, in turn, asking these informants for further recommendations and so on. Usually, the first tier of initial informants are not used as respondents so the data-gathering process commences with the second tier.

An important task

The above listing of sampling techniques ranges from probability sampling — where the participants are selected by chance — to non-probability sampling — where some bias could occur. However, the non-probability methods have the distinct advantage of quickly accessing participants who are most likely to provide rich information. For this reason, non-probability methods of sampling are more commonly used in qualitative research (Minichiello et al. 1990, p. 199).

Selecting a representative sample of respondents is an important task of an HRDNI investigator to ensure that no systematic bias occurs in the data gathered. At the same time, the investigator should not suffer from 'paralysis by analysis'. As Kruger (1994, p. 82) comments, the investigator needs to recognise that sometimes compromises are needed between the cost of finding the perfect participants and the likely increased quality of the data gathered. As a specific warning, Kruger goes on to advise caution about participants who have expressed concern about the topic, who are clones of the supervisor, can be best spared by the supervisor because they are the least productive, or who are picked from memory by the supervisor or other 'expert'. The cautious investigator always reviews the sampling options for the most efficient and potentially worthwhile participants in the HRDNI.

Overall, then, the HRDNI investigator has to recognise that, when using the interview or focus group, he or she is involved in qualitative research and that certain protocols — achieving the high ideals and sampling in particular — should provide guiding principles to manage the process.

INTERVIEWING

One wit has suggested that everyone claims that they are good drivers, good lovers and good interviewers. The last claim, at least, is not true! Successful interviewing is the result of the complex interaction of high level skills, empathy and understanding of others and an abundant curiosity. Interviews may be conducted face to face, over the telephone or via a video link. While there are some minor variations, the same general principles apply, whatever the medium.

The interview provides a unique opportunity to uncover rich and complex information from an individual. The face-to-face interactive process can, under the guidance of an experienced interviewer, encourage the interviewee to share intrinsic opinions and to dredge previously unthought-of memories from the unconscious mind. This rich and rare material invariably includes tacit knowledge from the interviewee, knowledge that is often critical to the design of the developmental learning experiences needed for individuals and organisations to overcome the challenges and take advantage of the opportunities that are the hallmark of the business environment today.

The key to uncovering this rich information is a well-designed and professionally conducted interview. Socialisation and natural resistance means that people tend not to disclose information, particularly to a stranger. Further, we often 'grade' the information that we are willing to disclose. There is a difference in responding to such **questions** as:

'How did you travel to work this morning?'
'What tasks did you carry out at work yesterday?'

compared to questions such as:

'Have you ever been convicted of taking prohibited drugs?'
'Would you describe your feelings when you experience your worst nightmare?'

Now, whether interviewees would respond to any of these questions and how much they would disclose depends a lot on the context of the interview. However, certain interview skills will increase the likelihood that the interviewee will provide the desired information. Such a well-designed interview is based on six factors:
1. the pattern of the interview
2. listening
3. questioning
4. paraphrasing
5. probing
6. non-verbal behaviour.

THE PATTERN OF AN INTERVIEW

A well-patterned interview has a number of benefits. The basic aim of the interview is achieved in less time by removing communication barriers and encouraging the flow of information. The interviewee feels at ease and tends to provide more complete answers. Finally, a well-patterned interview looks professional. Figure 7.1 is an overview of the pattern of an interview and this model provides a general guideline for an interviewer involved in a one-on-one interaction.

The first challenge of an interviewer is to bring the interviewee into the *rapport zone*. This is the area of minimum stress where the interviewee will disclose all information. We all retain natural barriers so that we do not disclose personal information inappropriately. The first task of the skilled interviewer is to encourage the interviewee to lower these barriers so that information will flow more easily. This easy flow of information occurs in the rapport zone. The interview proper cannot start until the interviewee enters this zone and the interviewer will need to invest some time and energy in encouraging the interviewee to lower his or her natural barriers.

The interview pattern consists of four stages: the entrance investment time, activity no. 2, intimacy and the exit investment time.

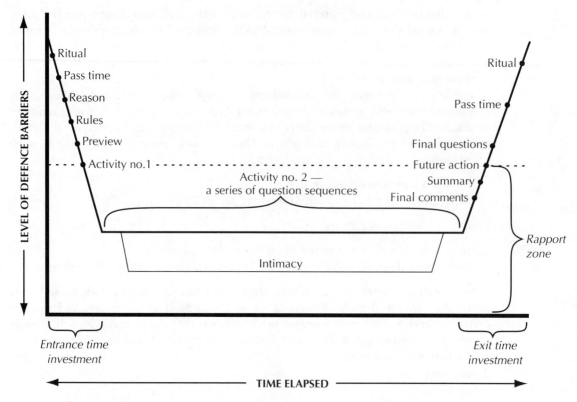

FIGURE 7.1 The pattern of an interview

Stage 1. Entrance investment time

This is the time invested at the beginning of the interview to ensure that the interviewee enters the rapport zone. It comprises six steps — the ritual, the pass time, the reason, the rules, preview and activity no. 1. The first two steps may seem to be superficial. However, far from being a waste of time, these exchanges provide information, as well as a time space, for the interviewee to start to become accustomed to the interviewer and the interview situation. Any attempt to 'short cut' the proceedings will often result in barriers reforming as a protection against insecurity.

- **Rituals** are the simple, stereotyped greetings that we use everyday and can be regarded as common good manners, for example 'Good Morning'. A frequent addition to the ritual is an introduction, for example 'My name is Yvonne'.
- A **pass time** carries on from the ritual and extends the time space available to the interviewee to adjust to the interview situation. Common pass times include the weather ('It's a windy day today, isn't it?') and health ('How are you today?'). The point of the pass time is that it does not expect a reply — in fact, a reply to a pass time is usually considered quite odd. However, a pass time should be reasonably relevant to the situation. A comment on the immediate environment may be more acceptable than the health pass time for example, 'It's quite cool in here, isn't it?', or if the interviewee has travelled to the interview location a comment such as 'Ah, good, you found the room then' would suffice.

- By this time the interviewee's mind should be coming off any events that occurred before the interview with his or her curiosity becoming piqued about *the reason* for the interviewer's presence. Needless to say, this curiosity should be satisfied immediately by sharing with the interviewee the objectives of the HRDNI. However, a decision needs to be made about the degree of specificity to be shared about the objectives of the HRDNI. If the interview is to be unstructured, then the interviewer may prefer to give a more generalised description as anything specific may bias the direction of the interview.

- Interviews are a somewhat artificial situation. In an interview, two strangers are coming together to share information in an open relationship that would normally take some time to establish. Therefore, there is a need to establish *basic ground rules* early. One frequent concern of interviewees is the confidentiality of the information and how the information will be used. Assurances need to be given at this stage. Permission on the type of recording — whether note taking or audio recording — needs to be obtained from the interviewee.

- Very briefly, *preview* the interview by telling the interviewee how it will proceed. This may simply be: 'I have six questions to ask and expect that this will take about 45 minutes'. More detail can be given, depending on the context, but be careful not to talk for too long. The sign of a good interview is a very high proportion of interviewee activity.

- The ritual, the pass time and the reason would have occupied a time space of about 60 seconds and the rules and the preview perhaps another 30 seconds. While the interviewee now may be willing to disclose some information, it would be naive to assume that no filtering would take place. It is now time for **activity no. 1**.

The role of activity no. 1 is to bring the interviewee fully into the rapport zone. Once people start on a perceived relevant activity information flows increasingly more easily as the natural barriers are forgotten and trust increases. However, activity no. 1 needs to be designed to meet two conflicting goals. On the one hand, activity no.1 has to be related to the objective of the HRDNI as any hint of artificiality will increase the interviewee's natural barriers, not lower them. On the other hand, it has to be recognised that the interviewee is not yet into the rapport zone so the initial information, at least, of activity no. 1 will be filtered by the interviewee. In addition, activity no. 1 needs to be a based on a question that the interviewee can answer easily and is willing to answer — lack of early success on the part of the interviewee is likely to increase the barriers to the free information flow. So, activity no. 1 needs to be carefully planned.

One good stratagem is to ask a question about the interviewee's most recent job: 'I see from your application that you have worked as a technical instructor on the coal fields in Central Queensland. Would you tell us about some of your experiences you enjoyed the most?' When involved in an HRDNI, most people expect to discuss their most recent job, so they have usually thought of possible answers. In addition, what they have done recently in their job is usually fresh in their minds, so they can usually answer quite readily. Further, most of the important information about their current job is often available elsewhere (for example, in organisational records), so if they forget some aspect through stress, there are minimal problems for the investigator.

As indicated in figure 7.1, activity no. 1 sits on the boundary between stage 1 (entrance investment time) and the rapport zone. This positioning indicates that activity no. 1 helps the interviewee enter the rapport zone and, at the same time, can also provide some useful information. However, this information would need checking, through triangulation, as there is a possibility that stress or lack of trust may have filtered the data.

The entrance investment time is needed to help the interviewee reduce the natural barriers to sharing information. The entrance investment time has two conflicting roles. It needs to be detailed and take sufficient time to allow the interviewee to lower his or her natural barriers but should not take so much time that the interviewee becomes exasperated.

Stage 2. Activity no. 2

As the interviewee enters the rapport zone (and this can be seen by the nonverbals) the interview proper can start. **Activity no. 2** is where the interviewer uses the skills of questioning, paraphrasing and probing. These skills will be discussed later in this chapter.

HRDNIs that are investigating explicit knowledge will remain at this activity no. 2 step. As discussed later in this chapter, interviews that stay at the activity no. 2 level are usually more structured and rely on questions that are pre-planned and content based.

Stage 3. Intimacy

HRDNIs that are researching knowledge that is deeper than explicit will usually encounter complexity, uncertainty and emotions. This suggests that such an interview will need to progress deeper into the rapport zone. Such a step involves genuine caring and authenticity and requires expert interviewing skills and sensitivity. Interviews at the intimacy level are usually more unstructured and rely heavily on the investigator's interview skills.

It should be noted that interviews moving this deep into the rapport zone will need to go through the steps of ritual, pass time, activity no. 1 and activity no. 2 before the interviewee will be deep enough into the rapport zone to risk full disclosure of emotions and inner feelings.

Stage 4. Exit investment time

Just as an investment of time was required to lower the defences of the interviewee at the beginning of the interview, so another time investment is needed to allow the interviewee to rebuild his or her natural defences. It is quite unethical for an interviewer not to provide this time space as no interviewee should be pushed defenceless into the cold outside world. There are six steps to this exit time investment:

1. When the interviewer considers that all the information has been gathered a comment can be made such as: 'Well, that is all the questions that I have. Do you have any *final comments*?' This achieves three aims. Firstly, the interviewee can add any further information that he or she considers important. This often leaves the interviewee with a feeling of satisfaction that he or she has completed a good job.

Secondly, it sometimes uncovers unexpected information which the interviewer may or may not choose to follow up. Thirdly, the word 'final' gives the interviewee a cue that the interview is coming to a close.

2. Some interviewers prefer to give a *summary* at this point, highlighting the main issues discussed. Again, this may encourage the interviewee to add some finer points and, by explicitly demonstrating all the issues covered, emphasises that the interview was very worthwhile. On the other hand, particularly if the interviewee is concerned about the amount of time the interview has taken, this step may take up too much valuable time and therefore may be omitted.

3. The interviewee may be curious and/or concerned about what will happen to the information that he or she has supplied. It is good practice to advise the interviewee of the *future actions* that you will take. This is also a good time to re-emphasise the confidentiality of these actions.

4. To check if there are any other issues or concerns held by the interviewee, a comment can be made such as: 'Do you have any *final questions*?' This gives the interviewee the opportunity to satisfy any curiosity and also indicates that the interview is just about finished.

5. A *pass time* gives the interviewee the chance to prepare to leave. Some interviewers like to use the same pass time that was used at the beginning of the interview but such a perfectly rounded ending is most probably not needed. This pass time can also be accompanied by nonverbal behaviours, such as standing up and moving towards the door of the interview room.

6. In a similar fashion to the entry *ritual*, this is common good manners and a 'goodbye and a thank-you for the time' is usually all that is necessary.

Each of these steps in the exit investment time signals to the interviewee that the interview is coming to a close and allows the interviewee to rebuild his or her defences in an orderly and dignified fashion.

LISTENING

Listening is the most important skill of an interviewer. Seidman (1991, p. 56) suggests that there are two levels of listening. Firstly, the interviewer listens to what the interviewee is saying — the content of the reply as constructed by the words used. The interviewer must concentrate on the substance to make sure that the message is understood and to assess whether the answer is on the right track, and is as detailed and complete as expected. Secondly, the interviewer listens for the 'unstated message' — what is not being said or what is being said verbally but is being contradicted by nonverbal messages. Does the interviewee continually avoid answering questions on a specific topic? Does the tone of voice match the verbalised message? Is he saying 'Yes, it's OK?' while looking despondent or even shaking his head?

As Fowler and Mangione (1990) comment, in an interview the participants have different roles — and it is the interviewee who answers. The answers are the raw data for the investigation so the interviewer must listen very carefully. This means that the interviewer must be comfortable with silence — allowing the interviewee to think — rather than rushing in and contaminating the outcome.

QUESTIONING

While the pattern of the interview defines the overall strategy of the interview, questioning is the real heart of the process. Well-designed questions allow the interviewer to control the direction of the interview and investigate areas of relevance and interest — to say nothing of ensuring that the objectives of the HRDNI are achieved. There are two types of questions — open questions and closed questions.

Open questions

There are two aspects to the open question (Delahaye and Smith 1998). Open questions allow the interviewee a wide choice of possible answers. While the interviewee may have only one opinion or remember only one point, as far as the interviewer is concerned, the *possible opinions* or points are many. Secondly the open question should be arranged in what is called the *stem-plus-query design*. So, an open question may look like:

'I am interested in the concerns you may have about the new financial system. Would you tell me about some of the concerns that you have, please?'

Compare this to the style of questioning that is often used in ordinary conversations:

'What are your concerns about the new financial system?'

Compared to the ordinary style, the stem-plus-query structure of open questions gives the interviewee the subject to be investigated early in the question. This allows the interviewee to start focusing his or her attention on the topic. It also 'softens' the question as the ordinary style can become inquisitory when used in a succession of questions. In addition, as we will see later in this chapter, the stem-plus-query design fits in well with the skill of probing.

Closed questions

Closed questions are used for identifying explicit facts or for confirmation, for example:

'How many times have customers complained?'
'So, in your opinion, blue would be a better colour for the background?'

Because of the very short interviewee response the stem-plus-query structure is usually inappropriate for the closed question.

In combination

During the interview, the first question is usually referred to as the *primary question*. All other questions are called *secondary questions*. The type of questions used as primary and secondary questions lead to different questioning sequences that have different uses.

A question sequence that starts with an open question and, in turn, has a secondary question as a less open question, then a relatively closed question and finally a closed question is called a *funnel sequence*. The funnel sequence is the most commonly used for investigations such as an HRDNI. The *inverted funnel sequence* starts with a closed question and the questions then become broader until the sequence finishes with an open question. An interviewer uses the inverted funnel sequence where the interviewee is reluctant to be interviewed or if there is some uncertainty that the interviewee has any knowledge of the topic area. Theoretically, the inverted funnel sequence allows the interviewer to stop the interview early so that time is not wasted. However, as discussed later under probing, there are more sophisticated ways of gathering data under these difficult situations that have a higher probability of success. The *tunnel sequence* is made up of either a series of closed questions or a series of open questions. A series of closed questions becomes an interrogation and this type of tunnel sequence is rarely used in an HRDNI (although it is a favourite of the police force!). A tunnel sequence of open questions requires high levels of interviewing skills as the interviewee can easily become bored or frustrated with the inability to cover any particular area in depth.

PARAPHRASING

From the point of view of the interviewer, questions are the key to the interview as they provide the cues to which the interviewee responds. However, from the interviewee's point of view, the answers are the most important component — and who can argue? The answers provide the required material that will become the raw data of the HRDNI.

So, let us look at the interview from the interviewee's perspective. The interviewee hears the questions and provides a detailed answer. The interviewer then asks another (possibly unrelated) question. The interviewee is left wondering. Has the interviewer heard the detailed answer? More importantly, has the interviewer understood the real meaning of the reply? These unspoken queries will divert the interviewee's attention and, worse, demotivate the interviewee so that less detail is given to the next question. This is not the ideal interviewing environment.

Of course, what the interviewee needs is confirmation that the interviewer has heard and does understand. This confirmation is achieved by *paraphrasing*. With paraphrasing, the interviewer repeats back to the interviewee, in a concise form, the essential message of the interviewee's reply. If there has been a misunderstanding the interviewee can then correct the interviewer's perception. As well as reassuring the interviewee that the message has been understood, paraphrasing has three additional benefits. Firstly, as the interviewer is paraphrasing, the interviewee is often reminded of some additional information and will then provide this when the interviewer finishes paraphrasing. Secondly, paraphrasing establishes a caring atmosphere within the interview that increases the trust between the participants. Thirdly, paraphrasing allows the interviewee a little time to think, giving the interview a slightly slower but methodical, measured and professional quality.

A special type of paraphrasing is called *reflection of feeling*. Whereas ordinary paraphrasing concentrates on the content of the message, reflection of feeling acknowledges the emotions of the interviewee. Reflection of feelings often becomes more important during the intimacy stage of the interview. Being able to reflect feelings is a much more complex skill than ordinary paraphrasing as it demands of the interviewer the ability to empathise with the interviewee's emotions — and, in turn, empathising with another's feelings needs an ability to be in touch with one's own feelings. In most Western societies, feelings and emotions are second-class citizens to the more factual pursuits, so developing the skill to reflect feelings often requires some considerable effort. (See Cormier and Cormier 1991, pp. 95–100, for an excellent discussion of reflection of feeling.)

PROBING

Probing combines the funnel sequence of questions with paraphrasing and allows the interviewer to delve into the memories of the interviewee. The steps in probing are as follows:

1. The interviewer asks the primary, usually open question, using the stem-plus-query structure.
2. The interviewee responds.
3. The interviewer makes note of the salient points of the interviewee's answer to the first primary question.
4. The interviewer paraphrases the salient points back to the interviewee.
5. Selecting one of the salient points, the interviewer asks the first secondary question, using the salient point as the stem of the question.
6. So the process continues on that first salient point, with each issue paraphrased and with the questions becoming more closed, until the interviewer is satisfied that the point has been explored fully.
7. The interviewer then briefly summarises the main issues that have come out of the first salient point. This overall summary is a special type of paraphrasing that briefly brings together what has been covered to this stage.
8. The interviewer then goes to the second salient point, using it as the stem for the next secondary question and continues to explore this second salient point, using the funnel sequence so that the questions become more closed and more factual information is uncovered.
9. The interviewer then progresses to the third salient point of the first primary question or goes on to the next primary question. Thus the interview becomes a series of funnel sequences.

Several points should be made about the probing process. Paraphrasing in the early stages of each funnel sequence is a must but, as the interview progresses down each funnel, paraphrasing may become too annoying for the interviewee. Therefore, as the questions become more closed, paraphrasing usually becomes more redundant. Secondly, the interviewer decides which salient points of the interviewee's response to explore. Some points may be explained fully as part of the response to the primary question; other points may not be worth following up. Only those points which help with objectives of the HRDNI are the ones on which the interviewer chooses to invest the time of the interview. Thirdly, the interviewer can decide how far down the funnel the questions should commence. For an interviewee who has limited knowledge of the topic, it may be easier to start with a less open question — i.e., start lower down the funnel. With interviewees who have a better knowledge of the topic the interviewer can afford to start with a broader, more open question — i.e., start higher up the funnel. Finally, the interviewer decides how far down the funnel the interview should progress. Remember, closed questions are used to confirm an issue or to gather a specific fact. If confirmation or a specific fact is not needed, then the interviewer finishes that funnel sequence (usually with a summary) before the closed questions and then goes onto the next area to be explored.

Probing

The following is an example of an interview in which probing has been used to discover more information.

Er: As you know, there are a number of problems with the human resource information system we use in the company. What type of problems have you come across when using the system?

Ee: Well, trying to access information is always a problem. You know, you need to find out various bits and pieces. I guess it is to do with the system not linking the various parts. When someone takes leave without pay then the system does deduct the right amount from their pay but it does not deduct the day from their leave records. You would think that the system would do the lot, wouldn't you? And another thing, when someone goes to a training course, the system does note their training record but nothing is transferred to their department's skills matrix. We have to enter that information by hand a second time.

Er: So the main problem with the current human resource information system is that the various parts are not linked. There are two specific problems; let's concentrate on the first. Tell me more about the problems between the pay record and the leave record.

Ee: Well, when someone goes on leave without pay they fill out a form. This leave form goes to the leave clerk who enters the information into the computer under the Individual Leave Record. But then the leave clerk has to complete another form which he sends to the pay office. The computer system should automatically deduct the amount from both the leave record and the person's salary.

Er: So the leave clerk has to do two actions — enter the leave into the computer and also complete another form. This other form that the leave clerk completes, what is it called?

Ee: Oh, that's the Salary Deduction form. It has to be signed by the manager as well.

Er: Ok, the leave clerk enters the information and also completes the Salary Deduction form when someone has leave without pay. You also spoke about the problem when someone goes on a training course. Would you tell me more about that?

Ee: Yes, when someone gets trained we have to update their personal record on the HRIS. But the personnel records of each department are separate. It's the same problem, really. We then have to open another field in the HRIS and enter the same information. It's a waste of time. And, of course, sometimes it is not always done, so it makes problems when we have to look up information — and it can cause quite a bit of confusion.

Er: So, it is the same general problem — you have to do two actions when only one entry should be all that is needed. I would just like to go back to the Salary Deduction form. You said that the manager had to sign it. If the computer did both jobs — note the leave record and also deduct the salary, how would the manager approve the salary deduction?

[and so the interview would continue]

Some points to note

1. The interviewer started with an open question in the stem-plus-query format.

2. The interviewee has provided information. The reply is fairly typical in that the first few sentences are not very clear. The interviewee is trying to make some sense of his or her thoughts and often, in the initial stages, this is not too logical. However, as the answer progresses, the interviewee becomes more articulate.

(continued)

3. The interviewer paraphrased the information back to the interviewee.
4. The interviewer chose to follow the first point about the leave and salary record.
5. The interviewer used a closed question to identify a fact — the name of the Salary Deduction form.
6. The interviewer summarised the main information from this first point, then followed up on the second point with another open question in the stem-plus-query format.
7. This information was again paraphrased. There was no need for a summary on the second as the paraphrasing did this role.
8. The interviewer then investigated a new point disclosed by the interviewee from the earlier closed question. The interviewer could have followed up this point when it was raised but this would have interfered with the flow of the interview. Instead, the interviewer has chosen to make it a major third point, as the interviewer considers it to be a very important issue.

SUMMARISING

Summarising provides a break in the relentless search for information — a break for both the interviewer and the interviewee. Zima (1991, p. 47) defines a summary as a restatement of the major ideas, facts, themes, and/or feelings that the interviewee has expressed. He suggests that summaries are like internal summaries in a good speech. From our knowledge of adult learning, a summary can be seen as a good example of at least two principles of learning (see chapter 2). The recency element refreshes the interviewee's memory. Secondly, the feedback provided is of the two types — informational and motivational. The advantages of recency and feedback alone emphasise the importance of the skill of summarising.

a closer look   7.2

Summarising

An example of inadequate summarising

Er: Yes, well, that was very interesting. You have made some very good points. They should be very useful for my enquiry. Thank you very much. Now I have some more questions.

An example of good summarising

Er: Good, thank you. Looking at my notes here, you have made four very good points about helping customers at the library. Firstly, on the return of books. The customer has no record of the return of their books and, if there is a later enquiry, the customers cannot prove that they have returned their books. Secondly, the returned books are not put back on the shelves quickly enough. You have found that, even though the library records indicate that a book is available, it is not on the shelves and some- times you have found it on the return trolleys. Thirdly, when checking out books, you have noticed that some staff seem to be confused by the 'hold system' and have to find and then ask the supervisor what to do. However, as a fourth point, you do like the friendly and helpful atmosphere in the library. You always feel that you can go to staff members and ask questions.

Ok, is there anything you would like to add to those points? No? Right, I would like to go onto the next point which is about the computer services.

[and so the interview would continue]

Some points to note

1. In the inadequate summary, the interviewer has given motivational feedback and has indicated that the interview will move on to further questions but little else has been achieved.

2. In the good summary, the interviewer has provided positive motivational feedback and then gone on to list and paraphrase the four points the interviewee made. The interviewer has also referred to the notes, thereby sharing the notes with the interviewee, indicating that the notes are not a secret record but can be shared.

3. In the good summary, the interviewer has given the interviewee an opportunity to add more information.

4. In the good summary, the interviewer has previewed the next area of questioning.

Interviewers should summarise at the end of each questioning sequence (for example, at the bottom of the funnel). This allows the interviewer to highlight the important points covered and to refresh the memories of each party of the salient points. The interviewee also has the opportunity to correct any misinterpretations that have occurred.

NONVERBAL BEHAVIOUR

The interviewer needs to be aware of nonverbal behaviour on two fronts. Firstly, the nonverbal behaviour exhibited by the interviewer can have a dynamic effect on the interview. Secondly, reading the interviewee's nonverbal behaviour can provide useful insights into the progress of the interview and also useful cues on when to press for more information or when to proceed more carefully on a particular topic.

Egan (1994, pp. 91–92) has provided a robust model that can be used successfully for either appropriate interviewer behaviour or for interpreting the interviewee's orientation. This model is called the **SOLER system**:

- (S)quare on. The interviewer needs to stand or sit so that he or she is fully facing the interviewee. This gives the message that the interviewer is paying full attention to the interviewee's responses.

- (O)pen posture. The interviewer should not be hunched down or 'close off' the interviewee (for example, by having arms or legs crossed so that they form a barrier). Sit up straight with an open profile. This gives the indication that the interviewer is willing to accept all the information that the interviewee will give and is usually interpreted as being non-defensive.

- (L)ean forward. Gently leaning forward slightly indicates involvement and interest. This posture says, 'I'm with you, I want to understand your message'. However, it should be noted that leaning too far forward has intonations of aggressiveness and should be avoided.

- (E)yes. In our society, the eyes play an important part in communication. There are two issues to consider here. Firstly, the distance from the eye of the interviewer to the eye of the interviewee should be at least a metre. This distance varies from culture to culture but a metre seems to be a comfortable distance for most people. Any less and the interviewee may become unconsciously defensive with a resultant suppression of information. Any more and the interviewee may feel that the interviewer is uninterested. Secondly, the amount of eye contact is important, although again this also varies between cultures. However, in most cultures there is an accepted level of contact, with too little being just as inhibiting as too much.

- (R)elax. A relaxed interview atmosphere is usually more conducive to easy information flow. If the interviewer models relaxed nonverbal behaviour — slower rather than jerky movements, a calm facial expression, slower speech patterns — then the interviewee is more likely to follow these examples.

The SOLER system provides a useful 'checklist' at the start of the interview. If the interviewer consciously concentrates on these nonverbal behaviours at the beginning, they tend to become more automatic as the interview progresses and the interviewer becomes more interested in the topic of the interview itself.

The SOLER system also provides a very useful guide to assess the involvement of the interviewee. The more defensive the interviewee is, the more the interviewee's behaviour will appear to be anti-SOLER — tends to stand or sit side on, tries to make their overall profile smaller by hunching down, does not keep eye contact and seems to be anything but relaxed. Such anti-SOLER behaviour is a sure sign that the interviewee is not in the rapport zone. This usually means that the interviewee has not reacted positively to the ritual and the pass time so the interviewer will need to spend more time on activity no. 1. Another option is for the interviewer to first mimic, very subtly, the anti-SOLER nonverbals of the interviewee and then gradually move to the SOLER posture. Frequently, if the changes in nonverbal behaviour are carefully gauged, then the interviewee will gradually model the SOLER posture of the interviewer and, concomitantly, become more open psychologically to allowing information to flow.

STRUCTURED AND UNSTRUCTURED INTERVIEWS

Interviews can be categorised as highly structured or highly unstructured, with these two points being considered as the poles of a continuum. Being on a continuum means that an interview can be described as, for example, less structured or more unstructured. In other words there are degrees of being structured or unstructured.

An *unstructured interview* is one in which the interviewer starts with a broad, open primary question and then relies entirely on the interview skill of probing — questioning, paraphrasing and summarising — to manage the process and the direction of the interview. An unstructured interview has the advantage of being unbiased by the preordained ideas interviewer and, theoretically, more truly reflects the world of the interviewee. The disadvantage of the unstructured interview is that it can be very time consuming and can wander away from the objectives of the HRDNI. This means that no two interviews are the same and the breadth of the investigation can become very wide.

In a *structured interview* standardised questions are carefully ordered and worded in a detailed interview schedule and each research subject is asked exactly the same question, in exactly the same order as all other subjects (Minichiello et al. 1990, p. 90). Each question is pre-planned and explores a specific topic — that is, it uses the content of the questions to manage the direction of the interview. Structured interviews are used in situations where the differences in the interviewees' responses can be compared and interpreted as indicating real differences in what is being measured. The structured interview ensures that each interviewee answers the same questions and that opinion is canvassed for specific areas of enquiry only. However, the interview direction is biased heavily by the predetermined questions and there is usually limited opportunity for the interviewee to provide further information.

The decision to use a structured or unstructured interview revolves around two variables. The first, and main, variable is whether there is a reasonable amount of information on the issues already known. If there is, then specific primary questions can be formulated for each of the issues. If there is only limited information available on the issues, then the interviewer will have no recourse but to use a more unstructured format and rely on interviewing skills to manage the process to ensure that the objectives of the HRDNI are accomplished. The second variable is the interview skills of the interviewer. The unstructured interview demands that the interviewer be highly experienced. On the other hand, the strict scheduling of the structured interview can often be used successfully by an unskilled interviewer.

Another option, of course, is to conduct a semi-structured interview. There are two basic strategies for this. The first strategy is to commence the interaction as an unstructured interview — present the primary, overall question and then concentrate on managing the process by using interview skills to elicit information. When the information sought appears to be coming less, the interviewer then switches to planned questions based on defined, pre-identified topics — that is, questions based on content. So, for example, the investigator may start the interview with a very open question such as:

> 'The records indicate that customer complaints for whole company have increased in the last 3 months by 32%. In your experience, what do you see as some of the possible reasons for these complaints?'

When the interviewer has used all her/his interview skills to explore the respondent's ideas, she/he may then choose to switch to some prepared questions on topics such as:
- the customer delivery systems
- the location of the complaints office
- the training of staff to handle difficult customers.

These are questions based on content. Where did the investigator find the content for these questions? Most probably from the beginnings of the investigation using other needs identification methods. For example, before conducting the interviews, the investigator may have examined organisational records and gained some insights into possible causes of the customer complaints.

Another strategy for semi-structured interviews is to use a pre-planned, logical approach to manage the interview process. Writers such as Tregoe (1983), Zima (1991) and Egan (1994) have each provided some insights that could be combined into a five-step model that can be used to manage the process of a semi-structured interview:
1. *Exploring the current situation*, where the interviewer probes for a description of the current situation by identifying, clarifying and exploring the problem situations and unused opportunities. The interviewer will tend to concentrate on:
   - what is actually happening and the identity of the issue
   - where it is happening or the location
   - when the event occurred
   - the extent of the event — how often; how serious/important.

2. *Possible causes/options*, where an HRDNI assumes that the people at the workfront have a wealth of knowledge and the interview should provide an opportunity for this knowledge to come to the fore. If the HRDNI is examining a problem then this step will concentrate on causes; if exploring an opportunity, the options will be the emphasis. Some techniques for assisting the process include:
   – listing the historical sequence of events, which will often highlight the link that was most at risk or had the highest impact on creating the problem or the link that is easiest to repair
   – brainstorming — asking people to come up with a long list of ideas, the more far-out the better, without assessing them
   – asking people to compare and contrast — how it used to be with now; this product with that one; utopia with reality
   – concentrating on what has changed.
3. *Identifying untrue causes/adverse consequences*, where the investigator finds out if the suggested cause would eliminate all the problem or if the suggested option would have other effects in another system.
4. *Preferred scenario*, where the investigator has people describe the preferred future scenario — defining activities that would occur, goals that would be achieved and people who would be affected. This is a good time to gather ideal examples, either in descriptive form or as actual artifacts. These ideal examples can often be used in formulating learning objectives or as part of the learning experience.
5. *Planning the future*, where the investigator gathers suggestions on how the proposed scenario should be planned — identifying the resources that will be needed, the timing of key events, the people who should be involved and any dangers that should be avoided.

THE THREE LEVELS OF INTERVIEWING

The interview is a dynamic vehicle for exploring rich and complex information in an individual. As an interaction, it is complex and dynamic, operating on three levels:
1. the *content level* where the interviewer listens to and records the data information that the interviewee provides
2. the *process level* where the interviewer uses the skills of questioning, paraphrasing, probing and attending to control the direction of the interview and encourage the interviewee to provide information
3. the *executive level*. As Seidman (1991, p. 57) points out, the interviewer must be conscious of time during the interview and must be aware of how much has been covered and how much there is to go. An interviewer must be sensitive to the interviewee's energy levels and continually make judgements on how to move the interview forward.

The interview is ideally suited for investigating information from an individual. Where qualitative information from two or more people is required, the focus group is used.

THE FOCUS GROUP

The focus group method is a research technique that collects data through group interaction on a topic determined by the researcher — the researcher's interest provides the focus while the data comes from the group interaction (Morgan 1997, p. 6).

As a data-gathering device for the HRDNI, the focus group has a number of similarities with the interview. Firstly, the facilitator of a focus group must operate at the three levels — the content, the process and the executive. As is the case with the interview, the management of the process is the most complex of these levels. Secondly, the conduct of the focus group is based on the same six factors:

1. The overall pattern is based on an entry investment time, with the steps of ritual, pass time, reason, rules, preview and activity no. 1, activity no. 2, intimacy (if needed) and exit investment time, with final comments, summary, future, final questions, pass time and ritual.
2. The ability to listen is still paramount.
3. Questioning by the facilitator still guides and controls the interaction.
4. The participants still need to hear paraphrasing to be reassured that their message has been received and understood.
5. The facilitator probes to uncover all the information required.
6. Nonverbal behaviour of the facilitator is used to encourage responses and the facilitator observes the nonverbal behaviour of the participants to check for levels of involvement and understanding.

However, the differences between the interview and the focus group highlight the roles that the facilitator will need to play in managing the process of a focus group. Morgan (1997, pp. 10–11) points out that the focus group method provides direct and immediate evidence about similarities and differences in participants' opinions and experiences as opposed to reaching such conclusions from post hoc analysis of separate statements from each interviewee. He goes on to acknowledge that the individual interviews have the distinct advantage with regard to (a) the amount of control the interviewer has and (b) the greater amount of time that each informant has to provide data. However, it is interesting to note that an investigation by Fern (1982) showed that focus groups did not produce significantly more or better quality information than an equivalent number of individual interviews.

In conducting a focus group, a facilitator has to be aware of a number of specific issues — among them being whether the focus group should be structured or unstructured, the logistics, group composition and the processes of conducting the focus group.

STRUCTURED AND UNSTRUCTURED FOCUS GROUPS

In a similar fashion to the interview, a decision needs to be made on whether the focus group should be structured or unstructured. A structured focus group is governed by predetermined, content questions while the unstructured approach uses an initial, open primary question and then relies on the skills of the facilitator to manage the process. A semi-structured focus group starts off being unstructured and then the facilitator brings in the predetermined, content-based questions.

LOGISTICS

A focus group brings together a number of people, at a common time, in a relatively large space that is comfortable, quiet and free from interruptions. Associated equipment such as chairs, tables, audio- or videotaping facilities, visual aids and writing material is usually needed. While the steps in planning a focus group are the same as those discussed for the interview, planning the **logistics**, so that a focus group runs smoothly, can take some considerable time.

Accessing financial resources is usually more involved. In discussing budgeting issues, Morgan (1997, p. 32) points out that major cost factors include salaries to facilitators, travel to research sites, rental of research workshop rooms, payments to participants and producing and transcribing tapes.

GROUP COMPOSITION

The investigator has to give careful thought to the membership of the groups. One of the assumed benefits of focus groups is that the individuals in the group can 'piggy-back' and 'leap-frog' off each others' ideas, thus generating a richer accumulation of data. Unfortunately, this interaction can also contaminate the outcome, if not carefully managed, particularly when stronger participants take over the group.

Another problem that can occur with inappropriate group composition is having a group where members have too diverse backgrounds. The diversity of interests often results in too many, and even inappropriate, issues being raised with the resultant time investment increasing significantly. Accordingly, there are several variables that need to be considered when assembling a group.

Homogeneity

The degree of homogeneity or sameness within the group will depend on the objectives of the HRDNI. If in-depth discussion is needed on a particular issue, then the members of the group will need to be similar on a number of elements. For example, if the perceptions of upper management on a particular situation are to be compared to those of operating staff, then there may be a need for at least two focus groups — one consisting of upper managers and another of operating staff. On the other hand, if the objective is to gather information from a wide variety of staff, then a mixture of participants may produce more relevant and richer data. Perhaps the final word can rest with Kruger (1994, p. 77) who suggests that the focus group is characterised by homogeneity but with sufficient variation among participants to allow for contrasting opinion.

Representation

Quite often the entire target population cannot be canvassed, so only a sample of representatives come together in the focus group. It is important to ensure that these representatives are likely to mirror the opinion of the target population. Previous comments on sampling should be considered here.

Strangers versus acquaintances

Whether it is preferable to select individuals who do or do not know each other is debatable. Morgan (1997) suggests that the rule of thumb favours strangers, although he acknowledges that this is not a necessity. Indeed, avoiding acquaintanceships within organisations is virtually impossible.

Size of group

There are conflicting issues to consider when deciding the optimum size of a group. The smaller the group, the more time each participant has to contribute views. However, the smaller the group, the less chance there is of representation of the target population and the more chance that one strong individual can hijack the agenda. Morgan (1997) considers that small groups can be disrupted easily by friendship pairs, 'experts' or uncooperative participants — therefore, small groups are likely to work best when the participants are interested in the topic and respectful of each other. Large groups, on the other hand, require considerable skill to manage the group processes simply because of the tyranny of numbers. In addition, as groups increase in size, they tend to become more complex and formally structured (Forsyth 1990).

Kruger (1994) suggests that a rule of thumb specifies a range of six to nine, although one should not feel confined by this upper and lower boundary.

CONDUCTING THE FOCUS GROUP

Figure 7.1 also provides a very good outline for the conduct of a focus group and allows the facilitator to work though the stages of entry investment time, activity stage and exit investment time. Focus groups rarely descend to the intimacy level as the public domain usually inhibits such disclosures. Fontana and Frey (1998) believe that the skills required by a group facilitator are not significantly different from those needed by an interviewer of individuals. The facilitator will also use the same process skills — questioning, probing and encouraging nonverbal behaviour.

Fontana and Frey (1998) go on to report that a facilitator of focus groups has three specific goals: first, the facilitator must keep one person or a small coalition of persons from dominating the group; second, he or she must encourage recalcitrant respondents to participate; and, third, he or she must obtain responses from the entire group to ensure the fullest possible coverage. To achieve these goals there are five specific considerations that need attention while conducting focus groups.

Facilitator team

Kruger (1994) recommends considering using a **facilitator team** — perhaps with a facilitator and assistant facilitator. The facilitator can concentrate on directing the discussion and recording the group's views on a white board, while the assistant can take more comprehensive notes.

Recording

Consider if technology is needed to assist with data gathering. Audio- or video-recording devices can record a variety of detail and be a significant memory aid during the analytic stage. However, recognise that such recording can cause participants to suppress information.

Use of visual aids

When talking to a group, it is difficult to be sure that you have the attention of everyone. It is also more difficult to recognise feedback from so many people. Using visual aids (i.e. multiple sense learning) can help overcome these problems, particularly when used on the three occasions discussed on the following page.

1. During the introduction, the *objectives* of the HRDNI can be shown on the overhead projector.
2. Each *new question* can also be displayed on the overhead projector. If the question is just presented orally, misinterpretations can occur. In addition, the question can remain on the overhead projector for some time, so the participants can refer to it and also helping to keep the discussion on track.
3. The *ideas* offered by the group should be recorded on a white board or similar device. This has at least three advantages. The offeree is rewarded by seeing her or his idea accepted visually. This reward is doubled if the facilitator paraphrases at the same time. Secondly, other participants can use an idea displayed on the white board to generate new ideas. Thirdly, the list can be easily used to summarise at strategic points during the focus group interaction.

Thinking time

It is often advisable to allow group members to think of and write down ideas individually, on a piece of paper, when each question or cue is presented (this is borrowed from the nominal group technique). This gives everyone a chance to collect their thoughts and tends to mitigate the overbearing predilections of the opinionated individual who likes to take over the focus group agenda. If someone has written down an idea, he or she usually shares it with limited encouragement, thus assuring contribution from all members.

Group dynamics

There are a variety of forces that operate within a group and these forces are known collectively as group dynamics. Early work by such researchers as Benne and Sheats (1948) and Bales (1950) suggested that there are two important functions carried out by groups — task and maintenance — and within these functions there are a variety of roles undertaken by the group members. The *task roles* encompass all behaviours that help the group achieve the goal or objective. In a focus group this task activity is the answering of questions. They contribute to the good working-relationships of the group by encouraging a collaborative attitude. A number of more recent authors have expanded on this earlier work on group roles (for example, Dunphy with Dick 1981; Forsyth 1990; Napier and Gershenfeld 1993). Roles within each of the functions that are important to focus groups are described in tables 7.1 and 7.2.

The facilitator must be able to differentiate between the task and maintenance functions and recognise the roles within each. Schein (1969) recommends that group facilitators should stay at the process level and not stray into the content. Using this recommendation as a basic theme, the facilitator of focus groups should not become involved in any of the task roles. Rather, the facilitator should recognise and encourage the contributions of each role within the task function. So, if the group is not making any progress, the facilitator may ask the person who has been filling the initiator role for a contribution. However, it is important to recognise that any group member may fill any of the roles at various points — for example, as the discussion moves from topic to topic, different members may fill the information-giver role.

TABLE 7.1

Task roles in
focus groups

ROLE	FUNCTION
Initiator	Provides new ideas or solutions about the problem at hand or suggests different ways to approach the problem. Is often deferred to by the group.
Information giver	Being a topic expert, provides facts and data. Acts in an advisory capacity to the group.
Information seeker	Calls for background, factual information from other members.
Elaborator	Gives additional information in the form of examples or rephrases others' contributions.
Opinion giver	Provides opinions, values and feelings.
Opinion seeker	Seeks more qualitative data, such as attitudes, values and feelings.
Coordinator	Points out the relevance of each idea and its relationship to the focus group objective.
Evaluator	Appraises the quality of the group's offerings, logic and results. Questions the validity or relevance of the facts raised by the group. Seeks clarification of vague ideas or issues.
Representative	Acts as a spokesperson for others outside the group and speaks for the group as a whole.

TABLE 7.2

Maintenance
roles in focus
groups

ROLE	FUNCTION
Encourager	Rewards others through agreement, warmth and praise. Asks for additional examples or inquires if others have a similar opinion.
Harmoniser	Mediates conflict between group members or between different points of view.
Gatekeeper	Ensures equal participation from members. Establishes procedures and ground rules that encourages smooth communications.
Orienter	Refocuses discussion on topic when necessary.
Energiser	Stimulates the group to continue working when discussion flags.
Expresser	Expresses the emotions the group is feeling and sometimes 'triggers' emotional responses from other members.
Confronter	Tends to take the 'hardnose' approach and exposes interpersonal conflicts. Is impatient with delays and confusion.
Tension reliever	Introduces humour when group tension is high; encourages a relaxed atmosphere.
Recorder	Provides a record of the information provided by the participants. This record is of two types — a visual record to help the group in processing the data and a permanent record for later analysis.

If the facilitator attends to the maintenance roles, then he or she will fulfil Schein's recommendation to concentrate on managing the process. However, group members will also often perform some of the maintenance roles. The facilitator, therefore, needs to decide when to use one of the roles or when to allow or encourage one of the participants to fill the role. Typically, the facilitator tends to use the roles of recorder, encourager, gatekeeper, orienter and energiser. While the facilitator does enter the other roles, it is sometimes better to allow one of the group members to take on the responsibility. For example, tension reliever is sometimes best occupied by a participant particularly if the tension reliever is also the expresser. Of course, the facilitator may find the need to become the tension reliever but must be careful that this is not viewed as being flippant or as demonstrating a lack of concentration on the goal of the focus group.

Benne and Sheats (1948) and Bales (1950) also suggested that some individual idiosyncratic behaviours can mitigate the achievement of the group goals. The facilitator needs to be on the lookout for these behaviours and plan ways of overcoming them. Napier and Gershenfeld (1993, p. 257) suggest being aware of five of these behavioural types. The *aggressor* questions the very use and existence of the focus group with thinly veiled sarcasm and makes personal attacks on the facilitator and individual group members. The *blocker* criticises every suggestion and idea. The *self-confessor* uses the audience to express personal problems seeking sympathy and atonement. The *recognition-seeker* boasts of personal conquests and past successes. The *dominator* likes to be 'top dog' and uses strategies such as interrupting, flattery and asserting superior status. The thing to remember about these dysfunctional behaviours is that they are personal agenda that run contrary to the needs and goals of the group. The behaviours are games that satisfy the needs of the aberrant individual. The facilitator has a number of strategies to cope with the situations, among them the following:

- Allow the group the chance to retain control. Often the confronter is good at this role.
- Use nonverbal behaviour to discourage the individual, for example go against the SOLER method — do not look the aberrant individual in the eyes and stand sideways to him or her.
- Do not paraphrase their aberrant offerings but reward them for positive contributions.
- Remind the group of the question by pointing to the overhead projector and restating the question.
- Summarise the progress so far and go back to the question.
- As a last resort, confess that you cannot see how the aberrant contribution helps the focus group achieve its goals. Be careful of this option as it can have negative repercussions.

Three of these considerations in particular — use of visual aids, thinking time and group dynamics — and the associated skills separate the focus group from the interview. They are also what makes the facilitation of focus groups both exciting and challenging.

ANALYSING QUALITATIVE DATA

The overall purpose of analysing qualitative data is to identify the themes and sub-themes in the raw data, which will provide an understanding of the issue, opportunity or problem that is being investigated. For an HRDNI it is well to keep firmly in mind that the most basic outcomes sought are learning objectives. Themes can be identified in two basic ways — based on the pre-planned questions or by content analysis.

PRE-PLANNED QUESTIONS

In structured and semi-structured interviews and focus groups, pre-planned questions were used to explore certain specific topics. These cue questions, then, automatically provide themes for investigation. For example, if a question used was:

'Staff expect their supervisors to take on several roles. What do you think some of these roles are?'

then the researcher would have gathered a list and description of a variety of roles based on the expectations of the respondents. So one theme in the HRDNI report would certainly be a list and description of the expected roles. This theme would then be converted into a learning objective, such as:

'Describe the five main roles expected of a supervisor.'

Of course, using the pre-planned questions as the analytic 'blueprint' places an *a priori* structure on the outcome of the analysis. However, if the pre-planned questions have been devised carefully and are accurate cues representing the concept or issue being investigated, then any resultant contamination will be minimal.

CONTENT ANALYSIS

The unstructured interview or focus group does not have the advantage of pre-determined themes. Of course, even with the structured interview or focus group, additional data that does not conform to the predetermined questions is often gathered as well.

Content analysis is the process of identifying, coding and categorising the primary patterns in the data (Patton 1990). This type of analysis allows the themes to emerge from the raw data. There are nine steps in conducting a content analysis. Recognise, however, that these steps are not necessarily followed in a strict linear order as interaction and overlapping do occur.

1. *Read* through your notes, transcripts and other evidence.
2. As you read through the notes and other evidence, themes will emerge for you. *Code* these themes as they surface. A coding system is a means of reorganising the data according to conceptual themes recognised by the researcher (Minichiello et al. 1990, p. 293). Coding can be achieved in a number of ways — putting an abbreviation, representing the theme, next to the sentence or paragraph which contains the theme; using a number, rather than an abbreviation, next to the

relevant sentence or paragraph; or using a highlighter pen to accent a theme. This coding process is the central activity of content analysis. As Patton (1990, p. 381) comments, coming up with topics or themes is like constructing an index for a book or labels for a filing system; look at what is there and give it a name, a label.

3. When you find what you think is a second theme, *compare* it to the first theme. When you find a third theme, compare it to the first and second themes, and so on. This process is called 'constant comparative analysis' (Samuelowicz and Blain 1992).

4. *Maintain a list* of the abbreviations and brief descriptions of the themes on a separate sheet of paper. Keep adding to this list as you discover new themes. This provides a *data index* and is the first stage of *classification*.

5. At reasonable intervals during this process (say, every couple of hours or so) or at the end of the process, *transfer the indicated passages to a file* — one file for each theme. These days this is usually achieved by using a computer and word processing package. Another option is the 'cut and paste' technique — simply cut the coded segments from your notes or transcripts and paste them onto other sheets of paper under the appropriate categories. As this destroys the original documents, the cut and paste process needs to be undertaken with copies.

   This transferring process classifies the data into specific *categories* and provides fuller descriptions and examples of the themes. Usually, one category consists of one theme. Guba (1978) suggests two criteria for judging a theme or category:
   - *internal homogeneity* — the extent to which the data in the theme 'dovetails' or holds together in a meaningful way;
   - *external heterogeneity* — the extent to which differences between themes are bold and clear.

   Do not be concerned if a sentence or paragraph contributes to more than one theme. Just incorporate the sentence or paragraph in all the themes to which it contributes. However, re-examine these themes to see if this commonality indicates a relationship.

6. Steps 1–5 describe what Neuman (1997) calls *open coding* — the first pass through the raw data when the researcher locates themes and assigns initial codes or labels in the first attempt to condense the mass of data categories.

7. The second reading of the raw data is for *axial coding* (Neuman 1997). While additional or new ideas may emerge during this pass, the researcher's primary task is to review and examine the initial codes assigned during the open coding step. During this second pass, the researcher asks about causes and consequences, conditions and interactions, strategies and processes, and looks for categories or concepts that cluster together.

   Read through each of the theme files and look for sub-themes within each. Again, re-read several times and see if there appear to be relationships between the sub-themes or even with another theme. Do not be surprised if one theme splits into one or more new themes or if two themes combine to make one. Your judgement is the critical element here as it is you who is trying to make sense of the wealth of raw data.

8. *Selective coding* (Neuman 1997) occurs during the third reading of the raw data. The researcher, firstly, looks selectively for evidence that illustrates or justifies themes and, secondly, makes comparisons and contrasts between sub-themes and between themes.

During this third stage, Morgan (1997) suggests that the number of participants who mentioned a particular code be noted and whether each group's discussion contained a particular code. In other words, numerical scores can indicate the strength of opinion on a particular theme — although this should not be confused with importance, which is more a judgement of the analyst. Neuman (1997) suggests that negative evidence should also be identified, in that the non-appearance of something can reveal a great deal and provide valuable insights. For example, an event not occurring, or the target population not being aware of certain issues, can have some significant meaning.

9. The researcher *writes the report*. Surprisingly, this step is also an important last step in the analytic process — simply because of the knowledge-generation process of externalisation. The researcher is forced to convert tacit knowledge to explicit knowledge and logic deficiencies often come to the surface during this period. Once again, this can be an iterative process, with the researcher often visiting the theme files and also the raw data to check, question or support various arguments to be enunciated in the report.

A RICH, MESSY AND COMPLEX PROCESS

Six important comments should be made about the analysis of qualitative data:

1. Analysis of qualitative data is a messy process. Even the nine steps of content analysis discussed above are relatively clean representations of reality.

   Firstly, analysis tends to start during the data gathering phase. It is difficult for the analyst not to see trends and categories as the data unfolds. Some authors argue that the analyst should ignore the urge to start analysing at the data-gathering stage. This is unrealistic. The best strategy is to acknowledge that this early analysing is natural and record any ideas on trends or categories. However, acknowledge that these early ideas are tentative, use them as possible sources for probing questions, but do not fall into the error of assuming that reality has been found. Maintain a healthy scepticism. Secondly, the analyst will work back and forward between the themes and sub-themes, and even between the themes and the raw data, again and again, until a level of satisfaction is felt that the reconstituted data is a true and accurate reflection of the phenomena being studied.

2. Further, Minichiello et al. (1990, p. 290) suggests that there can be at least two levels of data — the manifest content and the latent content. The *manifest content* is the data that is physically present and accountable in the evidence (for example, the words in a quote from an interviewee). The *latent content* is the symbolism underlying the physically present data — or reading between the lines, if you like. The analyst may choose to interpret the manifest or the latent content, or even both. However, Minichiello et al. emphasise that, when reading between the lines, it is essential to continually ask whether our reading is consistent with the informant's perspective.

3. The decisions are yours. Do not be overwhelmed by this. Look for the evidence that supports your choices of themes and go with it. Most people severely underestimate their ability to identify trends or themes in data — yet, the human brain is superbly designed for just this purpose.

4. Computer programs, such as NUD*IST, can be used as an aid in the content analysis. Decisions on themes (and the resultant codes), and also relationships between themes, between a theme and its sub-themes and between sub-themes, have to be decided on before such packages can be used. For an excellent discussion of the use of computers in qualitative data analysis see Richards and Richards (1998).

5. Gathering data, analysing the data and writing the report are not mutually exclusive activities. As Morgan (1997) comments, decisions about how to collect the data will depend on decisions about how to analyse and report the data. So, when planning an HRDNI, the investigator needs to project forward and consider the implications of data analysis and the make-up of the final report as well as planning the data-gathering techniques.

6. For a detailed and in-depth examination of qualitative data analysis see Miles and Huberman (1994).

It is a fact of life that the best instrument to analyse qualitative data is the human brain. This is the only instrument that possesses the required breadth of perception, complex appreciation and ability to reduce data. There is a danger of contamination. However, the principles of qualitative research are the means of mitigating this danger. Always striving for the utopian ideals of accuracy and replicability and following the conventions of content analysis are the hallmarks of good qualitative research.

THE BEGINNING OF LEARNING

The HRDNI is, in fact, the beginning of the learning experience for the individual and the organisation — and this is particularly so with the qualitative research methods of interviewing and focus groups. The interactions between the investigator and the participants are the epitome of communicative learning — two parties are striving to understand the other's values, beliefs and points of view while simultaneously trying to ensure that their own beliefs, values and points of view are understood.

In addition, both parties are involved in the knowledge-generation processes of externalisation and internalisation. The facilitator listens to the explicit knowledge of the participant and internalises the ideas and beliefs. The participant dredges information from deep within the tacit knowledge level and, in converting this knowledge to explicit knowledge, often gains new insights into the problem, opportunity or issue.

The qualitative approaches to HRDNI also uncover a variety of variables and concepts, a number of which need further investigation. In particular, confirmation is needed as to whether certain ideas validly coalesce to form a theme or if one variable does have a relationship with another variable. This confirmation and validation process is the realm of quantitative research.

GLOSSARY

accuracy — one of the twin pillars of scientific research, means that the research tools and analytic processes used are as precise and correct as possible

activity no. 1 — the activity used in the introduction of the interview to encourage the interviewee to talk

activity no. 2 — the first level in the rapport zone, where the interviewer uses interviewing skills to encourage the interviewee to provide information

content analysis — a way of analysing the qualitative data gathered during an interview or a focus group

entrance investment time — the time invested by the interviewer to bring the interviewee into the rapport zone

exit investment time — the time invested by the interviewer to bring the interview to a close

facilitator — the person who conducts and manages the focus group

facilitator team — the group of people who conduct and manage the focus group

focus group — a means of gathering data from a group of people

group composition — the make-up of the membership of the group

group dynamics — the forces that operate within a group

interpretation — drawing conclusions about the complex behaviours, messages, forces and conditions of an event

interview — a one-on-one interaction where one person is gathering information from another

interviewee — the person being interviewed

interviewer — the person conducting the interview

intimacy — a deeper level in the rapport zone where the interviewee is willing to discuss emotions

logistics — organising the resources needed to bring a focus group together

nonverbal behaviour — the gestures and body language used by the interviewer and the interviewee during the interview

painting the path — ensuring that the HRDNI report provides a sufficiently detailed description of the research process

paraphrasing — repeating back to the interviewee, in a concise form, the essential elements of the interviewee's reply

pass time — part of the introduction of the interview, used to decrease the stress levels of the interviewee

pattern of the interview — the model of an ideal interview structure that enhances the interview results

probing — the combination of questioning and paraphrasing to explore the interviewee's ideas to a deeper level

questions — the queries asked by the interviewer to control the direction of the interview

rapport zone — the time in an interview when the interviewee experiences minimum stress and is more likely to voluntarily disclose information

referential adequacy — ensuring that comments and descriptions are a sufficiently detailed and rich representation of the respondents ideas

replicability — one of the twin pillars of scientific research, means that the research should be able to be repeated with the same results

ritual — the polite greeting used to commence the interview

sampling — investigating a percentage of the whole population, and then drawing conclusions about the population from that sample

SOLER system — a way of categorising and interpreting nonverbal behaviour

structured interview — an interview where the interviewer relies on pre-planned questions that are asked in the same order

summarising — where the interviewer reviews the information provided by the interviewee

trustworthiness — the quality of a qualitative researcher who reports with integrity and honesty

unstructured interview — an interview where the interviewer relies on managing the process to control the direction of the interview

verification — cross-checking research evidence and interpretations

QUESTIONS

For review

1. List and discuss at least five ways that an interviewer ensures accuracy and replicability.

2. List and describe at least five ways of sampling.

3. Describe, and explain the benefits of, a well-patterned interview.

4. Using examples, describe how you would use probing in an interview.

5. Explain the three levels on which the interviewer must operate.

6. What is the difference between a structured and an unstructured focus group?

7. Discuss four variables that should be considered about the group composition of a focus group.

8. Describe how the task and maintenance roles can be used to help the facilitation of a focus group.

For analysis

9. What are the differences between preparing for an unstructured interview compared to preparing for a structured interview?

10. Explain how listening, questioning, probing and the use of the SOLER system interact.

11. Discuss how the appropriate use of recording, visual aids and thinking time can help control individual idiosyncratic behaviours in a focus group.

For application

12. Give an example, for each, where you would use systematic sampling, purposive sampling and snow ball sampling. Justify why you would use that type of sampling in each example.

13. Interview a friend or a relative about their favourite hobby and make an appropriate record during the interview. After the interview, firstly reflect on the experience and list all the skills that you used. Secondly, refer to the interview record and analyse the information, using content analysis.

14. Arrange for a group of university or college friends to come together as a focus group. Facilitate the focus group to achieve the objective 'List and describe at least six ways to study more efficiently', appropriately recording the information. After the focus group, firstly reflect on the experience and list all the skills that you used. Secondly, refer to the focus group record and analyse the information, using content analysis.

REFERENCES

Bales, R. (1950). *Interaction Process Analysis.* Reading Mass.: Addison-Wesley.

Benne, K. D. and Sheats, P. (1948). 'Functional roles of group members.' *Journal of Social Issues*, 4(2), 41–49.

Burns, R. B. (1994). *Introduction to Research Methods.* (2nd ed.). Melbourne, Vic: Longman Cheshire.

Cohen, L. and Manion, L. (1989). *Research Methods in Education.* (3rd ed.). London: Routledge.

Cormier, W. H. and Cormier, L. S. (1991). *Interviewing Strategies for Helpers.* (3rd ed.). Pacific Grove, Cal.: Brooks/Cole.

Delahaye, B. L. (1982). 'The structure of an interview.' *Update*, Issue 29, March. Brisbane: Australian Institute of Management.

Delahaye, B. L. and Smith, B. J. (1998). *How to be an Effective Trainer* (3rd ed.). New York: Wiley.

Dick, R. (1990). *Convergence Interviewing.* Chapel Hill, Qld.: Interchange.

Dunphy, D. C. with Dick, R. (1981). *Organizational Change by Choice.* Sydney: McGraw-Hill.

Egan, G. (1994). *The Skilled Helper: A Problem-Management Approach to Helping.* (5th ed.). Pacific Grove, Cal.: Brooks/Cole.

Eisner, E. (1991). *The Enlightened Eye: Qualitative Inquiry and the Enhancement of Educational Practice.* New York: MacMillan.

Fern, E. F. (1982). 'The use of focus groups for idea generation: The effects of group size, acquaintanceship and moderator on response quantity and quality.' *Journal of Marketing Research*, 19, 1–13.

Fontana, A. and Frey, J. H. (1998). 'Interviewing: The art and science.' In N. K. Denzin and Y. S. Lincoln (Eds), *Collecting and Interpreting Qualitative Data.* Thousand Oaks: Sage.

Forsyth, D. R. (1990). *Group Dynamics.* (2nd ed.). Pacific Grove,Cal.: Brooks/Cole.

Fowler, F. J. and Mangione, T. W. (1990). *Standardized Survey Interviewing: Minimising Interviewer-related Error.* Newbury Park: Sage.

Gubar, E. G. (1978). *Toward a Methodology of Naturalistic Inquiry in Educational Evaluation.* CSE monograph series in evaluation, no. 8. Los Angles: Centre for the Study of Evaluation, University of California.

Huberman, A. M. and Miles, M. B. (1998). 'Data management and analysis methods.' In N. K. Denzin and Y. S. Lincoln (Eds), *Collecting and Interpreting Qualitative Materials.* Thousand Oaks: Sage.

Kruger, R. A. (1994). *Focus Groups: A Practical Guide for Applied Research.* (2nd ed.). Thousand Oaks: Sage.

Miles, M. B. and Huberman, A. M. (1994). *Qualitative Data Analysis: A Source Book of New Methods.* (2nd ed.). Thousand Oaks: Sage

Minichiello, V., Aroni, R., Timewell, E. and Alexander, L. (1990). *In-Depth Interviewing: Researching People.* Melbourne: Longman Cheshire.

Morgan, D. L. (1997). *Focus Groups as Qualitative Research.* (2nd ed.). Thousand Oaks: Sage.

Napier, R. W. and Gershenfeld, M. K. (1993). *Groups: Theory and Experience.* Boston: Houghton Mifflin.

Neuman, W. L. (1997). *Social Research Methods: Qualitative and Quantitative Approaches.* (3rd ed.). Boston: Allyn and Bacon.

Patton, M. Q. (1990). *Qualitative Evaluation and Research Methods.* Newbury Park: Sage.

Richards, T. J. and Richards, L. (1998). 'Using computers in qualitative research.' In N. K. Denzin and Y. S. Lincoln (Eds), *Collecting and Interpreting Qualitative Materials.* Thousand Oaks: Sage.

Samuelowicz, K. and Blain, J. D. (1992). 'Conceptions of teaching held by academic teachers.' *Higher Education*, 24, 93–111.

Schein, E. H. (1969) *Process Management.* Reading Mass.: Addison-Wesley.

Seidman, I. E. (1991). *Interviewing as Qualitative Research.* New York: Teacher's College Press.

Sekaran, U. (1992). *Research Methods for Business: A Skill-building Approach.* New York: Wiley.

Tregoe, B. J. (1983). 'Questioning: The key to effective problem solving and decision making.' In B. Taylor and G. Lippitt (Eds), *Management Development and Training Handbook.* (2nd ed.). London: McGraw-Hill.

Zima, J. P. (1991). *Interviewing: Key to Effective Management.* New York: MacMillan.

The external consultant

Tony Nairb offered a management development service through his small business, Workplace Consulting. He had been asked by a large manufacturing company to conduct an initial needs investigation to 'identify the issues in improving front-line supervisor development'. The company had suggested that a series of focus groups would best suit their needs and that they expected a more detailed human resource development needs investigation to be conducted at a later stage.

Tony decided that he would base his focus groups on samples from the population. He thought that, first, he would have four focus groups — one from management, one from upper supervisors, one from front-line supervisors and one from production staff. Each focus group would have between eight and ten participants. Within the managers' focus group, he decided that he would need at least one representative from each of the functional areas — marketing, finance, engineering and supply. For the other focus groups, he thought that he would ask the human resource department to identify every tenth person from the payroll within each group.

Tony planned to conduct an unstructured focus group. He jotted down some ideas for the introduction:

1. Introduce self.

2. Say 'Good. You have all passed the first test — you have all found the room'.

3. Explain the reason for the focus groups. Have general manager or production manager say a few words?

4. Expect the focus group to take about 1 hour. Coffee/tea available at the back.

5. Advise that the session will start with a question. [*Note*: Make an overhead with 'What issues should we consider when developing front-line supervisors?'] Will then give them a few minutes to think about the question. Will then put their ideas on the white board.

6. Ask if any questions.

He thought that would set the session up well and realised that in the rest of the session he would have to manage the process. Tony was confident of his questioning and probing skills but was aware that he often forgot to summarise. He thought that he would write 'SUMMARISE' in large capitals at the end of his introduction notes to remind himself.

Discussion questions

1. What is your opinion of Tony's preparation? What has he done well? What else should he have done?

2. If you were to conduct these focus groups with Tony, how would you prepare yourself for the sessions?

The traineeship

The following is an excerpt from an interview (**Er** = the interviewer; **Ee** = person being interviewed):

[The introduction has been completed.]

Er: OK, if you have no questions we will get into it. As I said, we have about a half hour so take your time with the answers. Now, as part of your traineeship you have just completed 3 weeks on the front desk. Would you tell me about some of your good experiences?

Ee: Well, it was a bit nerve-racking at first. I didn't expect the counter to be so wide and it was made of this really expensive polished wood. I was afraid to even lean on it. Then the customers come up and you can only see their heads and shoulders. I kept wondering what they were wearing — you know, from the waist down. And you seemed to be so far away from them.

Er: Yes, yes, I guess it was a bit new. But I am really interested in the good experiences that you had.

Ee: Oh. Um, yes, well, the other people were nice to me. They didn't seem to mind explaining the same thing to me several times. That was another thing. You just did not know where all the records were, you know the stationery and things. And I was just dreading the computer. I could see the screen and it looked so complicated. Oh, dear.

Er: OK, it seems like the initial few hours were a bit anxious for you. The front counters do seem to be rather imposing, don't they? It sounds like you were a bit churned up inside and nervous. That's understandable, it was your first time.

Ee: Yes, I was really wondering if I had made the right choice for a career. I do like helping people, but all I could feel was that I wanted to hide behind the counter. Did you feel like that the first time? [Er nods and gives an understanding smile.] So, you think I can be a success at this?

Er: Yes, I think everybody is overwhelmed at first. I am sure you will do fine.

Ee: Good. I did enjoy it, though. You see people come in, looking tired. They just want a place to rest after travelling so far, some of them. A bit of a kind word, have all the forms so they can fill out everything quickly and hand them over to the concierge. You feel like you have done something good.

Er: So, giving a kind word, doing all the paperwork efficiently, making sure they get up to their room promptly. You enjoyed doing that.

Ee: Yes, of course others like to talk, tell you where they have come from, what they are going to do, sometimes about their families. It is very interesting. Of course, you cannot let it go on too long, there is a lot of other stuff to do.

Er: I can see you like to interact with the customers, hear about their travels. You also said that there was a lot of other stuff to do. Would you tell me more about that?

Ee: Yes, well, there are the phone calls from the rooms. It might be a complaint, or they need something, or they want to know about the local theatres or restaurants. Actually, I had one couple, their electric jug was faulty so we had replaced it. They came back from being out, put the new jug on to make a cup of coffee and it did not work either. He rang down. Well, he was not really angry but you could tell he was fed up. I said that I would have another jug sent up right away and then I had a thought. I told him we would send up two complimentary cups of coffee. He sounded so relieved. But when I hung up, I suddenly thought, oh no, how do I arrange for the coffee and can we make it complimentary? I went to Kylie, you know the night supervisor, and she said I had done the right thing, she sounded really pleased. She took me around to food services and showed me how to arrange it. Gee, that felt good.

Er: Well, you handled that situation well. See, you are doing fine. So, just to summarise, you greet the new customers when they come in and also receive telephone calls from the rooms. Your good experiences are meeting the new customers and making them feel welcome and fixing the coffee problem for one of the customers. OK, you said earlier that you did not know where the records were and you were concerned about the computer. What other areas did you find daunting or a problem?

[and the interview continues]

Discussion questions

1. Identify the good interviewing techniques used.

2. What would you have done differently? Justify your answer.

3. Using content analysis, analyse the information gathered so far.

4. What areas of information need further data gathering?

Questionnaires

CHAPTER OBJECTIVES

At the end of this chapter you should be able to:

1. explain why it is important for HR developers to know how to design questionnaires and analyse quantitative data

2. identify the types of information included in a questionnaire

3. identify and describe the types of data that are gathered by a questionnaire

4. discuss the six issues to consider when designing a questionnaire

5. describe the concepts of face validity, content validity, construct validity, internal reliability and temporal reliability

6. discuss how a pilot study can be used to prove the structure of a questionnaire

7. describe how data is collected using a questionnaire

8. describe how quantitative data can be analysed.

The chapter begins by emphasising two important points. Firstly, designing questionnaires is hard work and is based on a number of strict requirements. Secondly, contrary to the opinion of some academics and practitioners, HR developers do need a fundamental and professional knowledge of the processes used in designing questionnaires and in analysing quantitative data.

A questionnaire has five different parts — the **instruction section** to tell the respondents how to complete the questionnaire; a **classification section** to categorise the respondents; a section that seeks **factual data**; a section that seeks **opinions**; and a numbered scale for each opinion item for the respondents to record the strength of their opinion. Once the information has been gathered by the questionnaire it is called data. There are four types of data — **nominal data** simply assigns a number to each person or object (for example, numbers on a football jersey); **ordinal data** occurs where the number assigned indicates that one object has a higher value than another (for example, when rating a preference for a list of objects); **interval data** not only indicates that one object has a higher value than another but that the interval between the judgements is also equal; and **ratio data**, which is similar to interval data but the measurement starts from zero.

When designing a questionnaire, six issues need to be considered. The instructions to respondents on how to complete the questionnaire need careful thought. The classification section allows the researcher to demonstrate that the sample collected is a reasonable representation of the population being surveyed and also provides the opportunity to analyse different groups. When designing the factual data items, the researcher will need to decide whether exact figures are needed or whether categories (for example, age groupings rather than everyone reporting their exact age) would be acceptable. A lot of careful preparation and thought needs to go into the design of the opinion items. Being able to prove content validity is an important issue. Further, the designer will need to make decisions on theoretical scales, the wording of items and the number of items to be included in the questionnaire. For each opinion item a **response scale** is needed and there are several issues to be considered, although most HR developers choose the Likert scale method. Finally, the designer will have to make a decision on the **sequencing** of the opinion items, as positioning of an item within the questionnaire may influence the respondent's reaction.

Once the questionnaire is designed it should be pre-tested. There are three types of pre-testing. A small sample of possible respondents can be asked to look at the questionnaire and advise if any items are inappropriately formulated. This provides **face validity** for the questionnaire. **Content validity** is proven by demonstrating that the items are a reasonable representation of the concept they are supposed to measure by ensuring that the pedigree of each item is reported. The pedigree can be shown by demonstrating the source of each item — either from previous qualitative research or from the literature. Another way of demonstrating content validity is to seek the opinion of the questionnaire from a panel of experts. In a **pilot study**, the questionnaire is completed by a sample from the intended population. The resultant data are then examined, initially by examining the frequencies. Specifically, the mean, standard deviation and skewness, at least, are scrutinised to see if each item has had a reasonable response from the sample. In addition, the opinion items are subjected to a factor analysis to examine the **construct validity** of the questionnaire — that is, that the items making up each of the theoretical constructs did indeed cluster together in the expected groupings. Finally, the researcher will examine the reliability of each theoretical construct. Internal reliability indicates how well the items in each theoretical scale cluster together and a statistic called Cronbach's alpha is used to make this judgement. Temporal reliability indicates whether the items are consistent over time (that is, if a respondent completed the questionnaire this week, would he or she complete it the same way next week or next month or some other time in the future?). A statistical technique called correlational analysis is used to make this judgement.

When using a questionnaire to gather data, the HR developer as a researcher can administer the questionnaire personally or by mailing it out. Various techniques are suggested to ensure a large response from the entire sample with either of these methods. When analysing the data, the researcher will use non-parametric statistics (such as frequencies, cross-tabs and chi-squared) with nominal and ordinal data and parametric statistics (such as the t-test, correlation analysis and factor analysis) with interval and ratio data. It is strongly suggested that, if the HR developer does not have the requisite level of knowledge, then a statistician be used to conduct these techniques.

WHY ARE QUESTIONNAIRES IMPORTANT?

A questionnaire? Yes, that sounds easy — jot down a few ideas, type them up and send the survey out to everyone. What could be more simple? Actually, designing organisational survey questionnaires properly is hard work and is based on a number of strict requirements.

However, some practitioners and academics in HRD often ask, 'Do we really need to know how to construct and use questionnaires properly?' The answer is a resounding 'Yes!' Firstly, HRDNI is a research process and, as professionals, HR developers must have a working knowledge of the common research processes, of which the use of questionnaires is one. Secondly, in a business environment where litigation is becoming more common, a HR developer who uses a questionnaire without a reasonably professional knowledge of questionnaire design and analysis is running a grave risk. Thirdly, if a decision is made to use a limited questionnaire — perhaps without a pilot study or perhaps only using a frequency analysis of single items — then the HR developer must be aware of the weaknesses of the resultant data from that limited questionnaire. These weaknesses mean that less confidence can be placed on the findings and that caution must be exercised when making decisions based on the findings. So, knowing the basics of questionnaire design and the analysis of quantitative data is essential for the professional HR developer. While the

HR developer may not necessarily be able to carry out some of the procedures — for example, conducting the necessary statistical routines — they do need a level of knowledge that allows them to understand what is happening and, perhaps more importantly, to know when to call in experts to provide assistance.

A well-designed questionnaire will provide accurate and usable data that will allow you to write confidently the HRDNI report — which, remember, you are going to sign. Unlike the interview and the focus group, with questionnaires the investigator is not always present to make any adjustments or answer any queries from the respondents. Once a questionnaire is mailed out, it is at the mercy of the respondents — whether they decide to complete it; whether they interpret the questions as intended; and whether they answer the questions honestly. Designing the question-naire is about ensuring that these barriers are overcome — before the questionnaire is sent out.

A questionnaire allows the HRDNI to progress from gathering the ideas and sug-gestions of a few people in the qualitative stage to confirming whether the ideas and suggestions are widely held throughout the whole organisation.

QUANTITATIVE RESEARCH

Questionnaires come under the heading of quantitative research in that the data they uncover can be represented as numbers. HRDNI questionnaires are different from marketing surveys and psychometric questionnaires. Marketing surveys are often aimed at measuring the reactions of customers and are not always noted for their rigour of design. On the other hand, psychometric questionnaires are designed to measure very deep and complex human characteristics. Their detailed and lengthy construction is, often, not cost effective for HRDNI questionnaires. So, HRDNI ques-tionnaires fall somewhere between marketing surveys and psychometric tests. Also, it can be noted here that the acronym 'HRDNI' is often dropped for convenience and this convention will be followed in the remainder of this chapter.

THE TYPE OF INFORMATION

Figure 8.1 shows some sample items from a typical questionnaire called the Learning Orientation Assessment. If you examine the sample, you will see that it includes five different parts of a questionnaire.

Instructions provide information to the respondent on how to complete the ques-tionnaire. These instructions should be short but complete; that is, they should give the respondent sufficient direction without including unnecessary words. The instructions should also be worded in a manner that is readily understood by the target audience. This may mean that the wording may change slightly when the questionnaire is used for different clients.

In figure 8.1, the *classification* section is represented by items 9 and 10 which ask for details on the department and gender. These items solicit information that will be used by the researcher to classify the respondents. Classification items are often pos-itioned at the end of a questionnaire, as sometimes respondents prefer not to answer these items. If the classification items are at the beginning, the respondent will often not proceed any further.

INSTRUCTIONS: For each statement, circle the number on the response scale which best indicates your belief about the statement. The number represents a response scale of 'almost always' to 'almost never'.

	Almost always	Often	Occasionally	Seldom	Almost never
1. The trainer should be in control of the learning situation.	1	2	3	4	5
2. I should evaluate my own learning.	1	2	3	4	5
3. Competition between trainees is important.	1	2	3	4	5
4. The trainer should encourage me to design my own learning agenda.	1	2	3	4	5
5. The trainer should stay within the workshop objectives.	1	2	3	4	5
6. The trainer should allow for individual differences among trainees.	1	2	3	4	5

Training courses

7. How many training courses have you attended in the last year? _____
8. How many days of in-class training have you attended this year? _____

The following information will help us analyse the survey. Please tick one box in each category.

9. The department I work in is: ❑ Advertising
❑ Customer Services
❑ Production

10. Gender: ❑ Female
❑ Male

FIGURE 8.1
The Learning Orientation Assessment (sample only)

Items 7 and 8, asking for information on the number of courses attended and number of days of training, is seeking *factual data*. However, recognise that the accuracy of the respondent's information is heavily dependent on the respondent's memory. If available, the investigator may be better served by gleaning this information from the organisational records. Items seeking factual data can be placed immediately after the instructions or nearer the end (as in figure 8.1). Again, the researcher may place factual items nearer the end, if it is believed that providing the information may demotivate the respondent.

The section with six questions (items 1 to 6), in the form of a sentence with an attendant numerical scale, is seeking the *opinions* of the respondents. The sentence is called the *question item* (or 'item' for short) and the numbered scale is called the *response set* or *response scale*. We have a more in-depth discussion of these two features later in the chapter.

The sections discussed — factual information and opinions — highlight an important differentiation in the information sought by questionnaires. Information can be either fact or opinion. *It is important not to assume opinion is fact,* so make sure that you separate fact from opinion in whatever research you are doing.

THE TYPE OF DATA

Once information has been gathered by a questionnaire, it is called *data*. This collected data is then classified as belonging to one of four types: nominal, ordinal, interval or ratio data.

Nominal data is the most basic form of data in that the numbers assigned to the objects being measured merely differentiate them. For example, the numbers on the jerseys of a football team only separate one player from another for identification purposes. Having the number 1 on your back does not signify you are the best on your team. At the most, the number may indicate the position you play on the field and, with today's interchange rules, the number may not even provide that additional information.

In our example in figure 8.1, the factual data (on the training courses) and the classification data (on the department and gender) are nominal data. For example, working in an advertising department does not have a greater value than working in a production department — despite what the people in advertising think! Similarly, it does not matter whether a 1 is assigned to 'female' and a 2 to 'male' or vice versa — the numbers merely signify that each category is different.

Ordinal data is the next level up. The numbers assigned indicate that one object has a higher value than another object, based on some variable. So if we grade twenty people in a class from 1 to 20 based on the marks they achieved in an examination, then the person with the '1' has higher marks than the person with '2', who has higher marks than the person with '3' and so on.

Interval data has the distinguishing feature that, not only does one object have a higher value than another, but the interval between the various objects so measured is equal. If we examined peoples' ages in terms of years only, then the resultant data would be classified as interval data — as we would have people categorised as being 20 years old, 21 years old, 22 years old and so on. Each of the years would signify a 1-year difference between ages. However, in reality, the respondents will not be exactly 20 or 21 or 22. They may be 20 years 2 months and 3 days, 21 years 7 months and 28 days or 22 years 11 months and 16 days. So, in actual fact, there are very few examples of interval data in the natural world.

Ratio data is similar to interval data with the additional qualities that the measurement starts from zero and that any single measurement is a ratio of any other single measurement. Height is a classic example of ratio data. Height starts from zero and can continue to infinity. In addition, someone who is 2 metres tall is twice as high as someone who is 1 metre tall and is four times taller than someone who is 50 centimetres tall and so on.

These levels of data — nominal, ordinal, interval and ratio — are important considerations when the time comes to analyse the data. So the HRDNI investigator needs to be aware of the type of data that is appropriate to a given situation. There are at least two issues that the investigator needs to bear in mind:

1. Factual information is usually nominal or ordinal data. As such, any statistical analysis is confined to what are called **non-parametric tests**, such as the chi-squared test. Don't worry too much about the names of the tests at this stage. We discuss them later in the chapter.

2. The opinion information sought in the Learning Orientation Assessment questionnaire in figure 8.1 is, strictly speaking, ordinal data. Looking at the example, we cannot absolutely guarantee that the interval between 1 and 2 on the response scales is exactly the same as the interval between 3 and 4. However, in the social sciences, it is conventional to treat such data as interval data as the amount of error that can accrue is minimal (Bryman and Cramer 1990; Emory and Cooper 1991). This stance allows the investigator to use the more powerful **parametric** (sometimes called multivariate) **statistics** techniques such as correlation, factor analysis and regression analysis.

Now let us look in more detail at designing a questionnaire.

DESIGNING THE QUESTIONNAIRE

There are six issues to consider when designing a questionnaire — designing instructions, incorporating classification questions, incorporating factual items, constructing opinion items, constructing response sets, and sequencing.

INSTRUCTIONS

Most questionnaires are self-administered. This means that the questionnaires are posted to the respondents, either through the internal mail system of the organisation or via the government postal service.

The instructions for the self-administered questionnaires need careful thought. The instructions are usually conveyed by a covering letter or are incorporated in the questionnaire itself, usually on the front page. Writers such as Dillman (1978) and Sekaran (1992) suggest that the instructions should:

1. be clear and concise
2. be in a language understood by the target population
3. tell the respondent the reason for the questionnaire
4. motivate the respondent to complete the questionnaire by explaining the benefits from the respondents' perspective
5. include a reassurance that the data will be used only for the purposes of the HRDNI
6. include a telephone number or e-mail address, so that the respondent can have any queries answered.

CLASSIFICATION ITEMS

Classification items elicit basic information that can describe the population being surveyed — for example, gender, age and profession — and are included for two reasons. Firstly, it is essential that the researcher can show that the survey sample was a reasonable portrayal of the target population. For example, quite often it is important to show that there was an equal, or at least reasonable, representation of females and males. Other important characteristics of the target population, depending on the HRDNI objectives, should also be included.

The second reason for the inclusion of classification items is that the research objective may demand that various groups be compared. So, the investigator may wish to see if a particular need is more prevalent in supervisors than in middle managers. In this case, the questionnaire designer will include an item, with appropriate response squares (or other space in which to respond), that covers a categorisation including supervisors and managers. It is worth noting that other types within the categorisation (for example, senior management, operators or sales representatives) may also be gathered. In addition, if the designer is uncertain whether other alternatives are present in the population, the use of a final 'Other' is often included to ensure that there is a response category for every respondent.

FACTUAL ITEMS

Frequently, the investigator will want factual data for background information (for example, how much training are the staff receiving?) or to provide an objective measure of the problem or issue under research. To gather this information, the factual items will be included in the questionnaire.

The investigator will need to decide whether exact figures are required or if categories of data will suffice. So, with items 7 and 8 in the sample questionnaire in figure 8.1, the investigator has asked for exact figures. Now, most respondents will have no trouble in indicating how many training courses they have attended — most people in organisations attend only about three or four each year. However, the respondents may have difficulty in remembering how many hours of in-class training they attended (item 8). In this case, the respondents may need to make the additional effort to look at their records, or they may simply respond with their best guess, or they may put the questionnaire aside to complete later and then forget it.

So, in constructing factual items, the investigator has to assess the benefits of gathering exact data, as certain costs will be present (for example, a lower return rate of questionnaires; trying to decide whether the response given is factual or only a best guess). If exact factual data was not needed by the research objective of the HRDNI, then a better design for item 8 may have been categories of responses (for example, boxes with the numbers '0–2 hours', '3–5 hours', '6–10 hours', 'More than 10 hours'). However, in taking this category option, the investigator will pay the price later when analysing the data — less robust statistical processes can be used, thereby decreasing the confidence slightly in the final recommendations. As usual, costs must be paid somewhere and the investigator must construct the questionnaire that best suits the HRDNI objective.

OPINION ITEMS

If needing to go beyond factual data, the HR developer as the investigator will be researching opinions on an issue or on multiple issues. In questionnaire design, issues are usually called 'concepts' or 'themes'. Usually, the opinion concept or concepts being examined are reasonably complex, so often one question item for each concept will not suffice. The investigator will need to formulate several question items that will adequately explore each concept being investigated.

When designing the opinion items in the questionnaire, there are several conventions that the researcher should keep in mind — among them content validity, theoretical scales and theoretical constructs, the wording of the items and the number of items in the questionnaire.

Content validity

A questionnaire is designed to achieve a specific research objective. It is from this research objective that the issues to be investigated in the questionnaire are derived. In turn, each issue (at this stage of the questionnaire, often termed a 'concept') is explored by a number of question items. This attribute is called *content validity*.

This means that the HRDNI investigator must be able to show where each item originated — a process that could be called *demonstrating the pedigree* of each item. This is a two-step process — firstly identifying the concepts that will explore fully the research objective and, secondly, identifying the items that will explore each of the concepts. There are three main ways that this two-step process is achieved:

1. *From qualitative data.* The qualitative data (the interviews, focus groups, observations and organisational records) gathered earlier in the HRDNI are all sources of potential concepts and their related items for the questionnaire. The investigator examines all the qualitative data and identifies the main concepts raised. The qualitative data is then re-examined to identify the comments and ideas which make up and describe each concept.

    For example, the HRDNI may be investigating the research objective 'The preferred supervisory practices of managers' in a particular organisation. Earlier qualitative investigations in the HRDNI (for example, interviews and focus groups) may have found that the staff consider five practices are important:

    • Has good verbal communication
    • Provides adequate and appropriate resources
    • Has good delegation skills
    • Has high concern for the development of staff
    • Acts responsibly in conflict situations.

    Each of these preferred practices can become a concept to be explored further in a questionnaire. In examining the qualitative data from the earlier investigations, the investigator can then go further and identify what the interviewees and groups meant by each of these concepts. So, for example, when discussing 'good verbal communication' the interviewees and focus group members may have commented on such behaviours as:

    • Has positive nonverbal behaviour
    • Asks clear questions
    • Listens when the other person is speaking
    • Asks questions about the other person's concerns.

These four preferred behaviours, then, can become the basis of four items in the questionnaire — providing the investigator believes that the four items will adequately cover the issue of 'good verbal communication'. Similarly, each of the other four issues will also be given a number of items so that respondents can provide their opinions on their preferred importance. In this way a number of items can be designed to create a questionnaire that provides the investigator with data on the opinion of staff throughout the organisation.

2. *From the literature.* The research objective may ask the investigator to conduct an HRDNI on a more theoretical subject — for example, 'The preference for self-directed learning in the organisation'. The investigator would then examine all the appropriate textbooks, journal articles and other writings on the topic and identify the main concepts involved. In the example, the investigator may decide that the main concepts are andragogy and pedagogy. The literature would then be examined for ideas and comments that represent andragogy and pedagogy. If you look at the Learning Orientation Assessment questionnaire in figure 8.1, you will see that each odd numbered item (1, 3 and 5) is a specific statement about pedagogy while each even numbered item (2, 4 and 6) is representative of andragogy. The investigator would need to justify the pedigree of each item and this explanation is usually contained in an appendix in the HRDNI report. A closer look 8.1 is an example of an explanation of the content validity of item 2 of the sample questionnaire in figure 8.1. Each item is justified in a similar fashion until each concept or theme is explored to the investigator's satisfaction.

3. *A combination.* Quite often, the investigator will need to refer to both the previous qualitative data gathered and also relevant literature. Such a combination can result in a very robust questionnaire.

For a more in-depth discussion of content validity see Oppenheim (1992).

Theoretical scales and theoretical constructs

So far, we have loosely referred to several items forming a concept or theme or issue. Strictly speaking, when several items are constructed to survey a particular concept, the grouping of items is called a **theoretical scale** and each of these theoretical scales is said to measure a **theoretical construct**. So, items 1, 3, and 5 in the Learning Orientation Assessment questionnaire form a theoretical scale and this scale is being used by the researcher to measure the theoretical construct called 'pedagogy'. Researchers are encouraged to use such multiple item scales as the concept under investigation is more fully represented and the resultant measurement is more reliable (see, for example, the discussions in Converse and Presser 1986 and McIver and Carmines 1981).

Wording of the items

There are a number of accepted conventions to consider when formulating the items and choosing the wording (see, for example, Babbie 1990; Kidder and Judd 1986; Jolliffe 1986; Jones and Bearley 1995; Oppenheim 1992; Triandis 1971).

1. Use language that is closely related to the respondents' personal experience and is suitable for the population being targeted.

2. Avoid leading and ambiguous questions and complex phrasing.

3. Have only one basic idea for each item.
4. Avoid negative words (for example, 'not') and formulations. This recommendation is particularly relevant with a response scale with poles such as 'agree' and 'disagree'. The problem is that, in order to disagree with a negative statement, the respondent must engage in a double negative.
5. The key idea in the item should come last.
6. Items should simplify the respondent's task and not call for a lot of effort or rely on memory or working something out.
7. The item should be within the respondent's ability to answer. For example, it is of little use to ask the respondent what others think or feel.

Overall, then, the designer attempts to keep the question items short, simple and direct so that the respondent has a clear idea of the question being asked but is not bored with superfluous or ambiguous wording.

Number of items

The question then arises: 'How many opinion items should there be in a questionnaire?' Given a preference, most investigators would opt for a rather lengthy questionnaire so that all theoretical constructs are explored fully. The problem with a lengthy questionnaire, of course, is that the respondents become quickly discouraged.

There is no strict rule on the total number of items that a questionnaire should contain and the motivation of the respondents and their interest in the research project are considerable influences. However, as a general rule, thirty to fifty items seem to be handled comfortably by most respondents. The next question is: 'How may opinion items should be used to measure a theoretical construct?' Of course, the more items used, the more confident the investigator becomes that the construct is well measured. However, the 'fifty item' rule can be quickly reached. If there are five constructs to be investigated, then each theoretical scale could consist of ten items, at a maximum; if there are ten constructs then each theoretical scale could consist of between three and five items. Three items are generally considered to be the least number of items recommended for a theoretical scale (see discussion in Spector 1992). However, bear in mind that the most important first step is to 'ensure that the water front has been covered' (Robinson, Athanasiou and Head 1969, p. 4) — that is, make sure that the theoretical scale does adequately measure the construct.

Three other issues

In addition to content validity and decisions on the number and formulation of items, there are three other issues that the questionnaire designer should bear in mind:

1. *Differentiation.* Generally, the designer should avoid statements that are likely to be endorsed by almost everyone or no one. Usually, the investigator is interested in the spread of opinion and/or differences of opinion between nominated groups. Such differences cannot be measured if everyone chooses one of the two poles of the measurement scale. However, if the designer wishes to see if everyone does indeed agree (or disagree) with a particular statement, then such an item is sometimes included.

2. *Response bias.* A response bias occurs in two ways. Firstly, it occurs when the respondent answers an item in a socially desirable way instead of recording an honest, personal belief. So, when asked 'Should a learner take self-responsibility?' the respondent answers in the negative in the belief that this is the response that the organisation values at this point in time, rather than answering in the positive, which is the respondent's real belief. The second type of response bias is a general tendency towards assent or dissent — called 'acquiescence'. The respondents circle all the positive or all the negative options, often indicating laziness or lack of motivation on the part of the respondent.

   These two issues are most probably impossible to overcome completely. Formulating some items that reverse the meaning of the idea may be of some assistance. So, instead of an item 'I learnt a great deal in this course', an opposite option may be 'I learnt very little in this course'. However, be very careful of this type of rewording as it can cause confusion in the mind of the respondent. It would be best to 'pilot' the two options first to see if the rewording has made the questionnaire weaker.

3. *Layout.* Of particular importance when the questionnaire is to be self-administered, the physical presentation of the questionnaire can affect both the initial willingness of the respondent to answer the questionnaire and the motivation of the respondent to continue. Babbie (1990) strongly recommends that 'white space' be maximised. This imparts an uncluttered look and tends to provide a more relaxed atmosphere. Jones and Bearley (1995) believe that the questionnaire should have a distinctly professional look — uncluttered, printed well and incorporating the company's colours and logo.

RESPONSE SETS

Response sets are the scales that allow the respondent to record a preference in an opinion item. They measure the intensity, hardness or potency of a variable (Neuman 1997). There are a variety of types of response scales available to the researcher — Thurstone differential scale, semantic differential, Guttman scaling to name a few. The most common and widely used response scale is the Likert scale. The response scales in figure 8.1 are Likert scales.

Likert scales have several characteristics:

1. The scale is numbered and each number has an accompanying descriptive anchor.
2. The scale is odd numbered — for example, 3, 5, 7 or 11.
3. The ends of the scale are opposite poles — for example, strongly agree versus strongly disagree.
4. The middle value — the 3 in a 5-point scale — is either neutral ('neither one nor the other') or on the positive side at a 'passing' level ('average ' on a five-point scale of 'excellent', 'good', 'average', 'fair', 'poor'.

Likert scales are most easily constructed and are quite robust. In addition, it is possible to total the responses to individual items to achieve a measurement for a theoretical scale. In the sample in figure 8.1, which has three items measuring andragogy and three items measuring pedagogy, each theoretical scale can measure between 3 and 15. Such a breadth of measurement allows a wide variety of possible responses with high potential to differentiate between individuals and also groups of respondents.

Another type of response scale is the one which asks the respondent to provide 'factual' opinion. In construction, it is similar to the Likert scale. For example, the question 'How many times a week do you encounter abusive customers?' may have a response scale of 'none', 'one', 'two', three', 'four or more'. However, recognise that this type of scale measures opinion as it relies on the respondents' view of at least two 'facts'. Firstly, the concept 'abusive customer' may vary between respondents, as what may be abusive to one person may be just a robust enquiry to another. Secondly, while the response scale appears precise, it relies heavily on the respondents' memories. Of course, other data-gathering methods may have given facts — observation or record keeping, for example. However, these types of data gathering would have been a deal more expensive than the one item on the questionnaire. If the one item on the questionnaire achieved the research objective (which may have been more interested in the staff's perception of the extent of customer abuse, rather than an exact measurement), then that option is perfectly acceptable. Keep firmly in mind, though, that the data gathered is really opinion and not fact.

SEQUENCING

There are two considerations when making decisions on sequencing the items in a questionnaire. The first is deciding whether the classification and factual items come before the opinion items. Several writers (Babbie 1990; Jones and Bearley 1995; and Oppenheim 1992) recommend that the classification and factual items come *after* the opinion items. The sensitivity of some classification items (for example, on personal salary and wages) and their sometimes dull and routine nature may affect the respondent's motivation, if asked early in the questionnaire. By placing these items last, the respondent has completed the opinion items so at least this data has been gathered. To help with the response rate, some of the more sensitive classification data can be made voluntary.

The second sequencing issue is the order in which the opinion items should be displayed — in particular, whether to randomise the item order or group items measuring specific theoretical constructs together. The theoretical concern is that a previous item can affect the way the respondent answers a following item. Generally, the advice of various writers (Babbie 1990; Kidder and Judd 1986; Neuman 1997) is to group items into appropriate, understandable and similar topic areas. It is considered that a wholly randomised item order creates a high risk of confusing the respondents. With items grouped into the same topic areas, the respondents can concentrate on answering fully one concept at a time. However, as with any general rule, random or some other order can be used effectively. The sample questionnaire in figure 8.1 uses alternate items — odd numbers measuring pedagogy and even number measuring andragogy. As the items are all measuring a learning orientation, the respondents are unlikely to find this sequencing disconcerting.

PRE-TESTING

Once designed and before using the questionnaire to gather data on which to make decisions or recommendations, the prudent investigator will conduct pre-tests. There are several types of pre-tests that can be carried out — among the most important are face validity, content validity and a pilot study.

FACE VALIDITY

Face validity addresses the concern as to whether the questionnaire does *appear* to measure the concepts being investigated (Burns 1994). Of particular interest is whether the respondents will find the wording of the items clear and understandable. Accordingly, the investigator should arrange for a small sample of the respondents to answer the questionnaire and then interview them to see if any items caused confusion.

CONTENT VALIDITY

Content validity is the representativeness or sampling adequacy of the questionnaire regarding the content or the theoretical constructs to be measured (Burns 1994). We have already encountered this concept when discussing the construction of the questionnaire items. The investigator reports the origins or pedigree of each of the items (see 'a closer look 8.1').

a closer look   8.1

Justification of item 2

2. I should evaluate my own learning
Knowles (1980, 1990) has frequently pointed out that the andragogical learners have a self-concept of being responsible for their own learning.

Knowles emphasises the need for the adult learner to self-rate at the beginning and at the end of a learning episode (see, for example, Knowles 1983, p. 7). Further, Rogers (1983) is quite insistent that self-evaluation is

basic while evaluation by others is secondary. Full references, for these articles and texts are provided in the References section, page 226.

A further test of content validity is to send the questionnaire to a group of experts who examine each item and make a judgement on whether each item does measure the theoretical construct nominated. Other names for this process are panel or expert judgement validity.

PILOT STUDY

If possible, a questionnaire should be piloted with a reasonable sample of respondents who come from the target population or who are closely similar to the target population. Unfortunately, in an HRDNI, a pilot study of a questionnaire is sometimes not possible because of the finite number of people in the target population. As we shall see, some of the analytic procedures in a pilot study demand quite a large number of respondents. If a significant number of respondents are 'used up' in the pilot study then the investigator has very few people left from whom to gather data. As is often the case in the messy world of field research (research carried out in the real world as opposed to that conducted in experimental laboratories), the investigator needs to acknowledge two considerations — the requirements of an ideal research design and the realities of what the field situation will allow. Let us look at the requirements of an ideal research design for a pilot study.

Ideal research design

The first consideration is the number of respondents needed for a pilot study. If the questionnaire contains several opinion items which make up one or more theoretical scales (designed to measure one or more theoretical constructs) then a statistical procedure called *factor analysis* will be needed. To conduct a factor analysis, an investigator needs a ratio of respondents to items of between 4:1 to 10:1. For example, if the questionnaire has 20 opinion items (do not count the factual and classification items) then the ideal number of respondents will be between 80 and 200 — quite a large number to find! However, if the questionnaire only contains factual items, then a pilot study of 30 respondents is common. Of course, opinion items, particularly those which form a theoretical scale, provide such rich data most HRDNI do incorporate them.

Reality — less than ideal

So, what does the investigator do if there are insufficient numbers in the target population to carry out a pilot study as well as an investigation? Well, a less than perfect design will have to be used. The investigator may use less people in the pilot study — for example, twenty instead of eighty — and accept that the results will only be somewhat indicative. As another alternative, the investigator may be able to find a population that has most of the important characteristics of the target population — for example, general office staff if sales personnel are the target population. The characteristic that these two populations have in common is that neither are production staff and, providing this is the only important variable that could contaminate the result, the general office staff will provide a reasonable substitute. A final alternative is not to do a pilot study and to analyse the robustness of the questionnaire on the raw data gathered from the actual study itself. Recognise, however, that the further away from the ideal pilot study design the investigator moves, the greater the risk is that the questionnaire will not produce the desired result. However, such accommodations are the reality of an investigator's life.

Collecting and analysing the data

If a pilot study can be conducted, then the questionnaire is sent out to the respondents, returned to the investigator and the answers on completed questionnaires are entered onto a database suitable for a statistical analytic program, such as the Statistical Package for the Social Sciences (SPSS). Then a number of statistical analyses are conducted on the data by the investigator.

STATISTICAL ANALYSIS

Once the database for the questionnaires in the pilot study has been compiled, the investigator then analyses the data to see if the questionnaire has gathered data accurately and effectively. The investigator conducts this analysis by using statistics.

Of course, the whole basis of quantitative research is the use of statistics. However, some people become rather concerned when faced with statistics, their self-perceived inadequacies rising quickly to the surface. If you believe that you belong to this group, read 'a closer look 8.2'.

a closer look 8.2

Scared of statistics?

It is surprising the number of people who feel inadequate when it comes to statistics. Recognise these self-perceived inadequacies for what they are — they are frames of reference or meaning perspectives. If these frames of reference are interfering with your ability to cope with statistics, then they have become hegemonic assumptions.

A good starting point to overcoming this hegemonic assumption about statistics, acknowledge that no one in the world knows everything about statistics. I recently met a world-

respected professor of statistics — and he readily acknowledged the limitations of his own knowledge of statistics. My three enduring memories of this man were, one, his humbleness; two, his deep interest in statistics; and, three, his willingness to help anyone with a query about or a problem with statistics.

Everyone knows something about statistics and some people know more than others. When you feel your limitations have been reached, look around. It is surprising the number of people who will share their statistical

knowledge and expertise with you. Why is this? Well, anyone who has been involved in research that uses statistics knows that, sooner or later, they will exhaust their statistical knowledge and will need the help of someone more knowledgable. In turn, these researchers invariably are willing to help another struggling, would-be statistician.

You may now wish to review the material in chapter 2 on adult learning and recognise that you are not only an adult educator but also an adult learner.

A closer look 8.2 suggests that everyone knows something about statistics. Have a look at opinion item 1 in the sample questionnaire in figure 8.1. If eighty people had completed this short questionnaire, what might the researcher be interested in? Well, perhaps the number of respondents who had circled each of the scale points. This is fairly easy — simply go through the data and count the number of people who have circled '1', '2', '3', '4' and '5'. This statistical procedure goes by the grand name of *frequency analysis* and the SPSS package has a program called 'Frequencies' to do just this task. If you look at figure 8.2, you will see a table at the top which shows the number of people who circled each point on the response scale (under the heading 'Frequency'). Another heading, 'Per cent', converts these figures into a percentage for each point — so, the six respondents who circled '1' represent 6.3% of the total respondents. This table is a typical output that can be produced by most statistical analysis packages. Further, the frequencies can be converted to a visual representation, such as bar charts. Figure 8.2 also shows the results of a frequency analysis in a bar chart.

Value label	Value	Frequency	Per cent
Almost always	1	5	6.3
Often	2	20	25.0
Occasionally	3	30	37.5
Seldom	4	20	25.0
Almost never	5	5	6.3

Mean 3.000   Std dev 1.006   Skewness 0.000

BAR CHART

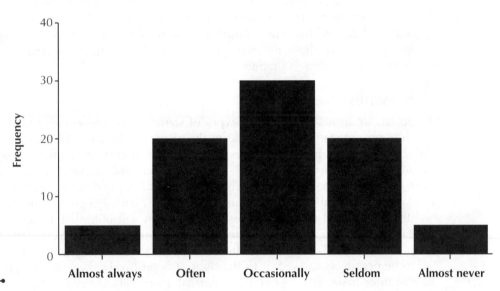

FIGURE 8.2
A normal distribution curve, using the data gathered for opinion item 1 in figure 8.1

Use of frequencies

Frequencies are used to examine three parts of the questionnaire. Firstly, the investigator will see how many respondents there are in each category of the classifications and compare these numbers with the number of questionnaires sent to the respondents in each category. Has one category returned fewer questionnaries than the other categories? If so, the investigator will need to find out why, to ensure that the problem is remedied before the main investigation stage.

Secondly, the investigator will examine the frequencies for the factual data. What is the range (the highest and lowest scores)? Is this range within the expected? If categories of factual data were used (remember the suggestion earlier that item 8 in figure 8.1 could be changed to boxes with the numbers '0–2 hours', '3–5 hours', '5–10 hours', 'More than 10 hours'), were the categories adequate? For example, if all of the respondents in the pilot study ticked 'More than 10 hours', a new set of categories may be needed — perhaps 'Less than 10 hours', '10–14 hours', '15–19 hours', '20 hours or more'.

Thirdly, frequencies are used for an initial examination of the opinion items. By examining the frequencies and bar charts for each opinion item, the investigator can see how the respondents have answered each scale. Is it a fairly even distribution, high in the middle and lower at the two ends? Or is there a hump at one end? Have more people responded for one point than the others?

The mean

Now, by itself this table in figure 8.2 reporting frequencies is only the start. Look again at one of the opinion items from the sample questionnaire: what else might the investigator be interested in? Most people would suggest the average. In other words, for each item, add all the answers by the eighty respondents and divide this total by 80. Statisticians call this average the *mean*. If we had submitted the sample questionnaire in figure 8.1 to two different groups of people and one group had a mean for item 1 of 2.1 and the other group had a mean of 4.3, then we would suspect that the two groups may have different perspectives about whether a trainer should be in control of a learning situation.

Skewness

So far, we have discussed two types of statistics — frequencies and the mean. The third type of statistics used looks at the 'shape' of the data. All data that is measured across three or more categories (for example, points on a Likert scale) will form some type of curve. A perfectly symmetrical bell-shaped curve is called a *normal distribution*. The shape of the bar chart in figure 8.2 approximates a normal distribution. An asymmetrical curve is described as skewed. Figure 8.3 gives examples of a normal distribution and two skewed distributions. You will note that a skewed distribution can be either negatively or positively skewed. Strangely, the description of negative or positive is based on the tail of the skew. If the tail is to the left, the distribution is said to be negatively skewed; if to the right, it is positively skewed. So, figure 8.3 shows the three basic types of curves — normal, negatively skewed and positively skewed. Further, looking at the curves in figure 8.3, the mean of the normal distribution is '3', while the mean for the negatively skewed curve would be about '4' and that for the positively skewed curve would be about '2'. So, the mean can provide some indication about the shape of the curve as well. However, the mean gives only a rough idea of whether the curve is positively or negatively skewed.

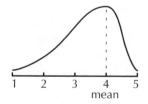
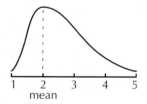

FIGURE 8.3 Normal and skewed distributions

A normal distribution   **A negatively skewed distribution**   **A positively skewed distribution**

Statistical packages such as SPSS give much more precise values for skewness. For the normal distribution curve, the skew value will be '0' with negative and positive values being given for anything that moves away from the symmetrical formation. Theoretically, the value of skewness can go to infinity, but in reality it is unusual for data to show more than plus or negative five. In addition, as a general rule of thumb, most analysts accept any skew value of under + or −1 as being close enough to a normal distribution for most analytic purposes. Figures 8.4 and 8.5 show negatively and positively skewed distributions with full statistical information. Note that the skewness of figure 8.4 is −1.531 while figure 8.5 has a skewness of 0.726, indicating that figure 8.4 is more skewed than figure 8.5.

Value label	Value	Frequency	Per cent
Almost always	1	1	2.5
Often	2	4	3.8
Occasionally	3	8	8.6
Seldom	4	29	35.8
Almost never	5	38	48.1

Mean 4.250   Std dev 0.948   Skewness −1.531

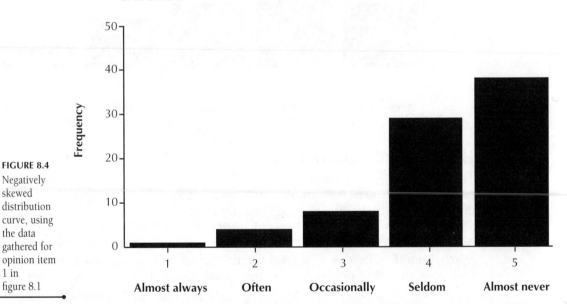

FIGURE 8.4 Negatively skewed distribution curve, using the data gathered for opinion item 1 in figure 8.1

Frequencies, the mean and the skewness help to describe the data gathered. Accordingly, these three statistics comprise what are called **descriptive statistics**.

Value label	Value	Frequency	Per cent
Almost always	1	14	16.0
Often	2	37	46.9
Occasionally	3	14	17.3
Seldom	4	11	13.6
Almost never	5	5	4.9

Mean 2.438   Std dev 1.077   Skewness 0.726

BAR CHART

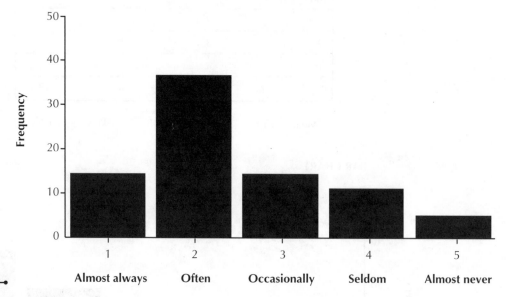

FIGURE 8.5
Positively skewed distribution curve, using the data gathered for opinion item 1 in figure 8.1

The standard deviation

The final descriptive statistic that the investigator uses to analyse the pilot study questionnaire depicts the spread of the curve. Have a look at figure 8.6. Each of the normal distributions have the same mean of '3'. But, each curve is obviously different — (A) is wider and flatter than (B). The statisticians would say that (A) has a larger *variance* than (B). What is meant by variance? Well, if you drew a square from the line that represents the mean, and so that the upper corner of the square touches the curve, then the area of the square is a reasonable portrayal of the variance (see figure 8.7). As you can see, the area of the square (representing variance) for (A) is much larger than that for (B). So, variance is one measure of the spread of the curve. Another, more common statistic used to measure spread is called *standard deviation*. The standard deviation is simply the length of the side of the square that represents the variance. Hence, the standard deviation is the square root of the variance (remember, the area of a square is the side squared). Again, you can see that the standard deviation for (A) is much longer than that for (B).

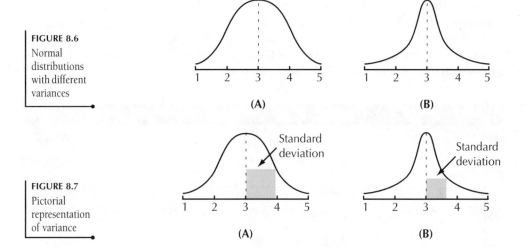

Some additional thoughts

In examining data gathered by the pilot study questionnaire, the investigator is interested in the success of the items in gathering that data. For factual data and opinion items, the investigator is usually interested in the frequencies, the means, standard deviations and the skewness for each item to see that there has been an acceptable spread of responses. Usually, the investigator prefers a normal distribution as this indicates a 'normal' spread of responses. With classification data, the investigator examines the frequencies for each category within the classification to ensure that a reasonable coverage of these characteristics within the sample has been taken (for example, is there a roughly equal number of people from each department?).

Employing user-friendly statistical packages such as SPSS, most people can analyse data for frequencies, means, standard deviations and skewness, with minimal instruction. The trick in using such statistical packages is to remember that you cannot harm the original data as you conduct the various analyses. So, try out options on the menu and you will quickly learn the basics.

The structure of the opinion items

For the opinion items, the investigator needs to conduct some further analysis — this time using *inferential statistics*. Rather than just describing the database for each item, inferential statistics analyses the database and infers or surmises certain, perhaps previously unrealised, qualities. Now, inferential statistics is more complex than descriptive statistics, so many investigators arrange for a statistician to conduct the analyses. Whoever does the analysis, the investigator still needs to understand the general process and to be able to interpret the results of the analysis.

With the opinion items, the investigator is interested in whether the planned structure has held true; in other words, whether the respondents saw the specific items that made up each theoretical construct as, in fact, clustering together. The statistical technique to test this clustering is called *factor analysis*. Factor analysis examines the way in which each respondent completed all the opinion items and compares this with the way in which every other respondent completed each and every item and then suggests that certain items have come together on particular factors (or clusters, if you like). Table 8.1 shows an example of the output of a factor analysis on a questionnaire called the Evaluation Questionnaire.

TABLE 8.1	ITEM	FACTOR A	FACTOR B	FACTOR C
Output of a factor analysis for the evaluation questionnaire	01	0.22346	−0.07300	**0.56741**
	02	0.22173	0.11086	**0.72553**
	03	−0.11021	−0.13279	**0.81159**
	04	**0.61291**	−0.18332	−0.11947
	05	**0.66958**	0.02347	0.20299
	06	0.07750	**−0.61141**	0.20597
	07	**0.72003**	−0.00131	0.00424
	08	**0.77667**	0.19312	0.12914
	09	0.01284	−0.24331	**0.58230**
	10	**0.62759**	−0.26720	−0.10879
	11	**0.43661**	−0.15479	**0.39083**
	12	**0.48110**	**−0.44660**	0.03393
	13	0.03974	**−0.70698**	0.17139
	14	−0.00829	**−0.81637**	0.12066
	15	−0.06771	**−0.93732**	−0.08814

The figures under factor A, factor B and factor C (for example, 0.22346, −0.07300 and 0.56741 for item 1) are called *loadings*. When examining the output of a factor analysis, the first activity is to highlight or underline all the loadings that are greater than 0.3. Some texts recommend only using loadings greater than 0.4 but, in the early stages of the analysis, if you highlight those greater than 0.3, you can come back and decide whether you wish to be more parsimonious. As you can see in table 8.1, items 1, 2, 3 and 9 all load on factor C; items 4, 5, 7, 8 and 10 load on factor A; and items 6, 13, 14 and 15 load on factor B. It is said that these items *load cleanly* — they load on that factor and that factor only.

Item 11 loads on factor A and factor C, while item 12 loads on factor A and factor B. This is called *leakage* — they are leaking across two factors and are not loading cleanly. Leakage indicates that the respondents were confused about the item and the investigator has the choice of deleting these items from the final questionnaire or designing two substitute, but more understandable, items. Preferably, if new items are included, then another pilot study is conducted. However, in reality, some investigators will take the risk of including two or three new items in the final questionnaire rather than using resources to conduct a new pilot study. Once again, the investigator has a choice!

This Evaluation Questionnaire, which was used to collect the data factors analysed in table 8.1, was constructed originally from material in textbooks. This gave *content validity* to the questionnaire. Remember, content validity describes the intended theoretical constructs. The Evaluation Questionnaire was designed to measure three theoretical constructs — the trainer (items 4, 5, 6, 7, 8, 9 and 10), the benefits to the trainees (11, 12, 13, 14 and 15) and the management of the course (1, 2 and 3).

A factor analysis is used to examine another type of validity — *construct validity*. Construct validity is used to examine the actual constructs as perceived by the respondents. Once the factor analysis is completed, the investigator compares the factors (the construct validity) with the intended structure (content validity). As you can see in table 8.2, the construct validity mirrors the content validity, except for four items.

TABLE 8.2
Items under each factor for the Evaluation Questionnaire

FACTOR A

4. The trainer has provided adequate feedback on student performance.
5. The trainer has provided an adequate flow of ideas in this course.
7. The trainer seems to know when trainees did not understand the material.
8. The trainer made a major contribution to the value of this course.
10. The trainer has been creative in developing materials for this course.

FACTOR B

6. This course has been adapted to trainees' needs.
13. I learnt a lot in this course.
14. This course generally fulfilled my goals.
15. This course stimulated me to want to take more work in the same or related area.

FACTOR C

1. Class time was well spent.
2. The course was well organised.
3. There was considerable agreement between announced objectives and what was taught.
9. The goals and objectives for this course have been clearly stated.

THE LEAKING ITEMS

11. The teaching methods used in this course have been suitable.
12. This course stimulated interest in the subject content.

Items 6 and 9, meant to be part of the 'trainer' construct, have moved — item 6 to measure the 'benefits to the trainees' construct and item 9 to the 'management of the course' construct. In addition, items 11 and 12 caused confusion. So, not only has the investigator to decide whether to delete items 11 and 12 or redesign them, he or she has to decide whether to stay with the content validity (items 6 and 9 stay with the 'trainer' construct) or accept the construct validity version. As a general rule, investigators tend to go with the construct validity as this is the way that the respondents perceive the structure of the questionnaire.

Let us assume that the investigator using the evaluation form has decided to go with the construct validity version and also to delete items 11 and 12.

Reliability

When the investigator is satisfied with the overall structure of the questionnaire (i.e. the constructs being measured), the attention turns to whether the instrument will be a consistent measure. This consistency is called **reliability**. There are several types of reliability for questionnaires, but only two are of interest for an HRDNI:

1. The factor analysis showed the items that cluster together to form a construct, but that is all the investigator knows — that certain items cluster together. The question remains: 'Are the items clustering sufficiently to form a consistent measure of the construct?' This consistent measure is called *internal reliability*. To measure this characteristic, the investigator uses a statistical analysis technique called 'Cronbach's alpha'. SPSS conducts this analysis quite simply when the investigator nominates the items to be included and provides a statistic called *Cronbach's Alpha coefficient*. This coefficient can hold a value of zero to 1. Generally, an alpha coefficient of 0.8 or higher is accepted (Bryman and Cramer 1990, p. 71) although some texts (for example, Nunnally 1978) suggest 0.6 and above is acceptable, especially for initial investigations. Again, the HRDNI investigator would have to decide on the quality of outcome that is desirable and the degree of risk that he or she is willing to take.

   The alpha coefficients for the three constructs of the Evaluation Questionnaire were: trainer construct (0.87), benefit to trainees construct (0.82) and management of course construct (0.79). The investigator would be happy with these results.

2. *Temporal reliability* is often called 'test–retest reliability' because this describes the process of identifying this type of reliability. In temporal reliability, the investigator has a small group of people (preferably thirty or more) complete the questionnaire twice, with a reasonable time period between the completions. A reasonable time period is usually considered to be at least a week. This process tests whether the respondents complete the questionnaire differently the second time around — in other words, whether the questionnaire measures the constructs consistently over time. Obviously various incidents could occur between the two completions that could affect an individual's response. However, the assumption is that, everything else being equal, people's opinions tend to remain relatively constant over a reasonable period of time.

   When the second completion has been finished, the data is entered into the database. The investigator can then score each construct (i.e. add up all the scores for each person for each construct — for example, add the scores for items 4, 5, 7,

8 and 10 on the 'trainer' construct for the Evaluation Questionnaire). Each score for each person can then be compared. For example, if respondent no. 1 scored 22 on the first completion and 21 on the second completion for the 'trainer' construct, we would say that the temporal reliability for that construct was consistent over time. If however, a respondent scored 22 on the first completion and 11 on the second completion, we would have to suspect that the construct was not reliable for that respondent. Of course, making such judgements for each person for each construct (even though there are only three of them) would strain the mental capacity, if not the concentration, of the investigator. Once again, a statistical package such as SPSS can come to the rescue.

The procedure used this time is called *correlation analysis*. A correlation analysis will compare each of the two completions for each person for each of the constructs, examine all the results and come up with a statistic, called a *correlation coefficient*, for each theoretical construct. A correlation coefficient has a value of −1 to +1. A +1 value means that the second completion by each respondent had exactly the same first score for each respondent on that construct. A −1 value means that all the respondents scored exactly the opposite of their first score. A zero value means that there was no relationship between the first and the second completions; that is, every respondent scored completely differently on the second time around. Again, the rule of thumb is a value of +0.8 and above for the correlation coefficient (Bryman and Cramer 1990, p. 71) and texts are very uniform on this recommendation.

However, with correlation analysis, there is another statistical consideration that must be taken into account. The concern is the likelihood that the correlation coefficient value may have been achieved by chance. Fortunately, the statistical packages also provide an estimate of this occurring and provide a statistic in the form of a probability statement. So, as well as ensuring that the correlation coefficient value is 0.8 or higher, the investigator checks to see that the probability statement is less than 0.05 (i.e. that there was less than a 5% probability that the correlation coefficient value was achieved by chance).

PROVING THE STRUCTURE OF A QUESTIONNAIRE

As you can see, the analysis of data from a pilot study to prove the structure of a questionnaire is a serious and rigorous process, especially for the opinion items. All items need to be examined for the frequency of responses and the investigator needs to pay particular attention to the descriptive statistics of the mean, the standard deviation and the skewness of the data for factual and opinion items. In addition, for the opinion items, the investigator has to prove the construct validity, compare this with the content validity, and then go on to examine both the internal and temporal reliability.

This analysis is a lot of work but, without the effort, confidence in the resultant recommendations in the HRDNI report would be limited. In chapter 7, it was suggested that the twin pillars of scientific research are accuracy and replicability. In quantitative research, accuracy is verified by ensuring that the three types of validity are proven — face, content and construct. Replicability is confirmed by testing for internal and temporal reliability. With these requirements met, the investigator is confident that the questionnaire is a robust instrument that will gather the desired data effectively and efficiently.

THE INVESTIGATION

Strangely, there is a difference in the time investment between a qualitative and a quantitative research at the design and investigation stage. In the qualitative design, such as interviews and focus groups, most of the time is taken in analysing the data. With a quantitative design, most of the time is invested in designing the instrument. With a quantitative design, once the investigator is satisfied that the questionnaire is an accurate and replicable instrument, the investigation itself takes a surprisingly short time. On the other hand, if short cuts have been taken in designing and constructing the questionnaire — for example, not conducting a pilot study — then the risk of the data gathered in the investigation proper being faulty, or even useless, can escalate alarmingly.

GATHERING THE DATA

When the sample of respondents who are to represent the target population has been identified, the questionnaire can be administered. There are two ways of administering a questionnaire — personally by the HRDNI investigator or by mail (Neuman 1997; Sekaran 1992). As the names suggest, for the personally administered questionnaires, a group of respondents are gathered together in one location and the questionnaire is administered to the group by the investigator who remains at the location until all the questionnaires are completed. In the mail-out questionnaire, the questionnaire, accompanying instructions and an introductory letter are sent by mail to the respondents.

Personally administered questionnaires are useful when groups of respondents can be assembled easily and they have the advantage of having the HRD investigator present to answer any queries. Usually there is a much higher response rate with personally administered questionnaires and the investigator can motivate the respondents to give honest answers. However, the presence of the investigator can give feelings of coercion which can contaminate the answers of some respondents.

Mail questionnaires have the advantage of being able to cover a wide geographical area and the questionnaire can be completed at a time and place convenient to the respondent. The questionnaire can also be sent to a very high number of respondents. Recognise, however, that the investigator does not have control over the conditions under which the questionnaire is completed — was the respondent watching TV at the time or at a party? In addition, mail questionaries are notorious for their low response rates. For this reason various techniques for improving the response rates are recommended — among them being a motivational letter to introduce the questionnaire, careful instructions, providing an addressed and stamped return envelope, follow-up letters and even monetary or other rewards (for example, eligibility for a valuable prize).

The introductory letter is generally considered to be an important component of the mail-out questionnaire. According to Jones and Bearley (1995), the introductory letter should impress on the respondents that their opinions are important, that everyone will be meaningfully involved in working through the results, that the data will remain anonymous and that the goals of the intervention are to improve organisational practices. It is also a good idea, if practicable, to undertake advising all respondents of the results of the analysis.

With the personally administered questionnaires, the completed questionnaires are immediately available for recording onto a data set ready for statistical analysis. Neuman (1997) suggests that the majority of mail questionnaires are returned within 2 weeks. If time allows, the investigator may then conduct follow-up action to increase the number of responses. At some stage, however, the investigator has to decide that enough time has elapsed and have the responses 'punched into' a data set. At this point, the second stage of the investigation can begin — the analysis of the data.

ANALYSING THE DATA

As discussed earlier, quantitative research inevitably involves the use of statistics. The type of statistical analysis and procedures used will depend on the objectives of the HRDNI. While investigators often employ a statistician for the more complex analyses, a basic knowledge of statistics is useful so that the investigator's expectations can be explained to the statistician and also so that the investigator to understand the results of the statistical analysis. There are two types of statistics — non-parametric and parametric.

Non-parametric statistics

Non-parametric statistics are used with nominal and ordinal data. The information gathered in items 9 and 10 of the Learning Orientation Assessment Questionnaire in figure 8.1 is nominal data. Looking at items 9 and 10, we may ask: 'What questions may the investigator examine?'

Well, certainly, the investigator will want to know how many respondents there are in each category and also what percentage each category represents. To provide this information, the investigator would use *frequencies*, a process we have already met when analysing the structure of the questionnaire in the pilot study.

The investigator may also want to have a cross-analysis of the two items — how many female respondents are from the advertising department? how many males are from the production department? and so on. The *cross tabs process* provides this information. Cross tabs simply creates a matrix with 'male' and 'female' at the top and the three departments down the side. The total numbers of respondents are recorded in the appropriate 'box' or 'cell'. The investigator may wish to go further and find out if any cell or cells of respondents are significantly different from the other cells, i.e. whether females or males are under- or over-represented in any of the departments. A statistician would phrase this question as: 'Is there a relationship between the variables of gender and department?' Now the investigator could make a guess simply by looking at the figures in each box and for a simple two-by-three matrix this may be adequate. For a larger matrix, the statistical analytic process called *chi-square* performs this task. Chi-square simply compares the observed number of cases in a cell with the expected number of cases in that cell. If there is a difference, chi-square decides whether the difference could have occurred by chance or is, in fact, caused by systematic bias.

Parametric statistics

Parametric tests can be performed where at least one set of data is interval or ratio data. There are a wide variety of parametric statistics, each of which answers a different question. Some of the more common used in an HRDNI are discussed below:

- The *t*-test is used when the investigator wishes to see if two groups are different on a particular variable. So, for example from the data in the sample questionnaire in figure 8.1, the investigator may wish to see if there is a difference between males and females on the andragogical theoretical construct. A *t*-test examines the means of each group (male and female) and decides whether they come from the same or a different population.

  The results of a *t*-test are given with a *t*-score, ranging from 1 to several hundred (although more than 50 is rare), and with a probability statement. The probability statement indicates the extent to which the *t*-score could have been achieved by chance. A general rule of thumb is to accept a probability statement of less than 5% — or, as it is usually shown, less than 0.05. In other words, the result has less than five possibilities in 100 of occurring by chance. So, in our sample questionnaire, we may find a result with a *t*-value of 9.57 and a probability of 0.02. In a statistician's parlance, this would indicate that the male sample comes from a different population than the female sample — i.e. the females are either more or less andragogical than the males. To see if the females were more or less andragogical, we would simply look at the mean scores for each group. If the females had a higher mean, then they are more andragogical, and vice versa.

- The Evaluation Questionnaire whose factor analysis appears in table 8.1 consists of three theoretical constructs — the trainer (items 4, 5, 7, 8 and 10), the benefits to the trainees (items 6, 13, 14 and 15) and the management of the course (items 1, 2, 3 and 9). If we were using this Evaluation Questionnaire on a large number of trainees who had attended the same type of training workshop, we could analyse the data to see if the males assessed the course differently to females. One way to see if there was a difference would be to conduct three *t*-tests. However, each *t*-test result would have nearly five possibilities in 100 of occurring by chance. With three separate *t*-tests, this adds up to an unacceptable risk. What is needed is a statistical process that conducts the three tests at once. Such a process is called *single-factor analysis of variance* — usually shortened to ANOVA.

  In our example, the single factor is the Evaluation Questionnaire which is divided into three levels or elements. We will not worry about the mathematical calculations involved. Suffice to say that the ANOVA process results in a statistical value called an *F* statistic and a probability statement and it is read in the same way as the *t*-test. So, if the result for our example for the Evaluation Questionnaire was an *F* value of 3.27 and a probability of 0.032, we could again say that the females evaluated the workshop differently from the males. We would then again resort to the mean to see which group had evaluated the workshop higher.

- The final parametric statistical process that we will discuss is the *correlation analysis*. A correlation analysis can be conducted on two sets of interval or ratio data. Suppose, for example, that we wished to see if those who scored the workshops highly on the evaluation form were also those who preferred an andragogical approach to learning (as measured by the sample questionnaire in figure 8.1). A correlation analysis will answer this type of question.

We have previously examined correlation analysis when discussing temporal reliability. To briefly review the concept, a correlation analysis results in a statistic called a *correlation coefficient*, which can have a value between −1 and +1. In our example, if the correlation analysis of the two questionnaires showed a correlation coefficient of +0.87, and a probability statement of less than 0.05, then we would conclude that those who had a high andragogical orientation also rated the workshop highly. If the correlation coefficient was close to zero then we would say that there was no relationship between andragogy and evaluation of the course; if it was closer to −1, then we would conclude that those with an andragogical orientation did not evaluate the course highly.

Of course, it would also be interesting to conduct a correlation analysis on the pedagogical orientation. If this also had a positive correlation coefficient that was within the 0.05 probability standard, then people with either orientation rated the workshop highly. We could then conclude that the workshop suited both types of learning orientations.

Further reading about statistics

This chapter has provided only a very brief introduction to statistics. If you would like to progress further, the texts by Bryman and Cramer (1990), Kranzler and Moursund (1995) and Williams (1992) are recommended (see References, page 226, for full references).

THE QUESTIONNAIRE — A VERY USEFUL TOOL

Designing and using questionnaires is a careful and rigorous process. The investigator must have every confidence that the results of the survey are accurate and truthful. There are four key decisions that have to be made:

1. *Whether the questionnaire will focus on factual or opinion information or a combination of both.* If opinion information is being sought then the questionnaire designer will need to ensure content and construct validity as well as internal and temporal reliability.
2. *Whether the questionnaire is to be personally administered or mailed out.* If personally administered, then the logistical planning becomes a prime consideration. If mailed out, then the introductory letter and the instructions require careful composition.
3. *Whether a pilot study will be conducted.* Perhaps not so important when only factual data is targeted, a pilot study becomes a serious issue when opinion information is sought. The investigator needs to weigh up the costs of conducting a pilot study against the risks of using a worthless instrument for the actual investigation itself.

4. *Which are the most appropriate statistical analyses to be used.* If in doubt, the services of a competent statistician should be considered.

When interpreting the results of the data analysis, the investigator should constantly bear in mind that the figures produced are only indicators. Jones and Bearley (1995, p. 75) offer four caveats based on the limitations of statistics:

1. Numbers, either singly or as a total score, can never adequately describe how people experience a phenomenon or event.
2. Numbers masquerade as truth. Numbers are convenient representations only.
3. What we can measure precisely often does not matter.
4. Paralysis by analysis — resist the temptation to gather more data unless there is good reason.

For all these concerns, the questionnaire is a very useful tool. Recognise that interpretation and wisdom are still needed when writing the report. However, questionnaires are very useful tools for the HRDNI investigator. A large number of staff can be assessed and subjective insights from the qualitative research stage can be confirmed or dismissed. Indeed, the quantitative results often need further investigation. Further insights may be achieved only by further qualitative research — and so the cycle continues.

GLOSSARY

classification section — the part of the questionnaire that calls for information that allows the respondents to be categorised

construct validity — a statistical process that demonstrates that the items do cluster into the theoretical constructs, commonly using factor analysis

content validity — the process that demonstrates that each item does represent the theoretical construct it is supposed to represent

descriptive statistics — the statistical techniques that allow the gathered data to be illustrated, includes frequencies, mean, standard deviation and skewness

face validity — the quality of an item appearing to measure the theoretical construct it is supposed to measure

factual data — data provided by the respondent that is verifiable

instruction section — provides the respondent with information on how to complete the questionnaire

interval data — the second highest type of data gathered by a questionnaire, indicates that one person or object is of higher value than another and that the interval between the degrees of difference are the same

nominal data — the most basic data, merely differentiates between the respondents or objects

non-parametric tests — statistical procedures that are used on nominal and ordinal data, includes frequencies, cross-tabs and chi-squared

opinions section — items on the questionnaire that seek the beliefs of the respondent

ordinal data — the second lowest level of data, indicates that one person or object has a higher value than another

parametric statistics — statistical procedures that are used for interval and ratio data, includes *t*-test, correlation analysis and factor analysis

pilot study — having a group from the target population complete the questionnaire so that the questionnaire can be analysed for content validity and reliability

ratio data — the highest level of data, similar to interval data but the measurement starts at zero

reliability — the questionnaire consistently measures what it is supposed to measure

response scale — the numbered scale after each item on the questionnaire that allows the respondent to indicate the strength of their opinion on that item (also called the response set)

response set — the numbered scale after each item on the questionnaire that allows the respondent to indicate the strength of their opinion on that item (also called the response scale)

sequencing — the order that the items are positioned in the questionnaire

theoretical construct — the theoretical concept or issue or theme to be investigated

theoretical scale — the sum of the several items that are designed to represent the theoretical construct.

QUESTIONS

For review

1. Explain the difference between nominal, ordinal, interval and ratio data.
2. What is the difference between factual data and opinion?
3. Discuss the reasons that a researcher would include classification items in a questionnaire.
4. How does a researcher achieve content validity in a questionnaire?
5. Describe the difference between internal reliability and temporal reliability.
6. Discuss the issues that need to be considered when deciding on the sequencing of items in a questionnaire.
7. Briefly describe three descriptive statistics.
8. Explain the difference between parametric and non-parametric statistics.

For analysis

9. Compare and contrast content validity and construct validity.
10. Examine the opinion items in the questionnaire in figure 8.1 on page 199. Comment on the quality of the wording of the items.
11. Consider the option of using a less-than-ideal pilot study design (for example, using a sample that is not exactly the same as the target population). What other actions could you take to decrease the risks of an inaccurate result.

For application

12. Using the literature in chapter 7, design a questionnaire that would investigate the level of interviewing knowledge in an organisation.
13. Describe how you would conduct a pilot study for the questionnaire designed in question 12. Justify at least three critical decisions you have made.

REFERENCES

Babbie, E. (1990). *Survey Research Methods*. (2nd ed.). Belmont, Cal.: Wadsworth.

Bryman, A. and Cramer, D. (1990). *Quantitative Data Analysis for Social Scientists*. London: Routledge.

Burns, K. D. (1994). *Introduction to Research Methods*. (2nd ed.). Melbourne, Vic: Longman Cheshire.

Converse, J. M. and Presser, S. (1986). *Survey Questions: Handcrafting the Standardized Questionnaire*. Thousand Oaks: Sage.

Dillman, D. A. (1978). *Mail and Telephone Surveys: The Total Design Method*. New York: Wiley.

Emory, C. W. and Cooper, D. R. (1991). *Business Research Methods*. (4th ed.). Homewood, Ill.: Irwin.

Jolliffe, F. R. (1986). *Survey Design and Analysis*. New York: Wiley.

Jones, J. E. and Bearley, W. L. (1995). *Surveying Employees*. Amherst, MA: HRD Press.

Kidder, L. H. and Judd, C. M. (1986). *Research Methods in Social Relations*. (5th ed.). New York: Holt, Rienhart and Winston.

Knowles, M. S. (1980). 'How do you get people to be self directed learners?' *Training and Development Journal*, May, 96–99.

Knowles, M. S. (1983). 'Developing the training professional: part II.' *Training and Development in Australia*, June, 3–9.

Knowles, M. S. (1990). *The Adult Learner: A Neglected Species*. (4th ed.). Houston: Gulf.

Kranzler, G. and Moursund, J. (1995). *Statistics for the Terrified*. Englewood Cliffs, NJ: Prentice Hall.

McIver, J. P. and Carmines, E. G. (1981). *Unidimensional Scaling*. Beverly Hills, Cal.: Sage.

Neuman, W. L. (1997). *Social Research Methods: Qualitative and Quantitative Approaches*. (3rd ed.). Boston: Allyn and Bacon.

Nunnally, J. C. (1978). *Psychometric Theory*. (2nd ed.). New York: McGraw-Hill.

Oppenheim, A. N. (1992). *Questionnaire Design, Interviewing and Attitude Measurement*. London: Pinter.

Robinson, J. P., Athanasiou, R., and Head, K. B. (1969). *Measures of Occupational Attitudes and Occupational Characteristics*. Ann Arbor, Mich.: Institute for Social Research.

Rogers, C. R. (1983). *Freedom to Learn in the 80s*. Colombus, Ohio: Merrill.

Sekaran, U. (1992). *Research Methods for Business: A Skill Building Approach*. (2nd ed.). New York: Wiley.

Spector, P. E. (1992). *Summated Rating Scale Construction*. Newbury Park: Sage.

Triandis, H. C. (1971). *Attitude and Attitude Change*. New York: Wiley.

Williams, F. (1992). *Reasoning with Statistics: How to Read Quantitative Research*. (4th ed.). Fort Worth: HBJ.

Decisions about the structure of a questionnaire

The tables presented on this page show the results of analysing the data from a pilot study of an HRDNI questionnaire. The questionnaire consisted of eighteen opinion items, each with a five-point Likert scale.

From the frequencies analysis:

Item no.	Mean	Standard deviation	Skewness
1	4.2	0.833	1.239
2	2.5	1.210	0.737
3	1.6	0.471	−0.429
4	2.3	1.101	0.329
5	4.3	0.869	−1.739
6	3.7	1.021	−0.581
7	3.8	0.879	−0.812
8	3.8	0.952	−0.689
9	3.5	0.951	−0.488
10	3.4	0.897	−0.753
11	4.2	0.687	−1.011
12	3.8	0.748	−0.473
13	3.3	1.241	−0.048
14	3.3	1.069	−0.271
15	3.4	1.301	−0.119
16	3.8	0.861	−0.910
17	3.2	0.976	0.079
18	4.2	0.832	−1.240

From the factor analysis:

Item No.	Factor 1	Factor 2	Factor 3
2	−0.0223	0.1911	0.7128
3	0.1158	0.6329	0.0079
4	0.4581	0.4312	0.2389
6	0.0981	0.6726	0.1121
7	0.7835	−0.1899	0.1362
8	−0.2611	0.0736	−0.2433
9	0.0344	0.1311	0.8122
10	0.1287	0.0021	0.7895
12	0.6439	0.2381	0.1311
13	−0.0315	0.4712	0.1099
14	0.5814	0.0689	−0.2469
15	−0.1539	0.4211	0.4301
16	0.5614	0.1481	0.0927
17	−0.0749	0.4891	0.2437

Cronbach's alpha coefficient for:
Factor 1 = 0.87; factor 2 = 0.81; factor 3 = 0.78

The correlation analysis:

	Factor 1	Factor 2	Factor 3
Correlation of first and second completions	0.89 ($p = 0.01$)	0.58 ($p = 0.09$)	0.80 ($p = 0.04$)

Discussion questions

1. Scan the results of the frequency analysis and decide if the reported data is correct.
2. Which items would not be acceptable for further analysis? Justify your answer/s.
3. Discuss the construct validity of this questionnaire.
4. Discuss the reliability of this questionnaire.

Questionnaire design analysis

Rebecca Chapelli made the following decisions on a questionnaire that she was designing:

- All the thirty-two opinion items had come from the qualitative data of twenty-eight interviews that Rebecca had conducted the previous month.

- There were four theoretical constructs to be tested, each made up of eight items.

- None of the opinion items had more than twenty words. There were three that she was doubtful about:

  Item 6 Managers in this organisation feel concerned if they have to work more than 10 hours overtime.

  Item 15 Managers should not show any negative emotions.

  Item 28 Managers should attend at least one management development course each year.

- The items would be sequenced with one item coming from each construct as item 1, item 2, item 3 and item 4 and this order would be repeated (i.e. item 5 — construct 1; item 6 — construct 2; item 7 — construct 3; item 8 — construct 4; item 9 — construct 1; item 10 — construct 2; item 11 — construct 3; item 12 — construct 4; and so on).

- A Likert scale of six points would be used for the response sets.

- Three classification items on age, gender and salary scale would be placed at the end of the questionnaire.

Discussion questions

1. Discuss the decisions that Rebecca has made, making reference to good questionnaire design.

2. Are there any other critical decisions that Rebecca should have made? Justify your answer/s.

Design — the two main considerations

CHAPTER OBJECTIVES

At the end of this chapter you should be able to:

1 describe the five major categories of programmed knowledge, task, relationship, critical thinking and meta-abilities in the hierarchy of learning outcomes (HLO)

2 explain how the HLO can indicate the preferred learning strategy

3 explain the effect of the learner's current level of knowledge on the design process

4 describe how learning experiences can be designed to encourage higher levels of learner motivation

5 explain the effect a learner's learning orientation can have on the design process

6 describe how learning styles can be incorporated into the design process.

CHAPTER OVERVIEW

The chapter begins by suggesting that the HR developer as a designer of learning experiences for adult learners must consider three variables — the learning strategies to be used, the learning outcomes to be achieved and the **learners** who will experience the learning episode. Further, it is suggested that two of these variables — the learning outcomes and the learners — can be used to predict the most appropriate and beneficial learning strategy.

The **learning outcomes** provide a preliminary sieve for identifying possible appropriate **learning strategies**. As a way of classifying learning outcomes and linking them to appropriate learning strategies, a **hierarchy of learning outcomes** (HLO) is proposed. This hierarchy is made up of five categories — programmed knowledge, task, relationships, critical thinking and meta-abilities — with programmed knowledge being the least complex and meta-abilities the most complex. Further, these categories occupy four levels as the task and relationships categories are at the same level.

The programmed information category consists of three elements — basic facts and skills, professional/technical information and procedural skills. The most appropriate learning strategies for the programmed information category are the theory session, the lecture and the skill session.

At a deeper level of complexity, the **task category** has three subgroupings — analytical, logistical and implementing. The **analytical subgrouping** consists of four elements — linear analysis, diagnostic analysis, complex analysis and analysis under uncertainty. Linear analysis is best developed by the theory or skill session while the learning strategies of choice for the other three elements are the discussion, the case study or the role play. The **logistical subgrouping** contains four elements — goal identification, administrative proficiency, resources allocation and efficiency. Goal identification can be learned best through the theory or skill session while the other three elements respond best to the discussion, case study or role play. At a deeper level in the task category is the **implementing subgroup**. This subgroup involves five elements — work **motivation**, a bias for action, purposeful action, appropriate use of unilateral power, and effectiveness. All of these learning outcomes are best developed by experiential learning or mentoring or problem-based learning.

At the same level of complexity as the task category, the **relationships category** also has three subgroupings — interpersonal, intrapersonal and concern for others. The **interpersonal subgrouping** consists of five elements. The first two — communication and interacting at the objective level — can be developed by the theory or skill session or even the lecture. The remaining three — interacting at the emotional level, using group processes and using social power — are better served by the role play, the discussion and the case study. The **intrapersonal subgrouping** has six elements. Again, the first two — spontaneity and accurate self-awareness — can be learned best via the theory session or skill session. The next three — self-confidence, inner strength and self-discipline — need the role play, the discussion and the case study for full development. The sixth element — emotional resilience — is a deeper level of outcome and responds best to experiential learning, mentoring or problem-based learning. At a deeper level in the relationships category, and on the same level as the implementing subgroup in the task category, the **concern for others subgroup** consists of four elements — developing others, empathy, leadership and managing conflict. These complex elements need the flexible approaches afforded by experiential learning or mentoring or problem-based learning to be fully developed.

Critical thinking relies more on tacit knowledge and incorporates five elements. The first three (problem solving, creativity and evaluation) can be developed by using the dynamic processes of experiential learning or mentoring or problem-based learning. However, the fourth and fifth elements — dialectic thinking and logical reflection — usually require the more long-term strategies of contract learning or action learning that emphasise self-responsibility.

The **meta-abilities category** comprises three very complex elements — mental agility, helicopter perception and self-perpetuating learning — that are usually deeply within the tacit knowledge area of the individual. Accordingly, the disciplines of self-responsibility and reflective practice that are incorporated within the learning strategies of contract learning and action learning are usually needed for the developmental processes.

So, for the HR developer who is designing a learning experience, the desired learning outcomes (usually defined in the HRDNI report) provide a preliminary, albeit tentative, process of selecting likely learning strategies. The HLO provides the designer with a basic model to make this tentative selection process.

The next main consideration for the HR developer in the design process is the learner. Indeed, bearing in mind the central role of the learner in the learning process, the learner should be consider the major variable the HR developer, as the designer, must consider. The challenge, of course, is that the learner is a very complex being. However, there are a number of characteristics of learners that must be considered when designing learning experiences.

Firstly, the learner needs a reasonable level of **current knowledge** in the topic area to successfully undertake the unstructured or self-directed learning strategies. Those with low levels should be first exposed to the topic area through the more structured learning strategies. The motivation of the learner is another key variable. Various theories of motivation provide insights into the motivation of learners. The **two-factor theory** suggests that hygiene factors (for example, supervision and physical conditions), if absent, can cause dissatisfaction while the motivator factors (such as recognition and relevance) can increase motivation. The **expectancy–valence theory** indicates that motivation is a process of four sequential steps — whether the task is achievable; whether the expected rewards will follow the effort; whether the reward, when it eventuates, is observable; and whether this reward can be converted into something valuable (that is, has valence) to the learner. Finally, the **three levels of motivation** indicate that a learner may have utility motivation (will use the learning for some other purpose), achievement motivation (receives intense satisfaction in achieving some goal) or interest motivation (intensely interested in the topic content itself).

The other two characteristics of learners that should be considered by the designer are the learning orientation and learning styles. There are four possible stages of a learner's **learning orientation**. Stage 1 (high pedagogy/low andragogy) indicates that the learner would be more comfortable with the highly structured learning strategies of the skill session, theory session or lecture. Learners at stage 2 (high pedagogy/high andragogy) are often disenchanted with the structured learning strategies but are not yet ready for the self-responsibility of the unstructured approaches. Fortunately, learners at this stage are usually adaptive and curious so explanations of the choices of learning strategies and time invested in resolving conflicts should be incorporated in the learning experiences for these learners. Stage 3 (low pedagogy/high andragogy) describes the quintessential self-directed learners. They are analytical, free thinking, and creative, and the self-directed learning strategies of contract learning and action learning suit them admirably. Those at the stage 4 (low pedagogy/low andragogy) level are highly mature and experienced learners. Sometimes described as personally auton-omous, these learners will select whatever learning strategy will most suit their needs. The concept of **learning styles** suggests that learners have a preference for a particular type of learning process. The diverger/reflector is a thoughtful person who likes to generate alternative ideas and consider all possibilities. The assimilator/theorist uses inductive reasoning and assimilates disparate facts into coherent theories. The con-verger/pragmatist likes to make practical decisions and act quickly and operates best in situations where there is one best answer. The accommodator/activist likes to be involved in new experiences and is action orientated.

These two main considerations — the content to be learned and the characteristics of the learner — provide the HR developer as the designer with pragmatic decision indicators when selecting appropriate learning strategies for developmental experi-ences for adult learners. A broad checklist of the issues discussed is included at the end of the chapter.

DEFINING THE ROLE OF THE HR DEVELOPER

Having finished the first of the HRD stages, the HRDNI, we now move onto the second stage: the design of learning experiences — sometimes called curriculum design or curriculum development. Before we begin, though, an early word of advice. In this text, for the sake of logical understanding, we are examining each of the four stages in turn. However, there are strong links and significant overlaps between the four stages. Accordingly, we will frequently make reference to the material discussed in the previous chapters on HRDNI and also to chapter 2, 'Adult learning'.

Print (1993) believes that curriculum design should consider the knowledge that is of most worth to the learners; the activities that are most effective in enabling the learners to acquire this knowledge; and the most appropriate way to organise these activities. A fourth feature could be added — the knowledge should be of worth to the organisation. Therefore, it could be said that the task of the designer is to create a learning experience consisting of a series of linked and appropriate learning strategies that will provide the maximum opportunities for the learners to achieve the desired learning outcomes effectively and in the most efficient manner.

There are three important variables in this definition:

1. The *learning strategies*, which will provide the learners with the opportunities to learn;
2. the *learning outcomes*, which define the levels of knowledge, skills and abilities that the HRDNI has deemed the learners should achieve;
3. the *learners*, whom the HRDNI has identified as needing the development.

The learning strategies are discussed in chapters 10 and 11 as these strategies describe the third stage of HRD: implementation. These learning strategies include the skill session, theory session, discussion, case study, role play, experiential learning, contract learning and action learning, to name a few. If you are unfamiliar with these strategies, you may prefer to have a quick look at chapters 10 and 11 before reading further. The other two variables identified in the definition — the learning outcomes and the learners — are the topics for this chapter.

The learning outcomes are derived from the HRDNI report. As discussed in chapter 5, these learning outcomes may also be framed in terms of learning objectives or learning competencies. The learning outcomes are derived from the knowledge, skills and/or abilities that the HRDNI has identified as being essential for the development of the targeted learners. The HRDNI has also identified and defined the targeted learners. Designing a learning experience, then, is linking the learning outcomes and the learners via the appropriate strategies. Now that seems simple enough! Unfortunately, the life of the designer is not that easy. The link between the learning outcomes and the learner, on the one hand, and the learning strategies, on the other hand, is surprisingly intricate. Further, there are other intervening considerations such as the resources available, the organisational strategic orientation and the organisational culture.

In this second stage of the HRD process, the HR developer takes on the role of the designer. In this role, the HR developer will find that designing a learning experience for adults is part science and part art. The 'art' input comes from the tacit knowledge of the designer and this complex understanding can be gained only by experience. However, scientific research has given us insights into the way adults learn and these insights provide an integrating paradigm on which to make informed decisions. This chapter will examine two of the main components of this paradigm — the learning outcomes to be learned and the learners. Chapter 10 will discuss the other intervening considerations.

THE HIERARCHY OF LEARNING OUTCOMES

The first important variable to be considered in the design stage is the learning outcomes. The content to be covered in a learning experience is defined in the HRDNI report by the list of learning outcomes and by the descriptions of the types of information, skills and abilities within the report itself. It has already been suggested in chapter 5 that the HRDNI investigator can help the designer by prioritising the learning outcomes between those relevant to instrumental learning or to communicative and emancipatory learning. This provides a very basic start to prioritising the learning outcomes.

One of the most used approaches to categorising learning outcomes was provided by Gagne (see Gagne, Briggs and Wager 1988). Gagne suggested that learning outcomes could be grouped under the headings of intellectual skills, cognitive strategies, verbal information, motor skills and attitudes. This categorisation provides some indications of appropriate learning strategies (for example, the use of the skill session for motor skills) but does not cope well with the wide variety and complexity of potential learning outcomes.

After reviewing a number of studies into managerial and professional competencies, Delahaye (1990) has compiled a hierarchy of learning outcomes (HLO) that can be linked to learning strategies. This hierarchy, while originally based on managerial and professional competencies, can be generalised to form a useful hierarchy for any learning outcomes (see figure 9.1).

This HLO indicates that there are five major categories — programmed knowledge, task, relationships, critical thinking and meta-abilities. These categories occupy four levels with programmed knowledge being the least complex, moving to meta-abilities at the most complex. The task and relationship groupings are at the same levels of complexity.

The five categories are presented as a hierarchy for four reasons. Firstly, in moving from the top to the bottom, the categories become more complex. Secondly, the top category, 'programmed knowledge', has more to do with explicit knowledge while the further towards the bottom, the more the categories enter the realm of tacit knowledge. Thirdly, those categories at the top respond best to structured learning strategies and those at the bottom to unstructured learning strategies. Finally, each category is dependent on an individual achieving competence in the categories above it.

However, while these five categories are presented as discrete entities, overlaps and interactions between the sub-groups, and between elements within the categories, do and must occur. Each of the categories will now be discussed, with comments in a 'closer look' indicating the most appropriate learning strategy that can be used to develop the various elements. However, bear in mind that the HLO provides an initial indicator of possible learning strategies only. The learner, the second main consideration discussed later in this chapter, must be given prime consideration in the design decision.

THE PROGRAMMED KNOWLEDGE CATEGORY

Programmed knowledge can either reside in the textbooks and journals in any library or be the knowledge declared by experts (Revans 1982). Nonaka and Takeuchi (1995) refer to this type of knowledge as explicit knowledge. As shown in figure 9.1, programmed knowledge can consist of basic facts and skills, professional/technical information and procedural skills. Examples of basic facts include the number of staff in an organisation or the exchange rate of the dollar. Basic skills are the psychomotor skills — those that are completed automatically such as writing or using a screwdriver. Of more complexity is professional/technical information which may be factual (for example, water is made up of hydrogen and oxygen) or more complicated, having detailed complexity. Senge (1990, p. 120) defines detailed complexity as occurring when many variables are involved. These variables are usually interactive but can be assessed and calculated to predict a cause-and-effect sequence (for example, an engineer designing a bridge to meet certain load and wind force conditions). This idea of a cause–effect sequence suggests that certain detailed complex information is basic to the whole sequence and provides 'building blocks' for more advanced information later in the sequence.

FIGURE 9.1 A hierarchy of learning outcomes

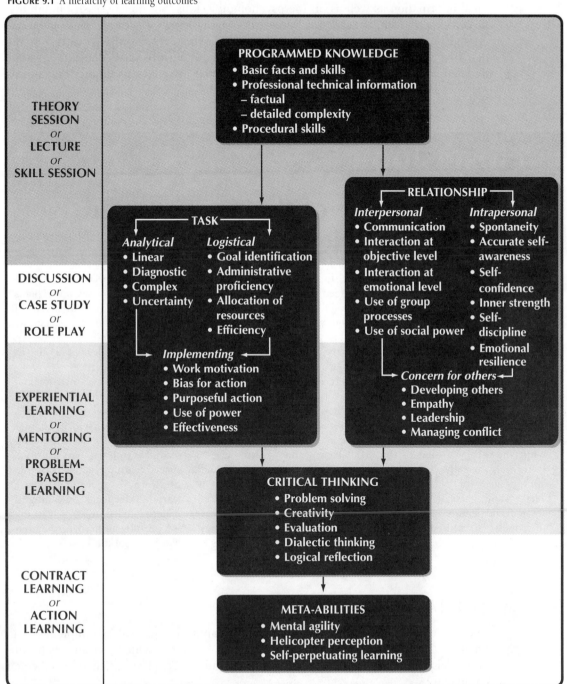

Procedural skills have been nominated as the final element in this category. Delahaye and Smith (1998) define procedural skills as those involving procedures, or psychomotor skills linked in a series, and where the order of psychomotor activities is crucial. Defusing a bomb would certainly come under this element of procedural skills! It should also be noted that procedural skills often rely on professional/technical information as well as on the psychomotor skills. So, the successful bomb disposal expert would need to know the engineering, electronic and chemical composition of the bomb as well as having the procedural skills to carry out the defusing safely. Indeed, selecting certain procedural skills may depend on some detailed complexity information — one could well imagine that different chemicals may need different approaches to be rendered safe.

a closer look 9.1

Application of the programmed knowledge category

The programmed knowledge category is at the level of instrumental learning — the knowledge is meant to give the learner facts, information and skills that are needed to manipulate the workplace environment. However, the designer needs to differentiate between skills and information. The skill session is used for skills acquisition while the theory session or the lecture is usually the most appropriate for information. The skill session, theory session and lecture are seen as the most structured of the learning strategies.

A further differentiation is between information that can become basic 'building blocks' for more advanced information. The designer needs to ensure that these basic building blocks are learned before the more advanced information is presented to the learners.

When this differentiation has been made, the designer then completes session plans (see Delahaye and Smith 1998, pp. 97–111) for each of the skill sessions, theory sessions and/or lectures, along with associated support material, such as overhead projector transparencies, board plans and specifications of

required material and equipment. These session plans describe and cover the details of information and skills that the presenter (trainer, lecturer, teacher or HR developer) has to impart to the learners.

As with any instrumental learning, the designer should ensure that the basic principles of learning discussed in chapter 2 — start with the unknown, readiness to learn, part learning, spaced learning, active learning, overlearn, multiple sense learning, feedback, meaningful material and transfer of learning — are fully utilised throughout the design of the sessions.

THE TASK CATEGORY

The task category has three subgroupings — analytical, logistical and implementing. Each of these subgroupings has a number of elements which, within each subgroup, also form hierarchies. The analytical and logistical subgroups are of equal complexity.

The analytical subgroup

The analytical subgroup consists of four elements; linear analysis, diagnostic analysis, complex analysis and analysis under uncertainty. *Linear analysis* consists of simple information processing skills (for example, collating and identifying trends) and the ability to understand cause-and-effect relationships. *Diagnostic analysis* is the ability to use existing programmed knowledge to explain or interpret an assortment of data. For example, a TV repair technician may use an algorithm (sometimes called a 'yes–no' chart) to explore the cause of a breakdown, with the algorithm providing assistance with the diagnostic analysis. In *complex analysis* an individual uses a store of problem-solving and decision-making procedures or programs from which relevant selections can be made to solve a problem. For example, a HRDNI investigator may use Dewey's seven-step scientific problem-solving model (define the problem, identify possible solutions, evaluate each solution, select a solution, plan, implement, evaluate). *Analysis under uncertainty*, the most complex of the analytical subgroups, is the ability to identify, analyse and solve problems under conditions of incomplete information. Senge (1990) refers to this as 'dynamic uncertainty', where cause and effect are distant in time and space and where the consequences are subtle and not obvious.

The analytical subgroup often interacts with the programmed knowledge category. Once the programmed knowledge has been learned, the individual is usually required to put the information into practice. This practical use relies heavily on the analytical elements. However, while this interaction exists, there is no doubt that acquiring analytical competence is more difficult and more complex than learning programmed knowledge. Learning programmed knowledge is more about memorisation and repetition, while the analytical elements usually require an acquisition of protocols and decisions on options. Hence, the task category is placed a more complex level than the programmed knowledge category.

The logistical subgroup

At approximately the same complexity level as analytical, the logistical subgroup consists of four elements: goal identification, administrative proficiency, resource allocation and efficiency. *Goal identification* is about concisely and accurately defining the goal or target that must be achieved. *Administrative proficiency* covers the interactive skills of planning and organising. Planning includes the ability to foresee what activities need to be completed to achieve a goal and also the ability to make logical decisions. When organising, an individual brings together the various resources that are needed to achieve a specified goal, in a logical sequence. While administrative proficiency is a more cerebral activity, *resource allocation* needs the courage to actually place the resources in the planned location. Allocating resources is a watershed element, as the logistics go beyond thinking and into observable and committed action. *Efficiency* is the concern with doing something better and using efficient methods, realistic goals and standards of excellence. While an individual can carry out the elements of goal identification, administrative proficiency and allocating resources, doing these actions efficiently requires a deeper level of commitment and ability.

While the analytical subgroup and the programmed knowledge category often interact directly, the logistical subgroup usually plays a supporting role. To analyse a technical or professional problem, the individual needs to identify preferred goals, plan and organise resources, and do the analysis in an efficient manner. For the TV repair technician, a knowledge of the electrical circuitry and an understanding of appropriate diagnosis protocols will be insufficient if the technician does not plan, organise and allocate resources (time, spare parts, equipment). If efficiency is not present, then one would have to wonder at the future employment prospects of the technician!

Application of the analytical and logistical subgroups

The HRDNI report will often concentrate on the programmed knowledge that the learners need to acquire. The designer may then be left with the need to deduce whether the learners also need to assimilate analytical and logistical abilities. If the learners will be required to put the information and skills to practical use, then they will usually have to be developed in the appropriate analytical and logistical abilities. Of course, a good HRDNI report would have already covered this eventuality, but the designer should not take for granted such extrapolation.

The initial elements, particularly linear and goal identification, are usually most appropriately developed by the theory session, the lecture and the skill session. Diagnostic analysis and administrative proficiency may be imparted best by one of these structured learning strategies. However, if the HRDNI report indicates that these two elements are reasonably complex, then a discussion or case study may be the method of choice. Certainly, however, the more complex elements of the task subgroup — complex analysis, analysis under uncertainty, allocating resources and efficiency — tend to need communicative learning, for example as offered by the discussion session strategy or the case study. The designer can also bear in mind the knowledge generation processes of internal-

isation and externalisation as the discussion session is aimed at encouraging these processes.

When considering the design of a full learning experience (for example, a workshop or course extending over a number of days), the usual sequence of learning starts with the imparting of the information through the theory session or lecture and then the deeper exploration of this information through reading case studies, or practising in a controlled environment using a 'complex task' skill session, and then conducting a discussion session to identify successful options, approaches and sequences as well as distinguishing paths that will lead to failure.

The implementing subgroup

The implementing subgroup of the task category is a deeper and more complex set of five elements — work motivation, bias for action, purposeful action, unilateral power and effectiveness. This is very much a results-orientated subgroup, having a high concern for ensuring that a positive outcome is achieved. *Work motivation* is an attitude that emphasises self-motivation and enthusiasm with a strong belief in the primacy of work. A *bias for action* concentrates this work motivation towards a desire to accomplish something, such as solving problems and overcoming obstacles. *Purposeful action* channels the individual's energy towards a specific goal to ensure a positive outcome. However, this drive is tempered with common sense and an appreciation for the larger picture. A significant but more sophisticated competence is the appropriate use of *unilateral power* — the ability to give directives and gain compliance. Unilateral power derives its energy from a variety of sources — knowledge expertise, position in the organisation and logical ability are the most common. Finally, ensuring *effectiveness* — that the goal is achieved fully and successfully with the least expenditure of resources — is the overall aim of any task-orientated process.

a closer look 9.3

Application of the implementing subgroup

With the implementing subgroup, the HR developer as a designer is entering the challenges of emancipatory learning. All the elements of the implementing subgroup deal with frames of reference, although more with causal and procedural assumptions than with paradynamic assumptions.

Accordingly, the learning strategies of choice tend to be experiential learning and mentoring or perhaps problem-based learning. These strategies confront the learner with irrefutable evidence of inconsistencies in personal causal and procedural assumptions and encourage the reflection needed for deep internalisation and externalisation. In addition, particularly with mentoring, there is the opportunity for socialisation.

THE RELATIONSHIPS CATEGORY

The relationships category consists of three subgroups — interpersonal, intrapersonal and concern for others. Like those in the task category, these three subgroups are on two levels with the interpersonal and intrapersonal seen as equivalent in complexity. As with the analytic and logistic subgroups, there is a strong interaction between the interpersonal and intrapersonal subgroups. Further, there is often a strong interrelationship between analytic/logistic and interpersonal/intrapersonal.

The interpersonal subgroup

The interpersonal subgroup consists of five elements: communication, interaction at the objective level, interaction at the emotional level, use of group processes and use of social power. Very few people in the workplace operate in isolation and this means that some form of *communication* must occur. Communication can take three basic forms — written, oral and nonverbal. Frequently, oral and nonverbal communication operate in tandem. Competence in communication is the most basic requirement for interpersonal abilities. To communicate logically and meaningfully, an individual must be able to *interact at the objective level*. Objectivity means being relatively impartial and unbiased about others' views and not being limited by subjectivity. A more complex ability is being able to *interact at the emotional level*, recognising that there is a fundamental difference between working with 'things' and working with 'people'. *Using group processes* needs high competence at the three preceding elements — communication and interacting at the objective and emotional level as well as knowledge of group processes. The appropriate *use of social power* is often not acknowledged in polite circles, but is a necessary, strong yet subtle tool in interpersonal relations. Social power comes from other peoples' acceptance that an individual can influence them and this acceptance may be based on charisma, 'likeability' and trust. Together with its partner in the task subgroup, unilateral power, social power used inappropriately can be very destructive so it is an energy that must be handled with care.

a closer look · 9.4

Application of the interpersonal subgroup

The basics of the first two elements — communication and interacting at an objective level — can often be learned through the structured strategies of the theory session and, to a lesser extent, the lecture. The theory session has the advantage of incorporating active learning which provides opportunities of converting cognitive understanding into practical application. The more complex levels of these two elements usually require more complex learning strategies such as the discussion and the case study.

The other three elements — interacting at the emotional level, use of group pressure and use of social power — usually need the development or change of causal and procedural assumptions. Because these three elements assume that there will be interactions with other people, the learning strategy of the role play is particularly effectual. Mentoring and experiential learning are also viable options. When using the role play, mentoring and experiential learning, full use should be made of modelling, as this is ideal for learning large, integrated patterns of behaviour (see discussion in chapter 2).

The intrapersonal subgroup

The intrapersonal subgroup deals with the ability of the individual to manage his or her self, 'intra' meaning within or inside. This subgroup is on a similar complexity level to the interpersonal subgroup and, indeed, a number of the elements within each subgroup often develop in tandem. The intrapersonal subgroup has six elements: spontaneity, accurate self-awareness, self-confidence, inner strength, self-discipline and emotional resilience. *Spontaneity* is the ability to express oneself freely and easily and has strong links with the interpersonal subgroup element of communication. *Accurate self-awareness* is the ability to assess one's strengths and weaknesses honestly and realistically while *self-confidence*, the ability to express confidence and be decisive, is a closely allied element. Both self-awareness and self-confidence are needed for interacting at the objective and emotional level. *Inner strength* means having a tolerance for uncertainty, being resistant to stress and being willing to handle ambiguity. Closely aligned to inner strength, but at a slightly deeper level, is *self-discipline* — the ability to subordinate one's personal needs or desires for a greater good (the needs of another or for the organisation or for a principle or for a higher order goal). Both of these elements — inner strength and self-discipline — are linked to the interpersonal subgroup elements of use of group processes and use of social power, as well as with the analytical category elements of analysis under uncertainty and efficiency. The final element, *emotional resilience*, is at a deeper level and could possibly be regarded as a separate subgroup. Emotional resilience is the capacity to be stimulated by emotional and interpersonal crises rather than exhausted or debilitated by them, and the capacity to bear high levels of responsibility without becoming paralysed.

Competence at the emotional resilience level is situational. The situation is most probably dependent on the programmed information category, to a large extent. So, an engineer may have high emotional resilience with engineering conundrums but may become much less so in the unfamiliar territory of psychological counselling. The deeper level outcomes of the subgroup concern for others and the categories critical thinking and meta-abilities are also highly reliant on the same situational context.

a closer look 9.5

Application of the intrapersonal subgroup

Similar to the interpersonal subgroup, the basics of the first two elements of the intrapersonal subgroup — spontaneity and accurate self-assessment — can often be learned through the structured strategies of the theory session and, to a lesser extent, the lecture. The more complex levels of these two elements usually require more complex learning strategies such as the discussion and the case study.

For the next three elements — self-confidence, inner strength and self-discipline — the role play is particularly useful because the learner has to examine current causal and prescriptive assumptions. However, extreme care has to be taken during the 'de-roling' and debriefing stages of the role play. Frequently, mentoring and experiential learning as follow-up strategies are also needed. Again, the use of

modelling is highly recommended.

Emotional resilience is reliant on paradynamic assumptions and more intensive and lengthy learning strategies are needed. Problem-based learning is often quite effective in raising awareness of possible hegemonic assumptions but supportive mentoring and caring feedback from another party are usually needed to develop this intricate and subtle element.

The concern for others subgroup

The subgroup 'concern for others' is very dependent on the other two subgroups in the relationships category — the interpersonal subgroup and the intrapersonal subgroup. Unless these two subgroups are developed to a reasonable level the individual does not have the skills to show concern for others. In addition, the less-developed individual usually does not have the inclination to be concerned as he or she is more interested in perceived inner deficiencies: 'How can I interact with these people?' or 'This problem is just stressing me out too much!' So, before an individual can be genuinely concerned for others, she or he has to have high levels of interpersonal competence and a well-developed sense and acceptance of self.

Concern for others is made up of four elements: developing others, empathy, leadership and managing conflict. *Developing others* involves not just training staff, but having a genuine interest in helping and watching others change and become more competent; having a belief in others' ability to perform and improve; being able to provide others with accurate and honest feedback; and knowing the optimal time to give this feedback. *Empathy* is the ability to get along with people, to become close to them and 'feel what others are feeling' but still to be able to maintain a strong recognition of right and wrong, what is needed and what is not needed. There are many definitions and theories of *leadership* but of particular relevance is to be a good judge of people, to be able to delegate and mould together a team, yet be able to supervise autonomous and independent individuals. Linked closely to leadership is the ability to *manage conflict* to ensure positive outcomes. Good leaders assume that conflict is a source of energy and a good leader uses this energy to the benefit of all concerned.

Rather than having links between elements, the subgroups of 'concern for others' and 'implementing' (from the task category) are a twosome that ensures a project will be carried to completion. Combining work motivation, a bias for purposeful action and effectiveness with the ability to develop and lead others empathically, overcoming obstacles with the appropriate use of power and managing conflict positively, are the hallmarks of good project management. So much workplace effort these days is based on projects with teams and groups sharing a variety of professional/technical information. Project work has now become the ultimate application of professional/technical information.

a closer look 9.6

Application of the concern for others subgroup

Similar to the implementing subgroup, when considering the concern for others subgroup, the designer is entering the challenges of emancipatory learning. All the elements of the concern for others subgroup deal with frames of reference, although more with causal and procedural assumptions than with paradynamic assumptions.

Accordingly, the learning strategies of choice tend to be experiential learning and mentoring or perhaps problem-based learning. These strategies confront the learner with irrefutable evidence of inconsistencies in personal causal and procedural assumptions and encourage the reflection needed for deep internalisation and externalisation. In addition, particularly with mentoring, there is the opportunity for socialisation.

THE CRITICAL THINKING CATEGORY

The second to last category is critical thinking, which was discussed at some length in chapter 2 applying to adult learning. To review, critical thinking is based on a combination of:

- *Problem solving*, which is a process of logically and accurately overcoming challenges. There are several protocols available and one of the most common in use is Dewey's seven-step scientific model. Of course, this was a component of the element complex analysis in the analytical subgroup. However, in critical analysis problem solving interacts strongly and frequently with the other components of critical thinking.

- *Creativity*, which involves novel responses and identifying new concepts by bringing together previously unconnected factors, in new or unusual or adaptive ways. Creativity includes the ability to think laterally.
- *Evaluation* by testing for what is both relevant and significant. Evaluation relies on some predetermined standard, which comes from the individual's explicit knowledge or tacit knowledge or even from his or her frames of reference.
- *Dialectic thinking*, which allows the mind to accept that an entity may have opposing attributes (for example, electricity can provide light and keep us warm but it can also kill us). Having dialectic thought allows the individual to imagine a wider variety of possibilities and options.

a closer look   9.7

Application of the critical thinking category

The learning strategy of problem-based learning was specifically designed to develop critical thinking and this is the strategy of choice. However, mentoring and experiential learning (with honest and accurate feedback) can also play a part.

Contract learning is another option as this approach gives the learner the responsibility for making all the choices during the learning experience. Making these choices about learning alternatives, and having the responsibility for accepting the consequences, tends to exercise the individual's critical thinking ability.

The advantage of problem-based learning and contract learning is that they involve the emotions and critical reflection components (see figure 2.2 in chapter 2). Thus, the complex interplay of these three components — critical thinking, critical reflection and emotions — is brought into operation, providing a full and rich learning experience.

However, highly experienced facilitators and mentors are needed to manage this sensitive and sophisticated learning process and designers will need to specify this requirement in any design.

THE META-ABILITIES CATEGORY

The category of meta-abilities is the deepest and most complex level in the hierarchy and comprises three elements — mental agility, helicopter perception and self-perpetuating learning. *Mental agility* refers to both the mental capacity for understanding complex situations and the speed at which this is done. It means being able to grasp problems quickly and think about them, to think of several things at once, to switch rapidly from one situation and problem to another and 'to think on one's feet'. *Helicopter perception* is the ability to draw back and see the larger picture and how the specific problem or project, that is the current focus of attention, fits into the overall scheme of things. This broader focus also includes the ability to read the political climate and to have a feel for what the community is looking for. *Self-perpetuating learning* engenders a thirst for new knowledge and holds an attitude that one's learning never ends. It allows one to be capable of using all the various learning processes and selecting the most appropriate learning process for the particular situation. A self-perpetuating learner can move from the abstract to the practical and back again and can generalise learning by applying new knowledge from one situation to a different situation.

This category is called 'meta-abilities' to indicate that the three elements form a deep-seated, nearly invisible network that operates at a subconscious level. The three elements are well within the tacit level of knowledge and are connected to the individual's basic frames of reference, the paradynamic assumptions. The meta-abilities allow the individual to simultaneously focus on his or her personal internal operations while simultaneously monitoring the overall external situation so that the other categories of programmed knowledge, task, relationships and critical thinking will be combined to ensure the most efficient and effective outcome.

a closer look 9.8

Application of the meta-abilities category

The adult learning strategies of contract learning and action learning place the learner in a situation where all the categories of programmed knowledge, task, relationships and critical thinking are needed. In fact, these categories are usually needed in combination to deal with these strategies. For example, when experiencing contract learning, the learner has to research the relevant programmed knowledge; needs the analytical abilities to conduct the research, and the logistical abilities to plan, organise and operate efficiently; has to ensure that the plans to learn are implemented; has to operate well on an interpersonal level as contract learning depends to a large extent on group work and contacting experts; needs the strength of the intrapersonal abilities to keep operating in the face of adversity; often has to manage conflict; and depends significantly on critical thinking. This combination of categories needs the meta-abilities as a managing process and to monitor simultaneously the external situation to ensure the learning contract keeps on track. Action learning exercises all the categories in a similar fashion.

THE PRACTICAL USE OF THE HIERARCHY

Any model is a rudimentary representation of reality. For this reason, no model should be followed slavishly to the exclusion of judgement, and the HLO is no exception. The overall design of categories and subgroups in the HLO seems to be relatively robust. That there is a gradient of elements within each of the subgroups is also plausible. However, there could be argument over the placing of some of the elements. For example, the placement of 'self-discipline' as marginally deeper and more complex than 'inner strength' could be challenged. Fortunately, as the design of adult learning experiences is not a precise science, such minor quibbles are of no great importance.

The HLO does bring some initial logic and predictability to the selection of suitable learning strategies by focusing the designer's attention on a reasonably specific domain of potentially appropriate learning strategies. For example, it was suggested that the role play would be the strategy of choice to develop the element of 'interact at the emotional level'. However, the designer may see that a case study may be a better way to introduce the concept and then to follow this with a period of interactions with a mentor in the workplace. However, perhaps a more important advantage is that the hierarchy does indicate clearly which learning strategies are inappropriate and that the designer should think carefully before using such inappropriate strategies. The hierarchy certainly indicates that the lecture is most inappropriate for developing 'emotional resilience', an error that is unfortunately overlooked by some organisations which attempt quick fixes in the name of cost savings.

For these reasons, the HLO is presented as a guide for both the novice designer and the experienced designer.

- For the novice designer, the hierarchy will prove useful in two ways. Firstly, it helps the designer to avoid costly errors in choosing very inappropriate learning strategies. Secondly, the hierarchy provides a useful model within which the designer can safely gain experience.
- The experienced designer will find the hierarchy useful as a reality check to counterbalance the creative enthusiasm which sometimes leads us astray.

THE LEARNERS

We now come to the second important variable: the learner. That people are complex and multifaceted is an axiomatic statement. While the designer should never under-estimate the power of individual differences, some order has to be made amongst the competing and myriad demands of the learners to ensure the strongest possibility of the success of the learning experience. Further, most learning experiences in an organisation assume that a group of people will be involved in the learning experience. This means that some of the individual differences will have to be subordinated to the greater good of the group.

Within this constraint, there are a number of characteristics about the learner that have been shown to have an effect on selecting appropriate learning strategies. In chapter 3, the issues of age, health, gender and culture were discussed and the HR developer as a designer must continually review these issues to ensure that the diversity in the organisation is harnessed as a positive and creative force. For example, adult learners from a high context, high power distance culture will expect that the HR developer as a presenter will be an authority figure who will share her or his expertise. This expectation is quite appropriate for the initial levels of the HLO (for example, professional knowledge) but runs counter to the logic of the HLO approach for the deeper levels of outcomes (for example, developing the 'concern for others' or the 'implementation' subgroups). The designer will need to consider how learners from such cultures can be developed to accept the more unstructured learning strategies.

Adult learners also exhibit a number of specific variables that need to be considered. These include the level of current knowledge of the topic content, motivation, learning orientation, learning cycles and learning styles. Having already made some decisions about possible learning strategies from the HLO, these characteristics of the learner should be considered as an 'overlay'. This overlay allows the designer to fine-tune the selection process, perhaps by omitting some options or perhaps by indicating that a particular learning strategy option is now highly preferred.

CURRENT KNOWLEDGE

Several authors (Biggs 1989a; Candy 1991; Harris 1989; Knowles 1990) have suggested that the ability to undertake unstructured (often referred to as self-directed) learning strategies, such as contract learning and action learning, may depend on the level of knowledge that the learner has about the particular programmed knowledge that is the focus of the learning endeavour. Delahaye (1990) found there were significant differences between those with high and low prior knowledge, with resultant implications for selecting a learning strategy.

a closer look   9.9

The effect of the learner's current knowledge

As learners with limited programmed knowledge are likely to have difficulty in operating within the unstructured strategies, they need to be guided through the programmed knowledge. The most effective and efficient options are the skill session, theory session or lecture and the structured discussion methods, until the learners reach a level where they can seriously examine the more advanced features and interrelationships of the programmed knowledge. Then unstructured discussions and perhaps case studies can be used.

MOTIVATION

There have been several motivational theories discussed through the years, mostly emanating from the fields of psychology and management. Two that are relevant to our discussion of the motivation of learners are the two-factor theory (Herzberg 1968) and the expectancy–valence theory (Vroom 1964).

The *two-factor theory* suggests that there are two major but different considerations to take on board when examining motivation. There are *hygiene factors* which, if absent, cause dissatisfaction. Of interest to designers are the hygiene factors of supervision, the physical conditions under which the learning takes place and relationships with peer learners. If any of these are too low, the learners are likely to become dissatisfied with resultant negative effects on learning. Interestingly, increasing the value or quality of these hygiene factors does not motivate learners; it just takes away the dissatisfaction. So, the learning environment should be comfortable, but do not expect plush and expensive surroundings to increase motivation to learn. The *motivator factors* include achievement, recognition, the relevance of the topic content being learned, responsibility and growth. The designer should look to enhance these motivators wherever possible.

a closer look 9.10

Design and the two-factor theory of motivation

The HR developer as a designer needs to ensure that the learning experience:

- includes opportunities for the learners to meet each other and interact so that good relationships are developed between the peer learners
- provides opportunities for the learners to see what they have achieved (for example, through tests of ability of knowledge learned)
- allows the learners to take some responsibility for deciding what should be learned and how it should be learned.
- provides opportunities for the learners to reflect on what

they have achieved during the learning experience so that they are aware of just how much personal growth and development has occurred

- covers the knowledge that is relevant to the learners. This issue of relevance has been discussed in chapter 2 when examining the work of Knowles and has also been emphasised as an important issue to be analysed in the HRDNI. That relevance is again raised under motivation just underlines what an important issue it is.

In addition to these design components, the designer needs to consider the physical location

where the learning will take place. For example, if the learning experience is a course or workshop such physical necessities as comfortable seating, sufficient light, air conditioning/heating and suitable space need to be provided.

The relationship between facilitator or trainer and the learner and the way the facilitator or trainer provides recognition to the learners is beyond the control of the HR developer who is the designer. However, the designer should designate the type and quality of the facilitator or trainer needed to manage the learning experience.

The *expectancy–valence theory* is a more complicated impression of motivation. This theory suggests that motivation is a process of four sequential steps. If, when taking this decision path, the learner believes any step is below an acceptable threshold then the motivation of the learner decreases. The steps, in sequence, are:

1. *expectancy one*, where the learner decides whether the learning task is achievable but challenging or if it is too easy or too hard. If the task is considered too easy or too hard the learner will become demotivated.

2. *expectancy two*, where the learner makes an educated guess on whether, once the task is achieved, the expected rewards will follow. If there is a belief that the expected reward will not eventuate then the motivation of the learner to become involved in the learning task will decrease.

3. *outcome one*, where the observable (to the learner) reward does eventuate. Skinner's operant conditioning (discussed in chapter 2) suggests that a behaviour only exists because of the reward following.

4. *outcome two*, where the observable reward does have some internal value (or valence) to the learner. If the reward does not have any valence, then the learner is unlikely to perform the learning task again.

a closer look   9.11

Design and the expectancy–valency theory

The designer needs to ensure that:
- any learning tasks are achievable but challenging for the learners
- observable rewards will be forthcoming (for example, that the results of any performance tests will be given to the learners)

- based on outcome two, any rewards are of value to the learner. While rewards are an individual issue, there are a number of recognised rewards that are valued by most people. These recognised rewards were identified in the two-factor theory — achievement, responsibility and growth. The designer needs to provide opportunities for these rewards to be incorporated into the learning experience.

One important motivational theory, developed by John Biggs (1989b), has come out of the educational literature. Biggs has suggested that there are three levels of motivation. While Biggs did not consider the three levels to be an hierarchy, it can be useful to consider them as such. The three levels are:

1. *utility motivation*, where the learner consents to be involved in the learning experience because the exercise will result in some utilitarian benefit other than the content learned. This type of motivation occurs when a learner attends a training course and tries only hard enough to achieve a basic pass, knowing that a basic pass is sufficient to receive a raise. The content covered by the training course does not hold any interest for the learner.

2. *achievement motivation*, where the learner receives intense satisfaction in achieving some measurable goal. This goal may be based on competing against a personally set standard (for example, achieving a high distinction or answering every question correctly) or on an external standard (for example, receiving a higher score than a peer or being in the top ten per cent of the class).

3. *interest motivation,* where the learner is intensely interested in the topic content itself. The details and interrelations are all fascinating to the learner with this level of motivation.

Now, it tempting to believe that interest motivation is more valuable than utility motivation. However, this decision is really that of the learner. If utility motivation achieves the goals of the learner then utility motivation is the best level for that learner. Designers and HR developers sometimes believe that others should share their interest motivation in a particular topic when, in reality, learners have other agenda that hold precedence for them.

Design and the three levels of motivation

The learner with utility motivation will prefer an efficient transmission of information, such as the theory session or lecture. A discussion will be tolerated, especially if it is a structured discussion, but it must not deviate into areas that are not essential. However, care must be taken by the designer that any summative tests (see chapter 12) are of a standard high enough to ensure quality performance on the job. The learner with utility motivation will not voluntarily achieve a level of performance higher than that designated.

The learner with achievement motivation needs tests that provide quantitative feedback. It is only with figures that comparisons can be made by the learner — comparisons that are the foundation of achievement motivation. So, the designer should incorporate some processes that provide quantitative feedback for learners with this level of motivation.

The learner with interest motivation needs freedom — in time, sources of information, opportunities for reflection — to plumb the full depths of the knowledge being covered. The self-directing approaches of problem-based learning, contract learning and action learning are the strategies of choice for learners with the interest level of motivation.

LEARNING ORIENTATION

As discussed in chapter 2, Knowles suggested that learning strategies can be categorised under two basic approaches — pedagogical or andragogical. Other words are often used to describe these two basic approaches — trainer/teacher or learner–controlled, traditional or self-directed, structured or unstructured. Delahaye (1987) and Delahaye, Limerick and Hearn (1994) showed that pedagogy and andragogy have an orthogonal relationship — that is, they are at right angles to each other. These authors also suggested that the resulting two-dimensional space can be divided into four orientations to learning — see figure 9.2. Extending this work, Delahaye (1995) found that the learners in each orientation stage showed different characteristics and, from these characteristics, preferred learning strategies can be inferred.

FIGURE 9.2
The four stages of learning orientation

Stage 3 (Low pedagogy/high andragogy)	Stage 2 (High pedagogy/high andragogy)
Stage 4 (Low pedagogy/low andragogy)	Stage 1 (High pedagogy/low andragogy)
PEDAGOGY	

Stage 1 (high pedagogy/low andragogy)

Learners in this stage tend not to be interested in 'intellectual' analytical thought. They are certain in what they have been taught to believe and accept the 'tried and true', even when something else might be better. They respect established ideas and are more tolerant of traditional difficulties (for example, the inadequacies of the lecture when used inappropriately). These learners tend to oppose and postpone change and spend a longer time in the 'cusp of change' — they leave the old and approach the new, find the new too imposing and try to go back to the old, find the old is no longer there and approach the new again, only to repeat the process (Cattell 1989). Some learners who have difficulty with close interpersonal relationships sometimes choose stage 1, simply because such structured learning strategies preclude interactions among learners.

a closer look   9.13

The learner in stage 1 of the learning orientation

The first challenge for the designer is to decide to which stage of orientation the learners belong. While there is a questionnaire designed for the purpose (Christian 1982), it is not readily available. However, the designer can refer to the characteristics of the typical learner described and make a judgement.

For those learners at the stage 1 orientation, two of the characteristics are distinctive. The first is a disinterest in 'intellectual' analytical thought — these learners often just want the minimal amount of information to be able to do the job reasonably competently or to just pass the test or examination. This minimalist approach seems to be caused either by a utility level of motivation or because the learner knows very little of the programmed knowledge and his or her priority is ensuring the basics of the knowledge are understood. The second distinctive characteristic is a fairly strong negative reaction to change. Stated preferences by the learner (during the HRDNI or at the beginning of the course) for lectures and 'not these airy fairy

talk fests', when discussions are proposed as learning strategies, are indicators.

Learners at the stage 1 learning orientation prefer structured (or pedagogical) learning strategies such as the theory session, lecture and skill session. Use of structured discussions are tolerated, provided there is not too much interaction between learners. If the topic to be learned is appropriate (i.e. at the introductory level of programmed knowledge), then there is no conflict with using these strategies.

However, if the topic is more in the realms of the deeper elements of the analytical, logistical, interpersonal or intrapersonal subgroups of the HLO, then the designer has a difficult decision to make. One option is that the learners are not ready to be developed to these deeper elements. This is a tough decision because of most HR developers' belief in equity for all and also because of the organisational political pressure that everyone has to be developed.

The other option is to develop the stage 1 learners to become

stage 2 learners. The designer will need to provide support and encouragement for the learner to progress into stage 2. Providing this support and encouragement is not easy because considerable time and effort is needed — resources that the organisation may be unwilling to invest. Providing a course program (or a weekly subject outline if in the educational sector), albeit one that has less topic content detail, can help. The designer and the educator/trainer/facilitator will find strong dependence needs ('It is your job to decide what I need to learn, not mine') and even the transition to less dependence (as compared to full independence) needs to be handled in a caring manner. Providing opportunities to develop supporting relationships with peer learners and the educator/trainer/facilitator can also help with those learners who do not have difficulties with close interpersonal contact.

Fortunately, with most learners, the human strengths of flexibility and adaptability allow a transition to stage 2, as long as some supporting mechanisms are provided.

Stage 2 (high pedagogy/high andragogy)

The learners in this group are very complex. They are quite perceptive and would prefer to understand a point rather than make hasty judgements. They are also curious and adaptable. They have a preference with the practical and are driven by their immediate learning needs. However, they tend to be suspicious and will avoid anything far-fetched. They can also have a relatively lower self-regard and lower self-acceptance but any feelings of inferiority may be masked by aggressiveness and stubbornness, attack being considered the best form of defence. A key characteristic is competitiveness. Learners at this stage crave competition which is displayed by a high achievement motivation. They display a need to achieve an internally established personal target (for example, a certain level of correct responses, usually 80% to 100% or a certain grade point average, again usually set a high level) or some external comparison (for example, achieving a higher score than a friend — or enemy!). As discussed under achievement motivation, such comparisons usually need a quantitative marking process. A give-away indicator for learners in stage 2 is that, when given some qualitative feedback on a test or examination, they will ask for a quantitative score ('If this was marked out of 20, what would you give me?').

a closer look 9.14

The learner in stage 2 of the learning orientation

The heightened perception of learners in stage 2 have often made them question the inappropriateness of the structured strategies in certain situations. This is an advantage if unstructured strategies are going to be used and the learning strategies of the unstructured discussion, case study, role play and research project are usually well tolerated. However, if any of these strategies are new to the learners, then their suspicion and aggression could be triggered. So, if the learners are likely to question the learning strategies chosen, whether they be structured or unstructured, the designer needs to consider how the selected learning strategies will be presented.

The big advantage for the designer is that the learners in this stage are curious and adaptive. Using their willingness to understand a point of view, the designer should incorporate full explanations of the objectives and processes of the proposed learning strategies. Time also needs to be built into any design to allow for conflict management and discussions when aggressiveness and stubbornness come to the fore.

Of concern to the designer is their need for competition. If there is no need to develop these learners to become self-directed learners then the designer can build in processes so that quantitative feedback is given. However, if the intent is to develop these learners so that they can progress to stage 3 then this dependence on extrinsic feedback will need to be changed.

Stage 3 (low pedagogy/high andragogy)

These learners are the quintessential self-directed learners — or andragoges as Knowles would call them. They are experimenting, analytical, creative and free-thinking and can be described as 'rebels with a cause'. The cause is usually an alternative to what they see as obstructive, unfair and oppressive traditional, structured strategies. They usually have the ability to develop meaningful, contactful relationships and prefer to operate within groups. Being in a group allows them to hear new ideas as well as to compare their ideas and values with others. While being imaginative and unconventional they can also be somewhat absentminded. They usually rate high on self-regard and self-acceptance.

a closer look   9.15

The learner in stage 3 of the learning orientation

The learners in stage 3 readily take to the unstructured learning strategies of problem-based learning, contract learning and action learning because of the freedom from obstruction and oppression, and the opportunities for analytical thought. Their high self-regard and self-acceptance see them through any challenges and constraints imposed by the organisation and powerful others. They are quite willing to accept self-responsibility for their own decisions and actions.

The challenge for the designer comes from two fronts. The first is when structured strategies are required (for example, the HLO indicates that the theory session or lecture would be the most efficient option). In this case the designer should use the structured approaches for the bare minimum of time to cover just the absolute basic of programmed knowledge. This should then be followed with discussions to give the stage 3 learners some freedom to think and interact in groups. The designer should then move into problem-based learning, contract learning or action learning as soon as possible.

The second challenge for the designer is that the stage 3 learners may become 'rebels *without* a cause'. Their experimental nature and self-confidence can engender a belief in their own learning immortality. This results in time spent on inappropriate or even unacceptable learning objectives. For example, a group could insist on watching pornographic videos for 2 hours after a lunch break, because they were suddenly overwhelmed by the feelings of freedom of choice and chose to exert this freedom — albeit in a somewhat feisty teenage manner. The designer needs to establish firm parameters (for example, through the non-negotiable objectives in contract learning) of what will be acceptable and what will not. Remember, these learners are experimenting, imaginative and unconventional. The designer will have to be in a highly creative and critical thinking mode to cover all bases. If there is a loop-hole, these learners will find it.

Stage 4 (low pedagogy/low andragogy)

These learners are highly mature and experienced learners. They are what Candy (1991) describes as personally autonomous — having an ability to conceive of goals and plans independently; having a high capacity for rational thought; exercising freedom in thought and action; fearlessly and resolutely carrying plans of action into practice; and rating high on self-mastery in the face of reversals and challenges. They have a systematic way of doing things and are decisive, although they tend to have settled opinions. While they can be easily upset by authority, they usually make few demands and are guided by an overwhelming desire to avoid conflict. This profile explains their low scores on andragogy and pedagogy as they will respond to inner demands.

The learner in stage 4 of the learning orientation

The key to this group is their high levels of learner maturity. They will select the most advantageous learning option available. For example, they are usually quite happy to sit through a lecture on a topic when their programmed knowledge is low, as they see that this is the most efficient way to gain mastery over the initial concepts of the topic.

The designer should be very aware of their reaction to authority and ensure that the reasons for selecting a particular learning strategy are explored. Further, providing other possible options allows this type of learner to choose the most personally effective approach. Fortunately, there is no problem in allowing these learners to operate individually once an agreed set of learning outcomes has been negotiated.

This work on learning orientations is interesting because the concept starts with learning strategies and links these to learner characteristics. The next concept we examine — learning styles — starts with learner characteristics and from these characteristics makes extrapolations to suggested learning strategies. While learning orientation indicates a preference for particular learning strategies, learning styles refer to a preference for particular information processing styles (Curry 1987).

LEARNING STYLES

Kolb (1984) believed that learning consisted of two dimensions. The first dimension, *prehension*, represents two different and opposing processes of the learner taking in or grasping information from his or her external environment. One process is 'concrete experience' (i.e. ap-prehension) where the learner relies on the tangible, felt qualities of the immediate experience of interacting with his or her world (for example, interacting with others or using a tool). The other process is 'abstract conceptualisation' (i.e. com-prehension) where the learner relies on the conceptual interpretation and symbolic representation (for example, reading the concepts in this book). The second dimension, *transformation*, deals with the way the learner transforms that 'grasped or taken in' information. Again, this occurs in two different and opposing processes. 'Reflective observation' occurs through internal reflection (for example, reading how to make a paper plane and, after abstract conceptualisation, making a scaled drawing). 'Active experimentation' is the active external manipulation of the information (for example, reading how to make a paper plane and then making one and seeing if it flies).

These two dimensions of prehension (concrete experience versus abstract conceptualisation) and transformation (reflective observation versus active experimentation) are seen as having an orthogonal relationship (at right angles) and intersect at the centre of each continuum. Further, Kolb believes (1984, p. 42) that learning requires both prehension (grasping information) and transformation (transforming the grasped information). This, then, forms four styles of learners:

1. *divergers*, who take in information through concrete experience and transform that information by reflective observation

2. *assimilators*, who take in information by abstract conceptualisation and transform it by reflective observation
3. *convergers*, who take in information by abstract conceptualisation and transform it by active experimentation
4. *accommodators*, who take in information by concrete experience and transform it by active experimentation.

Kolb also produced a questionnaire, 'The Learning Style Inventory', that allowed an individual to identify his or her predominant approach. Another popular learning style questionnaire is Honey and Mumford's 'Learning Styles Questionnaire' (1992). A comparison of these two learning styles is shown in table 9.1.

TABLE 9.1
A comparison of the learning styles: the Learning Style Inventory (Kolb 1984) and the Learning Style Questionnaire (Honey and Mumford 1992)

THE LEARNING STYLE INVENTORY	THE LEARNING STYLE QUESTIONNAIRE
Divergers generate alternative ideas and implications. They will view a situation from many perspectives and organise many relationships into a meaningful 'gestalt'. They are imaginative, feeling-orientated, aware of meaning and values and are interested in people.	*Reflectors* are thoughtful people who like to consider all angles and implications before making a move. Then they act as part of a wider picture to include others' observations as well. They tend to adopt a low profile and have a slightly distant, tolerant, unruffled air about them. They are cautious and tend to postpone reaching conclusions.
Assimilators use inductive reasoning and create theoretical models by bringing together diverse ideas into an integrated explanation. It is important that the theories or models be logically sound and precise, rather than of practical value. They are more concerned with ideas and concepts than people.	*Theorists* assimilate disparate facts into coherent theories and like to analyse and synthesise. They are keen on basic assumptions, principles, theories, models and systems thinking and prize rationality and logic. They prefer to maximise certainty and feel uncomfortable with subjective judgements, lateral thinking and anything flippant.
Convergers emphasise the practical application of ideas and operate best in situations where there is a single correct answer or solution. They tend to be controlled in their expressions of emotion and prefer technical tasks and problems rather than social and interpersonal issues.	*Pragmatists* are practical, down-to-earth people who like making practical decisions and solving problems. They like to get on with things and act quickly and confidently on ideas that attract them. They tend to be impatient with ruminating and open-ended discussion.
Accommodators like to be involved in new experiences and doing things. They are action orientated, take risks and seek opportunities. They happily change themselves along with changing immediate circumstances. Where plans or theories do not fit the facts, they will solve the problem in an intuitive trial-and-error manner. They will rely on other people for information (rather than use their own analytic ability) but are sometimes seen as pushy and impatient.	*Activists* involve themselves fully in new experiences. Their days are filled with activity but they are bored with implementation and longer term consolidation. They are open-minded, not sceptical, and this tends to make them enthusiastic about anything new. They tend to act first and consider the consequences later. They are gregarious, constantly involving themselves with others, but, in doing so they seek to centre all activities around themselves.

As you can see from table 9.1, there does seem to be a number of similarities between diverger/reflector, assimilator/theorist, converger/pragmatist and accommodator/activist. Undoubtedly, learning styles are very complex and the combined descriptions most probably give a clearer picture of each of the styles.

The concept of learning styles has an intuitive appeal. We all know some people who are more action orientated and other people who prefer to sit down and think an issue through before deciding what action to take. Further, Mezirow (1990) has suggested that one of the major sources of paradynamic assumptions is the epistemic influences and these include learning styles. So, it is reasonable to believe that a particular learning style will have some impact on the way an individual learns. However, the decision is not quite as straightforward as such a belief may indicate. There are three additional issues that must be considered:

1. The learning style questionnaires do identify a preferred style but most people have back-up or support styles. Humans, being the flexible creatures that they are, tend to be able to move from one style to another.
2. In any group, it is likely that there will be a variety of preferences and this variety could easily cover all four styles.
3. Both Kolb (1984) and Honey and Mumford (1992) believe that successful learners use all four styles. Learners, therefore, should be exposed to all four so that they can develop the requisite skills.

These three issues indicate that a designer should endeavour to incorporate all four learning styles in any learning experience. Indeed, Honey and Mumford (1992) suggest that a robust learning cycle should pass through the four steps of:

- *step 1:* having an experience (activist)
- *step 2:* reviewing the experience (reflector)
- *step 3:* concluding from the experience (theorist)
- *step 4:* planning the next steps (pragmatist).

a closer look   9.17

The effect of the learner's learning style

In general, designers should look to include all four types of learning styles in the learning experience and there are two ways to do this. Firstly, the various needs incorporated in the styles can be met by the content imparted and also by the strategies used. For example, pragmatists and those with a concrete experience preference would enjoy any film or demonstration of how a piece of equipment works (the content) and would see the skill session as a good opportunity for hands-on practice; reflectors and those with a reflective observation preference would see the case study as providing opportunities to analyse a situation logically and would appreciate the time given to reflect on the meaning of the concepts raised in the case study.

The second way of incorporating learning styles is to have group activities where each group has at least one representative from each of the four styles. It is often beneficial to ensure that each group member knows the benefits of each learning style so that the group members can see the contributions of each style. An interesting extension is to have two activities — one where the groups are homogeneous (i.e. comprise only members of each style) and a second activity where the groups are heterogeneous (i.e. have a representative from each style in each group). A comparison of the two activities often highlights the differences in the learning process and how valuable each of the learning styles can be.

A DESIGNER'S CHECKLIST

As Caffarella (1994) comments, planning learning experiences for adults is like trying to negotiate a maze. Despite this complexity, the designer must make decisions that are logical, credible and defensible. This chapter has suggested that there are two basic and important considerations when designing learning experiences for adults. The first is the content to be learned which is usually defined by the learning outcomes that the HRDNI indicates are most desirable. The second important consideration is the learners.

The easiest place for the designer to start is with the learning outcomes. The HLO provides a basis for some logical selections of appropriate learning strategies. While there may be some debate over some of the elements within the subgroups of the hierarchy, there does appear to be reasonable logic in the link between the subgroups of outcomes and preferred learning strategies.

Once an overall selection of preferred learning strategies has been made the designer can then turn to the needs of the learners. Certainly a judgement on the learners' current programmed knowledge is a base indicator as to whether unstructured (andragogical, self-directed, learner controlled) strategies could be tolerated. If the learners have a low level of knowledge then the more structured (pedagogical, traditional, trainer/teacher controlled) learning strategies would be the preferred option, at least until the levels of knowledge have improved. Then the designer can take into consideration other learner characteristics such as motivation, learning orientation and learning styles. Finally, reviewing the overall design to ensure that there is frequent use of the four stages of the learning cycle will provide a unifying theme throughout the whole design. A broad checklist is provided in figure 9.3.

1. Examine each of the learning outcomes listed in the HRDNI and decide which level of the HLO describes it best.
2. Identify the 'building blocks' — the basic programmed knowledge which needs to be covered first before advanced programmed knowledge is presented; the programmed knowledge needed before the learners can take on the task category elements; the relationship category elements needed and, if so, where are they needed in the learning experience; the critical thinking and meta-abilities categories that are needed so that these are placed near the end of the learning experience.
3. Identify the critical characteristics of the learners — level of knowledge, motivation, learning orientations and learning styles — and decide the effect that these characteristics may have on the overall design.
4. Explore how the learning cycle of step 1 (having an experience), step 2 (reviewing the experience), step 3 (concluding from the experience) and step 4 (planning the next steps) could be included in the overall design.
5. Ensure that opportunities for appropriate feedback are built into the design. This feedback should be:
   • a combination of qualitative and quantitative
   • from an external source, such as a HR developer
   • from an internal source (i.e., the learners should be given the opportunity to compare their own performances against standards and draw their own conclusions).

FIGURE 9.3
A checklist
for designers

analytical subgroup — consists of four elements (linear analysis, diagnostic analysis, complex analysis and analysis under uncertainty) and is one of the three subgroups of the task category in the HLO

concern for others subgroup — consists of four elements (developing others, empathy, leadership and managing conflict) and is the most complex of the relationships category of the HLO

critical thinking — consists of the elements of problem-solving, creativity, evaluation, dialectic thinking and logical thinking and is at the third level of learning outcomes in the HLO

current knowledge — the learner's present level of knowledge of a particular topic

expectancy–valence theory — a motivational theory describing a process of four sequential steps

hierarchy of learning outcomes (HLO) — a model that categorises learning outcomes into a hierarchy and links the categories to appropriate learning strategies

implementing subgroup — consists of five elements (work motivation, a bias for action, purposeful action, use of unilateral power, and effectiveness) and is the most complex of the subgroups of the task category of the HLO

interpersonal subgroup — consists of five elements (communication, interaction at the objective level, interaction at the subjective level, using group processes and using social power) and is one of the subgroups of the relationships category of the HLO

intrapersonal subgroup — consists of six elements (spontaneity, accurate self-awareness, self-confidence, inner strength, self-discipline, emotional resilience) and is one of the subgroups of the relationships category of the HLO

learners — the adult learners involved in the learning experience

learning orientation — a model that categorises learners into four stages that reflect their predisposition for certain learning experiences

learning outcomes — the levels of knowledge, skills and abilities that the learner should achieve at the end of the learning experience

learning strategies — the methods of instruction and/or facilitation used to provide adult learners with learning experiences

learning styles — four preferences (diverger/reflector, assimilator/theorist, converger/pragmatist and accommodator/activist) for particular types of learning experiences

logistical subgroup — consists of four elements (goal identification, administrative proficiency, resources allocation and efficiency) and is one of the subgroups of the task category of the HLO

meta-abilities category — consists of the elements of mental agility, helicopter perception and self-perpetuating learning and is at the fourth, and most complex, level of learning outcomes in the HLO

motivation — the internal force encouraging people to learn

programmed knowledge category — consists of the elements of basic facts and skills, professional/technical information and procedural skills, and is the least complex of the learning outcomes in the HLO

relationships category — consists of the subgroups of interpersonal, intrapersonal and concern for others and is at the second level of learning outcomes in the HLO, at the same level as the task category

task category — consists of analytical, logistical and implementing subgroups and is at the second level of learning outcomes in the HLO, at the same level as the relationships category

three levels of motivation — a motivational model describing utility, achievement and interest motivation

two-factor theory — a motivational theory, consisting of satisfiers and motivators

QUESTIONS

For review

1. Briefly describe the categories of the HLO, providing examples of elements and subgroups where appropriate.

2. Describe two motivational theories that the HR developer should consider when designing learning experiences for adult learners.

3. Discuss the four learning styles.

For analysis

4. Compare and contrast the task and relationships categories of the HLO.

5. Identify the learning strategies that you would be likely to select for a workshop consisting of the elements of professional/technical information, linear and diagnostic analysis, inner strength and self-discipline. Justify your answer.

6. Identify the learning strategies that you would be likely to select for a workshop consisting of the subgroups 'intrapersonal' and 'concern for others' and the elements of problem solving, dialectic thinking and logical reflection. Justify your answer.

7. In questions 5 and 6, what changes would you make for learners coming from stage 2 (high pedagogy/high andragogy) of the learning orientation model?

For application

8. Consider the course or learning experience you are undertaking at the moment. Analyse your motivation using the expectancy–valence theory and the three levels of motivation. What links do you see between these two motivational models?

9. Audit a learning experience (a training course or developmental workshop) from a workplace with which you are familiar, using the HLO and the learner variables discussed in this chapter.

10. Reflect on a recent unsatisfactory learning experience and use the motivational theories discussed in this chapter to analyse your dissatisfaction.

REFERENCES

Biggs, J. B. (1989a). 'Approaches to the enhancement of tertiary teaching.' *Higher Education Research and Development*, 8(1), 7–25.

Biggs, J. B. (Ed.). (1989b). *Teaching for Learning: The View from Cognitive Psychology*. Hawthorn, Vic: ACER.

Caffarella, R. S. (1994). *Planning Programs for Adult Learners*. San Francisco: Jossey-Bass.

Candy, P. C. (1991). *Self-direction for Life Long Learning*. San Francisco: Jossey-Bass.

Cattell, H. B. (1989). *The 16PF: Personality in Depth*. Illinois: IPAT.

Christian, A. C. (1982). *A Comparative Study of the Andragogical–Pedagogical Orientation of Military and Civilian Personnel*. Unpublished doctoral dissertation, Oklahoma State University, Stilwater.

Curry, L. (1987). *Learning Styles in Medical Education*. Ottawa: Canadian Medical Education.

Delahaye, B. L. (1987). 'The orthogonal relationship between pedagogy and andragogy — some initial findings.' *Australian Journal of Adult Learning*, 27(3), 4–7.

Delahaye, B. L. (1990). *Selecting Strategies for Quality Management Education*. A paper presented to the ANZAME conference, Launceston, Tas.

Delahaye, B. L. (1995). *The Effect of Personality on Orientation to Self-directed Learning*. A paper presented to the AARE conference, Hobart, Tas.

Delahaye, B. L., Limerick, D. C. and Hearn, G. (1994). 'The relationship between andragogical and pedagogical orientations and the implications for adult learning.' *Adult Education Quarterly*, 44(4), Summer, 187–200.

Delahaye, B. L. and Smith, B. J. (1998). *How to be an Effective Trainer*. New York: Wiley.

Gagne, R. M., Briggs, L. J. and Wager, W. W. (1988). *Principles of Instructional Design*. (3rd ed.). New York: Holt, Rinehart and Winston.

Harris, R. (1989). 'Reflections on self-directed adult learning: Some implications for educators of adults.' *Studies in Continuing Education*, 11(2), 102–116.

Herzberg, F. (1968). 'One more time: How do you motivate employees?' *Harvard Business Review*, January–February, 53–63.

Honey, P. and Mumford, A. (1992). *The Manual of Learning Styles*. Berkshire, UK: Peter Honey.

Knowles, M. S. (1990). *The Adult Learner: A Neglected Species*. (4th ed.). Houston: Gulf.

Kolb, D. A. (1984). *Experiential Learning: Experience as the Source of Learning and Development*. Englewood Cliffs, NJ: Prentice Hall.

Mezirow, J. (1990). *Fostering Critical Reflection in Adulthood: A Guide to Transformative and Emancipatory Learning*. San Francisco: Jossey-Bass.

Nonaka, I. and Takeuchi, H. (1995). *The Knowledge Creating Company: How Japanese Companies Create the Dynamics of Innovation*. New York: Oxford University Press.

Print, M. (1993). *Curriculum Development and Design*. (2nd ed.). St. Leonards, NSW: Allen & Unwin.

Revans, R. W. (1982). *The Origins and Growth of Action Learning*. Sweden: Studentlitteratur.

Senge, P. M. (1990). 'The leader's new work: Building learning organisations.' *MIT Sloan Management Review*, Fall, 112–128.

Vroom, V. H. (1964). *Work and Motivation*. New York: Wiley.

Designing a workshop

Kylie Delyvo looked at the HRDNI report before her. Last year's strategic plan had identified a new market for digital facsimile machines. The operational plans for increasing the supply of the machines, including constructing a new storage centre, were well under way and now attention was being focused on the human resources. As part of this focus, the eight client service consultants to be selected were to attend a 4-day developmental workshop. Lucy Fox, the manager, had decreed that all the new client service consultants would attend the 4-day workshop, no matter what their previous experience.

The HRDNI report listed the following concluding objectives for the workshop:

At the end of the workshop, the participants will be able to:

1. describe the main components and functions of the Model 4 to Model 8 Yameto Digital Facsimile
2. repair a simple type 2 breakdown to the standards required in the maintenance manual
3. negotiate a complex conflict situation with a dissatisfied customer
4. ensure that members of the Services Department completed repairs of customer machines within the service times and to the standards of the company
5. complete clear and concise written reports and write letters to the standards laid down in the company manual of procedures.

Kylie sat back thinking deeply. She would read the report again later but, first, she would identify possible learning strategies that may be suitable for each concluding objective. She thought to herself, 'Of course, there will be some less obvious outcomes under some of those concluding objectives. Look at number 4. They will have to make some use of power there and will also need to be emotionally resilient. But also they will need to know the company's policies on service times and standards and that is basic information they will have to learn.'

Discussion questions

1. Using the HLO, list the likely types of learning strategies that would be used for each concluding objective. Briefly justify your decisions.

2. Although Lucy Fox has decreed that all of the client service consultants would attend the workshop, some will be more experienced than others. What advice would you give to Kylie about this when she designs the workshop?

Motivating workshop attendees

Allan Fogarty sat in the bus quietly fuming. Why did he have to go to this blasted training course? A workplace assessor, what was that? It sounded like a disease. And he did not want to be teaching anyone. He really enjoyed his job in the drafting office. The work was interesting, he had daily contact with various tradespeople, he was allowed to use his judgement — and he could drive to work. No problem with parking. Now look where he was, in a bus going into the training centre in the city. He did not even like the city, particularly. If only he had not stayed back last night to finish that quote. Mark was sick. So what? Mark was supposed to go on the course. So what? If no one went, the company would still have to pay. So what?

'Ah, well. Look on the bright side', Allan thought. Another certificate would not hurt. You never knew what would happen in the future. Another string to the bow and all that. And really, that bit about not wanting to teach anyone was not really true. He did enjoy showing people how to do the job. It felt good watching them gradually grasp the ins and outs of quotation work and reading the plans. Really, when he thought about it, he was quite good at teaching and he was very patient with people. 'Of course, what assessing has to do with teaching I don't know', he said to himself. 'Perhaps I would be better going on that Trainer's Workshop. Hmm, OK, when I get into the training centre I will talk to the course coordinator. What was her name? Juanita Pierce, yes that was it.'

Discussion questions

1. Use the motivation theories to analyse why Allan did not want to go on the workplace assessor's course.

2. If you were Juanita Pierce, what points would you cover with Allen to motivate him to attend the workplace assessor's course? Justify your answers.

Other design considerations

CHAPTER OBJECTIVES

At the end of this chapter you should be able to:

1   describe the effect that the indirect factors of strategic orientation, organisational culture, key stakeholders, resources and the designer's personal frame of reference have on the design decision

2   describe the rational model, the interaction model, the cyclical models and the platform model of curriculum design

3   describe the program plan, the session plans, the resources plan, the product marketing plan, the budget and the evaluation plan and define the role of each

4   explain why transfer of learning, extended learning and the creation of knowledge are important processes.

In the previous chapter, we examined the two factors — the learning outcomes and the learner — that have a direct effect on the shape of the learning experience. However, when devising a learning experience for adults in an organisation, the designer also must consider factors that have an indirect influence on the ultimate programme.

For the HR developer, in the role of the designer, the decisions about these factors — both the direct and the indirect — will result in a learning plan. The learning plan is comprised of the learning program, the resources plan, the marketing plan, the budget and the evaluation plan.

This chapter, therefore, begins by examining the indirect factors that the HR developer must consider in the design decisions and then discusses the resultant plans that must be developed so that the learning experience will be successful.

The first indirect factor is the **strategic orientation** of the organisation. For staff operating in the legitimate system of the organisation, the strategic plan defines, firstly, the content to be learned. Accordingly, the predominant learning outcomes emphasised for the legitimate system are programmed information outcomes, and the structured learning strategies of the theory session, skill session and lecture often predominate. Secondly, for the legitimate system, the type of strategy being followed will also have an influence on the learning strategies that will be used. For example, the defender strategy will usually confine the designer to the structured learning strategies of the theory session, skill session and the lecture. For staff operating in the shadow system, the deeper level learning outcomes of the HLO usually predominate. Accordingly, the learning strategies of problem-based learning, contract learning and action learning, supported by mentoring, are usually the learning strategies of choice for developmental activities in the shadow system.

As a designer, the HR developer must be very conscious of the **organisational culture**. The organisational culture includes the shared meanings (made up of beliefs, values, rituals, myths and practices) which indicate how organisational members should behave. The organisational culture is particularly strong within the legitimate system and will often dictate what learning strategies can or cannot be used and sometimes even their content. **Key stakeholders** are people in the organisation who have political knowledge. Political knowledge consists of political power and knowledge of organisational procedures and processes. Using this knowledge and power, key stakeholders are in a position to help or hinder new initiatives. **Resources** in an organisation are always scarce and, accordingly, there is always competition within the organisation for the use of these scarce resources. The HR developer should accept this reality and plan the design of any learning experience so that reasonable resource limitations are allowed for. These resources include the time available to the learners, a more than optimal number of learners, the physical resources available and the quality of the HR developers who will conduct the learning experience. The final indirect factor to be addressed is the personal frame of reference of the HR developer who is designing the learning experience. As discussed in chapter 2, everyone is influenced by their frame of reference and designers are no different. Designers, therefore, should be aware of their own frames of reference and the likely effect that these may have on their design decisions.

Over the years a number of curriculum design models have been promulgated to explain the design process. While each of the models has limitations, each does provide an interesting insight into designing learning experiences for adult learners. The **objectives** or **rational model** emphasises a logical process of four steps — objectives, instructional strategies, organising the learning experiences, and assessment and evaluation. This is a very basic model but, other than providing an overview, is quite simplistic. The **interaction** and **cyclical models** use the same basic steps but highlight the interactive nature of the four steps and the fact that the process can commence with any of the four steps. The **platform model** suggests that the reality of design is a more complex and disorganised process. The platform model is said to represent the more natural human interactions where, firstly, the values and perceptions of all stakeholders are gathered (the platform stage) and then these values and ideas are defended and proselytised (the deliberation stage) before the final decisions about the components of the learning experience are made (the design stage). Various elements of each of these models have been incorporated in the chapters in the design for this book.

For the legitimate system, the end product of all the design work is a series of plans. The **program** and **session plans** explain the content to be covered in the learning experience, the learning strategies to be used and the expected assessment. The program and session plans that are designed for the HLO levels of programmed knowledge category and the more basic levels of the task and relationships categories tend to be time specific and rely on the structured learning strategies. However, for the deeper levels of the HLO, the more unstructured strategies of contract learning and action learning are often followed and the designer concentrates more on the process to manage the learning. The **resource plan** documents all the physical resources that will be required to mount the learning experience. The **product marketing plan** attempts to influence those who will be involved in the decision to use the learning episode and describes the promotional tactics to be followed. The **budget** estimates the expected income that will be generated from offering the learning experience and compares this with the expected cash expenditures and opportunity cost expenditures. Finally, the designer should present recommendations for assessing the learning experience in an **evaluation plan**.

For the shadow system, the designer can have some influence on the transfer of the learning back to the workplace using projects and follow-up training. However, the designer may need to use more indirect approaches, such as developing the learners as self-directed learners or developing the immediate supervisors in supervisory and management workshops. The opportunities for the learner should continue into workplace learning. The **extended learning** phase achieves this by providing the learner with further opportunities to develop non-routinised problem solving. In addition, the learners should become involved in an organisational climate that succours a learning community by encouraging the creation of new knowledge by using the processes of externalisation, combination, internalisation and socialisation.

THE INDIRECT FACTORS

The indirect factors are the second set of considerations that the HR developer as the designer has to contemplate when designing the learning experience. These factors include the strategic orientation of the organisation, the organisational culture, the key stakeholders in the organisation, and the amount and type of resources available. One other indirect factor is so obvious it is often overlooked — the personal frame of reference of the designer.

While these factors are indirect, they do not lack importance. Indeed, many a workshop or intervention has failed because one or more of these factors have not been taken into consideration. Further, the designer often finds that balancing and negotiating these factors takes up considerable time — time which the designer would prefer to invest in considering the two direct factors discussed in chapter 9. However, this is the real world of the design role for the HR developer.

STRATEGIC ORIENTATION

In chapter 1 and chapter 4, we discussed the idea that an organisation is made up of two basic systems — the legitimate system and the shadow system. The legitimate system is responsible for the day-to-day activities and for ensuring the organisation is efficient and is successfully servicing the market niche where it holds the most competitive edge. However, the legitimate system is effective at operating only under conditions close to certainty. The shadow system is that part of the organisation which continually prepares the organisation to survive in the future. What happens in the future, when viewed from the present time, is far from certain. Therefore, the shadow system is a highly fluid and creative part of the organisation which identifies, examines and provides possible solutions for the challenges and opportunities that may occur at some future time. Together, the legitimate and shadow system specify the current strategic orientation of the organisation. The legitimate system achieves this by defining the present market niche that is being serviced, the shadow system by exploring the future and by challenging the current philosophy, culture and strategic mission of the organisation. This fundamental conflict between the two systems creates a dynamic orientation called **bounded instability** — a healthy state of tension within the organisation where learning is continual, change is expected, thinking is pro-active but the bottom line of productivity is never forgotten. The developmental designs are usually quite different for the legitimate system and for the shadow system.

The legitimate system

As a general rule, the legitimate system gives much more emphasis to programmed knowledge than does the shadow system. After all, it is this programmed knowledge which often gives the organisation its current competitive edge. Further, the legitimate system wants organisational members to act and produce the goods or services in a predictable and organised manner, as this makes for an effective and efficient organisation which will continue to survive. The legitimate system is also quite dependent on its traditional strategic plans (as discussed in chapter 4) to define its HR development activities. The traditional strategic plan does this in two ways:

1. The strategic plan often defines the learning outcomes that become the content of what is taught in the learning experiences. For example, if an organisation decides to invest in new machinery, then the designer needs to create a learning experience (usually a series of training courses) that will cover the safe operation of that machinery. Now the learning needs for that change in machinery should have been researched in the HRDNI. However, designers should not take that risk and should be familiar with the new directions foreshadowed in the organisational strategic plan.

2. The strategic plan describes the types of strategies the organisation will follow. Chapter 4 suggested that the four basic strategies were the defender strategy, the analyser strategy, the dynamic growth strategy and the entrepreneur strategy. Each of these planning strategies will have associated preferred learning strategies.

a closer look 10.1

The effect of the legitimate system's strategic plan

When creating learning experiences for the legitimate system, the designer can expect to use predominantly the structured strategies of the theory session, lecture and skill session as these provide the means of imparting the programmed knowledge efficiently and effectively.

However, the type of strategy the organisation follows will also have an effect on the decision. The *defender strategy* will certainly constrain the designer to the structured learning strategies (theory session, lecture and skill session) as they are less costly. The *analyser strategy* will depend on staff learning the appropriate programmed knowledge but will also expect staff to have the more basic elements of the analytical, logistical, interpersonal and intrapersonal subgroups of the HLO. Usually, these basic elements can be developed quite effectively by the structured learning strategies and, again, this suits the cost-conscious analyser strategy. For the successful utilisation of the *dynamic growth strategy*, staff need to be developed in all the elements of the task and relationships categories of the HLO. So, the designer can expect to be using case studies, role plays and experiential learning to develop the more complex elements, especially those in the 'implementing' and 'concern for others' subgroups. The *entrepreneurial strategy* means that the legitimate system is operating very close to the shadow system. The entrepreneurial strategy depends on staff having the 'critical thinking' and 'meta-abilities' categories of learning outcomes, so the unstructured strategies of problem-based learning, contract learning and action learning will often used by the designer.

The shadow system

Staff operating in the shadow system need all the learning outcomes, from programmed knowledge to the meta-abilities. Usually, staff will not be operating in the shadow system unless they have extensive levels of programmed knowledge so the developmental activities emphasised are usually those that develop the more complex categories of 'critical thinking' and 'meta-abilities'.

While identifying, analysing and creating new knowledge that is critical to the organisation's future survival is its prime role, there is another important role for the shadow system. Once new knowledge has been created (whether this be in the form of a new product, new service, new strategic mission or new culture), the shadow system has to inculcate this idea into the organisation as a whole and into the legitimate system in particular.

a closer look 10.2

Learning and the shadow system

The designer will tend to concentrate on the unstructured strategies of problem-based learning, contract learning and action learning with the support of mentors. The staff in the shadow system are expected to continually challenge old methods and to envisage new scenarios and new approaches. The content to be learned is in fact these new challenges so the designer concentrates more on designing the process that will manage the learning.

For the second role of exporting new knowledge into the legitimate system, the members of the shadow system have to implement change. There are two choices — either the members of the shadow system have to facilitate the change or a facilitator has to be engaged. Either way, the designer can expect to be asked to create a learning strategy usually referred to as a 'change intervention'. This type of learning strategy is discussed further in chapter 12.

ORGANISATIONAL CULTURE

In every organisation, there are patterns of beliefs, values, rituals, myths and practices which combine into shared meanings. These shared meanings create common understandings among members as to what the organisation is and how its members should behave (Robbins and Barnwell 1998) and the result is commonly referred to as organisational culture.

Organisational culture is a subtle yet pervasive force which guides the behaviour and often the decision making in an organisation. While the strategic mission statement is constructed through the planning process, organisational culture grows imperceptibly over time until certain norms become the accepted way of operating. So, within the legitimate system in particular, the organisational culture and the strategic mission are the basic steering mechanisms that keep the organisation moving in a particular direction. However, while the strategic mission is reviewed in the strategic planning process, there is no overt evaluation of culture.

Culture plays a role in organisations that is similar to that played by frames of reference in individuals. It can be expected, then, that changing the culture is a difficult and time-consuming process. Yet this is one of the aims of the shadow system. The culture must be challenged and reviewed regularly to ensure that the organisation is preserved. The problem, of course, is that the legitimate system tends to remain loyal to the established culture, thus establishing one of the basic conflicts between the shadow and the legitimate system. As discussed in chapter 2, this conflict tends to surface in the form of organisational defence mechanisms. The management of this conflict will be explored further in the last chapter of this book.

The topic of organisational culture is a very large and pervasive one. For a more in-depth understanding, specific texts (for example Brown 1998; Turner 1990; Vecchio, Hearn and Southey 1996) are recommended.

a closer look   10.3

The effect of organisational culture

The organisational culture impacts on the designer in two ways. Firstly, the designer must be aware of what the culture will accept and what it will not accept in both the content to be learned and in the learning strategies used. The designer will often find various taboos within various organisations. For example, organisational defence mechanisms (see chapter 2) may dictate that certain issues will not be discussed even within the confines of a learning experience. In some organisations the name of the major competitor cannot be spoken and even good practices used by that competitor cannot be imported into the organisation. Taboos on types of learning strategies are less common, although the use of role plays is sometimes banned.

The second impact on the designer occurs when the organisational culture is seen as inappropriate. The 'inappropriateness' may have been recognised by the shadow system. More commonly, because most organisations do not manage their shadow systems well, the organisation is faced with undeniable proof that the organisational culture is no longer appropriate. Either way, the designer is faced with the need to design a change intervention (as discussed in chapter 12).

KEY STAKEHOLDERS

Sveiby (1997) suggests that there are two categories of knowledge within an organisation — professional knowledge and political knowledge. Professional knowledge is the knowledge on which the organisation depends so that it can produce its product or service. So, an accounting firm uses accounting knowledge to provide a service to its customers. **Political knowledge** comprises the political power and knowledge of the organisational procedures and processes. When referring to political power, we are not discussing government politics but the political struggles and decision making that goes on within organisations. Political power comes from having some control over certain assets (for example, knowledge of certain production processes or having the keys to the storeroom) or by having connections to people with legitimate power (for example, the personal assistant to the chief executive officer). Knowledge of the organisational procedures and processes, together with political power, gives a person within the organisation an ability to influence and manipulate what is done and how it is done. People with organisational political knowledge are called key stakeholders.

Key stakeholders who also have legitimate power tend to be the 'movers and shakers' within the organisation. Legitimate power comes from having some official capacity in the organisation and, usually, the higher up the organisational hierarchy an individual is, the more power she or he has. So, a manager tends to have more power than a first-line supervisor. HR developers, whether in the role of investigator, designer, implementor or evaluator, should be aware of key stakeholders and especially key stakeholders with legitimate power.

a closer look   10.4

The effect of key stakeholders

To be a successful designer, the HR developer has to be politically astute as key stakeholders can make or break a learning experience. A key stakeholder may decide that a particular program will not proceed or that a particular issue will or will not be discussed in a learning program. For example, you may have a situation where a chief manager refuses to allow accident targets to be discussed in a safety training program. He believes that there is only one accident target — zero accidents. The fact that decreasing the number of accidents from over 1000 to zero is unachievable, and therefore no one can be rewarded for achieving lower levels, does not come into consideration. One can empathise with the chief manager's thought process, but the decision does not help establish a safety program.

The designer needs to become aware of the peccadillos of the various key stakeholders in the organisation. A decision then has to be made about whether these peccadillos will be respected or will be transgressed. It is a brave designer who goes down the path of transgression, so if this path is chosen, the designer should be quite sure that the path is correct and that there are no other options. If, as a designer, you are faced with such an awkward decision, you may wish to review the discussion of changing frames of reference, in particular paradynamic assumptions, in chapter 2.

On the other hand, of course, the wise designer will also seek the support of key stakeholders when designing important or controversial learning programs. Such support will go a long way towards smoothing the passage of such plans.

RESOURCES

The resources available to the designer often seem to be a constraint on design, but this is a pessimistic view. The designer must be realistic and make decisions within the resources available. Some of the more significant resources a designer needs to monitor are time, physical resources and qualified HR developers.

The tyranny of time

Time is the constant enemy of the designer. There always seems to be so much to be learned and too little time for the learning to occur. Unfortunately, to exacerbate the situation, too many managers have little idea how time consuming learning can be. This is understandable as managers are invariably operating in highly uncertain situations but are expected to achieve targets that are, at times, set ambitiously high by the organisation. It is no wonder that managers are usually more swayed by the short-term needs of productivity rather than by the long-term benefits of developed staff.

This creates quite an internal conflict for the designer. On the one hand, there is the recognition that managers need their staff to maintain production schedules. On the other hand, the designer is aware that it would be professionally negligent to give learners a much less than minimally optimal length of time to learn a skill or to challenge a frame of reference. The hallmark of a high-quality designer is the ability to come to terms with this conflict by making decisions that are fair and of equal benefit to all and by negotiating time frames that optimise all needs.

Sometimes, the abilities of the learners (as discussed in chapter 9) can help the designer overcome some of the challenges of lack of time. Learners with mature learning abilities or with high motivation do not always need the time investment of the average learner.

The tyranny of numbers

Sometimes, a decision will be forced on the designer to accept more than the optimal number of learners on a learning program. This decision could easily come from a key stakeholder. If the decision cannot be reversed, then the designer has to make the best of a very challenging situation. The quality of learning will undoubtedly be harmed if the numbers of learners are too high. However, the designer has to be very creative and attempt to minimise the problem. For example, case studies can still be used in very large groups (even up to 100 learners). The problem is that the HR developer, who is the implementor of the program, cannot listen and provide feedback to every group. However, some of the learners can be designated 'observers' who report back to the total group at the end of the case study. The implementor can then overview the main points raised by the observers. This is not ideal, but under the circumstances, is much better than nothing.

Physical resources

A variety of physical resources are needed to mount a learning program. The first consideration is a location where the learning will take place. This may vary from a meeting room, when action learning is used, to a training room for most of the other learning strategies. Skill sessions sometimes need different types of accommodation, depending on the equipment needed to demonstrate the skill. I have seen an entire front end of an aeroplane in a training room on an airforce facility. These days it is not unusual to see whole training rooms devoted to computers.

These physical resources all need funding, so money is a basic resource for any learning experience. The organisation may own or hire the rooms and equipment, but this still means that some financial backing is needed. The designer has to work within the constraints of the physical resources and the finances of the organisation, although providing an early warning of future expenditure is often appreciated by higher level decision makers. At the same time, however, the designer should not be shy of pushing the boundaries of possibility!

Qualified HR developers

No matter what the learning experience, a design is merely a plan until operational-ised by a HR developer. HR developers need to be qualified in two areas — the content to be taught and the learning strategies to be used. Particularly when programmed knowledge is the focus of the learning experience, the HR developers need the content knowledge to explain the concepts and also for credibility. However, the best knowledge expert is worse than useless if he or she does not have the techniques and abilities to impart the knowledge. These techniques and abilities — sometimes referred to as the process of teaching or facilitating — become even more important when the learning strategies become unstructured. With the fully unstructured approaches such as contract learning and action learning, the HR developer cannot even operate unless he or she has exceptional facilitation abilities.

a closer look   10.5

The effect of available resources

A designer needs to pay very close attention to the available resources of time, physical resources and qualified HR developers. The best design can easily become a learner's nightmare if any of these resources fall below a critical level.

In addition, designers have to recognise that they are often in competition for scarce resources and will have to be prepared to fight for acceptable levels. Indeed, this is often where the backing of key stakeholders becomes important. So, even designers cannot be above the need to become involved in the political machinations of the organisation.

DESIGNER'S PERSONAL FRAME OF REFERENCE

Because it resides within, the designer often overlooks her or his personal frame of reference. Yet, as discussed in chapter 2, one's frame of reference has a significant impact on decisions and actions. Therefore, designers should critically reflect on their personal values and beliefs and consider what impact these values and beliefs may have on design decisions. For example, a designer may have experienced intense personal satisfaction using self-directed learning. This highly positive experience would have affected the designer's frame of reference. A problem occurs if the designer allows this positive frame of reference to unduly sway design decisions in favour of self-directed learning.

AN OVERVIEW OF THE DESIGN PROCESS

In an attempt to provide a logical conception of the design process, a number of models have been proposed over the years. The order of presentation, in chapters 8 and 10, of the decisions to be made in curriculum design have, to a large part, followed a number of these models.

The *objectives* or *rational model* (Tyler 1949) is the oldest and one of the most commonly used. This model suggests that there are four steps:

1. establishment of the objectives
2. determination of the instructional strategies
3. organisation of the learning experiences
4. assessment and evaluation.

The first decision of the designer is based on the first two steps of this rational model. In chapter 9, these two steps have been described under the HLO. The learning outcomes equate to the first step (establishment of the objectives) and the link to the appropriate learning strategies matches the second step (determination of the instructional strategies). The third step of the rational model, organising the learning experience, will be discussed in the next section of this chapter, 'The product'.

So far, no mention has been made of 'assessment and evaluation'. Planning the evaluation of the learning experience is the final duty of the designer (this is the topic of chapter 13). As indicated earlier, the four stages of the HRD process — the HRDNI, design, implementation and evaluation — not only overlap but are also highly interactive and it is overly simplistic to discuss them in a linear fashion. However, a textbook constrains an explanation to a linear presentation so we will continue to indicate where the major overlaps occur.

Tyler's model has received some criticism over the years but, as Print (1993, p. 65) points out, a lot of these negative comments are ill-informed. However, while this rational model is quite sound and robust, it is a mechanical view of the design process — more suited to learning experiences for programmed knowledge than the more complex categories of the HLO.

The *interaction model* (Taba 1962) and the *cyclical model* (Wheeler 1967; Nichols and Nichols 1978) attempt to overcome this mechanistic inflexibility by suggesting that curriculum development is a more dynamic process. The interaction and cyclical models still use the same four steps of objectives, instructional strategies, organising the learning experiences and evaluation. However, the models emphasise that the design process can start with any of the steps and follow any sequence. So, with the addition of new content, decisions are then needed on objectives, methods and assessment strategies (Brady and Kennedy 1999). Further, Taba (1962) argues strongly for the diagnosis of the needs of the learners. Chapter 9 has followed this recommendation, with the learner being considered as one of the two direct factors influencing the design decision. In addition, this text suggests that the design process is iterative — the initial decisions are based on the HLO, but these decisions are continually reviewed by the needs of the learners and the impact of the indirect factors.

The platform or naturalistic model (Walker 1971) is based on what is perceived as a more natural process of devising a curriculum and is based on three phases:

1. The *platform phase* incorporates a hotchpotch of the shared values, beliefs, and perceptions of all stakeholders (including learners and the designer) about what should be changed, how it should be changed and the levels of commitment to that change. These values, beliefs and perceptions may not be defined clearly or even logically. They may be based on facts or may even be politically motivated. Even so they form the basis, or platform, of future curriculum decisions.
2. In the *deliberation phase* the stakeholders defend their ideas and push for their own political advantage. Sometimes a decision may be achieved logically and quickly but, more often, the process may be chaotic and confused and full of

emotion (indicating frames of reference are involved). Further, this is the time when organisational defence mechanisms unfold. However, this phase is also a time of illumination and creativity and the designer should use this time to ensure that all possible avenues are explored.

3. The *design phase* begins when the key stakeholders have achieved consensus over the conflicting viewpoints and issues. In this phase, the designer can make final decisions about the components of the learning experience (the learning outcomes to be achieved, the content to be covered, the learning strategies to be used) and the sequence of these components.

a closer look   10.6

The design models

The rational, interactive and cyclical models tend to describe the design process for learning experiences in the legitimate system. Some aspects of the platform model are also present, of course, but the contentious issues tend to be about specific matters or about preserving and/ or gaining 'territory'. For example, it is quite common in educational institutions for vexed arguments to be based on the need for a particular curriculum design to include subject matter from a particular department — the aim being to have more students exposed to that department's subjects and hence that department receiving more money.

The platform model is particularly relevant to the shadow system when new ideas are to be incorporated into the organisation. In fact, the platform model becomes a robust foundation for the design of the change intervention that the designer has to devise and, sometimes, even facilitate. Change interventions will be discussed more fully in chapter 12.

THE PRODUCT

The result of the designer's efforts and deliberations will be a series of learning episodes. The most noticeable effects are in the legitimate system, as this is where the official plans for learning are instituted. However, the impact of the design process is also felt in the shadow system although, sadly, many organisations do not invest anywhere near the resources and energy required.

The legitimate system tends to be more interested in learning episodes that concentrate on what Billett (1999) describes as 'routine problem solving'. Such learning episodes focus on the everyday workplace knowledge and skills that ensure the organisation's survival in the near future. These learning episodes are also predominantly single-loop learning and are largely instrumental learning, although communicative learning (for example, in management development) can also be involved (see chapter 2). The content covered — whether the facts or the analytic processes to be used — presents a fairly uniform approach to problem solving or work behaviours. Accordingly, these learning episodes rarely go beyond the 'implementing' and 'concern for others' subgroups of the HLO (see chapter 9). These learning episodes for the legitimate system tend to be presented in formal training courses and developmental workshops within classroom situations.

The shadow system tends to be more interested in learning episodes that concentrate on what Billett (1999) describes as 'non-routine problem solving'. Such learning episodes develop problem solving and other workplace behaviours that are uncommon and/or complex. Accordingly, they tend to cover the more complex aspects of the HLO, from the deeper levels of the analytical, logistical, interpersonal and intrapersonal subgroups down to the meta-abilities category.

THE LEGITIMATE SYSTEM

For the legitimate system, the designer provides a series of plans. The exact type of plans expected by the organisation varies, but tends to include an overall program and session plans, a resource plan, a marketing plan, a budget and the evaluation plan.

The program and session plans

The program and session plans explain the content to be covered in the learning experience, the learning strategies to be used and the expected assessment. A program is made up of a series of sessions that are presented in a specific order.

For the designer, *sequencing* sessions which provide meaningful and effective developmental opportunities involve using both personal tacit and explicit knowledge. The tacit knowledge is developed over time and with experience. Explicit knowledge is available from the memory of the designer or in textbooks or other writings — for example, see chapter 2. A well-designed program is based on the theories discussed in that chapter. In particular, the designer should consider the following:

- *Use building blocks.* Ensure that the learners cover the basic knowledge and skills early in the learning program and that this basic information becomes the basis for the later learning.
- *Move from the simple to the complex.* Provide a simple model initially and then make this model more complex as the learning program progresses.
- *Ensure that part learning, spaced learning and active learning are used sequentially.* Present one small part of the knowledge or skill and follow this with a reinforcing activity to provide a space before the next small part of knowledge or skill.
- As a basic model, *use the learning cycle* of:
  - having an experience
  - reviewing the experience
  - concluding from the experience
  - planning and mentally rehearsing the next step.
- *Assure transfer of learning* by ensuring that all learning is contextually based and is highly relevant to the workplace (for an excellent discussion of transfer of learning see Tennant 1999). In the design phase, the HR developer must ensure that:
  - the learners are continually reminded of the need to transfer the learning back to the workplace

- the learners are provided with a variety of examples of the application of the concept, task or skill in the workplace
- the learning aids are a close replication of the workplace situation (for example, if the session is to teach the learners how to complete a form, then a copy of the form has to be made available to the learners)
- the learners are provided with opportunities to reflect on how they will transfer the learning back to the workplace
- practice time is provided in situations as close to possible to the real workplace environment.

- *Incorporate opportunities for both informational and motivational feedback.* (See chapter 2.) These feedback processes should present the learner with 'task feedback clues' (Evans and Butler 1992) where the learner is given opportunities to observe their own performance and draw conclusions. This feedback process should be combined with 'successive approximations of targeted expertise' (Gott 1995) where the learner is encouraged to iteratively complete the learning cycle, coming closer to the required standard on each iteration.

Programs that cover only programmed knowledge tend to be quite explicit about the amount of time to be invested (usually from a few hours to a few days) and about the content to be covered. These programs are usually called 'training courses' and may include information only or skills only or a combination of information and skills. The learning strategies are usually confined to the theory session or lecture and the skill session. Figure 10.1 (p. 276) shows a typical program for a training course. 'Workshops' tend to cover programmed knowledge and the less complex elements of the task and relationship categories. Typically, workshops have a defined time frame and content and the program itself is usually presented in a similar fashion to the training course.

Both training courses and workshops are made up of a series of sessions — predominantly the theory, the lecture, the skill, discussions, case studies and roles plays. The designer will also need to create the session plans and other associated material (for example, overhead transparencies, handouts, board plans) for these sessions. The requirements for session plans will be discussed in chapter 11.

For the learning outcomes from the deeper levels of the task and relationship categories and also those in the critical thinking and meta-abilities categories, the unstructured learning strategies of problem-based learning, contract learning and action learning are used. Each of these learning strategies have their own approach to managing the learning process (see chapter 12) and it is difficult to prescribe a time frame. Accordingly, a tightly defined program is usually not possible and the designer follows the learning management process recommended for each of these unstructured learning strategies.

The resource plan

The resource plan covers all those physical and human resources (other than the learners) needed to mount the program. Typically, the resource plan will include:
- the internal and external HR developers and guest speakers
- the training rooms, store rooms, meeting rooms and even personal accommodation during residential or 'live away' courses

Research Interviewing Workshop

Course objectives: To conduct a 10-minute research interview using an appropriate pattern of interview, questioning techniques and responding skills.

8.00 a.m.	Administration & introductions	**Doug Hansford** Senior consultant
8.30 a.m.	The pattern of an interview * *Explain the four stages of an interview.* (A theory session)	**John Stewart** Senior instructor
9.30 a.m.	Questioning techniques * *Discuss the difference between open and* *closed questions.* * *Explain the funnel sequence of questioning.* (A theory session)	**Jan Carroll** Senior instructor
10.00 a.m.	Morning tea	
10.15 a.m.	Practice questioning techniques	**Trainees**
10.30 a.m.	Responding skills * *Explain the responding skills of paraphrasing,* *probing and summarising.* (A theory session)	**John Stewart** Senior instructor
11.00 a.m.	Practice responding skills	**Trainees**
11.30 a.m.	Nonverbal behaviour * *Discuss personal reactions to the use and* *abuse of the SOLER system.* (Experiential learning and discussion)	**John Stewart** Senior instructor
12.00 noon	The finer points of interviewing * *Discuss ways of using interview skills.* (A discussion)	**Doug Hansford** Senior consultant
12.30 p.m.	Lunch	
1.15 p.m.	Plan a 10-minute interview	**Trainees**
1.45 p.m.	Conduct a 10-minute interview *(with a 5-minute feedback session from* *fellow trainees and facilitator)*	**Trainees and** **Jan Carroll**
4.00 p.m.	Review of personal experience * *What went well.* * *What can be improved.* * *Personal goals for improvement.* (A discussion)	**Trainees and** **Jan Carroll**
5.00 p.m.	Closure	**Doug Hansford** Senior consultant

Note: The session type in brackets is placed after each session for the information of the HR developers who will implement the program, but is deleted on the programs given to the trainees.

FIGURE 10.1
A program
for a training
course

- equipment and training aids needed — it is also a good idea to indicate whether these are to be purchased or hired
- stationery and other materials.

In addition to listing the quantities, the plan should indicate the time the resources are needed (for example, the exact time the guest speakers are required and their travel arrangements; when a particular video should be picked up and the supplier of the video).

The product marketing plan

The sole business of some organisations, such as private colleges and consulting groups, is to provide training, HR development and educational services. For these organisations, marketing their programs (or product) is a basic necessity of survival. However, it is becoming quite common for internal HR departments to see a need to market their services. As Cafferalla (1994) points out, marketing is important for educational and HR development programs where participation is often voluntary and potential participants may not be affiliated with the sponsoring organisation. Accordingly, most designers these days have to have some input to the marketing plans.

Kotler (1996) has identified five possible roles in a purchase decision:
- The *initiator* is the person who believes that there is some need for the product.
- The *influencer* can persuade others that the product will satisfy a critical need.
- The *decider* is the person who has the power to make the 'yes-we-will or no-we-will-not' decision.
- The *purchaser* is the one who has the delegation, budget or money to make the purchase.
- The *user* is the person who uses the product.

Five separate people may occupy each role or one person may be involved in two or more of the roles. A product marketing plan identifies the people who occupy these roles, where they are located and what benefit the product (for example, training course) will bring to each of them.

Any number of people, from inside or outside the organisation, may fill these roles. A union delegate, a potential learner or the manager are often the initiators and influencers. The decider is usually an upper level manager, and this person often fills the role of purchaser as well. The most obvious users of a learning program are the learners themselves, although one could argue that the manager or supervisor of the learners benefits as well (trained staff make the job of a manager that much easier). Of course, for an internal HR developer, a lot of this information will be available from the HRDNI. Outside HR developers and consultants rely on feasibility studies for the information.

The second part of a marketing plan covers the promotional tactics for the learning program. There are two major parts to promotional tactics — the advertising content and the media. The advertising content includes descriptions of the needs to be satisfied by the program. These descriptions should be targeted to the particular buyer role. The choice of media tactics identifies the communication methods to be used — internal memorandum, advertising poster, advertisements in newspapers and journals (and, specifically, which newspapers and journals), radio or television. Again, the choice of media should be dictated by the particular buyer role that is being targeted.

The budget

For a single product such as a learning program, a budget consists of three main areas — the expected income, the cash expenditures and the opportunity cost expenditures.

The *expected income* is an estimate of the income that the program is expected to generate. Calculating expected income is usually the prerequisite of organisations whose sole business is providing educational and HR development programs. Most internal HR departments of an organisation do not bother with estimating expected income.

The *cash expenditures* include all items on which the organisation will spend cash. Such items would include the payment of external consultants and guest speakers, the hire of equipment and training aids and the rental of floor space (for example, training rooms), consumable materials, travel expenses and the costs of marketing the program. Most organisations expect that cash expenditures will be included in the budget, at the very least.

Opportunity cost expenditures involve all those disbursements that the organisation has already made a commitment to, that would have been used on work other than the learning program. These expenditures include the wages of the learners (who would have been doing their normal work) and of the HR developers and the depreciation on buildings and equipment. Some organisations may not require the inclusion of opportunity cost expenditures.

The evaluation plan

The final, but not the least, important task of the designer is to plan how the learning program is to be evaluated. Evaluation is discussed in chapter 13.

THE SHADOW SYSTEM

There are three domains of learning that occur in the shadow system — learning transfer, extended learning and creating new learning. These three domains are considered to be part of the shadow system as the learning is highly individualised by being focused on the learner concerned. Further, the learning establishes long-term benefits for the organisation and is part of the knowledge storage process that is important to the management of knowledge capital (see chapter 14).

In reality, there is only limited opportunity for the direct involvement of the HR developer as a designer in any of these three domains. The HR developer tends to have a more direct involvement as an implementor or facilitator of unstructured learning strategies (see chapter 12).

Learning transfer

It should also be acknowledged that some people consider that the first of the three domains, learning transfer, is really the prerequisite of the legitimate system. However, any such argument is more about the grey boundary between the legitimate and shadow systems so, for the sake of convenience, the three domains will be dealt with under the heading of the shadow system.

The HR developer as a designer of learning programs must avoid the trap of **encapsulation**. Encapsulation occurs when the learners do achieve the desired learning objectives or learning outcomes in the training course or workshop but do not take the learning back to the workplace. The learning is encapsulated in the learning situation and stays there. As Tennant (1999) comments, historically in education there has been a greater value placed on decontextualised knowledge with a concomitant schism between 'knowing' and 'doing'. Knowing was seen as the mandate of the privileged and doing the role of the labouring class. However, recent research and literature irrefutably demonstrates that deep learning depends on the combination of both knowing and doing. Therefore, the designer must constantly focus on the need to ensure that the planned learning will be transferred back to the workplace situation.

As discussed under 'the program and session plans', the designer can encourage transfer of learning during the program itself. However, the most enduring effect on transfer occurs after the programmed learning episode when the learner returns to the workplace. The learner needs what Tennant (1999) calls a positive transfer climate. In a positive transfer climate, the learner:
- is provided with opportunities to reinforce and further develop the 'routinised problem-solving' knowledge and skills covered in the learning program
- is given both informational and motivational feedback
- operates in a supportive atmosphere. This support comes from both the supervisor and the learner's peers.

In this **transfer of learning** stage, the knowledge generation process of combination is emphasised, although internalisation tends to predominate automatically as well.

The designer may be able to incorporate activities in the learning program (for example, have the learners commence projects, which have to be completed on-the-job, during the learning program) or even arrange some follow-up training once the learner returns to the workplace. Such follow-up training is usually more successful if the supervisor of the learner is fully involved.

Extended learning

With the learner being able to reinforce the learning from the learning program under a positive transfer climate, the next phase of the individual learner's development can be initiated. This extended learning phase is the responsibility of the learner and the immediate supervisor. Accordingly, the HR developer as a designer has only an indirect influence. This indirect influence may be in terms of developing the learner as a self-directed learner or by developing the immediate supervisor (for example, in the design of supervisory or management development workshops). The HR developer as an implementor may have a direct influence by being engaged as a facilitator (see chapter 12).

This extended learning phase enters what Billett (1999) calls 'workplace learning'. Learning activities in which individuals engage in the workplace influence what knowledge the individual constructs as such activities are framed by the workplace's norms and values (Billett 1999, p. 155). The combination of engaging in work tasks of increasing complexity and accountability, the close guidance of other workers and experts and the more indirect ongoing guidance provided by the setting appears to be the basis for robust knowledge in the workplace (Billett 1996). Further, the extended learning phase allows the dynamic combination of both theory and practice (see Tennant 1999) and the development of knowledge and skills in the 'non-routinised problem solving' arena (see Billett 1999). Accordingly, the immediate supervisor should ensure that the learner is:

- provided with opportunities to become engaged in tasks, based on the knowledge and skills originally developed in the learning program, that are progressively more complex and hold more accountability
- given feedback that is both informational and motivational
- given opportunities to observe models of expert performance
- encouraged to develop expertise using the process of successive approximations.

During this extended learning phase, the learner should be encouraged to indulge in externalisation. Socialisation is also a powerful influence as the learner associates with experts and models of excellence. Again, internalisation is an automatic process, provided sufficient time is allowed for reflection.

Creating new knowledge

The transfer of learning and the extended learning phases tend to create reservoirs of already known knowledge — knowledge that is used by the legitimate system to conduct the everyday activities of the organisation. The supervisor needs to ensure that the learning progresses much further than this by converting the work group into a learning community. Such a learning community can be initially established by encouraging the involvement of all staff in the transfer of learning and the extended learning phases of all learners returning from a learning program. However, as discussed in chapter 1, an organisational climate that encourages staff to create new knowledge through the knowledge generation processes of externalisation, combination, internalisation and socialisation is the real hallmark of a learning community. This issue will be discussed further in chapter 14.

A HOLISTIC VIEW

As Billett (1999, p. 151) comments, workplace contributions to learning are held to be different in kind to those furnished by educational settings. Further, these contributions are not necessarily better or worse, but they are different. Accordingly, organisations must take a holistic view to learning by ascribing to the four interconnected levels. The formal learning of the well-designed programs that are sponsored by the legitimate system must be followed and complemented by the three phases in the shadow system — transfer of learning, extended learning and the creation of new knowledge.

For the successful execution of such deep, complex and rich learning, several issues need to be noted:

- The HR developer as a designer has high involvement in the learning program, and this involvement becomes less as the learning progresses through the shadow system.
- The less the HR developer is involved, the more responsibility the immediate supervisor has in providing opportunities and designing learning experiences for the learner.

- The organisation must be willing to invest energy in all four phases of the learning process — the learning program, the transfer of learning, extended learning and the creation of new knowledge. This is particularly so for the shadow system, where this energy will take the form of time for the learner to be involved and to reflect and also time for other key players, namely the supervisor and other experts to be involved.

THE HR DEVELOPER AS A DESIGNER

For the HR developer, the role of the designer is quite wide and complex. For the legitimate system, the HR developer bases the design of the learning program on the information from the HRDNI. The designer makes initial decisions based on the HLO and then moves, in an iterative process, through the learning needs of the learners and the indirect factors of strategic orientation, the organisational culture, the key stakeholders and the resources available. This iterative decision-making process results in the production of a number of plans — the program and the session plans, the resources plan, the product marketing plan, the budget and the evaluation plan. The checklist for designers presented in the previous chapter has been extended to incorporate the indirect factors in this chapter and also the various plans that need to be produced — see figure 10.2.

1. Examine each of the learning outcomes listed in the HRDNI and decide which level of the HLO best equates with each learning outcome.
2. Identify the 'building blocks'. Ask questions such as: what basic programmed knowledge is needed to be covered first before advanced programmed knowledge is presented? What programmed knowledge is needed before the learners can take on the task category elements? Are relationship category elements needed and, if so, where are they needed in the learning experience? What critical thinking and meta-abilities categories are needed and where should these be developed in the learning experience?
3. Identify the critical characteristics of the learners — level of knowledge, motivation, learning orientations and learning styles — and decide the effect that these characteristics may have on the overall design.
4. Explore how the learning cycle of step 1 (having an experience), step 2 (reviewing the experience), step 3 (concluding from the experience) and step 4 (planning the next steps) could be included in the overall design.
5. Ensure that opportunities for appropriate feedback are built into the design. This feedback should be:
   - a combination of qualitative and quantitative
   - from an external source, such as a HR developer
   - from an internal source (the learners should be given the opportunity to compare their own performances against standards and draw their own conclusions).

(continued)

FIGURE 10.2
A checklist
for designers

FIGURE 10.2
(cont'd)

6. Check that the proposed learning strategies are compatible with the organisational strategic plan. If there is a discrepancy, verify the logic of the choice of learning strategy. If a more expensive learning strategy is proposed, seek support from key stakeholders.

7. Analyse the organisational culture for activities or issues that are or are not acceptable. Check the impact of these on the proposed learning experiences. If fundamental changes are needed to the organisational culture, examine the alternatives of change interventions. Discuss such expected fundamental changes with key stakeholders.

8. Negotiate sufficient time for the learning experience with affected managers.

9. Design the learning program. For training courses and workshops, devise a program plan similar to that in figure 10.1. If unstructured learning strategies are to be used, devise program plans that will manage the learning processes (see chapter 12). Decide appropriate lengths of time for each session. Juggle these times so that all sessions fit into the time available for the program.

10. Design the session plans, including all the support material. Recognise that this step will take some considerable time. Delahaye and Smith (1998) suggest allowing a ratio of 1:4 — for every hour that a session lasts, 4 hours of session planning will be needed.

11. Define the qualifications needed by the HR developers. Identify the sources (internal or external) of potential HR developers.

12. Draw up the resources plan.

13. Create the product marketing plan.

14. Calculate a budget for the resources needed. Ensure that all expected cash expenditures are included (for example, hire of rooms, rental of films, payment to external HR developers). Seek support from key stakeholders.

15. Design the evaluation plan.

For the learning that occurs in the shadow system, the HR developer's role tends to blur between that of a designer and that of an implementor. This is discussed further in chapter 12. The craft of the designer is based on a solid foundation of scientific research. However, the decisions are so complex, and surmounting the political influences of the organisation so potentially hazardous, that science alone is not always enough. The designer needs experience — but experience comes only from practice. The novice designer will find the issues discussed in chapters 9 and 10 substantial and tangible bases for gaining that experience. However, finding a knowledgable and competent mentor will certainly assist with personal development — and will also help to avoid some of the more serious dangers!

GLOSSARY

balanced instability — a healthy state of tension within the organisation where the need for high productivity is balanced with a continual search for learning and change

budget — a plan documenting the expected income and expenditures of the designed learning experience

cyclical model — a model which suggests that the curriculum design process can start at any of the four steps of the rational model

encapsulation — the phenomenon where learners leave the learning in the classroom

evaluation plan — a proposal for assessing and evaluating the designed learning experience

extended learning — where the learner is encouraged to increase and further the learning in the workplace

interaction model — a model of curriculum design which suggests that the four steps of the rational model are interactive

key stakeholders — people with political knowledge who influence decisions within the organisation

objectives model — another name for the rational model

organisational culture — the shared meanings of values, beliefs, rituals and myths that create common understandings between organisational members

platform model — a model of curriculum design which reflects the more natural process of negotiation in human interactions

political knowledge — is made up of political power and knowledge of the organisational procedures and processes

product marketing plan — a plan to market and advertise the designed learning experience

program plan — a time plan of the designed learning experience

rational model — a model suggesting that curriculum design consists of four steps — objectives, instructional strategies, organising and evaluation

resources — the assets available to the HR developer to conduct a learning experience, including time, physical resources and other HR developers

resource plan — a plan that describes the resources needed to mount the designed learning experience and when these resources will be needed

session plan — a plan that describes the content to be covered in sequence and the associated overhead transparencies and board plans

strategic orientation — the market niche that the organisation is servicing

transfer of learning — overcoming encapsulation by ensuring that the learning in the classroom is transferred back to the workplace.

QUESTIONS

For review

1. Explain how the legitimate system and the shadow system help to define the strategic orientation and, in turn, how the strategic orientation influences the learning strategies.

2. Describe the most critical resources that the designer must consider and explain how the limitations of these resources can be overcome.

3. Describe the influence of the rational model, the interaction model and the cyclical model on the curriculum design process.

4. List and briefly describe the components of a program for a learning experience.

For analysis

5. Compare and contrast the rational model and the platform model of curriculum design.

6. Explain how the organisational culture and key stakeholders may interact to influence the design of a learning experience.

7. Explain how the legitimate system and the shadow system combine to provide a holistic approach to the learning of the individual.

For application

8. Consider the course you are undertaking currently. Identify the people in the five purchase roles and describe how you would design a product marketing plan for the course.

9. Examine a training course, workshop or university course with which you are familiar. Identify the cash expenditures and opportunity cost expenditures that the organisation offering the program would be liable for.

10. Review the discussion in chapter 2 on frames of reference. Identify important elements in your own frame of reference that may impinge, either positively and negatively, on your decisions when designing a learning experience for adult learners.

REFERENCES

Brady, L. and Kennedy, K. (1999). *Curriculum Construction*. Sydney, NSW: Prentice Hall.

Billett, S. (1996). 'Towards a model of workplace learning: the learning curriculum.' *Studies in Continuing Education*, 18(1), 43–58.

Billett, S. (1999). 'Guided learning at work'. In D. Boud and J. Garrick (Eds), *Understanding Learning at Work*. London: Routledge.

Brown, A. D. (1998). *Organisational Culture* (2nd ed.). London: Pitman.

Cafferalla, R. S. (1994). *Planning Programs for Adult Learners*. San Francisco: Jossey-Bass.

Delahaye, B. L. and Smith, B. J. (1998). *How to be an Effective Trainer*. New York: Wiley.

Evans, G. and Butler, J. (1992). *Thinking and Enhanced Performance in the Workplace*. A paper presented to the Fifth International Conference on Thinking, Townsville, Qld.

Gott, S. (1995). 'Rediscovering learning: Acquiring expertise in real world problem solving tasks.' *Australian and New Zealand Journal of Vocational Education Research*, 3(1), 30–69.

Kotler, P. (1996). *Marketing Management: Analysis, Planning and Control*. (9th ed.). Englewood Cliffs, NJ: Prentice Hall.

Nichols, A. and Nichols, A. H. (1978). *Developing a Curriculum: A Practical Guide*. (2nd ed.). London: Allen & Unwin.

Print, M (1993). *Curriculum Development and Design*. St. Leonards, NSW: Allen & Unwin.

Robbins, S. P and Barnwell, N. (1998). *Organisation Theory: Concepts and Cases*. (3rd ed.). Sydney, NSW: Prentice Hall.

Sveiby, K. E. (1997). *The New Organizational Wealth: Managing and Measuring Knowledge-based Assets*. San Francisco, Cal.: Berrett-Koehler.

Taba, H. (1962). *Curriculum Development: Theory and Practice*. New York: Harcourt Brace.

Tennant, M. (1999). 'Is learning transferable?' In D. Boud and J. Garrick (Eds), *Understanding Learning at Work*. London: Routledge.

Turner, G. M. (1990). *Organisational Culture*. Bristol, UK: The Staff College.

Tyler, R. W. (1949). *Basic Principles of Curriculum and Instruction*. Chicago: University of Chicago Press.

Vecchio, R. P., Hearn, G. N. and Southey, G. N. (1996). *Organisational Behaviour*. (2nd ed.). Marrickville, NSW: Harcourt Brace.

Walker, D. F. (1971). 'A naturalistic model for curriculum development.' *School Review*, 80(1), 51–65.

Wheeler, D. K. (1967). *Curriculum Process*. London: University of London Press.

The Gordian knot

Bob Hearn heaved a sigh of relief. Designing the 1-day workshop had been a challenge. He sat back with a satisfied grin. Well, that was his first workshop and, confident of success, he looked forward to many more design challenges.

'OK', he thought, 'let's just make sure that I have covered everything'. He had based the design on the HRDNI completed by the learning and development manager, Glen Edwards. Glen had emphasised that this was a procedural course as the counter staff had to operate the new computer system correctly and efficiently. Most of the sessions were either theory or skill sessions. Bob had carefully ensured that the initial sessions provided the basic information and that each subsequent session built on the preceding information and skills. He thought that the final session of a role play, where the learners had to use the computer and interact with a customer, provided a realistic final test before they went back to the workplace. Of course, the 1-day time frame had been a bit difficult but he had covered all the critical learning objectives identified in the HRDNI. The budget looked quite realistic, although it was 1% over the limit Glen had set. The program for the day read quite clearly and all of the session plans were in folders containing session plans, overhead transparencies, a board plan and all the material needed for the skill sessions. 'Thank heavens only one HR developer will run this',

Bob said to himself, 'There are no guest speakers to worry about. Now let's see, the room is booked, all the equipment is in there. Yep, everything looks good. OK, let's send everything into Glen and see what he says'.

Two days later Bob' feelings were mixed. Sure, Glen had been very supportive. He had really liked most of the design, particularly the session plans and the printed program. He also thought that the final role play was very creative and appropriate. 'But why, oh why, did I go with that Gordian knot for the ice breaker? Of course strangers would not want to hold hands and be that close to each other'. As Glen pointed out, it was a procedural course after all and people expect such a workshop to be more task orientated. They don't want to be touching each other. Bob thought, 'Thank heavens Glen saw that. It would have been a disaster. I just remembered doing that Gordian knot for my Train the Trainer course and that course meant so much to me. I suppose I wanted it in because of that.'

Discussion questions

1. Identify and explain the good design decisions that Bob made.

2. What errors did Bob make? Justify your answers.

3. From the information provided in the case study, what plans did Bob not design?

The continuing story: beyond the Gordian knot

'OK', thought Bob, 'Let's put that Gordian knot thing behind us. Glen has suggested that I see what other people think of the design. What should I do?'

Discussion questions

1. Using the platform model of curriculum design, what actions do you believe Bob should take?

2. If Bob is to design a product marketing plan, who else should Bob talk to and what should he find out from them?

3. How is the additional information gathered in questions 1 and 2 likely to affect the workshop Bob designed?

Implementing the structured learning strategies

CHAPTER OBJECTIVES

At the end of this chapter you should be able to:

1 identify and describe the important actions a HR developer must take to manage and coordinate a learning program

2 describe the micro skills of questioning, responding, using visual aids and constructing learning objectives

3 differentiate between structured and unstructured learning strategies

4 describe the structured learning strategies of the skill session, the theory session and the lecture

5 describe the semi-structured learning strategies of the discussion, case study, role play and experiential learning.

The chapter begins by suggesting that the implementation stage of HRD involves the interaction of three major operations — managing and coordinating the program, utilising micro skills and conducting the learning strategies.

While managing and coordinating a learning program is a rather invisible operation, any errors that do occur can have a very detrimental effect on the learners. The HR developer should ensure that all learners have been notified of their attendance, arrange the training room, check all equipment and ensure that guest speakers are available.

Micro skills are those taken-for-granted techniques that can enhance the learning experience for the learners. The micro skills include **questioning**, **responding** (paraphrasing, probing and summarising), using **visual aids** competently and constructing appropriate **learning objectives**.

The learning strategies available to the HR developer can be categorised as being on a continuum which is structured at one end and unstructured at the other. With structured learning strategies, the HR developer makes all the decisions on the learning objectives to be achieved, how the content will be learned and what evidence will be presented to prove that the learning objectives have been achieved. In unstructured learning strategies, the learner makes all these decisions. The most **structured learning strategies** discussed in this chapter are the skill session, the theory session and the lecture. The **skill session** is used for teaching a procedural skill and is based on the steps of show, show and tell, check of understanding and practice. The **theory session** is used to impart programmed knowledge. The body of the theory session is divided into segments (to coincide with the pieces of knowledge to be taught) and each segment is based on a three-step sequence of explanation step, activity step and summary step. The **lecture** is a modified theory session, in that the activity step is omitted.

In the **semi-structured learning strategies**, the learner takes more responsibility for decisions about the learning objectives and about the content to be covered, particularly. In the **discussion**, the HR developer as a facilitator of learning encourages the learner to contribute information and knowledge that will help the group attain the desired learning objectives. The **case study** learning strategy encourages the learners to go beyond their explicit knowledge. A case study consists of two parts. The narration combines a description of a real world event with sufficient background information to orient the learner. The second part, the questions, direct the thinking of the learner in the desired direction. A **role play** is similar to a case study in that, rather than listening to a narrative, the learners become involved in acting out roles. In both the case study and the role play the HR developer must debrief the learners to ensure that the knowledge-generating processes of internalisation and externalisation are exercised. **Experiential learning** covers a number of possible learning approaches. **Learning instruments**, usually a questionnaire, allows learners to examine their frames of reference, especially learning styles, management styles, team roles and decision techniques. **Simulations** allow the learner to act out real work-based situations and include flight simulators, computer-managed games and the 'in basket exercise'. A

project is a defined activity that occurs in the workplace but is studied and reflected on by the learner. Finally, **sensitivity groups** use group processes as a vehicle for individual learners to examine specific aspects of their behaviour and frames of reference by disclosing deep personal issues and emotions. Experiential learning depends on the motivation and energy of the learner, so success in using these learning approaches does depend on the commitment of the learner.

❧   ❧   ❧

THE ROLE OF THE HR DEVELOPER

After the design of the learning experience has been accepted and the appropriate approvals have been given, the implementation stage begins. To use a colloquial saying, the implementation stage is where 'the rubber hits the road'. In this third stage of the HRD process, the HR developer takes on the role of implementor and is often referred to as the facilitator, instructor, trainer, or teacher. In this role, the HR developer is responsible for implementing the design. In assuming this responsibility, the HR developer is accepting certain obligations — to be fully conversant with the programmed knowledge to be covered; to have the capability to conduct the learning strategies nominated; to be willing to help the learners meet the various challenges; to deal with the learners honestly; and never to place personal idiosyncratic needs above the best interests of the learners. There is also an expectation that the HR developer will stay within the planned design.

However, it must be recognised that the design is a plan and, as Print (1993, p. 217) comments, in implementing the designed learning experience, it can be expected that some modification may be required. The implementor needs to have the authority to make fine adjustments to the overall design. Most of these adjustments are based on the implementor's first hand experience of the learners. While the design may have made certain assumptions, the implementor has first hand knowledge of the learners' needs. So the implementor may make some modifications because of the learners' knowledge base or learning styles (see chapter 9) or because of their cultural backgrounds, gender or ages (see chapter 3). For example, recognising that in the indigenous Australian culture, asking questions is considered bad manners (see Byrnes 1993) but that adult learners from this culture are comfortable with communicative learning, the HR developer may increase the amount of time scheduled for discussions. Having said this, it must be stressed that major changes would be unexpected and could be justified only by significant and transparent reasons that were not acknowledged in the original design. (*Note*: The question of why such a variation was not accounted for in the original design would be addressed at the evaluation stage.)

Three major interacting operations occur during the implementation stage:
1. management and coordination of the program, where the various support resources are brought together to ensure that the learning program runs smoothly
2. utilisation of the micro skills of the HR developer, which support the learning strategies and increase the learning opportunities of the learners

3. Application of the learning strategies, where the HR developer uses accepted practices specific to the particular learning strategy.

A less than optimal performance in any of these operations can have a very deleterious effect on the learning experience. An acceptable level of performance in each leads to a reasonable learning experience for the learners. However, for a highly successful learning experience, these three operations interact to create a multiplier effect.

MANAGING AND COORDINATING THE PROGRAM

Managing and coordinating a program is a rather invisible operation — until something goes wrong. Some problems invariably arise during a program and most of these can be dealt with quickly and quietly. However, what can seem to be a minor irritant to the HR developer can be a discordant interruption to a learner. The possibilities for problems are many and varied — a learner's name misspelt, the incorrect designation of a guest speaker, a video not arriving or, perhaps the worst of all, morning tea not on time! The HR developer in charge of a program should check the following, at least:

- Ensure all learners have been notified of their attendance at the program and have received all preparatory material.
- Arrange the layout of the training room to maximise the effectiveness of the learning strategies to be used and for the comfort of the learners.
- Make sure the learners' name tags, programs and stationery are distributed or are readily available.
- Make sure all equipment and training aids are present and in working order. Remember the HR developer's adage: 'If anything will spoil your presentation it will be equipment breaking down.' It is worth checking all electrical equipment each morning before the sessions start.
- Check all safety aspects of the room and equipment.
- Each morning check that the guest speakers are still available.
- Check on the readiness of other HR developers and on their session requirements.

A lot of these tasks can be delegated by the implementing HR developer to a designated coordinator. However, the responsibility of ensuring that the tasks are completed is never delegated. The final responsibility always remains with the implementing HR developer, as he or she is the person who suffers the immediate consequences — and these consequences are invariably felt by the learners.

For a more detailed discussion of managing and coordinating a program see Caffarella (1994, pp. 209–225) and Delahaye and Smith (1998, pp. 387–405).

MICRO SKILLS

'Micro skills' refers to those taken-for-granted techniques used most successfully by experienced HR developers — questioning, responding, using the visual aids and creating learning objectives. Inconveniently, these micro skills take quite some time to develop to a competent standard. The word 'inconveniently' is used because these skills can enhance the learning process to a surprising extent. Conversely, when they are absent, or used ineptly, the learning process is usually diminished markedly.

QUESTIONING

Questioning skills were discussed thoroughly in chapter 7. The HR developer relies heavily on open questions with a 'stem-plus-query' structure and, particularly in the discussion, frequently uses the funnel sequence of questions.

RESPONDING

'Responding skills' includes the processes of paraphrasing, probing and summarising. Again, these were discussed extensively in chapter 7. From the HR developer's point of view, questioning and responding skills are tightly interwoven during any learning episode and this questioning-responding sequence is sometimes referred to as the 'trainer–trainee dynamic'. The word 'dynamic' is very appropriate as the interaction is usually fast and spontaneous so, for the HR developer, these skills need to be habitual as there is little chance to pre-plan the sequence of questioning and responding.

VISUAL AIDS

As discussed in chapter 2, the principle of learning called 'multiple sense learning' emphasises that humans perceive the major portions of their information through the sense of sight. HR developers must be adept at the appropriate use of visual aids.

Even in our high technology world, the most commonly used visual aids are the white board and the overhead projector. The white board is not a notebook for random scribbling. Information should be presented in a clear and logical sequence that enhances the assimilation of the information by the learners. The overhead projector can provide interest and impact to a presentation but is probably most effective when used in conjunction with the white board. This combination allows the HR developer to display the main points of the presentation on the white board and provide extended detail of each point via the overhead projector (Delahaye and Smith 1998).

A more modern and popular visual aid is the computer-assisted visual package such as PowerPoint. These packages confer a colourful, vibrant and dramatic edge to a presentation. While the presentations based on these packages are relatively flexible, they do require some specialised equipment and are difficult to combine with a white board. The overhead visualiser is another recent technological advance. It is very similar in construction to the overhead projector but incorporates a small video camera rather than a reflective prism in the head. This camera allows the display of a variety of photographs and graphs. It also provides a zoom capability so that particular points on the photograph can be highlighted and studied in greater detail.

Other visual aids include the chart, video, films, slides and audiotapes.

Recognise, however, that all these modern visual aids are only that — aids to learning. Spending a disproportionate amount of time on fancy visual aids will not improve learning significantly. It is the skills and abilities of a competent HR developer as an implementor that provide the most dynamic assistance to learning.

For a more detailed discussion of visual aids, the texts by Agnew, Kellerman and Meyer (1996), Delahaye and Smith (1998), Kemp and Smellie (1993), Reynolds and Anderson (1991) and Tarquin and Walker (1996) are recommended.

LEARNING OBJECTIVES

The construction of learning objectives was discussed in chapter 5. Based on the work of Mager (1984) and Tyler (1949), Delahaye and Smith (1998) recommend that learning objectives should describe:

- the *terminal behaviour* to be achieved by the learner at the end of the learning session (for example, theory, discussion) or learning experience (for example, training course — action verbs should be used to describe this terminal behaviour
- the *standard* to which this behaviour has to be performed — this standard describes the criteria for acceptable performance
- the *conditions* under which the learner will be expected to perform. A statement of conditions is sometimes superfluous (for example, if the learner is taking a paper-and-pencil test in a training room) but can become very important if the learner is expected to use a calculator half-way up a mast of a sailing ship on a windy day.

Well-stated learning objectives are critical to a HR developer for at least two reasons. They provide a clear goal which, in turn, gives a conspicuous direction for the HR developer to follow. This conspicuous direction allows decisions (on such matters as content to be learned and appropriate learning strategies) to be made quickly and precisely. Secondly, clear learning objectives describe the behaviour which, when displayed by the learner, indicates to the HR developer that the learning session or experience can conclude — as the aim of the learning session or experience has been achieved.

Now, in the structured learning strategies, the HR developer has the advantage of planning the learning objectives beforehand. However, during the unstructured learning strategies, the HR developer is often required to formulate or adjust learning objectives at a moment's notice. Having the ability to be this flexible is a trademark characteristic of the experienced HR developer.

THE IMPORTANCE OF MICRO SKILLS

The micro skills of questioning, responding, using visual aids correctly and effectively, and creating learning objectives are often unrecognised and undervalued. Yet, these skills are the catalysts which the HR developer uses to bring together the disparate concepts being covered. Further, it is with these micro skills that the HR developer helps the learner to generate knowledge through the processes of externalisation and internalisation. The absence of these skills invariably results in the learner being left floundering in directionless frustration. So, these skills are indeed a very powerful device in the toolkit of the HR developer as an implementor.

THE STRUCTURED LEARNING STRATEGIES

To this point, the terms 'structured learning strategies' and 'unstructured learning strategies' have been used and these terms represent the poles of a continuum. Other terminology is sometimes used to describe these poles — scientific/artistic;

teacher-controlled/learner-controlled; traditional/self-directed learning; pedagogy/andragogy. Each of these terms provide some insight into the difference between the concepts. Structured learning strategies are based on findings gleaned from quantitative research by researchers such as Thorndike (1931); teacher-controlled learning indicates that the teacher makes all the decisions on the learning process; self-directed learning signifies that the learner takes responsibility for all stages of the learning experience; pedagogy means the teaching of children while andragogy denotes the teaching of an adult.

Where a learning strategy transforms from structured to semi-structured is a moot point as the change is a gradual transformation. This chapter defines the following learning strategies as structured:

- skill session
- theory session
- lecture.

These three learning strategies are considered structured because the HR developer takes full responsibility for what will be learned, how it will be learned and what evidence will be produced to prove that the learning did occur.

THE SKILL SESSION

All communication models have a similar overall structure — an introduction, a body and a conclusion. All the structured learning strategies have this structure and the skill session is no different.

As the name implies, a skill session is used for teaching a procedural skill. A procedural skill is one involving procedures (based on some programmed knowledge) and a sequence of psychomotor skills, where the order of the activities is crucial. A skill session is based on a set series of steps that are controlled by the HR developer. Delahaye and Smith (1998) suggest that the body of the skill session should be divided into four steps:

1. *Show*, where the HR developer demonstrates the skill in an efficient and practised manner.
2. *Show and tell*, where the HR developer again proceeds through the skill but explains each step carefully to the learners. The HR developer re-explains any step where the learners are having difficulty and may demonstrate the skill several times.
3. *Check of understanding*, where the learners verbally describe each step, in the correct sequence, to the HR developer. This step ensures that the learners understand the skill before they are allowed to use the tools and materials and is an important component of safety training.
4. *Practice*, where the learners do the skill several times while being supervised by the HR developer. The practice step should occupy at least 50% of the time allotted to the body of the session.

At the end of the practice step, the HR developer should test the learners to ensure that they have achieved the learning objectives.

The HR developer needs to be highly competent at performing the skill, and the logistics of organising sufficient materials and tools requires careful planning. Safety should be high on the HR developer's agenda particularly when dangerous tools or hazardous materials are being used.

THE THEORY SESSION

The theory session is used to impart programmed knowledge. The structure of the theory session is shown in figure 11.1.

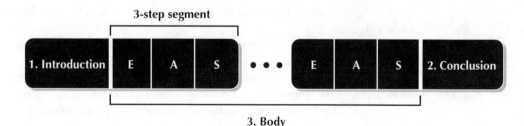

FIGURE 11.1
The theory session

E — Explanation
A — Activities by trainees
S — Summary

Source: Delahaye and Smith (1998), p. 30

When planning a theory session, the HR developer must decide how many segments will comprise the body. Each segment will cover a major component of the programmed knowledge to be learned. It is quite surprising how small each of these 'major' components can be and the learning principle of part learning (see chapter 2) should be used. As a general rule of thumb, five or six very minor points should make up a 'major' component.

Each 'major' component is then presented to the learners using a three-part sequence:

1. the *explanation step*, where the programmed knowledge is explained to the learners using visual aids, questioning and verbal descriptions;
2. the *activity step*, where the learners are given an activity to test whether they have understood the programmed knowledge described in the explanation step. This step can also test the learning objectives;
3. the *summary step*, where the information is briefly reviewed and any minor misunderstandings are cleared up.

Like the skill session, the theory session is a powerful learning strategy for programmed knowledge, largely because all the principles of learning discussed in chapter 2 are in operation. You might like to review these principles of learning and note exactly where each of them are used in the recommended steps of the skill and theory sessions.

THE LECTURE

Lectures are one of the most commonly used delivery methods as they are useful for transmitting large quantities of information, cost little to prepare, are easy to organise (Rothwell and Sredl 1992) and can be delivered to a large audience. However, most of the advantages of a lecture are to do with the transmission, not the learning, of programmed knowledge.

The lecture is really a modified theory session. It has all the components of a theory session except the activity step. Of course, this omission of the activity step does lessen the impact of the lecture as a learning strategy, as several of the principles of learning are thus lost. However, a well-planned and well-delivered lecture can result in significant learning to a well-motivated audience. Ali (1998) believes that a lecture is effective for:

- conveying organised information, when there is an accepted body of organised knowledge
- outlining and explaining concepts, to a knowledgeable audience to deepen the understanding of ideas and values
- stimulating people to think in new ways, although this is highly dependent on the motivation of the audience.

Accordingly, the lecture tends to be used most in the transmission of procedural knowledge.

THE SEMI-STRUCTURED LEARNING STRATEGIES

Moving along the structured–unstructured continuum, we come to the semi-structured learning strategies of:

- discussion
- case study
- role play
- experiential learning.

As discussed previously, in the structured learning strategies, the HR developer takes full responsibility for what will be learned, how it will be learned and what evidence will be produced to prove that the learning did occur. In these semi-structured learning strategies, however, some of these responsibilities are transferred to the learner and so there are elements of unstructured learning about them.

THE DISCUSSION

In a discussion, the HR developer encourages the learners to provide the knowledge that will achieve the desired learning objectives. The assumption is that, while each individual learner in the group does not have all the information, together the whole group does. It is up to the HR developer to unearth this information. So, the role of the HR developer is to encourage the learners to share their explicit knowledge, thereby using the knowledge generation process of combination. There is some opportunity in the discussion to stimulate the learners' tacit knowledge (externalisation) but this knowledge-generation technique does not always occur that frequently in the discussion learning strategy.

A discussion has many similarities to an interview, in that the HR developer:

- uses questions to elicit information
- records this information in a logical format, although with a discussion this is done on a white board rather than a notebook
- uses responding skills to encourage the learners to contribute information

- uses summaries at strategic points in the discussion to review the material covered and to help the learners think of new information.

In another similarity to the interview, discussions can be viewed as being on a continuum, being structured at one pole and unstructured at the other. In a structured discussion, the HR developer uses questions based on programmed knowledge to lead the learners down the path of discovery. With the unstructured discussion, the HR developer relies solely on the skills of questioning, responding, summarising and board work (placing the information in logical classifications on the white board) to manage the learning process so that the learners achieve the desired learning objectives.

Discussions are most appropriate for learning advanced programmed knowledge and the less complex elements of the task and relationship categories of the hierarchy of learning outcomes — linear analysis, some diagnostic analysis, goal identification, administrative proficiency, communication, interacting at the objective level, spontaneity and accurate self-awareness.

THE CASE STUDY

The case study learning strategy encourages the learners to go beyond their explicit knowledge by using the knowledge-generation processes of externalisation and internalisation. These deeper learning processes are aroused and stimulated by a cue known as a case study.

A case study consists of two parts — a *narration* and *questions*. A narration combines a description of a real-world event together with sufficient background information to orient the reader. The length of the narration varies from half a page to ten or more pages and is designed to bring the real world into the classroom. The second part of the case study is the questions that the learners need to answer.

The secret to selecting or writing case studies is the learning objectives to be achieved by the session. Firstly, the questions should be derived directly from the learning objectives. For example, the learning objective 'List three common unsafe acts that can lead to serious injury on a building site' would become 'What are the three unsafe acts that led to serious injury to Shane on the building site?' Secondly, the case study is written to include clues about the learning objectives (for example, the three unsafe acts) that are described in the narrative.

Case studies should be long enough to provide sufficient information to give the learners a challenge but not include so much useless information that reading the case study becomes boring. Reynolds (1998) suggests that the narrative should:
- be a short, written description of an actual situation
- include enough detail for the learners to gain the experience of relating facts to one another effectively in problem solving
- include enough detail that the learners have to judge between important and unimportant information
- stop short of describing the final key actions and decisions, thus leaving open to the learners the choice of actions to be recommended.

When conducting the session, the HR developer can ask the learners to read the case study beforehand or at the start of the session. Either way, individual learners should then be given time to write notes which will provide a considered base for contributions to the later group discussion. To maximise the use of this time, the following five steps can be recommended to the individual learners:

1. *Read the whole case study* for a general feel of the incident or incidents being presented.
2. *Re-read* the case study to identify facts and issues.
3. *Organise* these facts and issues into a logical sequence by asking the famous four Ws — what, where, when and why.
4. *Focus on the case study questions* to see how the facts and issues provide answers.
5. *Make notes*, to be used in the later discussion, under each of the case study questions.

At the end of this preparation time, the HR developer brings the learners together firstly in small groups. Goldstein (1993) believes that interacting in small groups increases feedback to individual learners and also allows individuals to learn by observing others developing their respective solutions. The HR developer then brings the whole group together and facilitates a discussion. This discussion can take a wide variety of paths. One of the most common options is a structured discussion based specifically on the case study questions. Other times, the small groups are asked to present their solutions before the HR developer facilitates a review of the most pre-ferred resolutions. However, when conducting the discussion, the HR developer needs to ensure that:

- the learning objectives of the session are achieved
- the learners can identify connections between issues and also any cause–effect relationships
- the learning that occurs is not just single-loop learning — the detection and cor-rection of error — but that double-loop learning is also addressed so that under-lying organisational values, assumptions and goals are examined and challenged (see chapter 2)
- the learners can generalise the learning outcomes from the specific case study to their real-life work context.

The case study is ideal for developing the diagnostic analysis, complex analysis, administrative proficiency and allocation of resources elements of the task category of the HLO. There can be the added benefits of also developing the accurate self-awareness and self-confidence elements of the relationship category, as the learners test their ideas against the results of the case study discussion and find that their conclusions are valid.

For an in-depth discussion of the case study learning strategy see Pigors (1976) and Reynolds (1998) and for a detailed examination of writing and conducting a case study see Delahaye and Smith (1998, pp. 203–215). For a thoughtful critique of the case study method see Argyris (1980).

THE ROLE PLAY

The role play is similar to a case study, in that the role play itself provides the cue for the generation of information that can be combined into new learning during the later discussion. However, rather than a narrative, some or all of the learners become actively engaged by acting out roles.

Delahaye and Smith (1998) suggest that there are two types of role plays. In the first, the pre-planned role play, the role players are given clear and detailed role descriptions depicting scripted behaviours that are usually quite different from the learners' usual deportment. These roles take the place of the narrative of the case study. The remaining learners in the group are given detailed observation guides that indicate what they should look for during the role play. These observation guides take the place of the case study questions. Both the roles and the observation guides are based firmly on the learning objectives for the session. In the second type, the spontaneous role play, the selected learner is given a role in which he or she basically plays himself or herself but tries out new behaviours to expand his or her range of options. This second type of role play is very close to experiential learning and further comments will be made on the approach under that heading.

Whatever type of role play is used, it is the direct involvement of the learners that creates the most significant difference as the role play engenders an emotional component in the learning experience. This emotional component is both the strength and the weakness of the role play as a learning strategy. It is the strength in that the emotional component triggers the deeper levels of learning (see figure 2.1 in chapter 2) encouraging critical reflection and critical thinking. It is the weakness in that, when not properly channelled by the facilitator, the energy created by the emotions can become self-destructive. Accordingly, the facilitator must ensure that the following steps are covered:

- The roles are written so that they are realistic and not heavily biased to release negative feelings. Negative feelings are easily initiated so the role play descriptions should be written so they are well balanced.
- The selection of the learners for the roles is taken with care and considered thought. On the one hand, the role players need some confidence that they can handle the role but on the other the role should not create such stress to the individual that learning is blocked out.
- The learners are thoroughly briefed in the roles they are to enact.
- The observation guides are very clear so that the observers are in no doubt about what they should heed.
- The actors are 'de-roled' carefully and thoroughly at the end of the play.
- The main themes are identified and examined fully during the discussion stage.
- The role players are observed closely during the discussion stage to ensure there is no regression back to the emotions of the role.
- The learners can generalise the learning outcomes from the specific to their real-life work context.

The discussion needs to be closely supervised by the HR developer and combined with a very sensitive analysis of the performance and actions of the role players. The HR developer should be careful to refer to the roles by the role name, not by the name of the learner playing the role, to ensure that the comments and actions made during the role play are divorced from the personality of the learner. The HR developer should emphasise that the choices made by the role players were made to enrich the role and are not regarded as being the usual performance of the person playing the role. Without such a sensitive review, the role play can easily become a damaging experience with learning outcomes directly opposite to those intended.

Conducted correctly, the role play is ideally suited to develop the deeper elements of the relationship category of the hierarchy of learning outcomes of 'interaction at the emotional level', 'use of group processes', 'use of social power', 'self-confidence', 'inner strength' and 'self-discipline'.

For a detailed examination of role plays see Maier, Slaem and Maier (1975) and Van Ments (1994) and for a discussion of writing and conducting role plays see Delahaye and Smith (1998).

EXPERIENTIAL LEARNING

The term 'experiential learning' covers a number of possible approaches, with various writers providing a variety of definitions. This text will include those learning approaches which allow the learner to experiment with or experience a specific situation and to reflect on that experience or experiment. Two conditions set experiential learning aside from other structured strategies. Firstly, the whole learner — his or her explicit knowledge, tacit knowledge, emotions and frames of reference — is involved. Secondly, the learning is generated by the first-hand experience of the learner, not by a vicarious or artificial event (such as in case studies and role plays). On the other hand, it is the situation-specific nature and the fact that the majority of the learning occurs within the classroom that differentiates experiential learning from the more unstructured learning strategies such as action learning.

There are four techniques that are usually discussed under the term 'experiential learning' — learning instruments, simulations, projects and sensitivity groups. One common theme of the four techniques is the use of the learning cycle (see chapter 9). Each technique starts with the learner being given an experience (step 1). The learner is then expected to review that experience (step 2) and, usually with the help of a HR developer and a learning group, to draw conclusions from that reflection (step 3). Finally, the learner is encouraged to plan changes in his or her future life (step 4).

Learning instruments

A learning instrument is a device, often a questionnaire, that provides an individual with insights about his or her frames of reference (see chapter 2). The learning instruments often measure the epistemic-based paradynamic assumptions such as learning styles, management styles, team roles and decision techniques. A good learning instrument provides thorough, reliable and systematic data-gathering and a valid analysis of that data. The analysis of the data should provide the learner with personal enlightenment or new perception of self.

Smith (1992a) suggests seven steps that the HR developer should follow in using learning instruments:

1. *Set the scene*, where the HR developer sets goals, explains terms, and clarifies the process. Establishing this base provides the motivation which encourages truthfulness in responses, discourages defensiveness and establishes the supportive atmosphere essential to the sharing of results.
2. *Administration*, where the instrument is distributed, clear instructions are given and questions clarified. The learners then complete the instrument.
3. *Theory input*, where an explanation is given of the theory or key concepts underpinning the instrument
4. *Scoring*, where the learners calculate their results on a scoring sheet
5. *Interpretation*, where the theory and concepts explained earlier are related to the scores

6. *Posting,* where the learners' scores are made public. Usually, scores are not related to individuals but the ranges and means of the group scores are disclosed to provide information for the later discussion.

7. *Processing,* when the discussion takes place. This discussion period is really the make or break of the learning instrument technique. A shallow discussion adds little more than a lecture while vigorous and open deliberations encourage critical thinking and critical reflection. A surprising level of emotional energy can also be generated as individuals become involved in introspection about personal values and future self-development.

Learning instruments are useful for developing and raising awareness about the relationship category element of emotional resilience and the initial elements of the implementing and concern for others subgroups, particularly work motivation, bias for action, developing others and empathy. Whether these elements will be changed or developed depends on the extent to which the individual is willing to become involved in critical thinking and critical reflection.

Simulations

A simulation allows the learner to act as if he or she were in the real work-based situation. To give the learner an opportunity to act out this real behaviour, the HR developer uses a model of reality. A simulation model takes a number forms. It may be a physical representation such as a flight simulator used for training pilots. It may be a computer-managed game as often used in management development. Another example is the 'in basket exercise' where novice managers are asked to make a number of decisions about pieces of paper (letters, telephone messages, hand written instructions) that are representative of a manager's normal workday.

In general, a simulation model should include a close representation of the usual work environment (at least the basic technology that is the norm for the role), sufficient information inputs to ensure that the learner has to make choices, and a mechanism to provide immediate feedback which, in turn, provides further information which forces the learner to make further choices. Hernes (1998) believes that successful simulations:

- provide a challenge to the learners so that they apply themselves, become motivated to seek new and innovative solutions and create a desire to use the new solutions
- have relevance to the learners' real needs (see comments by Knowles in chapter 2)
- are realistic so that the learners can recognise their work situation being reflected in the simulation.

Conducting simulations tends to be a much more interactive and dynamic exercise than those using case studies, role plays and learning instruments. The HR developer is usually constantly involved, providing feedback and advice to the participants. The de-briefings are usually made on an individual basis first (or at least the small group if a small group was the unit involved in the decision making) before bringing the whole group together to discuss common trends or ideas. The HR developer should ensure that the whole group discussion raises the learning outcomes from the specific solutions to general principles that can be used back in the workplace.

Simulations are designed to develop all the elements in the implementing and concern for others subgroups as well as those in the critical thinking category of the HLO.

Projects

A project is a defined activity that has limiting boundaries. These boundaries ensure that the project is not so large that the learner will be overwhelmed by the challenge. On the other hand, the project should be substantial enough to engender high levels of interest. The project should be workplace orientated but be of sufficient complexity to provide the learner with opportunities to see theory in practice. The experiential side of the activity often takes place outside the class room but time should be planned so that discussion with a facilitator and a learning group can occur.

Unfortunately, learning projects can degenerate into just another task to be completed as the urgencies of the workfront become paramount. So, for a project to be a successful learning technique, emphasis has to be given to reflection and feedback. The following steps are recommended for a successful learning project:

1. The project is explicitly defined with the limits described clearly and concisely.
2. The learner visits the work situation where the project is located to review the context, identify any significant features and locate key stakeholders in the project.
3. The theories and concepts that may impact on the project are reviewed.
4. The learner uses critical thinking and critical reflection to review and contemplate new information and to integrate theory and practice.
5. The learner discusses new insights with a HR developer and/or the learning group.
6. The above five steps are repeated, in any order, throughout the project.
7. The learner produces a report on the recommendations for the project.

To provide further opportunities for reflection and development a learning diary is often included. Smith (1992b) suggests that a learning diary should include a brief description of the experience, detailed observations of important events or issues, an analysis of these events or issues using relevant theories or concepts and a description of proposed future behaviour of the learner. A learning diary encourages a learner to reflect deeply on the experience and to challenge any hegemonic assumptions (see chapter 2) and is discussed further in chapter 12.

Projects, properly managed, can be useful in developing the critical thinking category and the mental agility element of the meta-ability category.

Sensitivity groups

Sensitivity groups (sometimes called laboratory groups or T-groups) came out of the research and studies of such people as Bion (1961) and Lewin (1951) into the use of group processes for psychotherapeutic and interpersonal developmental purposes. Bion developed his ideas while helping shell-shocked soldiers from the Second World War come to terms with their terrors while Lewin was interested in developing individual and group skills to create a harmonious and productive modern society.

Sensitivity groups are based on the belief that disclosure of deep personal issues and emotions within a highly supportive and caring group can lead to a more profound understanding of self and of one's personal relations with others. Accordingly, open and honest communication between group members and a willingness to disclose innermost feelings are the keys to productive sensitivity groups. In a symbiotic relationship, the well-known schools of therapeutic counselling of client centred therapy (Rogers 1983) and gestalt therapy (Perls 1973) added to the rich values and processes of the sensitivity groups. The guiding beliefs of self-analysis (encouraged by unconditional acceptance by the facilitator) and staying in the 'here and now' were imported from these two schools of counselling into the sensitivity group technique.

The key to successful sensitivity groups is the HR developer (usually referred to as a facilitator) managing the process but staying out of the content. This exhortation is a reflection of client centred therapy where Rogers never gave the client any advice but reflected meanings and feelings so that the client explored the issues and came to personally relevant conclusions. 'Managing the process' has become the catch cry of facilitators in sensitivity groups. We have come across the concept when examining interviewing (chapter 7) and the discussion (earlier in this chapter). In these, the HR developer uses processes (for example, questioning and responding) to help the learners externalise feelings and tacit knowledge. In sensitivity groups the processes became more complex than just questioning and responding with paradigms such as force field analysis and transactional analysis being used.

a closer look   11.1

Force field analysis and transactional analysis

Force field analysis (FFA) is a process suggested by Lewin (1951) as a method for analysing problems that involve people. An FFA has four steps:
1. State the *objectives* to be achieved in behavioural terms (for example, improve customer relations).
2. Identify the *driving forces* — the forces that are already present and encourage good customer relations (for example, staff greet customers with a smile).
3. Identify the *restraining forces* — those forces that inhibit the achievement of the objective (for example, staff lack product knowledge).
4. Plan *means of overcoming* the restraining forces (for example, staff to attend product training courses).

The basic premise of FFA is that, once the restraining forces have been identified and overcome, the driving forces will automatically encourage the achievement of the objectives. In managing the process, the HR developer simply has the group cover each of the four steps in FFA — the group then concentrates on the actual content (for example, 'staff lack product knowledge').

Transactional analysis (TA) is known as 'the poor person's psychology' and is a means of understanding what drives the inner self and of analysing interpersonal relations. The heart of TA was the belief that an individual was comprised of three 'ego states':
1. The *parent ego state* is made up of two parts — the

nurturing parent and the critical parent. The nurturing parent is made up of caring messages to the self, such as 'Look left and right before crossing the road' and 'Don't worry, everything will come out alright in the end'. The critical parent gives fault-finding messages such as 'You are so stupid' and 'You will never be a success'. Interestingly, parent ego messages are a simplistic understanding of frames of reference (see chapter 2).
2. The *adult ego state* is based on logic and takes in factual information which is then analysed in a cause-and-effect manner.

(continued)

3. The *child ego state* is made up of two parts. The natural child has all those childlike qualities of curiosity, excitement and living-for-the-moment. The adapted child assumes all those less-liked qualities of the manipulating child where tantrums and elements of cruelty can gain the rewards that the child-within-the-person seeks.

The HR developer would use examples from the real lives of the learners and utilise TA on these examples to firstly show what is going on and, secondly, to 'raise the interaction'. For example, TA could be used to examine two aspects of an individual: firstly, to identify the basic motivations of the individual (for example, a parent 'tape' from the parent ego saying 'Don't even bother trying, you are hopeless'); secondly, to analyse the interactions between two people. This second type of analysis depends on identifying which ego state in one person is 'hooking' which ego state in the other person. So, the parent 'tape' of 'Don't even bother trying, you are hopeless' could be aimed at another person who could respond from the adapted child ego state by starting to cry.

Alternatively, rather than responding by crying (i.e. from the adapted child) the second individual may respond from the adult ego state ('What evidence do you have that I will not succeed?').

In this way, the HR developer uses TA to manage the process, while the learners contribute the content.

TA is reasonably complicated, with other concepts such as 'games people play' being used to analyse interpersonal interactions. For further information see texts such as Harris (1967) and Jongeward and James (1973). TA dropped out of favour over the years as it can be used in a shallow and trite manner. However, there is a simplistic robustness about the concept of TA and, when used correctly, it provides an easily assimilated foundation for interpersonal relations. You may have also noticed the connection of the ego states with the frames of reference discussed in chapter 2.

Sensitivity groups were very popular in the late 1960s and early 1970s but have decreased in use over the years. Misuse of power by unskilled facilitators and the difficulty in demonstrating the relevance of the approach to workplace issues contributed to the lower interest. However, the values and techniques of sensitivity groups were transferred to the wider field of organisational change — a learning strategy that will be discussed in the next chapter. Indeed, it is often difficult to see where sensitivity groups finish and the organisational change strategies start, so close is the link between them.

Well-managed sensitivity groups were designed to develop the relationship category of the HLO in particular but also contribute to critical thinking and the mental agility and helicopter perception elements of the meta-abilities category.

The energy for experiential learning

Experiential learning has the potential to develop the deeper levels of the task and relationship and some aspects of the critical thinking and meta-abilities categories of the HLO. However, whether this potential is fulfilled depends largely on the motivation of the learners. This motivational force is the catalyst that decides whether the learner will honestly and energetically follow the opportunities for development or whether the learner will take the easiest course and just 'play along'. The experiential learning options do require a great deal of commitment and energy from the learner. A comprehensive discussion of experiential learning can be found in Higgs (1988).

THE CHALLENGE TO THE HR DEVELOPER

The discussion of learning strategies in this chapter commenced with the most structured approaches — the skill session, the theory session and the lecture — before progressing to the less structured approaches of the discussion and the case study.

The role play represents something of a watershed in this continuum of learning strategies in that the role play focuses strongly on the emotions of the learner as well as on the more objective or cognitive information to be learned. This means that the HR developer not only has to be adept with the programmed knowledge and the analytic procedures based on that programmed knowledge but also has to be comfortable with other peoples' emotions. Indeed, more than this, the HR developer has to regard these emotions as a form of energy and use them in a caring but productive manner when facilitating role plays and the more unstructured learning strategies.

Experiential learning involves the whole learner and the implementation of each of the techniques is based on the learning cycle of experience, review, conclude and plan. In conducting experiential learning, the HR developer becomes more of a facilitator of the learning process rather than didactically imparting content information.

To successfully implement these learning strategies, a HR developer needs to have highly competent micro skills. These skills — questioning, responding, using visual aids and constructing learning objectives — allow the HR developer to present information, elicit information, challenge and encourage the learners. Having both the ability to use each of the learning strategies appropriately and effectively and the micro skills to implement them gives the HR developer the competence to present individual sessions. However, a learning experience usually consists of a number of these structured learning strategies linked together into a training program or workshop. A HR developer must be able to manage and coordinate this assembly of sessions to ensure that the desired learning experience outcomes are achieved.

While the learning strategies described in this chapter often combine to form a course or workshop, the strategies discussed in the next chapter are usually total learning experiences in themselves.

GLOSSARY

case study — a learning experience where the learner reads a narration of a real life event and answers set questions and where the HR developer uses the discussion to encourage learning

discussion — a learning experience where the HR developer uses micro skills to elicit the required information from the learners

experiential learning — a learning episode where the learner experiments with or experiences a specific situation and then reflects on that experience, consists of several approaches including learning instruments, simulations, projects and sensitivity groups

learning instrument — an experiential learning approach where the learner completes an instrument, often a questionnaire, to uncover information about personal frames of reference

learning objective — a statement, usually written and consisting of a terminal behaviour, a performance standard and conditions under which the assessment is to take place, which provides the direction for, and the final destination of, the learning experience

lecture — a modified theory session which omits the activity step

micro skills — the skills of questioning, responding, using visual aids and constructing learning objectives used by the HR developer to enhance the learning experience

project — a defined activity from the workplace where the learner can experiment and reflect on the outcomes

questioning — a micro skill where the HR developer queries the learner to externalise that learner's ideas and thoughts

responding — a micro skill where the HR developer uses paraphrasing, probing and summarising to provide feedback and encouragement to the learner

role play — similar to a case study, where the narration is replaced by the learners enacting roles which are subsequently discussed

semi-structured learning strategy — a learning strategy where the learner takes responsibility for deciding the learning objectives, the content to be covered and the evidence that is to be presented to prove that learning objectives have been achieved

sensitivity groups — where the HR developer uses group process to allow the learner to disclose deep personal issues and emotions

simulation — an experiential learning approach which allows the learner to experience and reflect on a real work-based situation

skill session — a learning experience to teach a learner a procedural skill and based on the steps of show, show and tell, check of understanding and practice

structured learning strategy — a learning strategy where the HR developer takes responsibility for deciding the learning objectives, the content to be covered and the evidence that is to be presented to prove that learning objectives have been achieved

theory session — a learning experience that imparts information, the body of which is divided into logical segments, each segment consisting of three components: the explanation step, the activity step and the summary step

visual aids — resources such as the white board, overhead projector, computer-assisted computer packages and the overhead visualiser which the HR developer uses to maximise multiple-sense learning during presentations and learning sessions

QUESTIONS

For review

1. Describe the actions an HR developer should take to manage and coordinate effectively a learning program.
2. Briefly explain how three types of visual aids could be used by a HR developer to enhance a learning session.
3. Describe the skill session.

For analysis

4. Describe how an HR developer should combine learning objectives, questioning and responding to lead a discussion.

5. Compare and contrast structured and semi-structured learning strategies.

6. Compare and contrast the theory session, the discussion and the role play.

For application

7. Examine the theory session, the case study and the experiential learning approach of the simulation. Identify the principles of learning (see chapter 2) that are used in each of these learning strategies.

8. If you were asked to design a learning experience to achieve the HLO levels of programmed information, diagnostic analysis, administrative proficiency, interact at the emotional level and use of social power, what learning strategies would you be likely to use? Justify your answer.

REFERENCES

Agnew, P. W., Kellerman, A. S. and Meyer, J. M. (1996). *Multimedia in the Classroom*. London: Allyn and Bacon.

Ali, A. (1998). 'Lectures and presentation methods.' In J. Propopenko (Ed.), *Management Development: A Guide for the Profession*. Geneva: ILO, 291–303.

Argyris, C. (1980). 'Some limitations of the case method: Experiences in a management development program.' *Academy of Management Review*, 5, 291–298.

Bion, W. R. (1961). *Experiences in Groups*. New York: Ballantine Books.

Byrnes, J. (1993). 'Aboriginal learning styles and adult education: Is a synthesis possible?' *Australian Journal of Adult and Community Education*, 33(3), 157–171.

Caffarella, R. S. (1994). *Planning Programs for Adult Learners*. San Francisco: Jossey-Bass.

Delahaye, B. L. and Smith, B. J. (1998). *How to be an Effective Trainer*. New York: Wiley.

Goldstein, I. L. (1993). *Training in Organizations: Needs Assessment, Development and Evaluation*. Pacific Grove, Cal.: Brooks/Cole.

Harris, T. (1967). *I'm OK — You're OK*. New York: Avon.

Hernes, T. (1998). 'Simulation methods.' In J. Propopenko (Ed.), *Management Development: A Guide to the Profession*, Geneva: ILO, 251–271.

Higgs, J. (Ed.). (1988). *Experienced-based Learning*. Sydney: ACEE.

Jongeward, D. and James, M. (1973). *Winning with People*. Reading, Mass.: Addison-Wesley.

Kemp, J. E. and Smellie, D. G. (1993). *Planning, Producing and Using Instructional Technologies*. New York: Harper-Collins.

Lewin, K. (1951). *Field Theory in Social Sciences*. New York: Harper and Row.

Mager, R. F. (1984). *Preparing Instructional Objectives*. (3rd ed.). Belmont, Cal.: Davis S. Lake.

Maier, N. R. F., Slaem, A. R. and Maier, A. A. (1975). *The Role Play Techniques*. La Jolla, Cal.: University Associates.

Perls, F. (1973). *The Gestalt Approach and Eye Witness Therapy*. New York: Bantam.

Pigors, P. (1976). 'Case method.' In R. L. Craig (Ed.), *Training and Development Handbook: A Guide to Human Resource Development*, New York: McGraw-Hill, 35–1 and 35–12.

Print, M. (1993). *Curriculum Development and Design*. St. Leonards, NSW: Allen & Unwin.

Reynolds, A. and Anderson, R. H. (1991). *Selecting and Developing Media for Instruction*. (3rd ed.). New York: Van Nostrand Reinhold.

Reynolds, J. I. (1998). 'Case method.' In J. Prokopenko (Ed.), *Management Development: A Guide to the Profession*, Geneva: ILO, 272–290.

Rogers, C. R. (1983). *Freedom to Learn in the 80s*. Ohio: Charles E. Merrill.

Rothwell, W. J. and Sredl, H. J. (1992). *Professional Human Resource Development: Roles and Competencies Volume II*. (2nd ed.). Amherst, Mass.: HRD Press.

Smith, B. (1992a). 'Learning instruments.' In B. Smith (Ed.), *Management Development in Australia*. Sydney: Harcourt Brace Jovanovich, 129–139.

Smith, B. (1992b). 'Learning diaries.' In B. Smith (Ed.), *Management Development in Australia*. Sydney: Harcourt Brace Jovanovich, 149–154.

Tarquin, P. and Walker, S. (1996). *Creating Success in the Classroom: Visual Organisers and How to Use Them*. Englewood, Colo.; Libraries Unlimited.

Thorndike, E. L. (1931). *Human Learning*. New York: Appleton-Century-Crofts.

Tyler, R. W. (1949). *Basic Principles of Curriculum and Instruction*. Chicago: University of Chicago Press.

Van Ments, M. (1994). *The Effective Use of Role Plays: A Handbook for Teachers and Trainers*. London: Kogan.

The discussion plan

Sarojni Ehrich reviewed her session plan one last time. After lunch she was scheduled to conduct a discussion about designing questionnaires for the Marketing Services trainees. These trainees had all been customer service officers for at least 3 years and had been especially selected as having potential to move into the marketing area.

Sarojni thought that she would start with a 3-minute introduction briefly outlining the reasons survey questionnaires were used. The discussion session would then be divided into three parts. For the first part, she had two examples of a survey questionnaire — one good and one that contained a lot of errors. She thought that she would hand out the 'bad' questionnaire first and ask them to identify all the problems, before handing out the 'good' questionnaire as a comparison. Hopefully, this comparison would generate more thoughts.

In the second part of the discussion, Sarojni wanted to bring up ideas on validity and reliability. She did not want to use those words at first — 'validity' and 'reliability' sounded too much like jargon. However, she was sure that, through questioning, she could have the group identify the concepts and then at the end she could give them the words. For the third and final part of the session, Sarojni wanted to cover the strengths and weaknesses of questionnaires. By that time the trainees would have a good knowledge of questionnaires, so Sarojni was confident that her good questioning skills would help the trainees identify the strengths and weaknesses and, therefore, when it was appropriate to use questionnaires.

With the discussion session scheduled for one and a half hours, Sarojni did not anticipate too many problems.

Discussion questions

1. What are the strengths of Sarojni's plan for the discussion session?

2. What other issues should Sarojni consider?

3. Identify the learning objective and the primary question for each of the three parts of the proposed discussion.

The role play

Jason Mirza stared at the white board without really seeing it. What had he got himself into? He looked down at his hands and saw that they were so tightly clenched that the knuckles were white. 'That's funny', he thought, 'I have often read about that and this is what it feels like'.

'Hey Jason, are you alright?' Startled, Jason looked up and saw the HR developer looking at him, smiling. Jason was very aware that the rest of the group were looking at him as well and he felt himself flushing and was suddenly aware of how hot he felt. He gave a quick smile and assured everyone that there was no problem. The HR developer went back to the white board and said, 'OK, what else did you learn from that role play?' One of the other trainees started answering. 'It's alright for him. He was just an observer.', Jason said to himself.

It had been an awful experience. 'No, I really am a good HR person.', Jason argued with himself. 'I don't normally do those sort of things. I wouldn't yell at one of the staff like that. But that's what the role play script wanted me to do.

This is silly. It wasn't my fault. The script made me do it. But I did it so well and I really did feel angry. What if this happens when I get back to the office? If I lose my temper here, I could easily do it again back on the job. Oh, damn, why was I selected to do the role play? I felt such a fool out there. Usually, I have everything together. And when I was asked that question, I stuttered and carried on as if I was clueless. I do know the answer. I remembered it as soon as I came back here to my desk. Now everyone thinks I am an idiot. I have only been in the company for 2 months. Most of these others have been here for years. Oh, I hope my boss doesn't hear about it. I can just imagine it. I'll be out of a job next.'

Discussion questions

1. What did the HR developer either fail to do or do inadequately?

2. In detail, describe what you would have done after the role play to ensure this situation would not have happened.

Implementing the unstructured learning strategies

CHAPTER OBJECTIVES

At the end of this chapter you should be able to:

1 describe the role of the HR developer in facilitating the unstructured learning strategies

2 list the assumptions that underpin the unstructured learning strategies

3 describe the unstructured learning strategies of problem-based learning, contract learning, action learning, change interventions and mentoring

4 discuss the use of the unstructured learning strategies in the legitimate system and the shadow system.

This chapter begins by defining the role of the HR developer as an implementor of the unstructured learning strategies. This role is one of facilitation
where the HR developer uses the micro skills of questioning and responding,
actively listens to the learner by understanding and feeling what the learner is
explaining, provides a supportive atmosphere so that the learner can explore the
unknown, exhibits the essential quality of patience, encourages the learners to
evaluate their own learning, accepts the troublesome, innovative and creative ideas
of the learners and, above all, is also prepared to learn.

The unstructured learning strategies are based on six assumptions — the learners
have equal opportunity to participate; are free from coercion and distorting self-
deception; are open to alternative points of view; care about the way others think and
feel; have free and informed choice; and keep testing the validity of the choices
especially as the choices are being implemented.

The chapter discusses five unstructured learning strategies. **Problem-based learning**
is based on a real-life problem from the workplace. The selection of the problem is
critical, as this provides the trigger for learning. The problem must be more than an
application exercise, should be multidimensional and cover a complexity of issues. The
learners should then identify all possible issues and implications of the problem before
tracking down the programmed information which provides insights into those issues
and implications. These possible solutions then need to be reviewed closely by the
learners to identify any omissions of content or logic. Finally, the learners need to review
the problem-solving processes used to identify general principles of decision making.

Contract learning, as the name suggests, is based on a learning contract. The
learning contract covers six main sections — the learning objectives, the subject content, the learning methods, the evidence that will show that the learning objectives
have been achieved, the criteria that will be used to judge the evidence and the date
that the evidence will be submitted. In a typical contract learning episode, the learner
makes all the decisions on five of the six areas. The exception is the learning objectives. Often the institution or organisation in which the learning will take place wishes
to have some control over the direction of the learning. This control is achieved by
using non-negotiable objectives. The learner is required to achieve these non-
negotiable objectives at least — although the way these objectives are achieved and
the evidence that is presented is still the learner's responsibility. In addition, the
learner can also include further learning objectives that she or he wishes to achieve.
These are called negotiable objectives.

The driving force of **action learning** is the formula 'learning = programmed information + questions'. Programmed information is available in textbooks and from
experts. The real heart of learning is the ability to ask questions. Further, action
learning denotes a process that is more than passive acquisition of information.
Learning is an active process and must result in the implementation of a plan. In
action learning the learners wrestle with a relevant problem from the workplace and,
while solving the problem is part of the learning, the significant issue is for the learner
to identify the questioning processes that he or she used to solve the problem. The

learner becomes part of a **learning set** of other learners who encourage and extend each other. The **set adviser** does not solve problems for the learners but manages the process so that the learners ask the appropriate questions. Typically, this facilitation progresses through five stages — the survey stage, the trial decision stage, the action stage, the audit stage and the control stage.

There are a variety of **change interventions** that can be used to enhance the development of individuals, groups and organisations. The basic model used in change interventions is **action research**. The action research model begins with the objective to be achieved and from this the facilitator identifies the first cue (usually a question). The group responds to this cue by generating data. Usually a large quantity of data is developed by the group and this data has to be reduced into workable sizes. This reduction is achieved by prioritising or by collating the data into common areas. If the objective has not been achieved by the first cue, the facilitator creates another cue from the decisions made by the group on the reduced data.

Successful **mentoring** programs are based on an organisational belief system that values learning. In addition, mentors-to-be must be must be developed in the role, resources (especially time) need to be allocated to the mentor and the mentors must gain both extrinsic and intrinsic benefits. The **protégé** should ensure that her or his mentor is a superior performer, is willing to be a role model, is supportive, is willing to delegate appropriately and to encourage the protégé to value self-feedback. The mentor should use the various learning strategies appropriately, coach the protégé in specific skills, task and relationship competencies, be able to use counselling skills and sponsor the protégé.

The structured learning strategies of the skill session, theory session, discussion, case study and role play are used predominantly by the legitimate system, especially in planned learning programs. These learning strategies are most suitable for developing staff in the procedures, analytical processes and values paradigms of the legitimate system. The shadow system uses the unstructured strategies predominantly as these strategies develop the deeper competencies of the HLO and also are used in the exploratory nature of the activities in the shadow system. In addition to these unstructured learning strategies, the shadow system uses a **five-stage model** to enhance adult learning. These five stages are inquiring, modelling, experimenting and practising, theorising and perfecting and actualising.

THE ROLE OF THE HR DEVELOPER

The learning strategies in the previous chapter were termed 'structured' although, strictly speaking, this description only applies to the skill session, theory session and lecture. The other learning strategies — the discussion, case study, role play and experiential learning — were discussed in a specific order that went from less structured to more unstructured. Also in the previous chapter, an emphasis was placed on the connection between the learning strategies and the hierarchy of learning outcomes (HLO) — the highly structured being suitable to the programmed knowledge category while the less structured the learning strategies became, the more suitable to the deeper complex categories. Another way to look at this progression is that the highly structured learning strategies rely more on the knowledge-generation process of combination while the discussion, case study, role play and experiential learning also bring in aspects of the knowledge processes of internalisation and externalisation. In addition, all the learning strategies examined in the previous chapter place the responsibility on the HR developer to trigger these knowledge-generating processes.

The learning strategies discussed in this chapter place this responsibility for generating knowledge directly on the learner. There is less emphasis on combination and much more relevance is placed on internalisation and externalisation. Further, the learning strategies in this chapter encourage socialisation as a significant learning channel. You will also find that, while the structured learning strategies use instrumental and communicative learning, the strategies in this chapter highlight emancipatory learning.

The first four of the unstructured learning strategies — problem-based learning, contract learning, action learning and change interventions — use defined protocols that allow the HR developer to manage the learning process while allowing the learner to retain control over the learning itself. The final strategy — mentoring — has been designated as the most unstructured of all. In that mentoring is usually a one-on-one relationship between the mentor and the learner, the appropriate use of learning strategies can be very fluid. However, in dealing with these unstructured learning strategies, the HR developer takes on a very subtle role that concentrates on managing the process but rarely becomes involved in the specific content. This 'process management' or '**facilitator**' role is common to all the unstructured learning strategies and so we will examine this role first. In performing this role, the facilitator undertakes a number of activities.

SUPPORT

Structured learning strategies, particularly the theory session and the lecture, are very familiar to most learners. This familiarity, together with the material evidence of what the future will hold (for example, the course program or the semester subject outline), provide a solid sense of security to the learner. However, the unstructured learning strategies are often unfamiliar and, further, there is little observable material that tells the learner what will happen in the future. The facilitator, therefore, has to provide supportive mechanisms that will ensure that learner insecurities will not impede the learning process.

There are two **supportive mechanisms** that all the pioneering writers (Knowles 1990; Revans 1982; Rogers 1983) in the field recommend. The first is investing the time and encouraging supportive relationships between the learners so that they become what Revans calls 'comrades in adversity'. The second is to develop a positive relationship between the facilitator and individual learners. This relationship is not one of dependence, but one where the learner has sufficient trust to approach the facilitator as a 'sounding board' and counsellor.

MICRO SKILLS

The **micro skills** of questioning and responding are critical to the ability of the facilitator to stay at the process level. When learners ask questions, they often expect answers based on content but, by and large, the facilitator should avoid 'descending into the content'. Self-directed learners are independent learners and should be encouraged, with the facilitator questioning, reflecting, probing and summarising, to investigate options for themselves.

Knowles (1980a) believes that facilitators must acquire a different set of rewards — experiencing the joy of releasing learners rather than controlling them. This theme of 'releasing the learners' is one of the predominant constants in all the unstructured learning strategies. Of course, this means that the facilitator must have the maturity to be able to accept and help learners with this new-found power.

PATIENCE

For facilitators patience is more than a virtue; it is an essential quality. The internal craving of the facilitator to intervene, give a specific example or provide detailed advice is, at times, overwhelming. This craving must be resisted and to resist needs patience. Being novices to the concepts being investigated, learners will usually muddle around, procrastinate, explore dry gullies and take the line of least resistance even though such a line will eventually take twice the time. Resisting the craving to jump in and say, 'Look, this is the best way', requires patience.

To manipulate an old adage slightly, the role of the facilitator is to help the learners to learn how to catch fish, not to catch the fish for them.

ACTIVE LISTENING

Linked very closely to micro skills and patience is the skill of listening. Listening actively is not just using responding skills in the technical sense but really understanding and feeling what the learner is explaining. **Active listening** requires effort and concentration.

ENCOURAGE SELF-EVALUATION

Valuing **self-evaluation** above evaluation-by-others is the final bastion on the journey to becoming a self-directed learner. Most educational systems place a very high priority on evaluation-by-others. Breaking this nexus is one of the most difficult tasks of the facilitator, yet learners cannot become really independent until this transition occurs. Needless to say, we are attempting to change a very deep frame of reference here and the transition is not easy for the learner. However, by keeping this ultimate goal of the importance of self-evaluation always to the forefront of the learning experience, the facilitator provides a constant guiding theme for the learner.

ACCEPTANCE

Rogers (1983) first commented that good facilitators can accept the troublesome, innovative, creative ideas that emerge in learners. Providing caring support, being patient and encouraging self-evaluation releases powerful needs and forces within learners. They will experiment, they will examine issues in new ways and they will have what they believe to be omnipotent insights. Combined with a recognition that they do have a power to think, these insights will often be communicated forcefully and dramatically. The wise facilitator accepts and rejoices with the learner over these new-found abilities while also encouraging a judicious and healthy restraint.

PREPARED TO LEARN

The successful facilitator is always prepared to learn — about the content being investigated by the learner and about the very process of being a facilitator. Rogers (1983, pp. 138–142) believes that facilitators have to be less protective of their own beliefs, to be able to accept feedback, both positive and negative, and to use this feedback as constructive insight into themselves and their behaviour. It is only by being non-defensive that facilitators can deal successfully with those 'troublesome, innovative, creative ideas that emerge in learners'. Indeed, successful facilitators are always looking for opportunities to learn from the learners.

Brookfield (1995) in his text, *Becoming a Critically Reflective Teacher*, provides an excellent discussion of the developmental process needed to become a successful facilitator.

A DIFFERENT VALUE SYSTEM

Being a facilitator of the unstructured learning strategies requires a different value system. A facilitator uses open communication and encourages an honest relationship with the learners and between the learners. The learners are constantly challenged to examine hegemonic assumptions and to become truly independent learners by valuing self-evaluation above all else. This is not a frictionless journey for facilitators who must be secure enough in their own identity to honestly evaluate feedback about their behaviours and beliefs and forever enjoy each and every opportunity to learn.

THE ASSUMPTIONS

All the unstructured learning strategies are based on rational or democratic discourse. As discussed in chapter 2, Argyris (1992) and Mezirow (1994) believe that rational discourse is predicated on the critical assumption that the interaction is based on valid information. Further, they suggest that rational discourse is likely to be more successful when the participants:

- have equal opportunity to participate
- are free from coercion and distorting self-deception
- are open to alternative points of view
- care about the way others think and feel

- have free and informed choice
- keep testing the validity of the choices, especially as the choices are being implemented.

These assumptions, then, form the basic critical doctrine for the implementation of the unstructured learning strategies.

PROBLEM-BASED LEARNING

As the name suggests, problem-based learning is founded on a real-life problem from the workplace. Problem-based learning reverses the traditional view of presenting information, then asking the learners to apply this information in the workplace. The proponents of problem-based learning believe that learning should revolve around professional problems that the learner would face in real life, not around academic subjects that underpin the field (Boud 1985). So the essence of problem-based learning is that the problem is presented to the learners who are then expected to find the appropriate knowledge.

THE PROBLEM

The problem provides the trigger needed to make the learners think. Selecting the appropriate problem is critical to the success of the learning episode but, unfortunately, there are no hard and fast rules to govern this selection process. Indeed, this dilemma reflects the strength and weakness of the problem-based approach. On the one hand, the problem should lead the learners towards the successful achievement of the learning objectives. On the other hand, the problem has to be broad enough to provide a realistic representation of a complex issue in the real world.

The problem should be multidimensional and cover a complexity of issues. There is a difference between an exercise and a problem. An exercise applies knowledge that a learner already possesses. A problem asks the learner to go out and search for appropriate knowledge. As Woods (1985) comments, in an exercise the learner already has some idea of solving the puzzle and it will just take time to work carefully through the details. With a problem, however, the learner initially has no idea of how to proceed — it is difficult.

Usually, the facilitator locates and presents the problem although some writers (for example, Vilkinas and Cartan 1992) suggest the learners can bring 'problems' with them. These writers recommend a careful preparatory process where the learners first analyse their own work life by seeking feedback from peers and colleagues. The issues identified are then brought to the workshop where further analysis converts them into manageable problems.

THE PROCESS

The presentation of the problem to the learners can take many forms — a written description, videotape, computer simulation, audiotape or even a combination of these media. However, once again, the guideline for the presentation is that it should reflect the same presentation sequence and quality that is encountered in real life.

If the learning experience is with a group of learners then they should be split into small groups. These small groups may be based on self-selection although there is a danger of cliques evolving and also of the loss of being exposed to contravening ideas, as self-selected small groups are often formed on the basis of common values. Another option is for the facilitator to 'force' a selection, but this has the disadvantage that the facilitator is seen making decisions early in the process with a resultant increase in dependency. A unique option is to present the two options of forming small groups, with their advantages and disadvantages, to the learners and ask them to decide on a process of how to form small groups.

Once the small groups have been formed, or if the learning episode will involve only one learner, the following steps should be covered by the facilitator:

1. Have the learners read, view or listen to the problem.
2. Have the learners, firstly as individuals and then in their small groups, identify as many of the possible issues and implications of the problem as they can.
3. The facilitator may then ask each small group to present their findings. The idea here is to encourage each learner to identify all possible options that may need to be investigated. However, some facilitators prefer to miss this step and keep the learners operating within their own small groups.
4. The small groups then identify possible sources of programmed knowledge that will need to be identified. Each individual learner can then investigate these sources or the task can be divided amongst members of each small group.
5. The learners report back to their small group (and full group if the facilitator prefers) on what programmed knowledge they have gathered and its application to the issues and implications of the problem.
6. The small groups re-examine the problem to evaluate whether all the issues and implications have been resolved. The facilitator needs to be very active at this stage, asking questions and encouraging analysis by the learners, so that any omissions in logical analysis or programmed knowledge are highlighted. If omissions are identified, then the small groups return to step 4 and repeat the process.
7. Near the end of the learning episode, the learners are encouraged to review the problem-solving processes used. The discussions should be designed to identify general principles of decision making that can be used in the workplace or in their professional life.

PROBLEM-BASED LEARNING IN PRACTICE

Problem-based learning focuses on providing answers to real-life situations. The proponents of problem-based learning believe that the learning is more closely linked to the learner's needs (thereby increasing motivation) and provides a much broader learning experience. This breadth of learning is reflected in the amount of programmed knowledge covered — the learners tend to cover a broad range of interlinking topics — and the strong transference of learning to the workplace situation.

However, perhaps because of its very definition, problem-based learning tends to be more successful in situations where physical evidence of problems is evident. There are numerous reports of its use in the health professions, by medical doctors, nurses and opticians. Problems in these professions can be readily defined, measured and observed. In other areas, for example with the more subjective areas of management, problem-based learning has not been popular, with educators and HR developers leaning more towards the strategies of contract learning and action learning.

Problem-based learning is ideal for the more detailed, complex areas of professional/technical information and the task analytical and logistical subgroups of the HLO. Problem-based learning can be useful in developing outcomes in the relationship category and also the problem solving element of the critical thinking category, depending on the problem used as the catalyst.

CONTRACT LEARNING

In championing adult learning, Knowles (1990) realised that his concepts of andragogy would have to be operationalised. He achieved this practical interpretation of andragogy by promulgating an approach called 'contract learning'.

THE LEARNING CONTRACT

The heart of this strategy is a learning contract. Now this may seem to be an obvious statement, but so many HR developers do not fully appreciate the care needed to create the learning contract nor the central role it plays in managing the learning event. A learning contract has six main sections:

1. the *learning objectives*, which define the final outcome that the learner wishes to achieve. The learning objectives should be stated as terminal behaviours
2. the *subject content* the learner proposes to cover to achieve these learning objectives
3. the *learning methods* that will be used to learn the subject content
4. the *evidence* that will be produced to show that the learning objectives have been achieved
5. the *criteria* that will be used to ensure that the evidence achieves the appropriate quality standard — this criteria description will take the place of the 'standard statement' in the learning objectives and it is here the learner specifies how the evidence will be judged or validated
6. the *date* that the evidence is expected to be submitted.

An example of a learning contract is shown in figure 12.1. This example is really just that — an example. The design and layout of learning contracts are many and varied. The example given has a vertical layout. Learning contracts can also vary in the amount of information that is provided under each of the six sections. The example in figure 12.1 has given only minimal information. Some learners prefer more detailed descriptions, especially of the subject content.

Knowles (1990) provides a form, setting out the same information, but in a horizontal or landscape layout (see figure 12.2). The advantage of Knowles's form is that several objectives can be listed with the details of the content, learning methods, evidence, criteria and date being given for each objective across the page.

LEARNER'S NAME: Merv Ehrich

FACILITATOR'S NAME: Ian Wilkinson

LEARNING OBJECTIVE: To list and discuss the skills of good interviewing

CONTENT: 1. Questioning
          2. Paraphrasing
          3. Probing
          4. Summarising
          5. Nonverbals

EVIDENCE: A report to be read by the facilitator and the manager, Marketing
           and Sales

CRITERIA: 1. The report will be at least 2000 words long.
           2. All the major components of each of the interview skills will be
              discussed.

DATE: The report will be submitted by 30 March.

SIGNED: ....
           (Learner)   (Facilitator)

FIGURE 12.1
An example
of a learning
contract

Learning contract for:			
Name _____			
Activity _____			
Learning objectives	Learning resources and strategies	Evidence of accomplishment of objectives	Criteria and means for validating evidence

FIGURE 12.2
Knowles's
learning
contract

Source: Knowles (1990), p. 214

Knowles emphasises that the learning contract is infinitely re-negotiable up until the end of the learning episode. This exhortation acknowledges that often the learners initially complete the learning contract with limited information. However, as they progress through the learning episode, the learners' knowledge improves and certain aspects may become clearer. Under these circumstances the learner could easily identify new objects, or even realise that the original intentions were much too ambitious, and that a change in plans is prudent. So, the learners can re-negotiate up or down the learning spectrum.

THE PROCESS

While the learning contract is the heart of contract learning, Knowles gives quite detailed advice on the process that should be used by the HR developer in managing the process (Knowles 1980a, 1980b, 1983a, 1983b, 1984, 1990). He is quite adamant that the learner should not be 'thrown into the strange waters of self-directed learning and hope they can swim' (see, for example, Knowles 1980a, p. 98). Rather, the learner should be caringly and carefully prepared for the journey into andragogy (helping people to learn).

This preparation may vary on some specific points depending on the situation — for example, there are differing requirements for learning in a university compared with learning in the workplace. Further, the learner may be operating alone or as part of a learning group. However, most contract learning episodes cover the following steps:

1. The learners are introduced to the concepts of contract learning — a brief history of andragogy, the contract form, the idea of self-directed learning and self-responsibility, and a preview of the steps now being described.
2. The concept of learning objectives is discussed, both in the general sense (that learning objectives need to be stated in terms of terminal behaviour) and the specific sense (the actual learning objectives that the learner will achieve during the learning episode).

   Knowles readily acknowledges that some organisations, both educational and workplace, will not be in the position to allow the learner total control over what is to be achieved. Universities and colleges need to have some say over what will be learned and some workplace organisations will need to specify what outcomes are expected of the learners. To cover this angle, Knowles suggests the use of non-negotiable and negotiable objectives. Non-negotiable objectives are the lowest level of achievement that the learners must achieve. If the learners wish to delve deeper than this minimal requirement then they can formulate negotiable objectives. For example in university and college courses, the non-negotiable objectives are set at the pass level. If the students wish to achieve a level higher than a pass — honours or distinction — then the students suggest additional objectives that interest them but are also worthy of this higher award.

   In a situation where the learner is going to be fully responsible for the learning and where the educational institution or workplace organisation does not wish to set specified outcomes, then only negotiable objectives are used.
3. When non-negotiable objectives are being used, the facilitator provides what Knowles calls the 'broad brush' view of the content to be learned. A broad brush view covers the main points of the content that the learners will need so that they can achieve the non-negotiable objectives. This information can be covered using a lecture or handouts or readings (specific pages or perhaps a chapter) from textbooks.
4. For the negotiable objectives, Knowles suggests that the facilitator acts as a 'traffic cop'. The facilitator may recommend to the learner certain texts to be read or may

refer the learner to a noted expert. One very useful, but frequently overlooked, source is the list of contents from relevant textbooks. A list of contents provides a good broad brush view of a particular topic where key words and concepts can be identified very efficiently.

If they are facing self-directed learning for the first time, the learners are often feeling somewhat insecure at this point. The idea of doing something useful and tangible, such as examining relevant content, is very reassuring for the learners, so asking them to examine content is satisfying both intellectually and emotionally.

5. At this stage, some time for reflection can be very beneficial, allowing the learner to accumulate and internalise the appropriate content.

6. As well as internalising the content, most learners are reviewing the whole concept of contract learning during this reflective time. Issues, questions, concerns and doubts are starting to bubble and become disconcerting. This distraction can then interfere with learning, so the facilitator needs to deal with the distractions by encouraging the learners to discuss them.

If the contract learning is taking place with a group of learners, then they can be divided into small groups and asked to list all the issues, questions, concerns and doubts. If these are disclosed within a small group, then no negative queries can be attributed to an individual. So, the small groups are more likely to be forthcoming and produce more information. Once the small groups have completed their list, then the facilitator can combine the contributions (usually on a white board so that all can see). It is then a matter of confronting each point.

Some of the points can be addressed simply by providing information — for example, the query 'I'm not sure what you mean by terminal behaviour in the learning objectives' can be addressed by defining terminal behaviour more precisely. However, other points can be answered only by the learners experiencing the situation. For example, the concern of trust in the facilitator is always an issue, sometimes overt but usually covert. The learners will not be influenced by the facilitator exhortations of 'Sure, you can trust me'! Trust will only be built over time and after a close examination of the facilitator's behaviour by the learners.

A similar process can be used for individuals using contract learning, although the safety of anonymity within small groups is not available, of course.

7. With at least some of the anxieties abating, the learners can again turn to the learning objectives they wish to attain. At this stage, learning can be enhanced when the learners discuss their insights and findings with each other. As well as interchanging content (i.e. combination), the learners discover that the other learners are experiencing similar concerns and impediments, and feelings of loneliness tend to dissipate. Further, there is an opportunity for the knowledge-generating process of socialisation to occur.

At the end of this interaction, the full group of learners is encouraged to publicly generate a long list of possible competencies or issues or concepts that could be covered during the learning episode. This list is then used by individual learners to identify personally relevant matters that they can investigate.

8. The learners can then be encouraged to turn their attention to their learning contracts. They should be given a definite target date to submit their contracts as procrastination can suffocate the best of intentions. When the contracts are submitted the facilitator examines them and decides whether they do reflect the required intentions. If the contract is acceptable then the facilitator signs to signify agreement. If the contract is not acceptable, then the facilitator and learner will enter a

negotiation stage until the needs of the learner and the facilitator (who represents the educational institution or workplace organisation) are met.

9. With agreement on the learning contract reached, the learner then follows the plan described under the learning methods section of the learning contract, always moving towards producing the evidence promised. When a group of learners is involved, it is common for the facilitator to help them identify areas of common interest and assist the learners to identify efficient and effective learning events.

By following these nine steps, the facilitator manages the learning process while allowing the learner to concentrate on the content to be learned. Good support and encouragement is provided to the learner and the various decisions required for learning to continue are raised at the appropriate time.

CONTRACT LEARNING IN PRACTICE

During the discussion of contract learning, care has been taken to differentiate between process and content. Theoretically, the content can include any of the elements in the hierarchy of learning outcomes, from the programmed knowledge to the meta-abilities categories. However, in learning contracts, the learners tend to concentrate on the programmed knowledge category, the analytical and logistical subgroups of the task category and the interpersonal and intrapersonal subgroups of the relationship category. But, by being involved in contract learning, the learners are likely to develop competence in the implementing subgroup of the task category, the concern for others subgroup of the relationship category and the critical thinking category. There is also the possibility of developing the outcomes in the meta-abilities category, although this will depend largely on the motivation and perceptiveness of the learners. It is this wide range of possible outcomes that often attracts HR developers to contract learning as a robust learning strategy.

ACTION LEARNING

If the learning contract is the heart of contract learning, then the driving force of action learning is the formula: Learning = Programmed Information + Questions. Programmed information is available from books, journals and experts. However, true learning comes only from the ability to ask important questions. In reading the various texts by Revans (for example, 1980, 1982), one finally realises that Revans avoids supplying explicit definitions. Indeed, he is more noted for providing insights into what action learning is not! However, two of his writings (1983a, 1983b) offer characteristics of action learning that can be combined to create a workable paradigm. The characteristics of action learning are:

1. learning by doing, not just acquiring information
2. learning to take effective action rather than just analysing a situation — conclusions should not be just reported but implemented and this implementation has to be evaluated for effective learning to occur
3. working on a specific and defined project that is rooted in the real workplace — and is of significance to the learner. The project should be about attacking a problem or opportunity, not puzzles. A puzzle is an embarrassment to which a

solution already exists while a problem or challenge has no currently existing solution.

The selection of the specific and defined project can be based on two parameters — the task and its context. The task — the problem or challenge — can be familiar or unfamiliar to the learner. Similarly, the context from which the problem comes can also be familiar or unfamiliar to the learner. These two parameters establish four possible situations from which the project can be selected:

- *situation 1:* a familiar task in a familiar context (for example, if the learner is a sales representative, a marketing problem in the organisation in which the learner works)
- *situation 2:* a familiar task in an unfamiliar context (for example, if the learner is a sales representative in a manufacturing organisation, a marketing problem in a service industry)
- *situation 3:* an unfamiliar task in a familiar context (for example, if the learner is a sales representative, an accounting problem in the marketing department)
- *situation 4:* an unfamiliar task in an unfamiliar context (for example, if the learner is a sales representative in a manufacturing organisation, an accounting problem in a service industry). The learner is more likely to experience more meaning and deeper learning from situation 4, but the other situations also offer learning opportunities.

4. learning to identify the important questions to ask when attacking a problem or challenge
5. changing learners' perceptions of what they are doing and how they interpret their past experiences. (This is very similar to what was discussed in chapter 2 on changing frames of reference.)

As well as being defined by these five characteristics, action learning has two other essential elements — the learning set and the set adviser.

THE LEARNING SET

Revans firmly believed that the learning process was a social one as people learn best with and from each other. In action learning this social interaction is provided through a 'learning set' where a group of learners meet regularly to discuss their individual projects. The learning set becomes the support system, the sounding board and the devil's advocate where individual learners can raise issues, confess to a lack of understanding and have ideas tested and challenged.

THE SET ADVISER

The role of the set adviser is not to teach but to help the learners learn from exposure to problems and to each other. The set adviser encourages the learning set to become a learning community. Casey (1983) suggests that the set adviser has two basic tasks:

1. to develop the ability to *give* by formulating questions that provide maximum help rather than satisfying the curiosity of the questioner; by giving opinions, both positive and negative in an open, honest and effective manner; and by giving support, especially emotional support
2. to develop the ability to *receive*, by encouraging each learner to search diligently for help from their peers and other sources. This may seem to be a paradox to

some learners where, on the one hand, they are asked to be independent but, on the other, to seek help. The difference is that dependent learners depend solely on a significant person but in developing the ability to receive the learners are seeking to find clues to solutions from a variety of sources.

The set adviser holds regular meetings for the learners — the comrades in adversity — who discuss individual projects with an emphasis on identifying the types of important questions that provided the most productive results. Challenges and barriers encountered are noted and the strategies used to overcome these barriers are analysed for general principles that can be used in a variety of situations.

As an overall guide to keeping individual learners focused on their project, the set adviser uses System Beta, a process that Revans believes is needed to plan and implement a decision. System Beta comprises five steps:

1. a *survey stage*, where the learner identifies all possible options
2. a *trial decision stage*, where the learner examines each possible option as if it is the most likely to help with the decision, imagines the possible outcomes of each option and then selects the option that is most likely to succeed
3. an *action stage*, where the selected option is implemented, either in whole or in part, either in reality or in some simulated form
4. an *audit stage*, where the observed results of the action stage are compared to the planned outcome
5. a *control stage*, where appropriate action is taken on the comparison. This action may encompass accepting success and moving to the next stage of the plan, modifying the plan or rejecting it and starting again. Whichever action is decided upon, the learner then returns to the survey stage to repeat the process.

System Beta has some striking similarities to Dewey's scientific decision-making process (see chapter 2) and also to Honey and Mumford's learning cycle (see chapter 9). You may wish to review these two concepts and identify the commonalities.

ACTION LEARNING IN PRACTICE

In action learning, the emphasis is on questioning, implementing and reviewing. Mumford (1998) believes that action learning is different from other reality-based programs on several counts:

- The learners solve problems that entail taking risks and resolving uncertainties.
- The projects are open ended in that there is rarely one 'correct' solution. Thus the learners learn to cope better in situations of complexity and uncertainty.
- The learners are encouraged to develop their own abilities to solve problems.
- It is not just a method (for example, a case study or a simulation), but a set of methods whereby the learner learns through action in the real world.
- It is not used to perpetuate nor diffuse existing practice but to creatively modify and replace it.

When an action learning project is selected at the situation 4 level (unfamiliar task in an unfamiliar context), the learner is likely to develop the critical thinking and meta-abilities level. The less complex categories are also developed, of course, especially the implementing subgroup of the task category and the concern for others subgroup of the relationship category. However, the programmed knowledge category is relegated to a certain extent in that programmed information is used as a means to an end — to allow the learner to detect new relationships between thoughts, ideas and values.

CHANGE INTERVENTIONS

Managing change appropriately to enhance the development of individuals, groups and organisations has its origins in the sensitivity groups (see chapter 11). There was a recognition that the more mechanistic and structured training methods did not always allow individuals or organisations to cope with the speed or the complexity of change that was becoming evident in society as early as the 1970s. Gradually, more interest was taken in the power of people analysing and developing their own solutions to their own problems. This interest was based on a strong belief that the people involved in the change knew all the issues but their inability to solve the problems was caused by a block in the decision-making processes used. This strong belief has led to the key value in managing change interventions — the facilitator manages the process and stays out of the content. For a detailed discussion of managing process see Schein (1969).

One of the fundamentals of managing the process is the use of group dynamics and this was discussed in chapter 7. Another fundamental model used in managing the process is action research.

ACTION RESEARCH

In managing the process of a change intervention, the facilitator uses a basic model called action research (see figure 12.3). The action research model starts with the objective to be achieved. As usual, this objective should include a terminal behaviour statement but may or may not include standards. For example, an objective may be 'To increase customer spending by 10%' and this includes both a terminal behaviour statement — 'increase customer spending' — and a measurable standard — '10%'. However, the objective 'To decrease conflict within the group' does not have a standard as it is difficult to measure 'conflict'. Of course, some pseudo-measurements could be created — for example, 'There are 10% less arguments each day' — but such measurements are easily faked. Change interventions are based on open communication, and pseudo-measurements are often felt to be counter-productive.

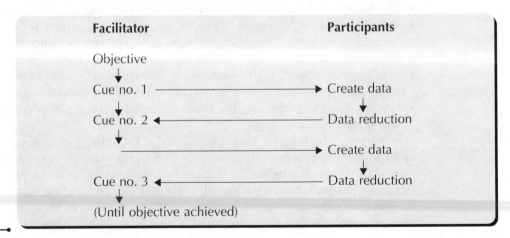

FIGURE 12.3
The action research model

From this objective, the facilitator creates 'cue no. 1'. A cue is a catalyst that guides the participants in the appropriate direction. So, how does the facilitator create this cue? Well, the decision may be based on logic. For the objective 'To increase customer spending by 10%', the facilitator may decide that the participants already have a number of ideas so the cue may be: 'In what ways could the customers be encouraged to spend more while they are in the store?' Another way that a cue could be created from this objective is to use theory. A very common theoretical base for cues is force field analysis (FFA) — see chapter 11. So, cue no. 1 could become: 'What currently encourages customers to spend money.'

This cue is then given to the participants — perhaps on a piece of paper, a white board or an overhead projector — and they are asked to generate data by listing a series of ideas. During this stage, the facilitator has to be very aware of group dynamics (see chapter 7) and ready to manage the task and maintenance roles as well as any idiosyncratic needs that may arise. Another technique that encourages deeper thought and analysis is the individual–small-group–large-group sequence. In this technique, the individual participants are given time to think and jot down ideas by themselves before being invited to join small groups (three or four people) to share their ideas. When finished, each small group reports to the main group on their accumulated ideas. To help promulgate the information efficiently across the large group, it has become traditional for the small groups to use 'butcher's paper' (sometimes called 'flip chart paper') — large pieces of white paper, approximately one metre by three-quarters of a metre — on which each group can write ideas and then hang it from a wall and refer to it while debriefing their ideas.

With all this information displayed and understood, the problem now faced by the whole group is that there is an embarrassment of data — there is too much to handle effectively. Accordingly, the data needs to be reduced. This data reduction can be carried out by the facilitator, although this option is usually taken only if time is of the essence. Preferably, the group should make this decision on what data is less important or what pieces can be collated or combined to make a significant issue. Because a number of people are involved and issues can engender in-depth discussion, this option is time consuming. Depending on the time available and the motivation of the participants, the facilitator will have to decide which option is most feasible.

Once the data has been reduced to a workable level, and if the objective has not been achieved by the first cue, the facilitator then creates cue no. 2. Again, this cue can be based on logic or theory. For example, the second cue may be based on FFA by concentrating on the hindering forces. This cue is again presented to the participants and so the action research process continues with cue no. 3 being 'How can the hindering forces be overcome?'

CHANGE IN A SOCIAL SYSTEM

Change interventions are used to transform any social system. A social system is one that includes people. As a learning strategy, a change intervention can be used in a classroom or in an organisation.

A change intervention in an organisation is usually referred to as organisational development. While all change interventions are based on action research, organisational development interventions also use a variety of other, specifically designed models. The choice of model selected to help manage the change process depends on the objective that is to be achieved. These models vary from conflict management to team building to strategic planning. For detailed description of these models see Dick (1988), French and Bell (1995), French, Bell and Zawicki (1994).

A change intervention in a classroom is often referred to as classroom democracy. While action research is still the base model used, there are no other specific, recognised models designed for classroom democracy. There is high reliance on managing group processes (see chapter 7) with a theme of devolving responsibility for learning to the learners. For a good description of classroom democracy see Dick (1992).

CHANGE INTERVENTIONS IN PRACTICE

Change interventions are designed to manage the learning process in any social system. While all change interventions are based on action research, organisational change interventions also use specifically designed models that suit particular situations, such as conflict resolution or team building. Change interventions in the classroom — called classroom democracy — are also based on the action research model but rely heavily on managing the group dynamics.

Most participants involved in a change intervention usually develop abilities in the implementing subgroup of the task category and the concern for others subgroup of the relationship category and the critical thinking and meta-abilities categories.

MENTORING

As Mumford (1988) comments, the idea of an older person acting as a coach, counsellor or sponsor is one that has long existed informally and even accidently. Indeed, the very word 'mentor' comes from ancient Greek mythology when King Odysseus selected Mentor as the tutor and friend of his only son.

The words 'mentoring', 'coaching' and 'counselling' are bandied around the literature with a variety of meanings and to describe a variety of relationships. Some authors (for example, Gonczi 1992 and Zey 1988) believe that mentoring is the dominant role with coaching being a subset, while others (for example, Landsberg 1996 and McLennan 1995) see mentoring as being a subset of coaching. The argument eventually comes down to semantics and, for practical purposes, it is more important that a writer has consistent definitions. This text will assume that mentoring is the dominant concept.

SUCCESSFUL MENTORING PROGRAMS

Mentoring is not just a set of techniques; it is also a philosophy. A successful mentoring program is based on an organisational belief system that values learning, where senior staff enjoy assisting talented staff to develop and where senior staff actively accept that responsibility.

Organisations, thinking of implementing a mentoring program, need to consider the following.

- Mentors-to-be need to be developed in the role of a mentor. Mentors do not just have appropriate programmed knowledge but are also adept at using structured and unstructured learning strategies.
- Organisations need to allocate resources to the mentor, especially the resource of time. The assumption that highly productive staff, who are usually the ones to become mentors, will somehow find sufficient time in their busy schedules is antiquated and short-sighted.
- The mentor must gain both extrinsic and intrinsic benefits from the program. This means that organisations need to consider meaningful rewards for those staff willing to take on the role of mentor. Just as important, each mentor should feel personal satisfaction in the improvement of the protégé. In addition, successful mentors expect to learn just as much as the protégé — in different ways, of course, but just as much in a quantitative sense.

THE MENTOR–PROTÉGÉ SYNERGY

Selecting a productive mentor–protégé team is a delicate task. The desired outcome is a complex combination of career and psychosocial functions. The protégé is not being developed in just the programmed knowledge required but in all categories of the HLO. In addition, these outcomes are being developed in the workplace for demonstrable improvement in the workplace context. As Odiorne (1985) comments, choosing a mentor is not exactly the same as hiring a new secretary, recruiting an engineer or even choosing a spouse!

So, what should a protégé look for in a mentor? Odiorne (1985) believes that good mentors have the following qualities:
- They are superior performers and thus represent a model to which the protégé may aspire.
- They realise that they set an example, and behave accordingly.
- While being very supportive, they avoid usurping or interfering too much.
- They are good delegators, defining the required outcomes specifically, providing appropriate resources and support — and then leaving the person alone to work towards the desired outcome.
- They encourage self-feedback so that the person becomes a self-directed learner.

Further, there has to be a compatibility between the mentor and the protégé but this compatibility has to be about balance. It could be argued, for example, that both parties should have similar learning styles so that they can communicate and avoid misunderstandings. But similarity of learning style will not 'stretch' the protégé. There will be few new insights, less challenging of thought processes and more limited exploration of alternative perceptions. On the other hand, too large a difference between the mentor and the protégé can lead to a less than harmonious relationship. There are two keys to a successful mentor–protégé alliance. Firstly, the two parties have to be able to communicate. This means each recognises and accepts individual differences and each goes out of his or her way to discuss issues using words and nonverbals understood by the other. Secondly, the protégé should be encouraged to interact with other 'experts' and 'superior performers'. Such encouragement requires a high level of maturity on the part of the mentor.

THE ROLE OF THE MENTOR

Smith (1992) suggests that there is no universal role description for a mentor, as requirements will vary according to the organisational factors, the stage of the mentor–protégé relationship and the needs of the protégé. The role of the mentor, though, goes beyond being a HR developer. The mentor is involved in the psycho-social development based on the organisation's culture. The mentor is also closely involved with career planning, preparing the protégé's advancement for several promotions. So the mentor–protégé relationship is usually of a fairly long term. The mentor can expect to do the following:

- Use the various learning strategies appropriately. Frequently, the mentor will commence with contract learning or action learning to manage the process.
- Coach the protégé in specific skills, task and relationship competencies. Coaching tends to be relatively performance orientated, is a very active role and concentrates on short-term, immediate requirements (Smith 1992).
- Counselling tends to concentrate on the relationship category of the HLO and the mentor would use counselling skills from recognised counselling approaches such as client centred counselling, rational-emotive therapy and gestalt therapy.
- Be a sponsor, by ensuring that the protégé is involved in career-building projects, by bringing the protégé to the attention of the key stakeholders in the organisation and opening the door to opportunities for advancement.

MENTORING IN PRACTICE

The role of the mentor is to set up an environment wherein protégés feel good about themselves, believe in themselves, care about others and feel empowered to make a meaningful contribution (Oncken 1997). Mentors are very special people. They delight in watching others fulfil their potential, see mentoring as a challenge which will provide opportunities for learning for both parties and are themselves highly developed in the competencies of the meta-abilities category of the HLO. The mentoring role itself is a complex set of interacting skills, knowledge and values. The mentor has to have high levels of appropriate programmed knowledge, be competent in managing the adult learning and have the compassion to accept the unique combination of strengths and weaknesses that make up an individual.

Hansford and Ehrich (1999) see a number of benefits accruing from mentoring. For the protégé, the benefits include career advancement, personal support, learning and development, increased confidence, assistance and feedback. For the mentor, the advantages are personal fulfilment, assistance on projects, increased self-confidence and revitalised interest in work. The organisation also benefits as staff are developed, turnover is reduced, there is increased commitment to the organisation and organisational communication is improved. However, the authors also warn that there is a dark side to mentoring. The protégé can have negative experiences because of unrealistic expectations, can be forced to neglect core aspects of his or her own job and can experience role conflict between his or her boss and mentor. The mentors often experience a lack of time and have very few of the supposed benefits accrue.

Mentoring can develop any one of the elements within the categories of the HLO or develop all the elements of the categories. Overall, though, mentoring is ideal for developing combinations of HLO categories and ensuring that this development is transferred into the workplace. It must be emphasised, though, that such development is a long-term investment. Organisations need to think carefully before entering mentoring programs and, once the decision is taken, ensure that appropriate resources are assigned.

THE LEGITIMATE SYSTEM

The learning strategies that operationalise the implementing stage have been discussed on a continuum starting with structured approaches at one end and unstructured at the other. As a crude rule of thumb, this continuum of structured–unstructured also provides an indication of the type of strategy suitable for the two basic systems of an organisation. The more structured strategies of the skill session, theory session, lecture, discussion, case study, role play and experiential learning are most suitable for developing staff in the procedures, analytical processes and value paradigms of the legitimate system. These more structured learning strategies are the most efficient when the content to be learned is relatively well-defined. These learning strategies also provide the legitimate system with the control needed to ensure the short- to medium-term viability of the organisation. Accordingly, the majority of planned programs designed for the legitimate system by the HR developer tend to comprise these more structured learning strategies.

This is not to say that the unstructured strategies are never used by the legitimate system. Use is made, at times, of problem-based learning and contract learning. These strategies allow the learner to make the most of the flexibility of self-directed learning but still allow the organisation some basic control. For example, in contract learning, the organisation will establish the non-negotiable objectives to ensure the learning steers what the organisation perceives as an appropriate course. Candy (1991) refers to this type of self-directed learning as *learner controlled learning*. Learner controlled learning indicates that there is some residual institutional control over the learning process and that not all the learning decisions are made by the learner.

THE SHADOW SYSTEM

The shadow system tends to use the more unstructured strategies for two reasons. Firstly, these strategies develop staff in the deeper categories of the HLO and these abilities are needed for staff to operate in the dynamic and unpredictable environment that is the mark of the shadow system. Secondly, these very unstructured learning strategies are frequently the vehicle that the shadow system uses to explore the environment and future of the organisation. For example, action learning can be used so that the learner challenges the current beliefs of the legitimate system and explores the future by asking critical and important questions.

As discussed in chapter 10, the role of the HR developer in these learning processes in the shadow system is more as an implementor than as a designer. Further, the HR developer's role is to facilitate the learning in the extended learning and the creation of new knowledge phases. To do this, the HR developer needs a model which will allow him or her to recognise and manage the learning processes that are operating within each individual actor in the shadow system. Such models should allow the learner to be involved in *autodidactic learning* (Candy 1991) — learning that is beyond the constraints of an institution and that allows the learner to dictate the direction and depth of the learning.

STAGES OF AN ADULT LEARNING EPISODE

Cavaliere (1992) has proposed a five-stage model of adult learning:
1. *Inquiring*, where the individual sees a need to solve a particular problem.
2. *Modelling*, where the learner casts around and observes similar phenomena (for example, watching birds fly before designing an aeroplane). Similarities and differences are noted and, gradually, a prototype model or solution is proposed. Undoubtedly, the observations of a similar phenomenon are used to build the individual's tacit knowledge and then metaphors, analogies and models are gradually made conscious. A number of these will be discarded until a viable model is identified.
3. *Experimenting and practising*, where the learner builds a model or representation of the solution and tests it against various standards of reality. This may mean trying out the prototype (for example, testing a model of the aeroplane) or having the solution critiqued by experts. For the actors in the shadow system, the proposed solution may be previewed by certain trusted members of the legitimate system.
4. *Theorising and perfecting*, where the model or solution is continually refined from a stage where it does just solve the problem in a barely acceptable manner to a stage where the model or solution gains high acceptance from the potential clients. The actor in the shadow system will continually ask the question 'What possible objections could be made to this solution?' or the actor could use a decision-making model such as force field analysis.
5. *Actualising*, where the individual (who has been both a learner and an actor in the shadow system) receives recognition for the product of their learning efforts.

Within each of these stages, there are four repetitive cognitive processes of goal setting, focusing, persevering and reformulation.

Thus, when working with the actors in the shadow system, the HR developer is operating at two levels. At the first level, the HR developer is using the unstructured learning strategies — such as problem-based learning or contract learning — to help the actor explore the content of the problem or challenge. At a deeper level, the HR developer can use the five-stage model of adult learning to help the actor understand the various stages of the learning process that must be navigated. For example, most learners become quite excited when they identify what they see as a viable model or solution. The HR developer can used the five-stage model to point out that the job is only half done — the proposed model or solution needs further experimentation, justification by theories and perfecting. Similarly, during each of the five stages, learners tend to become frustrated and even discouraged. The HR developer needs to point out that this is a natural cognitive process in the learning cycle and that perseverance is the name of the game.

THE IMPLEMENTING STAGE

The structured–unstructured learning strategy continuum discussed in the last two chapters moves from being highly content orientated at the structured end to a focus on the management of the process of learning at the other. Each of the learning strategies is appropriate for a particular situation. The situations were discussed in chapters 9 and 10 and were based on the combination of a number of variables — the hierarchy of learning outcomes (HLO), the learners, the strategic orientation of the organisation, the organisational culture, the key stakeholders and the resources available. It has been suggested in chapters 11 and 12 that particular learning strategies are more suitable to particular levels of the HLO.

So the appropriate use of the learning strategies is paramount to the success of the organisation by ensuring that effective learning does occur and that resources are not wasted on learning that goes nowhere. However, just as important as the appropriate use is having HR developers who are adept and competent in using the various strategies. Without the facilitative endeavours of experienced HR developers any learning strategy becomes a ghost of its effective self.

GLOSSARY

action learning — an unstructured learning strategy that emphasises questioning and the need to implement what is learned

action research — the fundamental model used in managing the process in change interventions

active listening — going beyond the technical skills of listening and responding to really understand and feel what the learner is explaining

change interventions — an unstructured learning strategy that uses group dynamics and action research to manage the learning process

contract learning — an unstructured learning strategy that uses a learning contract to manage the learning process

facilitator — the role the HR developer takes to manage the process of the unstructured learning strategies

five-stage model of adult learning — based on the stages of inquiring, modelling, experimenting and practising, theorising and perfecting and actualising, this model is used in the shadow system to develop staff and encourage learning

learning set — a group of learners involved in action learning

mentoring — an unstructured learning strategy where a senior member of staff who is a superior performer acts as a model, coach and adviser to the learner

micro skills — the questioning and responding skills used by the facilitator

problem-based learning — an unstructured learning strategy which allows the learner to work on a professional problem to develop knowledge and skills

protégé — the learner in the mentoring program

self-evaluation — where the learner evaluates his or her own learning and values this above evaluation by others

set adviser — the facilitator of action learning

supportive mechanisms — the actions the facilitator takes to provide the learner with the confidence needed to undertake the unstructured learning strategies

For review

1. List and discuss at least five activities undertaken by the HR developer in the role of a facilitator in the unstructured learning strategies.

2. What are the assumptions about the learners that underlie the unstructured learning strategies?

3. List and briefly describe the steps that the facilitator takes to manage the learning process in problem-based learning.

4. Describe the main sections of a learning contract.

5. Describe the role of the set adviser in action learning.

6. Briefly describe the five steps of System Beta.

7. Draw and describe the action research model.

8. Describe the role of the mentor in a mentoring program.

For analysis

9. Compare and contrast problem-based learning and action learning.

10. Imagine you are to be a facilitator in a contract learning program. List and discuss five key points you would keep in mind that would encourage the learners to be successful.

For application

11. If you were to be a protégé in a mentoring program, briefly describe the qualities you would look for in a mentor.

12. Plan a management development program that is based on action learning.

REFERENCES

Argyris, C. (1992). *On Organizational Learning.* Cambridge, Mass.: Blackwell.

Boud, D. (1985). 'Problem-based learning in perspective.' In D. Boyd (Ed.), *Problem-based Learning in Education for the Professionals.* Sydney, NSW: HERDSA.

Brookfield, S. (1995). *Becoming a Critically Reflective Teacher.* San Francisco: Jossey-Bass.

Candy, P. C. (1991). *Self-direction for Life Long Learning.* San Francisco: Jossey-Bass.

Casey, D. (1983). 'The role of the set adviser.' In M. Pedler (Ed.), *Action Learning in Practice.* Aldershot, Eng.: Gower.

Cavaliere, L. A. (1992). 'The Wright Brothers' odyssey; Their flight of learning.' In L. A. Cavaliere and A. Sgrol (Eds), *Learning for Personal Development.* San Francisco: Jossey-Bass.

Dick, R. (1988). *Enjoying Effective Team Work.* Brisbane: Interchange.

Dick, R. (1992). 'Democracy for learners.' In B. Smith (Ed.), *Management Development in Australia.* Sydney: Harcourt Brace Jovanovich.

French, W. L. and Bell, C. H. (1995). *Organizational Development.* Englewood Cliffs, NJ: Prentice Hall.

French, W. L., Bell, C. H. and Zawacki, R. A. (1994). *Organizational Development and Transformation: Managing Effective Change.* Burr Ridge, Ill.: Irwin.

Gonczi, A. (Ed.). (1992). *Developing a Competent Workforce: Adult Learning Strategies for Vocational Educators and Trainers.* Adelaide, SA: National Centre for Vocational Education.

Hansford, B. H. and Ehrich, L. C. (1999). *Mentoring: A Panacea for all Times?* A paper presented to the HR Practices Day, Australian Human Resources Institute, Brisbane, February.

Knowles, M. S. (1980a). 'How do you get people to be self-directed learners?' *Training and Development Journal,* May, 96–99.

Knowles, M. S. (1980b). 'The magic of contract learning.' *Training and Development Journal,* June, 76–78.

Knowles, M. S. (1983a). 'Developing the Training Professional'. *Training and Development in Australia,* March, 3–7.

Knowles, M. S. (1983b). 'Developing the Training Professional: Part 2.' *Training and Development in Australia,* June, 3–9.

Knowles, M. S. (1984). *Andragogy in Action.* San Francisco: Jossey-Bass.

Knowles, M. S. (1990). *The Adult Learner: A Neglected Species.* (4th ed.). Houston, Texas: Gulf.

Landsberg, M. (1996). *The Tao of Coaching.* London: Harper Collins.

McLennan, N. (1995). *Coaching and Mentoring.* Hampshire: Gower.

Mezirow, J. (1994). 'Understanding transformational theory.' *Adult Education Quarterly,* Summer, 44(4), 222–232.

Mumford, A. (1988). *Management Development: Strategies for Action.* London: Institute of Personnel Management.

Mumford, A. (1998). 'Experiential and action learning.' In J. Propopenko (Ed.), *Management Development: A Guide for the Profession.* Geneva: ILO.

Odiorne, G. S. (1985). 'Mentoring — An American management innovation'. *Personnel Administrator,* May, 63–70.

Oncken, W. (1997). 'A coaching key for any century.' *Executive Excellence,* 14(4), 12–14.

Revans, R. W. (1980). *Action Learning.* London: Blond and Briggs.

Revans, R. W. (1982). *The Origins and Growth of Action Learning.* Sweden: Studentlitteratur.

Revans, R. W. (1983a). *ABC of Action Learning.* London: Chartwell, Bratt, Bromley and Lund.

Revans, R. W. (1983b). 'Action learning: Its origins and nature.' In M. Pedler (Ed.), *Action Learning in Practice.* Aldershot, Eng.: Gower.

Rogers, C. R. (1983). *Freedom to Learn in the 80s.* Columbus, Ohio: Charles E. Merrill.

Schein, E. H. (1969). *Process Consultation: Its Role in Organizational Development.* Reading, Mass.: Addison-Wesley.

Smith, B. J. (1992). 'Mentoring, coaching and counselling.' In B. J. Smith, (Ed.), *Management Development in Australia.* Sydney, NSW: Harcourt Brace Jovanovich.

Vilkinas, T. and Cartan, G. (1992). 'Problem-based learning.' In B. J. Smith (Ed.), *Management Development in Australia.* Sydney, NSW: Harcourt Brace Jovanovich.

Woods, D. (1985). 'Problem-based learning and problem solving.' In D. Boyd (Ed.), *Problem-based Learning in Education for the Professionals.* Sydney, NSW: HERDS.

Zey, M. (1988). 'A mentor for all reasons.' *Personnel Journal,* January, 46–51.

Choosing a mentor

Consider the profiles of the following managers.

Manager 1

This person is 45 years old and has had extensive experience as a manager in a variety of organisations and industries. He/she completed a psychology degree 15 years ago and has attended several management development programs, both in-house and presented by the Australian Institute of Management, since then. He/she has already successfully mentored five protégés over the last 5 years but has never attended a mentor-development program. He/she has full responsibility for the department's budget. One of the previous protégés indicated that this manager scheduled weekly meetings every Friday afternoon for at least 1 hour. The protégé was expected to bring his/her learning diary and discuss the problems encountered during the week and how these problems were overcome. The manager would question the protégé extensively and then suggest readings in management that the protégé would be expected to read before the next weekly meeting. However, the manager would never answer questions directly but would encourage the protégé to suggest options and then help the protégé examine those options. It was then left to the protégé to decide on the course of action.

Manager 2

This person is 30 years old and has an Associate Diploma of Business (Accounting) as well as a Bachelor of Business degree which she/he completed 4 years ago. The organisational rumour is that this person is 'really going places' and is expected to rise through the managerial ranks rapidly. She/he attended the 1-day workshop on mentoring last month and is said to be very committed to being a mentor. However, she/he has never been a mentor before. One of her/his staff members has said that this manager is very organised but 'everything has to go like clockwork. If you are given a half-hour's appointment, then that is what you get — exactly 30 minutes. And you had better be there on time'. This manager has also spent several years as a trainer in the organisation and has a good knowledge of all administrative processes as well as good facilitation skills. She/he has an organisational reputation of designing and conducting excellent learning programs and has also been a facilitator in several organisational change interventions.

Discussion questions

1. Which of the two managers would you prefer as a mentor for your personal management development program? Justify your answer.

2. If one of the managers was of the same gender as you and the other of the opposite gender, would this affect your choice? Justify your answer.

3. What other characteristics would you look for in a mentor?

The self-directed learner

Shane was not too sure of this contract learning stuff. At first it sounded really good — lots of freedom to choose. Further, he did not have to go to classes. He was quite free to study when he liked and where he liked. Now he was starting to feel really insecure and this was only the first lunch time of the 4-day workshop.

The HR developer had explained the idea of contract learning and Shane thought that he had understood. But he was supposed to hand in his learning contract after lunch. The 1-hour discussion in his group before lunch had been helpful. He had not really understood the non-negotiable objectives but now he could see that he had to achieve these. The other group members had given him some good ideas on what to learn and he liked Olive's idea of doing a presentation for the class on the last day. This would give him time to learn and, after all, he was very confident about his presentation skills. 'Talking in front of this group would be a piece of cake', he thought.

But how was he going to learn all of this? Where could he get the information? And should he go for a 'satisfactory' or should he try to get an 'above requirements'? How did the negotiable objectives fit in with all of this? What would happen if he went for an 'above requirements' and could not achieve it? Did this mean that he would fail the workshop? 'Oh dear', he thought, 'This is going to be harder than I thought. I don't know about doing a presentation in front of class. I'll look an absolute turkey if I don't know anything.'

Discussion questions

1. If you were the HR developer conducting this workshop what would you do to help Shane overcome his concerns and problems?

2. With the benefit of hindsight, what should the HR developer have done differently in the morning period of the workshop?

Evaluation

CHAPTER OBJECTIVES

At the end of this chapter you should be able to:

1 describe the three misperceptions that surround evaluation

2 identify and describe the various types of assessment that can be used to evaluate the changes that have occurred within a learner

3 differentiate between criterion-referenced and norm-referenced scoring and also between formative assessment and summative assessment

4 list and describe Kirkpatrick's four levels of evaluation

5 list and describe Brinkerhoff's six stages of evaluation

6 discuss the scientific models of evaluation

7 discuss the role of cost–benefit analysis in evaluation

8 list the steps taken to plan an evaluation

9 list the components of an evaluation report

10 describe the role of evaluation in the legitimate system and the shadow system.

*T*he chapter begins by examining three misperceptions about evaluation. The first misperception is caused by an exclusive focus on the costs of the evaluation rather than balancing these costs with the costs of the risk of not conducting the evaluation. The second misperception is the assumption that the evaluation must provide exact and irrefutable measures. This is never the case in any decision support system, where the results have to be taken as indicators on which professionals base a decision. The third misperception is that evaluation pertains only to the legitimate system. While evaluation of the efforts in the shadow system are difficult, every effort must be made to ensure that the shadow system is not only viable but is also assisting the organisation to survive. Evaluation is essential for a number of reasons, among them the fact that the legal imperatives of the present day business environment demand proof that certain developmental activities have taken place and the need to demonstrate that HRD interventions have contributed to the organisation's success.

The initial focus of evaluation concentrates on the assessment of the extent that learning has occurred. Specifically, the assessment of learning addresses the question 'Just what changes have occurred in the learner's mind as a result of the learning episode?' There are six types of tests that are commonly used to assess learning — **skills tests**, objective written tests, subjective written tests, **performance tests**, **learning diaries** and **portfolio assessment**. These tests are discussed in an hierarchical order that follows the same principle as the HLO, in that they are on a continuum that moves from the most simple to the most complex. The parallel of the six tests with the HLO also indicates which type of assessment is most suitable for what type of learning outcome.

Kirkpatrick's four-level model has become a widely accepted basis for evaluation. The first level, results, measures the learners' satisfaction with the learning experience. The next level, learning, identifies the knowledge gained by the learners. The techniques used in this level have been discussed under assessment of learning. The third level, behaviour, examines the change of behaviour back on the job. The fourth level of evaluation is to assess whether the learning intervention has had an impact on the organisational outcomes. Kirkpatrick stresses that evaluation should occur at all four levels.

One criticism of Kirkpatrick's model is that it is output orientated. These critics believe that the **presage factors** — those factors which occur before the learning episode — should also be evaluated to predict whether the learning episode is likely to be successful. Accordingly, **Brinkerhoff** has presented a six-stage model of evaluation. Stage I concentrates on evaluating needs and goals. In this text this need has been discussed under the HRDNI. Stage II evaluates the design of the program before the program is implemented. Stage III suggests that the program should be evaluated while the program is being implemented. Stage IV (evaluate learning) equates to Kirkpatrick's **learning level**, while stage V (evaluate usage and endurance of learning) is the same as the **behaviour level** and stage VI (evaluate payoff) is essentially the same as the **results level**.

The Kirkpatrick and Brinkerhoff models provide indications of whether some change has occurred after the learning episode and also provide information on how the other three stages of HRD — investigation, design and implementation — may be improved. The **scientific models** answer the question 'Was the change attributable to the learning episode?' There is a range of scientific models that can be used and, again, these can be placed on a continuum moving from simple to complex. The more simple models are less costly while the more complex models provide richer data. The most simple model is the **post-test** — the learning episode is conducted and a measurement is taken afterwards. The **pre-test–post-test** provides some confidence that the improvement in learning could be attributed to the learning episode. The **time series evaluation** — a series of pre-tests and post-tests — remove the doubt that an unknown bias may have contaminated the results shown by the simpler pre-test/post-test. However, the time series evaluation does not prove conclusively that the change did result from the learning episode. The use of a **control group** does alleviate these concerns somewhat although the use of the **Solomon four** design — which involves three control groups — does come as close to certainty as possible. While the aim of the scientific models is to prove causality, some organisations do question the 'return on the investment' of the increased costs of the methods.

The use of a **cost–benefit analysis** attempts to answer the question 'Was the amount of change worthwhile?'. As the name suggests, this analytic technique attempts to convert the benefits and the costs to dollar terms so that a comparison can be made. The suggestion is that a positive ratio in favour of the benefits is the proof required. However, there are two major problems with cost–benefit analyses. Firstly, few of the benefits and some of the costs are difficult to convert to monetary terms. Secondly, it is often difficult to determine the cut-off point of where costs are attributable to the learning episode. If used as an aid to decision making, a cost–benefit analysis can be a useful tool in showing that the efforts of the HRD department or section have been worthwhile.

An **evaluation plan** should be established so that appropriate time frames are adhered to and so that relevant evidence is collected at the correct time. The result of an evaluation process is an **evaluation report**, which should be distributed to all interested parties. The evaluation report should comment on the reasons for the evaluation, provide descriptions of the evaluation methods used and list and explain the findings and recommendations.

The results of an evaluation are most directly useful to the legitimate system. The legitimate system can then make decisions about whether to continue the investment in the learning episode and what improvements to make. For the shadow system, the evaluation report tends to have a more indirect impact. For the shadow system, evaluation answers the more general question 'How can the CEO be assured that the shadow system is doing its job?' Any evaluation in the shadow system needs to concentrate on the values needed for that system to carry out its duties effectively.

MISCONCEPTIONS ABOUT EVALUATION

The fourth and final stage of HRD, evaluation, is by far the most controversial. While professionally and theoretically desirable, there are doubts about its accuracy and usefulness. Its add-on cost nature does not win it very many friends in higher management, either. These concerns, however, are based on a sadly misconstrued perception of evaluation's role in HRD.

Evaluation is a control system and, as with any control system, the likely pay-off has to be balanced with the cost. There are two types of costs associated with a control system. The first and most obvious cost is the expenditure of undertaking the evaluation itself — for example, the salary of the HR developer, the cost of materials and the down time of staff involved in the evaluation. These expenditures are also most immediate — the organisation has to undertake the expenditure at the time of evaluation. The other cost is the risk of not conducting an evaluation — not knowing if the learning episode achieved what it was supposed to; not knowing if the organisation has benefited from the investment; not knowing if any mistakes were made; and worse, not knowing how to avoid these mistakes in the future. However, the costs of such risks are not likely to surface until some time in the future and, at the current time, may seem questionable or even ephemeral. When balancing the advantages and disadvantages, it is easy to understand why some managers may decide to avoid the evaluation stage. However, brutal reality is that such risks will translate invariably into fact and the dues will then have to be paid. It is far better to overcome small deficiencies now rather than to let the problem escalate and become a major headache.

It is true that the techniques used in evaluation are not an exact science. The results do not always transpose into specific indicators for future action. However, such deficiencies are true of any decision support system. The medical doctor interprets an X-ray to make a best-guess decision. The techniques of evaluation operate in exactly the same way. They provide indicators that give the professional HR developer the facts on which to make an informed decision. The more difficult the measurement of a attribute, the more the evaluation has to rely on the professional judgement of the HR developer.

The third misconception that undermines evaluation is not so obvious. Because the legitimate system deals with that part of the external environment that is closer to certainty, any serious mis-judgement or lack of action is likely to show up reasonably quickly — within a year or two. Concomitantly, the evaluation techniques used in the legitimate system are likely to sense any aberrations as the signs are relatively noticeable. However, the shadow system operates in situations far from certainty and not only deals with change but encourages change. Further, the shadow system contemplates the distant future of the organisation. Therefore, evaluation of any learning in the shadow system is going to be extremely difficult, if not impossible. As we will note, some indicators of learning can be observed in the shadow system. Generally, though, the first notification that the organisation will have that its shadow system has not been performing, or has been starved of resources, is that the organisation does not have the new knowledge needed to meet the unknown challenges. Accordingly, most of the evaluation techniques discussed in this chapter apply directly to the legitimate system. However, some effort has to be made to evaluate the development in the shadow system. To the extent that the evaluation techniques discussed in this chapter can be adapted or used as surrogate measures in the shadow system, every effort should be made to evaluate the learning processes and outcomes in the shadow system.

So, despite the fact that evaluation techniques may not always provide exact answers and that these techniques are more applicable to the legitimate system, the evaluation stage cannot be ignored. There are at least four pragmatic reasons for conducting evaluations of the HRD effort. Firstly, as Goldstein (1993) comments, all HRD interventions will be evaluated, either formally or informally. Therefore, the concern has to be with the quality of evaluation rather than with the question of whether to evaluate. Secondly, legal imperatives have raised the awareness of organisations about evaluation. Some state and federal legislation require evidence that certain HR development activities (for example, health and safety) have taken place. In addition, some industrial relations decisions have shown that organisations have to demonstrate not only that HR development has taken place but that the development was successful (see Delahaye and Smith 1987). Thirdly, as Delahaye and Smith (1998) point out, evaluation is essential to the survival of the HRD function so that the contributions of that function can be demonstrated. So evaluation is, in fact, a vital part of the HRD endeavour. Finally, the evaluator must have an acute sense of the likely costs and benefits of the different evaluation approaches, but above all it should be clear whom, and what purposes, one is serving (Easterby-Smith 1998).

The role of the evaluation stage is four-fold:

1. to measure what change has occurred
2. to improve the other three stages — investigation, design and implementation — of the HRD system
3. to see if the change is attributable to the learning episode
4. to see if the amount of change was worthwhile.

The evaluation techniques that can be used to fulfil these roles will be discussed under six sections — the assessment of learning, Kirkpatrick's four levels, the presage elements, the scientific approach and cost–benefit analysis.

ASSESSMENT OF LEARNING

The assessment of learning addresses the big question 'Just what changes have occurred in the learner's mind as a result of the learning episode?'. This question presents the challenge of deciding how the change can be measured. After all, the change has occurred within the learner's mind and we cannot directly observe what has happened. So, most assessment procedures ask the learner to perform a behaviour and it is this behaviour that is then measured.

This conversion of a learning into a behaviour that can be observed has several potential weaknesses:

- The behaviour is only *a sample* of the total learning that has occurred. This limitation is best seen in a university or college examination where the learners have to answer a specific number of questions. For a start, the questions usually do not cover all the knowledge covered in the course. Secondly, the learners tend not to write down all their knowledge of the question, because few people can recall everything on a given topic at one specific time.

- The behaviour represents only *explicit knowledge* (see figure 2.2 in chapter 2). Tacit knowledge may not be reflected in any behaviours and yet tacit knowledge is an important reservoir of wisdom.
- The internalising process of knowledge generation for the individual may take place over quite a period of time, perhaps several years. So *timing* is very important in evaluation.
- The cue to convert the learning into a behaviour, usually some type of test, has to tap into the *appropriate knowledge* and not involve irrelevant knowledge. We have met this concept in chapter 8 where it was called *validity*. So validity is an important component of a test as the test must measure what it is supposed to measure.
- The cue to convert the learning into a behaviour (i.e. the test) has to tap into the *same potential knowledge* each time it is used and for each learner on whom it is used. Again, we discussed this concept in chapter 8 when examining *reliability*. The test must measure the same way each time it is used.

In summary, then, a cue that converts learning into a behaviour must be valid and reliable. It must also be recognised that the converted behaviour is only a possible sample of the learning that has occurred and usually only represents explicit knowledge. Finally, the cue must be administered at the appropriate time — and, for the learner, this appropriate time occurs at the end of the internalising process. Unfortunately, the appropriate time for the learner may not be the appropriate time for the organisation and this presents yet another quandary in the evaluation process for the HR developer.

TYPES OF ASSESSMENT

It is a fact of life that, the further down the hierarchy of learning outcomes (HLO) the learning is, the more difficult impartial measurement becomes. Measuring the successful performance of a procedural skill (in the programmed knowledge category) is much easier than measuring the gain in mental agility from the meta-abilities category. Accordingly, the six types of assessment — skills testing, objective written, subjective written, performance tests, learning diaries and portfolio assessment — are discussed in that order, from easiest to most difficult.

Skill tests

Skill testing is used for procedural skills. It is the most direct form of testing and follows, exactly, the learning objective. If the learning objective is 'To repair a basic fault in the slide mechanism of a Type 0411 photocopy machine in 3 minutes' then the test is simply that: repair the slide mechanism in 3 minutes. This behaviour can be observed directly and the slide mechanism must be working and repaired within the 3-minute time frame for the learner to pass the test.

Objective written tests

Delahaye and Smith (1998) differentiate between objective and subjective written tests. The scoring of **objective written tests** requires no interpretation by the examiner. There are four types of written objective tests:

1. *Multiple choice tests*, which pose a question, usually referred to as a stem, and then provide alternative answers from which the learner can make a selection, as shown in the example on the following page.

'An open question allows the interviewee to:
(a) Choose from a limited number of options from which the answer comes.
(b) Choose from a wide number of options from which the answer comes.
(c) Discuss some new area.
(d) Ask the interviewer for some additional information.'

When designing multiple choice questions, the answer options should be kept as short as possible by including as much information as possible in the stem, and all alternatives should appear to be equally likely to the uninformed reader. In addition, it is better to avoid negative constructions (for example, using the word 'not') in the answer alternatives as this tends to confuse the reader — and the aim is to test content knowledge, not mental agility or linguistic skills.

2. *True–false tests*, which provide a statement to which the reader has to respond 'true' or 'false', for example:

'The funnel sequence of questions starts with an open question. T/F'

There is a 50 per cent probability that the reader can guess the answer, so true-false tests have limited use. If using true-false tests, ensure that the statement is unequivocally true or false and avoid the use of qualifiers such as 'never' or 'always'. Qualifiers tend to make the statement either true or false, no matter what the content of the statement.

3. *Matching tests*, which examine relationships between pieces of information. In matching tests a series of stimuli is listed down the left-hand column and a series of responses is listed down the right hand side. For example:

'Canberra   USA
Paris   United Kingdom
Tokyo   France
London   India
Washington, DC   Japan
                   Australia'

The items in each list should be homogeneous and the lists should be of unequal length so that the last connection is not self-evident.

4. *Completion tests*, which are constructed by leaving a key word or phrase out of a statement. For example:

'_____ questions allow the interviewee to answer from a wide variety of options.'

The statement in completion tests has to be designed carefully so that the key word or phrase is the only logical option.

Objective written tests tend to verify recognition rather than recall. Each of the objective written tests provide enough clues for the knowledgeable respondent to recognise the possible answer. In addition, objective tests examine only very specific pieces of information. The advantage of objective tests is that they can be scored reliably as the answer is always the same. They are ideal for checking factual professional/technical information in the programmed knowledge category of the HLO. A good discussion of objective written tests is included in Thorndike (1997).

Subjective written tests

Subjective written tests are usually referred to as *essay tests*. The cue to an essay test is a reasonably detailed question which examines a complex topic that contains several interrelated concepts. The learner then has to write an essay to answer the question. These essays may be several pages long or just one paragraph, the latter being referred to as a 'short essay'. Unlike objective tests, essay test questions have few direct clues for the reader about the content being examined and therefore verify recall of information'. An example is:

'What is the difference between reliability and validity?'

Delahaye and Smith (1998) suggest that, when constructing an essay test, the designer should list the main issues and interrelationships first and then formulate the question so that the issues and relationships will be covered by the informed reader.

Essay tests are called 'subjective' as the scoring depends on the opinion of an expert. In an attempt to provide some reliability and validity to the scoring process, the examiner is often given a list of issues or concepts that the learner would expected to discuss. However, given the variety of individual approaches each learner may take, the examiner is still required to make complex judgements on the worth of the learners' offerings. It should be acknowledged that subjective tests are also assessing the learner's literacy ability and this very fact may contaminate the outcome or even preclude the use of the assessment method.

Essay tests are ideal for probing the detailed complexity level of professional/technical information of the HLO. Essay tests can also be used to explore the learners' knowledge of the linear and diagnostic analysis, the goal identification and administrative proficiency elements of the task category, as cue questions can include words that encourage analysis, synthesis or evaluation.

Performance tests

Performance tests are used where assessment of a complex process is needed. This complex process simulates an actual situation in the workplace and usually represents a major responsibility in the workplace. The complex process is a combination of programmed knowledge and outcomes in the task and relationship categories of the HLO. A good example of such a complex process would be an interview. So, if the learning objective is 'To conduct a 20-minute research interview', the learner would have to demonstrate a complex combination of programmed knowledge (for example, of the professional/technical information being investigated and also of interviewing techniques), task outcomes of diagnostic and complex analysis, interpersonal elements of interacting at an objective and perhaps an emotional level and intrapersonal elements of self-confidence and inner strength. Several other elements of the HLO could also be involved, depending on the type of interview.

In evaluating such complex processes, the examiner may assess the process itself (as in observing an interview) or the product of the process (as in a piece of artwork). If assessing the process itself, the examiner may observe the event live or may view a video recording. Observing a video recording has the advantage of the replay and the slow motion facilities.

Scoring performance tests is a very multifarious task and is heavily dependent on the professional ability of the examiner. In fact, nothing can replace this professional competence. Often, a pre-designed observation form is used to provide assistance. An example of a pre-designed observation form is shown in figure 13.1.

FIGURE 13.1 An example of a pre-designed observation form

SKILL-SESSION FEEDBACK SHEET

Name _____ Date _____

Session Title_____

Directions: Listen carefully to the session, and place a check mark in the column to indicate your option.

		No	Partly	Yes
Introduction: Did he/she				
1. Clearly and precisely state the session objective(s)?	1			
2. Include time/quality standards in objective(s)?	2			
3. Utilise past experiences to introduce the session?	3			
4. Check current knowledge?	4			
5. Motivate the group?	5			
Show (Demonstrate): Did he/she				
1. Do the job in a professional manner?	1			
2. Observe the time factors — good methods — safety — housekeeping?	2			
Show and Tell: Did he/she				
1. Tell — Show — Illustrate one stage at a time?	1			
2. Stress key points — pause between stages?	2			
3. Ensure that all trainees could clearly see?	3			
4. Follow the breakdown — no backtracking, etc.?	4			
5. Observe correct methods — good housekeeping — safety?	5			
6. Make adequate provision for trainees to ask questions?	6			
Check of Understanding: Did he/she				
1. Ask trainees to name stage and key points?	1			
2. Perform the task to trainees' instructions?	2			
3. Ensure that all trainees knew how to do the job?	3			
Practice: Did he/she				
1. Have everything ready and properly arranged?	1			
2. Correct errors as they occurred by *constructive* criticism?	2			
3. Ensure correct methods — good housekeeping — safety factors?	3			
4. Structure adequate trainee practice (50% +)?	4			
Conclusion: Did he/she				
1. Briefly review critical stages and key points?	1			
2. Ensure that trainees were aware of the standards expected?	2			
3. Ask for new ways or difficult parts?	3			
Job Breakdown:				
1. Did he/she provide each trainee with a job breakdown?	1			
2. Did the breakdown have sufficient steps?	2			
3. Did the explanatory points cover 'how', 'why', 'when', and 'where'?	3			
4. Was safety emphasised?	4			

Source: Delahaye and Smith (1998), p. 52

Thorndike (1997) suggests four steps in designing an **observation form**.

1. *Describe the process or end product that is to be assessed.* For most processes, this step merely involves displaying the learning objective to be achieved, but for a product a definition may be needed.
2. *List the important behaviours and characteristics.* Any behaviours or characteristics that everyone could achieve or that cannot be assessed should be omitted. In figure 13.1, there is no mention of 'standing in front of the class' (everyone could do this action) or 'comfortably analyses all situations' (cannot be assessed as it is too general). Rather, behaviours and characteristics that are critical to successful performance should be listed.
3. *Include common errors.* It is also important to note the presence of specific behaviours that are considered inappropriate.
4. *Put the list into an appropriate format.* The list of appropriate and inappropriate behaviours and characteristics should be organised into a sequence that is most useful to the observer and can be used easily in the 'heat of the moment' of the observation process.

As a further assistance in the scoring process, rating scales and rubrics are sometimes added to the observation forms. Rating scales were discussed in chapter 8 and similar structures can be added to the observation form. The example in figure 13.1 merely notes the presence or absence of the behaviour or characteristic. Rather than these columns, a five-point scale, for example, could be added. A **rubric** identifies the qualities expected for each behaviour or characteristic and also provides a hierarchy of potential responses. So, for questioning techniques, the following simple rubric may be given:

3 points:	Uses more than six open questions with 'stem plus query' structure. At least two demonstrations of a funnel sequence. Combines paraphrasing and open questions at least twice.
2 points:	Uses more than six open questions with 'stem plus query' structure. Combines paraphrasing and open questions at least twice.
1 point:	Uses more than six open questions with 'stem plus query' structure.

For a more detailed discussion of rubrics see Thorndike (1997, pp. 291–293).

Performance tests are used to assess the more complex outcomes in the task and relationship categories of the HLO and can also be used for the critical thinking category.

Learning diaries

Learning diaries are journals written by the learner to record events, and the thoughts and reflections of the learner. In a learning diary, the learner:

- describes the learning events that have occurred — this record is made fairly soon after the event has transpired, preferably before going to sleep that night.
- discloses the feelings and inner thoughts that the events engendered.
- reflects on the personal effect and personal meaning of the events.
- becomes involved in critical reflection (see chapter 2) to challenge and change hegemonic assumptions.

Learning diaries encourage the development of high levels of analysis and critical reflection and frequently highlight small, but important, incidents which would have been overlooked otherwise (Bennett and Kingham 1993). Smith (1992) suggests that there are three types of diaries:

1. The **analytic diary**, where four headings are used. The first, a brief description of the experience, records data that is gathered from as many observers as possible (for example, the learner, the facilitator, peers, other actors in the event). The data will include subjective (impressionistic) information and objective information. The second heading, detailed observations, classifies this data into four categories — what the learner observed about the experience, what the learner observed about his/her own feelings and behaviour, what others observed about the experience and what others observed about the learner. The third heading, synthesise, allows the learner to analyse and reflect on the outcomes compared to the expectations, the worth and use of formal theories and the worth and use of personal frames of reference. The fourth heading, future behaviour, concentrates on plans for the future — what changes can be made and how these changes will be instigated. The parallels of this structure with the Honey and Mumford learning cycle (see chapter 9) are most marked.

2. The **organised diary** is usually in prose format and is characterised by careful construction, clear expression, attempted objectivity and a preoccupation with cognitive logic. The organised diary is based on the assumption that people tend to be naturally logical and are more likely to see strengths and flaws in their thought processes when they write their thoughts down on paper. This writing discipline allows the learner to review the material gathered, identify key concepts and link concepts.

3. The **free flow diary** is a 'cathartic experience' allowing the learner to creatively express thoughts and feelings. The emphasis of this type of diary is on raw perceptions, emotions and reactions with little attempt on external objectivity. These diaries usually include a number of astute observations as the learner 'gets in touch' with him/herself. There are three advantages to the free flowing learning diary. Firstly, it allows the learner to clarify the reality of feelings. Secondly, this recognition of feelings, expressed appropriately, decreases the chance that they will interfere with learning (see chapter 2 for the role of feelings in changing hegemonic assumptions). Thirdly, the record preserves significant aspects of the original raw data. The free flow diary is often employed as a precursor to using the organised or analytic learning diary.

Learning diaries are powerful tools in the knowledge-generating process of externalisation. There are, however, some criticisms of this assessment approach. They are susceptible to being based on faked data, and, particularly with the free flow diary, there are serious questions about validity and reliability. Further, justifying decisions made for summative assessment is quite difficult. However, learning diaries are one of the few ways of assessing the meta-abilities category of the HLO and, correctly used, are invaluable as a means of progressing learning.

Portfolio assessment

Portfolio assessment is used extensively in the arts but can be useful in HRD. Portfolios are collections of the learner's work and often consist of a number of the other types of assessments described above. Portfolio assessment has become more common in HRD with the advent of awards (for example, certificates and diplomas) based on competencies. For example, in the Certificate IV in Assessment and Workplace Training, it is common for the learners to gather evidence of their achievements in a portfolio. The learners then have copies of their session plans, videos of sessions they have conducted, copies of the observation sheets completed by their trainees and a report from their assessor all gathered into a portfolio. It is common for the learner to include a report on their learning as a coordinating front document and all the evidence attached as appendices.

However, portfolio assessment is different to other forms of assessment on three counts. Firstly, it takes a long-term view to evaluating the learner's performance — sometimes up to 12 months. Secondly, it focuses on quality of work more than on some raw score. Thirdly, and perhaps most importantly, the learner has to reflect on his or her own work and thoughtfully evaluate their own history as learners. Learners are expected to identify not just strengths and weaknesses, but changes that have occurred over time, what they are satisfied with and why, and any personal negative reactions to their own work.

Portfolio assessment is susceptible to the same criticisms as the learning diaries but is a dynamic tool for developing and assessing the self-perpetuating learning element of the meta-abilities category of the HLO.

THE HR DEVELOPER'S CONUNDRUM

As with so much of HRD, assessment imposes on the HR developer a number of conflicting choices. Certainly at the easiest end, the skills tests, it is simpler for the HR developer to show reliability and validity based on the desired learning objectives. However, the skills tests reflect a simple situation. Moving towards the more difficult end, the behaviour observed becomes, more and more, a blurred shadow of the quality that is being assessed. When using portfolio assessment, the HR developer has to rely on the honesty of the learner. Accepting this honesty is of limited consequence, and indeed turns into a major strength, when the development of the learner is the main characteristic of the learning experience and, therefore, the assessment. After all, in this situation, any dishonesty will only damage the learner. However, when the assessment is for other purposes (for example, monetary gain for the learner, as in salary increment or the award of a qualification), then the use of the more complex assessment types, such as the learning diaries or portfolio assessment, becomes more problematical. So, once again, the HR developer is placed in a situation of making professional judgements.

THE MEANING OF SCORES

When a test has been examined and the result given in a quantitative score, the result is called a **raw score**. Now, this seems quite straightforward — after all, a score is a score. Well, not necessarily so. Suppose a learner has received 11 out of a possible 20. Is this a pass? If several hundred people have taken the test and the lowest any one else received was 18, one would have to wonder about the learner who received 11 out of 20. Or perhaps the test was for a rigger on tying knots. How would you feel halfway up a 200 metre cliff knowing that the person who tied the knots on your safety belt had achieved only 11 out of 20 on the knot tying test? In that situation, most people would opt for a test with a pass mark of 20 out of 20!

So test scores can be interpreted in a number of ways. One way is called **criterion-referenced scoring**. Criterion-referenced scores reflect the level of mastery of a certain content or domain of knowledge. A criterion-referenced score is the way people usually interpret a raw score. Marks are given for each correct answer and none for incorrect answers. The result is a raw score out of a total score (for example, 11 out of 20) and this ratio — usually given as a percentage — reflects the learner's supposed level of knowledge. Another way to interpret a raw score is called **norm-referenced scoring**. The raw score is compared to the average of a nominated group. The group may be the current class that the learner is attending or everyone in the organisation who has taken the test or even a nation-wide group. Usually, the comparison point is the average of the nominal group. This comparison point is called the standardised score. In norm-referenced scoring, the raw score is compared to the standardised score and, if it is above, the learner has passed.

A raw score can also be considered as a formative assessment or summative assessment. **Formative assessment** is used where the HR developer is interested in identifying the learner's strengths or weaknesses. The raw score is used in this instance as feedback. Firstly, the learner can gauge his or her progress. Secondly, the HR developer can adjust the learning experience. **Summative assessment** provides concluding evidence of the level of achievement of the learner and this is the usual accepted purpose of the raw score.

OVERLAP OF THE FOUR HRD STAGES

Previously in this book, the point was made that dividing the HR process into four stages — investigation, design, implementation and evaluation — may present an overly simplistic view. The four stages are, in fact, highly interactive. One such interaction occurs between the implementation stage and the assessment of learning in the evaluation stage.

In the implementation stage, the assessment of learning provides dynamic feedback. The feedback on the learning is often immediate. Indeed, good learning design provides a sequence of a learning experience followed by assessment (i.e. formative assessment) so that the learner can gradually improve over the period of the learning episode. Secondly, most assessment of learning provides irrefutable evidence that a learner finds difficult to ignore. Positive evidence gives satisfaction and support. Negative evidence provides the opportunity for the learner to challenge frames of reference.

McAllister (1997) believes that better learning and deeper commitment is enhanced when the HR developer and the learner begin to reframe assessment as an essential part of everyday learning. She presents real concerns that blanket application of assessment rules remove creativity for the HR developer–learner relationship, promote uniformity and blind adherence to rules, and reduce knowledge to the technical level — all in the quest for efficiency.

In the evaluation stage, on the other hand, assessment of learning provides some initial evidence of the success or otherwise of the learning experience. Recognising the two roles of assessment — developmental at the implementing stage and judgemental at the evaluation stage — is critical to the HR developer. These dual but conflicting roles have to become an important consideration when designing learning episodes and when planning the evaluation stage.

THE IMPORTANCE OF ASSESSMENT

The six types of assessment — skill, objective written, subjective written, performance, learning diaries and profile assessment — have been discussed in a hierarchy that corresponds roughly with the HLO to show the most suitable use of each type of assessment. Further, at the easiest end of the continuum (skills tests), the judgement of the assessor can be more objective while at the opposite end the assessor has to rely on professional, albeit subjective, judgement.

Assessment of learning is important for two reasons. Firstly, the measurement provides an indication of how well the learner understands the concepts. This is particularly valuable for the legitimate system which needs to ensure that acceptable levels of procedural knowledge are maintained for the continued viability of the organisation. The second important reason for assessment is that it provides feedback. This feedback allows both the learner and the HR developer to make adjustments to the learning process by identifying strengths and weaknesses.

KIRKPATRICK'S FOUR LEVELS

The most commonly used model of evaluation for HRD in organisations is Kirkpatrick's four levels of reaction, learning, behaviour and results (Kirkpatrick 1959a, 1959b, 1960a, 1960b, 1994). These four levels are arranged in ascending order of value of information. There is also an assumption that each level affects the following level.

REACTION

This level simply measures the reactions of the learners to the learning episode — their liking for and feelings for the program. The assumption of this level of evaluation is that, if the learners did not enjoy the learning experience, then this dislike will affect the amount that they will learn. The **reaction level** is usually measured with a questionnaire, sometimes derisively called 'happy sheets', which cover such areas as the content, the HR developer, the learning strategies used and the physical location in which the learning took place.

Wexley and Latham (1991) believe that measuring the reaction level is important for two reasons. Firstly, positive reactions encourage organisational support. Secondly, the feedback from the reaction questionnaires can be used by HR developers to improve future programs.

LEARNING

Evaluating learning has been discussed under the previous section, 'Assessment of learning', and is aimed at identifying the knowledge gained by the learners. The assessment of learning should be linked directly to the learning objectives of the learning episode. The assumption is that successful learning is needed before the increased knowledge can be transferred to the job.

BEHAVIOUR

The behaviour level of evaluation examines the change in the behaviour of the learner on the job. The behavioural level is concerned with actual ability, not potential ability as measured by the amount of learning. As Delahaye and Smith (1998) comment, this is the payoff for the organisation in investing in the learning episode. The assumption is that the behavioural change will have an impact on the organisation, improving its viability.

The issue that then arises is deciding how the behaviour level can be assessed. The simplest answer, but one that is often ignored by organisations, is to repeat the investigation methods used in the HRDNI. In particular, the performance appraisal system should play a big role in the behavioural level of evaluation. Firstly, the performance appraisal process can readily identify changes that matter the most — those at the workface. Secondly, a performance appraisal can evaluate changes in the more complex categories of the HLO, particularly at the task, relationship and critical thinking level. In addition, a performance appraisal is possibly the only approach to assessing the meta-abilities category. Thirdly, the performance appraisal process, particularly the interview, can extend the learning of the participant by focusing on the benefits of the learning episode. In addition, an experienced and astute appraiser can use the knowledge-generation processes of internalisation, externalisation and socialisation to reinforce and extend the learning. The other methods used in the HRDNI — organisational records, questionnaires, interviews, focus groups — also have the potential to identify improvements simply by comparing the facts and data when used in the HRDNI with that in the evaluation.

Brinkerhoff (1987) suggests that the behaviour level of evaluation produces a number of benefits:

- It gives positive and negative feedback, allowing the HR developer to *revise the learning program*, as knowing what went right is just as important as knowing what did not work. Further, while the learning program may have successfully improved performance in the desired area, it may now become obvious that the staff are having difficulty with the subsequent process. For example, the technicians now may be able to repair the equipment but are having difficulties with diagnosing repair needs. This would indicate that the original HRDNI did not analyse the situation deeply enough and another round of the four HRD stages is required. This example highlights the fact that the behaviour level evaluation not only evaluates the learning program but also evaluates the assumptions and methods used in the original HRDNI.
- It allows interventions to be planned to support *increased transfer of training*. While learners may graduate successfully from a learning program, the most that can usually be said at this point is that they have achieved some minimally accepted standard. The very fact that the on-the-job behaviour is being screened tends to concentrate the focus of the supervisor and the returning learner on the learned behaviour often resulting in opportunities that ensure the new skills are practised and used.

- It identifies *unintended consequences*. For example, new trainers are usually told that their introductions to sessions should include a motivational component. Unless specifically warned, these new trainers will often use negative motivational statements, such as 'If you do not learn this you will not have much chance of being promoted' and 'Customers can become very violent if you do not fill out this form correctly'. If not warned, then their behaviour of using negative messages can become an habitual part of their repertoire, giving their sessions a decidedly gloomy atmosphere — a consequence that was certainly not intended in their original development.
- It allows plans for the next level, *results*, to be formulated and for information from the behaviour level to be integrated. For example, the logic of the increase-in-value-to-the-organisation argument will often require a demonstration of changes in the on-the-job performance.

It should also be noted that the competency movement has contributed significantly to the recognition that learning must be transferred back to the job. The underlying theme of competencies is that they should be assessed several times under workplace conditions.

RESULTS

This level measures the impact of the learning episode on the organisation as a whole. So, the organisation may be looking for indicators such as improved profits, a decrease in accidents, an improvement in morale or a decrease in turnover.

Again, repeating the measures used in the HRDNI can identify the benefits at the organisational level, although organisational records tend to be the approach used predominantly.

COMMENTS ON KIRKPATRICK'S MODEL

Kirkpatrick's model is a simple and seemingly robust paradigm that recognises the impact of a learning episode should extend beyond the individual learner. It has provided an easily remembered checklist that has broadened people's perception of the role of evaluation. In addition, each of the levels certainly provides a unique examination of the worth of a HRD intervention.

There are criticisms of the model. Alliger and Janak (1989) have been the most cogent of the critics. They believe that the levels are not co-dependent — for example, successful learning can occur even if the participants did not like the location or the HR developer. Delahaye and Smith (1998) point out that the model concentrates on outcomes and process only and pays little attention to inputs.

In addition, if the four levels are considered a continuum from reaction to results, an interesting relationship exists with three issues (Delahaye and Smith 1998). Firstly, gathering data at the reaction level requires much less effort than gathering data at the results level. However, counteracting this, the data becomes more useful the further towards the results end of the continuum the evaluation progresses. Now, just to complicate the relationship, the more the evaluation moves towards the results end, the more the data can become contaminated. So, data gathered at the reaction level is easy to collect and tends to reflect the true representation of the learning episode because the information is specifically about the learning episode. However, other than providing feedback on how to improve the specific learning episode if it is repeated, the information is of limited use to the organisation as a whole. At the other end of the continuum, proving that the learning episode has had an impact on the results of the organisation (for example, increased profits, lower accident rate) is valuable information. However, gathering such data is often complex, and showing causality — that the learning episode was solely responsible for the organisational changes — is very difficult.

THE PRESAGE FACTORS

The evaluation processes discussed so far have concentrated solely on the outcomes of the learning episode — how much learning occurred; what changes to behaviour on the job eventuated; and whether the investment in the learning episode had any impact on the continued viability of the organisation. This post facto orientation has been criticised as not being dynamic and pro-active. There is a belief that certain presage factors should be evaluated. Presage factors are those factors or events which can be examined to predict a particular outcome. Further, examining presage factors can keep the program moving in the intended direction, as changes can be made during the planning and implementation stages. One writer, Brinkerhoff (1987), has proposed a six stage model that extends evaluation so that it includes a formative, improvements-oriented focus. The six stages are:

1. stage I: *evaluate needs and goals*, which we have referred to as the HRDNI. It is interesting that Brinkerhoff regards the needs investigation as part of the evaluation process. This stance underlines the interactive and overlapping nature of the HRD process.
2. stage II: *evaluate HRD design*, which focuses on evaluating the design of the program *before* it is implemented to ensure maximum payoff
3. stage III: *evaluate implementation*, which examines and provides feedback on the program as it is being implemented. This allows adjustments to be made as the program is being conducted.
4. stage IV: *evaluate learning*, which is similar to Kirkpatrick's learning level
5. stage V: *evaluate usage and endurance of learning*, which is similar to Kirkpatrick's behaviour level
6. stage VI: *evaluate payoff*, which is similar to Kirkpatrick's results level.

So, Brinkerhoff adds two presage factors to the evaluation model proposed by Kirkpatrick — evaluating the design and evaluating the program as it is being implemented. From the educational field, Kyriacou and Newson (1982) add another presage variable — the HR developer who conducts the learning program.

EVALUATING THE PROGRAM DESIGN

Brinkerhoff (1987, pp. 70–89) sees that, where stage I (the investigation) is concerned with whether HRD is a good idea in the first place, stage II focuses on the quality of the HR plan. A stage II evaluation should be conducted when the program design is unique or experimental, the costs are high, the HRD needs are crucial, or life or death issues or the participant groups are volatile, influential or demanding.

Conducting a stage II evaluation simply means having the design of the program reviewed by a variety of stakeholders — potential learners, the supervisors of potential learners, the customers of potential learners, managers, the CEO and other HR developers who are experts in both the content and the learning strategies. These reviewers should be asked to examine the theoretical adequacy of the design, the compatibility with the environment and culture, its practicality and cost effectiveness, its potential to satisfy the defined needs, the appropriate use of adult learning theories and techniques, any legal or ethical considerations and the overall clarity of communication of the plans themselves. Another option at this stage II evaluation is to conduct a 'pilot study'. Conduct the program with a small sample of potential learners with the prime objective being the evaluation of the program, rather than the development of the learners. However, for reasons of organisational politics, this option is not always viable.

The benefits of conducting a stage II evaluation include the following.
- The design can be improved prior to implementation.
- Opinions and advice from those who will be most affected by the program can be solicited. This increases the commitment of the key stakeholders (for example, the learners, managers, upper management).
- The transfer of training (see chapter 2) is facilitated as the learners and immediate supervisors are better informed about the purposes of the program and are more likely to look for opportunities to use the learning after the program.
- The stage II evaluation process is likely to reveal and shape the expectations of both parties — the HR developers and the learners and supervisors. In this way, unreasonable expectations can be resolved before the event, new ideas and interpretations can be tried out and the continuing dialogue between the HR development section and its clients will increase.

EVALUATING DURING IMPLEMENTATION

The primary purpose of the stage III evaluation is to monitor the implementation of the program and to provide the data that will help 'shepherd' the learning event to a successful conclusion (Brinkerhoff 1987, p. 94). Brinkerhoff's stage III performs at least one sterling service — it highlights one of the covert activities of the conducting HR developer. This covert activity is to continually monitor what is really happening as the program is progressing and compare this reality with the program plan. Did the learning strategy have the expected effect? Were there any unintended consequences? Are the learners alert? Is a dominant learner contaminating the experiences of the other learners? A variety of questions should be flowing through the mind of the HR developer. Being a classic control system, the stage III also incorporates an action step. If a discrepancy is identified, the HR developer has two courses of action. Either the discrepancy can be altered (for example, clearer instructions are given to the role players in a role play) or the outcomes can be accepted but a re-design of the program is undertaken. For example, if the role play has not gone as expected, the HR developer may decide to debrief what has happened and glean any possible lessons that can be learned, and then conduct a second role play that achieves the learning objectives missed by the first role play.

So, the stage III evaluation should be a natural activity of the conducting HR developer. However, the organisation may wish to invest more in this stage by using another HR developer to conduct the evaluation. This option, though, is usually undertaken only as a developmental activity for the conducting HR developer rather than an evaluation *per se*.

Brinkerhoff (1987, pp. 105–109) highlights some critical points that may be worthy of particular attention during a stage III evaluation:

- *functionally critical areas*, where, if a breakdown occurs, major damage or bottlenecks to a program will be caused (for example, if the learners do not understand the programmed knowledge presented in a theory session and this means that the learners would not be able to do the following skill session)
- *areas of theoretical shakiness or concern*, where a new idea is being tried out for the first time — this new idea may be new programmed knowledge or the trial of a new learning strategy
- where *experience* has shown that problems may arise (for example, where groups have had difficulty in confronting a long-held organisational cultural issue)
- where there is some *specific research and development interest* that the HR development section or upper management may wish to investigate (for example, if there are any gender or sociocultural differences in learners who prefer unstructured learning strategies)
- where there is a need for *special records* (for example, for government regulations on equity or health and safety).

THE CONDUCTING HR DEVELOPER

Being responsible for the management and implementation of the designed program, the conducting HR developer is obviously a key variable in the success of the program. Usually, evaluation emphasises that HR developers — whether they be trainers, facilitators or teachers — be assessed by the participants at the end of the program. More often than not, this data is collected by using questionnaires — reaction sheets, structured questionnaires and unstructured questionnaires. There has been quite a deal of literature on this issue over the years and a most detailed and concentrated analysis is offered in a special edition of the *Journal of Educational Psychology* (Perry 1990).

These measures are, again, post facto. They are only really useful for predicting whether that particular HR developer is likely to be suitable for the next similar program. This conundrum reflects the perennial problem of selecting staff. The selection decision can be made only on the past performance of the selectee. So, when evaluation is pro-active and concentrates on the presage variable of the conducting HR developer, the decision makers have to operate on the information about the past performance of that HR developer. If the HR developer has conducted similar programs to the planned program, and the developer has been assessed, then the information used in the subsequent decision is more valid. If the HR developer has not conducted a similar program, then the decision makers have to use less valid information — that is, use information from a somewhat similar program and extrapolate the likely behaviours of the HR developer in the planned program from that less valid information.

TO BE OR NOT TO BE

Brinkerhoff and other writers who have championed the evaluation of the presage variables have raised an interesting issue. In the perfect world, reviewing the design, carefully selecting the HR developer and conducting an on going evaluation while the program is in progress has the potential to ensure a close-to-perfect learning experience. As Brinkerhoff (1987, p. xiv) comments, HRD is like any other human activity — it is fraught with error, it is based on incomplete knowledge and understanding, it is difficult to control and it is as likely to run off course as it is to succeed, if not more so. Hence, the steering control of evaluating presage variables has definite attractions.

However, widening evaluation to include the presage variables increases the cost of evaluation. Organisations have to decide which cost they are willing to bear — the cost of increased evaluation or the cost of risk.

TIME OUT

Let us take time out to get our bearings. At the beginning of this chapter, it was suggested that the evaluation stage had four roles:
1. to identify what change has occurred
2. to improve the other three stages — investigation, design and implementation — of the HRD system
3. to see if the change is attributable to the learning episode
4. to see if the amount of change was worthwhile.

Basing an evaluation plan on Kirkpatrick's model — reaction, learning, behaviour and results — and also including an assessment of the presage factors (i.e. using Brinkerhoff's model) would provide answers to the first two of the four roles. Some information on the last two may have been gathered but usually further data has to be gathered to substantiate these two claims. That the change was attributable to the learning episode may be shown by using the scientific model and a cost–benefit analysis exercise has to be undertaken to see if the change was worthwhile.

THE SCIENTIFIC MODELS

The scientific models of evaluation are based on the experimental methods used in research laboratories and are aimed at demonstrating causality. The five models — post-test, pre-test–post-test, time series, control group and Solomon four — are discussed in order from the simple and less costly to the complex and more costly.

POST-TEST

The simplest scientific model, the post-test method of evaluation, can be represented as:

learning experience/evaluation

The learners experience a learning episode and an evaluation is then conducted. This evaluation may be conducted immediately after the learning episode or up to several months later. The post-test method proves whether the learners achieved a certain level of performance. However, there is no indication whether a change did occur as the levels of performance may have been achieved without the learning experience.

PRE-TEST–POST-TEST

In the pre-test–post-test method the same evaluation is taken before and after the learning episode, as follows:

> evaluation/learning experience/evaluation

The evaluation is referred to as a 'test' for two reasons. Firstly, the term is a residue from the physical sciences of laboratory experimentation where tests were performed on the subject, item or element being researched. Secondly, in the HRD sense, the learners are often given an examination or test to evaluate their performance or knowledge. The pre-test–post-test evaluation does show whether a change has occurred. However, we cannot say with certainty whether the change has occurred because of the learning experience or if some other fortuitous event intervened.

TIME SERIES EVALUATION

One such fortuitous event may be an unknown bias in the tests themselves or perhaps the whole group of learners made lucky guesses in the post-test. The time series method uses a number of pre-tests and a number of post-tests, as follows:

> pre-test/pre-test/pre-test//learning experience/post-test/post-test/post-test

The time series evaluation, while showing conclusively that a change has occurred, still does not prove that the change occurred because of the learning experience.

CONTROL GROUP

In the idealised version of the control group method, potential learners are assigned randomly to an experimental group and a control group. In less idealised versions, the members of each group may be matched on certain characteristics (for example, gender, level of responsibility in the organisation, profession or salary scale). Another less idealised option is the 'group of convenience' — whatever groups are conveniently available are used. In the less idealised versions, the opportunity for a rogue variable to cause systematic bias becomes increasingly likely.

However they are selected, both groups are submitted to a pre-test and a post-test — but only the experimental group undertakes the learning episode (or, in scientific terms, is given a 'treatment').

> Experimental group — pre-test//learning experience/post-test
> Control group — pre-test/usual duties/post-test

The control group method does provide improved confidence that the change did occur because of the learning experience and not because of extraneous factors. However, it is possible for other contaminating factors to bias the result. For example, the members of the control group were resentful because they did not receive the training (and therefore achieved a lower score) or perhaps the experimental group believed that they were an elite band because they were selected and therefore tried harder on the post-test. It is also theoretically possible that the experimental group learned from the pre-test and the control group did not.

THE SOLOMON FOUR

The Solomon four, the deluxe model of scientific evaluation, involves an experimental group and three control groups, as follows:

> Experimental group — pre-test//learning experience/post-test
> Control group A — pre-test/usual duties/post-test
> Control group B — no pre-test/learning experience/post-test
> Control group C — no pre-test/usual duties/post-test

The Solomon four design counters most of the possible arguments over causality and a successful demonstration of results provides high levels of confidence that the learning experience was successful. The Solomon four design does present the HR developer with practical problems, three of the more important being as follows:

1. It is a very expensive design with high levels of expenditure in terms of money and time.
2. The logistics can be quite formidable. Negotiating with managers for the release of the high number of people (three control groups and one group of learners) can be difficult, and then organising the pre-testing and post-testing can take quite some effort.
3. There are ethical considerations if one group receives developmental opportunities and the other three do not. The industrial relations implications also have to be considered.

A COMPLEX DECISION

The aim of the scientific models is to prove causality — that the learning experience did improve the changes at the learning level and/or the behaviour level and/or results level of evaluation. While the more simple approach — the post-test — is less costly and easier logistically, it only goes marginally towards proving causality. At the other end of the continuum, the Solomon four design does provide close to conclusive proof but the costs escalate considerably.

Accordingly, the HR developer needs sound justification for using the more costly methods. There may be legal reasons for proving causality — for example, in a safety course, not only was the training provided but it did, without question, change the behaviour and attitudes of the participants. Also, some HR departments need to show causality if they are to maintain their status, and therefore an appropriate budget, in the organisation.

Being able to use the scientific models depends heavily on the ability to measure change in individuals and/or organisations. As discussed in chapter 2, measuring improvements in tacit knowledge or changes in personal frames of reference can be very difficult, if not impossible. In addition, these evaluation measurements usually have to occur at a time that is decreed by the organisation. Whether these changes have in fact occurred by this decreed time depends on a variety of variables (for example, the individual ability of the learners, opportunities arising in the workplace for the learners to use the new skills or knowledge). These issues have been discussed previously when we examined the assessment of learning, and are a perennial concern in evaluation. Indeed, we will encounter them again in the next segment on cost–benefit analysis.

COST–BENEFIT ANALYSIS

The logic behind cost–benefit analysis is quite simple — identify the costs, in dollar terms, for the learning experience; identify the benefits accruing from the learning experience in dollar terms; the ratio between costs and benefits should be in favour of the benefits. The costs of mounting a learning experience can cover a multitude of items — the salary/wages of the learners, the salary/wages of the HR developers, the rental of the classrooms, the depreciation on the training equipment, copying costs, cost of stationery, payment to guest speakers, travel costs, hiring (for example, of videos), advertising costs, to name a few. Some benefits can also be reduced to a monetary value — for example, the reduction in accident numbers can be converted into time not lost on the job. Other benefits can be estimated with a 'shadow value'. For example, one way of calculating the value of the development an individual receives over the years is to assess the value of the promotions the individual achieves. However, at this point we quickly run into the two basic problems facing cost–benefit analysis.

The first problem encountered is converting benefits into monetary values. Most benefits from a learning experience, particularly with the more complex outcomes from the HLO (the task, relationship, critical thinking and meta-abilities), are difficult to measure, let alone convert to a monetary equivalent. Think of the most common sequence — a change in a learner (for example, increased emotional resilience) which produces a benefit in the workplace which can be measured and then converted to a monetary value. This is quite a tall order. Then add to this the perennial problem of when the benefit surfaces, which may be some considerable time after the learning experience.

The second problem with cost–benefit is deciding on the cut-off point, where the costs and the benefits stop. For example, when a learner attends a learning event, the cost of the learner's salary is usually included. However, what about the costs back at the workplace? The learner's duties still have to be performed. Often, the person one level below the learner is temporarily promoted to do the learner's job at an increased pay rate. Should this increased pay rate be included? What about the duties of the person who has been temporarily promoted? If someone else is promoted temporarily to perform these duties, is their increased pay rate to be included? What about the extra work that these temporary promotions have caused in the pay office? And so we could go on. A similar situation exists with benefits. For example, the learner's interpersonal skills have improved because of a designed learning experience and the learner performs customer relations better because of this new-found skill. What about the effects on the learner's peers? Perhaps their work becomes easier and more productive. Perhaps modelling occurs and the peers' customer relations improve also. Again, you get the idea. At some stage a decision has to be made on the cut-off points for both the costs and the benefits. Defining acceptable cut-off points may be a matter of:

- *logic* — for example, the time spent by the manager and the learner during the appraisal interview (the results of which are used in the HRDNI) is not considered part of the costs of the learning experience;
- *organisational culture* — for example, the organisation may have decided some decades ago that only the learner's salary will be included as the temporary promotion costs are the responsibility of the learner's workplace;
- *organisational politics* — for example, the manager of the HR department holds early discussions with the chief executive officer to decide on what will and will not be included in the costs and benefits.

WHY BOTHER?

With these real and well-documented difficulties, one has to wonder why a HR developer should bother with a cost-benefit analysis. As Delahaye and Smith (1998) comment, the answer is simple — survival! Particularly in the legitimate system, success is measured in monetary terms. A cost centre such as a HR department has to show that it is providing demonstrable assistance in ensuring the organisation is viable — in other words, showing that the learning episode has contributed to the 'bottom line' is generally regarded by management as an imperative (Owen with Rogers 1999, p. 277).

Another reason for conducting cost–benefit analyses is to select the learning programs that have the most impact. Few HRD departments are over-resourced, so the HRD manager needs some data on which to make decisions for selecting the programs that will have the most impact. So, despite the difficulties, the HR developers need to do everything in their power to ensure that defensible decisions are made on defining the appropriate costs and benefits involved in any planned learning event.

In addition, a professional cost–benefit analysis report acknowledges the problems with cut-off decisions and converting benefits to monetary values. The cut-off decisions should always be acknowledged in the report. Where it is not possible to convert benefits to a monetary value, the benefits should be fully described and such qualitative descriptions given full recognition in the final cost–benefit comparison.

THE EVALUATION PLAN

Earlier in this chapter we discussed the overlap that occurs between the assessment of learning and the implementation stage. Another overlap occurs between the evaluation stage and the design stage. Planning the evaluation starts during the design stage. As well as ensuring that appropriate evaluation occurs at appropriate times during and after the implementation, producing an evaluation plan during the design stage allows the two roles of the assessment of learning — developmental and judgemental — to be coordinated. This ensures that one role does not interfere with the other.

Planning for the evaluation of a learning episode should include the following:

- Develop the assessment of learning for developmental purposes first.
- Incorporate appropriate developmental assessments into the evaluation plan and add further assessment of learning processes as required for the evaluation at the learning (or stage IV) level.
- Decide what presage variables will be evaluated and when. If the design is to be reviewed, arrange for this to occur. If the conducting HR developer and the location are to be evaluated, plan for the process (for example, include items on the reaction sheets) and the personnel (for example, for another HR developer to review the conducting HR developer).
- Review the investigating instruments (for example, questionnaires, performance appraisals) used in the HRDNI and decide which will be used in the evaluation. Also ensure that the results of these investigating instruments are recorded for later comparisons in the evaluation report.
- Design daily and course/workshop reaction sheets.
- If the scientific models are to be used, plan the pre-test and post-test instruments. Decide when these tests will be implemented and plan logistics.
- Identify the methods that will be used to examine the behaviour (or stage V) and results (or stage VI) levels of evaluation. Plan the measuring processes to be used and plan the logistics.
- If a cost–benefit analysis is to be implemented, arrange for the details of the costs to be collected. Identify all possible benefits and arrange for the collection of objective (for example, monetary value) and subjective (for example, managers' opinions) data to be collected. Ensure exact definitions of cut-off points are promulgated.
- Prepare a budget for the evaluation plan (include financial, staff and time requirements) and submit it for approval.
- Send the evaluation plan to staff who are affected (for example, the conducting HR developer) or who will be involved (for example, evaluators).

THE EVALUATION REPORT

As the saying goes, the job is not complete until the paperwork is done. There is little sense in conducting an evaluation unless the results are communicated. An evaluation report should include at least the following:

- an *executive summary*, of about one page, which provides a precis of the report with an emphasis on the objectives of the report, the approach taken and the main findings
- a *findings/recommendations section*, which briefly describes the findings of the evaluation and the main recommendations and supporting recommendations
- a *contents list*, which lists the main topic headings and the associated page numbers
- the *main body*, which includes:
  - the reasons for the evaluation, leading to the objectives of the investigation
  - a list of the personnel involved in the evaluation
  - a discussion of the various types of evaluations undertaken and how the data were collected and analysed

- a discussion of the findings, an examination of the options and a presentation of the conclusions
- a list of, and a discussion of, the recommendations — the recommendations should flow logically from the findings and conclusions
- *appendices*, some of which will include supporting data from the evaluation and others which will provide a detailed discussion or examination of important issues. This allows a precis of this detailed data to be included in the main body.

The evaluation report can have three significant roles in an organisation. The first is a communicative role. The evaluation report is usually distributed to the key stakeholders of the learning experience, and particularly to those who occupy the influencing and decision-making buying roles (see chapter 10). Some parts of the report may be contentious and therefore abbreviated versions may be sent to other people. Secondly, of course, the report has a role in decision making — was the learning design useful? Should it be used again? What further learning is required? (Notice here the overlap between evaluation and the HRDNI.) Thirdly, the report becomes an historical record that can be used to prove that certain events did take place (for example, if there is a safety enquiry) or to analyse later for any organisational trends.

THE LEGITIMATE SYSTEM

A significant proportion of what has been discussed in this chapter on evaluation fulfils the needs of the legitimate system. After all, the legitimate system is concerned with the efficient use of organisational resources and with the organisation's immediate survival.

Owen with Rogers (1999) suggests that there are five categories or forms of evaluation and, in examining these forms, it can be seen that the evaluation techniques discussed so far in this chapter are involved in every one of these forms:

- Form A is described as *pro-active evaluation*. Pro-active evaluation includes Brinkerhoff's first stage — stage I, of evaluate needs and goals. This type of evaluation, which this book discussed under HRDNI, allows decisions about the type of program needed and how to best develop the program.
- Form B is called *clarification evaluation* and includes Brinkerhoff's second stage — stage II, of evaluate HRD design. This type of evaluation describes the structure and functioning as well as the logic or theory of the program.
- Form C, or *interactive evaluation*, provides information about the delivery or implementation of a program and has been discussed under Brinkerhoff's stage III — evaluate implementation.
- Form D, referred to as *monitoring evaluation*, is appropriate when the program is established or ongoing. Certain elements of Brinkerhoff's stage III are evident in this form but, for learning episodes, the predominant evaluation is the assessment of learning. This assessment process is present in Brinkerhoff's stage IV and in Kirkpatrick's learning level.
- Form E is described as *impact evaluation*. This form of evaluation is the equivalent of Brinkerhoff's stage V (evaluate usage and endurance of learning) and stage VI (evaluate payoff) as well as Kirkpatrick's behaviour and results levels. The scientific models and cost–benefit analysis are classic approaches to impact evaluation.

As Hall (1995) has commented, the introduction of competency-based learning (CBL) has highlighted the importance of evaluation and assessment in the workplace. For the legitimate system, one of the major advantages of CBL has been the recognition of the strong link between learning in a planned learning program and the application of that learning at the workface. Where learners are certified under the Australian Qualification Framework using the certified competency-based learning, careful assessment is critical to the legitimate system. Further, as Smith (1998) points out, if the assessment procedure fails to detect a lack of competence on the part of the learners, and serious consequences ensue (for example, injury or death), the HR developer could be held liable for the incompetence of the learners.

THE SHADOW SYSTEM

Evaluation in the shadow system is a very delicate affair. Evaluation has its genesis in the legitimate system where negative feedback systems are more relevant. Negative feedback systems (Stacey 1996) have a dampening effect and are designed to return an aberrant situation to 'normal'. So, for example, a quality control system detects that a machine is not completely filling a bottle. An adjustment is made to the machine and the bottles are then filled to the predetermined level of capacity. The evaluation processes discussed so far represent this principle of a negative feedback system — some aspect is found to have deviated from a predetermined path or standard so action is taken to return the event to the planned and expected direction. The shadow system, on the other hand, thrives on positive feedback systems. Positive feedback systems have an enhancing or amplifying effect (Stacey 1996). They escalate small changes — just what is required in the shadow system where creativity and free thought have to be nurtured. Any hint of a negative feedback process can discourage and even inhibit the creative energy of the shadow system.

However, the shadow system does use organisational resources so some assurance is needed that this investment is not being totally wasted. So, the question must be asked: 'How can the CEO be assured that the shadow system is doing its job?' The answer is partly based on extraordinary management and partly on the concepts of HRD. Wheatley (1994) suggests that, in the shadow system in particular, the predominant 'control' system is based on invisible forces. Hard-nosed managers are suspicious of any concept that cannot be measured, yet we are surrounded by invisible forces everyday. One of the most common is gravity. We do not know what gravity is (the scientific definition of a 'warp in the space–time continuum' does not seem to help!) and yet we accept it as an everyday part of our lives. Similarly, Wheatley suggests that such invisible forces can operate in an organisation. In universities, the assessment system is fraught with subjectivity and yet university qualifications are generally held in high esteem. This occurs because there is a widespread value system in universities of high professional standards. It is this value system that maintains the validity, and subsequent respect, of the assessment systems in universities. It is the loss of this value system in some college of technical and further education systems in Australia that is causing questions to be raised about the quality of assessment in some trade qualifications. So the first stage of evaluation in the shadow system is for the CEO to engender appropriate values in the shadow system, values that can be used as a comparative standard. So the CEO may ask for the predominant value to be one of continual learning but that this learning result in at least three new ideas, marketable to the legitimate system, being raised every 6 months. The CEO can also use the presage concept of evaluation by ensuring that only staff with high potential for creative thinking and learning are transferred into the shadow system on projects where there is significant resource investment. However, above all, the CEO has to give overt and positive support to the staff in the shadow system — often simply by communicating and encouraging them frequently. This simple activity is one of the main positive feedback processes in the shadow system.

The staff (or 'actors', as they are sometimes known) in the shadow system then use the techniques discussed in this chapter to evaluate their ideas and personal learning. For example, the actor in the shadow system can ask key stakeholders to assess any changes they have seen in the actor. The actor could also conduct an evaluation using one of the scientific models. Certainly, the actor in the shadow system would need to conduct a cost–benefit analysis, as this aids the decision making in the legitimate system.

THE NEED FOR DIALECTIC THINKING

At the beginning of this chapter, we discussed the misunderstandings that have plagued the evaluation stage over the years. In many ways, these misperceptions can be explained by a concept discussed in chapter 2 — dialectic thinking. It is believed that dialectic thinking may separate adults from youths. Dialectic thinking consists of the ability to view artifacts (objects, operations or concepts) as having more than one characteristic. Further, these characteristics of an artifact may be conflicting. So, for example, electricity has positive benefits (keeps us warm in cold weather) but can also have negative consequences (it can kill us).

Evaluation must be approached with the wider viewpoints provided by dialectic thinking. Evaluation has a number of opposing characteristics and we have discussed two of these:

1. Evaluation can be both developmental and judgemental.
2. The more objective the measure used, the less rich the insights. On the other hand, the more subjective measurements may provide richer, more contextual and realistic data, but the process of subjective analysis lacks validity and reliability.

Evaluation also shares a conflicting characteristic with the implementation stage. Chapters 11 and 12 were divided into structured and unstructured learning strategies based on two philosophies of learning. One, the traditional school, believed that knowledge was finite, could be passed on by experts and should be delivered in a controlled environment. The artistic school believed that learning should be holistic and at the behest of the learner. As indicated in chapter 11, both of these philosophies are correct, depending on the situation. Chapters 9 and 10 suggested that the situation could be gauged, to a certain extent, by such variables as the HLO, the learner, the strategic orientation of the organisation and the resources available. So, the evaluation at the learning (or stage IV) level should consider the conflicting assumptions of structured and unstructured learning.

Evaluation also brings to the surface one of the oldest arguments in education. Bantoch (1992) believes the distinction between liberal and vocational education goes back to ancient Greece where liberal education was for living and what we call today vocational education, was for earning a living. This belief has survived for centuries, where the slaves and craftsmen received an education that was trade-focused and gave society the products and services it needed. The upper classes became involved only in learning that trained the mind and cultivated the intellect (Sanderson 1993). Thus liberal education had a continuing popularity among the self-styled elite because of its original association with high culture and dignity. However, Thorndike (1931) deflated this balloon of pomposity somewhat by finding that studies in Latin and Greek did not necessarily generalise to other types of knowledge and abilities.

However, writers such as Barcan (1992) and Wiggins (1989) report that the more modern interpretation of liberal education focuses on the identification of general but controlling principles rather than techniques, and emphasises the world of values rather than uniform behaviour. Liberal education develops the ability to accept other people with more knowledge and listen to them, perceive which questions are the most important to ask, challenge values and hidden agenda and imagine that a new and strange idea is worth attending to. It has also championed learning for its own sake and placed a high value on academic freedom (Davies 1995) and this stance has brought stringent criticism in the 1990s where the emphasis has been on economic rationalism. Vocational education, on the other hand, is more specialised, technical and productivity orientated. It is much easier to prove causality with vocational education and the results of such learning tend to surface more quickly and readily. With the competency movement (see chapter 5) and economic rationalism, vocational education has received a resurgence of support from governments and other sources in the last few years.

However, as emphasised in chapter 1, indulgence in unitary thought — for example, that vocational education is more valuable and critical to organisational viability — is a luxury that cannot be afforded in these complex times. Dialectic thinking must be substituted. Key stakeholders in organisations (be they CEOs, managers or HR developers) must recognise that evaluation supports and serves a variety of dual roles. Evaluation has to be objective and subjective and judgemental and developmental. All the four HRD stages — investigation, design, implementation and evaluation — have to consider structured and unstructured learning as equally valuable and be based on the values of both liberal and vocational education.

Balancing these conflicting roles is the new challenge for organisations which have to accept that knowledge is a valuable but delicate resource that needs careful management. This is the topic of the next, and last, chapter in this book.

GLOSSARY

analytic learning diary — one type of learning diary, is based on four headings — description of the experience, detailed observations, synthesis and future behaviour

behaviour level — the third level in Kirkpatrick's evaluation model, examines the change in behaviour on the job

Brinkerhoff's model — a more extensive evaluation model than Kirkpatrick's, consists of six stages — stage I (needs and goals), stage II (design), stage III (implementation), stage IV (learning), stage V (usage and endurance of learning) and stage VI (payoff)

control group — the second most complex scientific model, uses a pre-test–post-test model with a control group as well as the group experiencing the learning

cost–benefit analysis — an analysis that identifies the costs and the benefits of a learning episode and then compares the results as a ratio

criterion-referenced scoring — the marks achieved against predetermined criteria, usually presented as a percentage of the total possible score

evaluation plan — the plan, showing time lines and what evidence needs to be collected, allows the developmental and judgemental roles of evaluation to be coordinated

evaluation report — records the decisions taken during the evaluation and presents the results and recommendations

formative assessment — assessing the strengths and weaknesses of a learner's knowledge and using this information as developmental feedback

free flow diary — one type of learning diary, is a 'cathartic experience', allowing the learner to creatively express thoughts and feelings

Kirkpatrick's model — the most common model used for evaluation, consists of four levels — reaction, learning, behaviour and results

learning diaries — journals written by the learner to record events, thoughts and reflections, consisting of three types — analytic diary, organised diary and free flow diary

learning level — the second level in Kirkpatrick's evaluation model, examines the amount of learning that occurred, using one of the testing processes — skill test, written objective test, subjective written test, performance test, learning diary or portfolio assessment

norm-referenced scoring — the comparison of the raw score to the average of a nominated group

objective written test — where the scoring requires no interpretation by the examiner, consists of four types — multiple choice, true-false, matching, completion

observation form — an aid used by the assessor in a performance test (see also rubric)

organised diary — one type of learning diary, is usually in prose format, with an emphasis on careful construction, clear expression, attempted objectivity and cognitive logic

performance test — assessment of a complex test, usually based on both the procedural and task and relationships levels of the HLO

post-test — the simplest of the scientific models, consists of conducting the learning episode and then conducting an evaluation

portfolio assessment — collections of the learner's work across a significant time period

presage factors — the factors to be evaluated before the learning episode commences, are included in Brinkerhoff's model but not in Kirkpatrick's model

pre-test–post-test — the second simplest of the scientific models, consists of conducting an evaluation, conducting the learning episode and then conducting the evaluation again

raw score — the overall quantitative score achieved in a test

reaction level — the first level in Kirkpatrick's evaluation model, examines the reactions of the learners to the learning episode

results level — the fourth level in Kirkpatrick's model, examines the impact of the learning episode on the organisational outcomes

rubric — an aid to the assessor in performance testing, identifies the expected qualities of each behaviour within a hierarchy of potential responses

scientific models — aimed at proving causality, consist of five types — post-test, pre-test–post-test, time series evaluation, control group and Solomon four

skill test — used to assess procedural skills

Solomon four — the most complex of the scientific models, uses the pre-test–post-test on three control groups and the group undergoing the learning experience

subjective written tests — sometimes called essay tests, this type depends on the opinion of the examiner

summative assessment — the sum of all the tests of assessment on a learner, provides concluding evidence of the learner's achievement

time series evaluation — in the middle of the simple/complex continuum of scientific models, this test consists of a series of pre-tests, followed by the learning episode, followed by a series of post-tests

QUESTIONS

For review

1. Identify two misconceptions about evaluation and explain why those misconceptions are incorrect.

2. Describe a learning objective that would be suitable for a performance test and explain how you would go about conducting the performance test.

3. Provide an example and then explain a rubric.

4. What is the difference between criterion-referenced scoring and norm-referenced scoring?

5. List and describe Kirkpatrick's four levels of evaluation.

6. Explain how a learning program could be evaluated while implementing the program. Identify at least three critical points where such evaluation should take place.

For analysis

7. Compare and contrast objective written tests with learning diaries.

8. What are the similarities and differences between an analytic learning diary and a free flow diary? Using the hierarchy of learning outcomes (HLO) explain when each would be most appropriate to use.

9. Compare and contrast the time series evaluation with the Solomon four model.

For application

10. Using the current subject or unit that you are studying at university or using the current learning program you are attending, design:

    (a) an evaluation process that would assess the amount of learning that has taken place

    (b) an evaluation process that would demonstrate suitable levels of causality.

11. Using the current subject or unit that you are studying at university or using the current learning program you are attending, conduct a cost-benefit analysis from the point of view of the university or the organisation sponsoring the learning program.

REFERENCES

Alliger, G. M. and Janak, E. A. (1989). 'Kirkpatrick's levels of training criteria: Thirty years later.' *Personnel Psychology*, 42, 331–342.

Bantock, C. (1992). 'Finn and vocational education.' *Education Monitor*, 3(1), 10–12.

Barcan, A. (1992). 'Is there room for liberal education?' *Education Monitor*, 3(2), 2–3.

Bennett, J. and Kingham, M. (1993). 'Learning diaries.' In J. Reed and S. Proctor (Eds), *Nurse Education: A Reflective Approach*. London: Edward Arnold.

Brinkerhoff, R. O. (1987). *Achieving Results from Training*. San Francisco: Jossey-Bass.

Davies, P. (1995). 'Time to tear down the universities?' *Australian*, 12 April, 27.

Delahaye, B. L. and Smith, B. J. (1987). 'Warning — Now you have to prove you have trained them.' *Human Resource Management Australia*, 25(1), March, 5–8.

Delahaye, B. L. and Smith, B. J. (1998). *How to be an Effective Trainer*. New York: Wiley.

Easterby-Smith, M. (1998). 'Training evaluation and follow-up.' In J. Prokopenko (Ed.), *Management Development: A Guide for the Professional*. Geneva: ILO.

Goldstein, I. L. (1993). *Training in Organisations*. (3rd ed.). Pacific Grove, Cal.: Brooks/Cole.

Hall, W. C. (1995). *Key Aspects of Competency-based Assessment*. Adelaide, SA: National Centre for Vocational Education Research.

Kirkpatrick, D. L. (1959a). 'Techniques for evaluating training programs: Part 1 — Reaction.' *Journal of ASTD*, 13(11), 3–9.

Kirkpatrick, D. L. (1959b). 'Techniques for evaluating training programs: Part 2 — Learning.' *Journal of ASTD*, 13(12), 21–26.

Kirkpatrick, D. L. (1960a). 'Techniques for evaluating training programs: Part 3 — Behaviour.' *Journal of ASTD*, 14(1), 13–18.

Kirkpatrick, D. L. (1960b). 'Techniques for evaluating training programs: Part 4 — Results.' *Journal of ASTD*, 14(2), 28–32.

Kirkpatrick, D. L. (1994). *Evaluating Training Programs: The Four Levels*. San Francisco: Berrett-Koehler.

Kyriacou, C. and Newson, G. (1982). 'Teacher effectiveness: A consideration of research problems.' *Educational Review*, 34(1), 3–12.

McAllister, M. (1997). *Enriching Values: An Educational Criticism Approach to the Role of Assessment in Teaching Mental Health*. Unpublished doctoral thesis, Queensland University of Technology, Brisbane.

Owen, J. M. with Rogers, P. J. (1999). *Programs Evaluation: Forms and Approaches*. (2nd ed.). St. Leonards, NSW: Allen & Unwin.

Perry, R. P. (1990). 'Special section: Instruction in higher education.' *Journal of Educational Psychology*, 82(2), June, 183–274.

Sanderson, M. (1993). 'Vocational and liberal education: A historian's view.' *European Journal of Education*, 28(2), 189–196.

Smith, A. (1998). *Training and Development in Australia*. (2nd ed.). Sydney, NSW: Butterworths.

Smith, B. J. (1992). 'Learning Diaries.' In B. J. Smith (Ed.), *Management Development in Australia*. Sydney: HBJ.

Stacey, R. D. (1996). *Strategic Management and Organisational Dynamics*. (2nd ed.). London: Pitman.

Thorndike, E. L. (1931). *Human Learning*. New York: Appleton-Century-Crofts.

Thorndike, R. M. (1997). *Measurement and Evaluation in Psychology and Education*. (6th ed.). Upper Saddle River, NJ: Prentice Hall.

Wexley, K. N. and Latham, G. P. (1991). *Developing and Training Human Resources in Organizations*. (2nd ed.). New York: Harper Collins.

Wheatley, M. J. (1994). *Leadership and the New Science: Learning about Organisation from an Orderly Universe*. San Francisco: Berrett-Koehler.

Wiggins, G. (1989). 'The futility of trying to teach everything of importance.' *Educational Leadership*, 47(3), 44–48.

The safety program

Ravi Sidhu, the HR development officer for Fremantle Minerals and Metalworks, had been asked to design a safety program for the new workshop. The modern building housing the new workshop had the latest in communications design and would house machinery that was new to all the staff. The CEO of Fremantle Minerals and Metalworks was highly committed to safety, so Ravi had taken a lot of care over the design of the safety program. He now wanted to plan an evaluation process that would demonstrate beyond any reasonable doubt the effectiveness of the program. With the support of the CEO he knew that the budget for the evaluation would be reasonably generous.

Ravi looked at the HRDNI report on which he had based the design of the safety program. The questionnaire that had been used looked very sound. The Cronbach alpha was 0.81 although the test-retest was 0.58. The validity looked quite strong as well. The interviews with the CEO and the production manager had emphasised a 'strong safety attitude' and good interpersonal communication between all staff members in the new workshop. Ravi was glad that he had

included case studies and role plays in the safety program. The production manager had also emphasised the need for weekly safety audits that would be conducted by any member of the staff. Ravi smiled to himself as thought of the production manager's SAFETY AUDIT CHECKLIST — the production manager always referred to it in capital letters. Still, it was a good procedural form and 3 hours of the program had been devoted to it. 'That final role play which used it was good', Ravi thought. 'And there is just the right amount of conflict in the role play.'

'OK, now how will I evaluate the program? Shame the CEO is so down on all that scientific stuff, as he calls it.'

Discussion questions

1. What do you think Ravi should include in the evaluation of the program?

2. How would you justify the costs to the CEO?

3. If the CEO told you to reduce the budget on the evaluation by about one-third, what would you leave out? Why?

An ineffectual learning program?

Niki Nucifora was quite puzzled. The day the 'customer service' training course finished, she had read the 'happy sheets', as they called the questionnaires that asked the learners to record their reactions to the program. The comments were all so positive. So why was the marketing manager saying that the training course was so useless 3 weeks after the course had finished?

Niki thought back to the training course. It had been held every Tuesday morning for 8 weeks. The skills workshops on questioning and listening had been fun and all the trainees seemed to grasp the ideas well. The lectures on the products had been given by various guest speakers who were experts in the products. Sure, a couple of the speakers were a bit boring, but the information they gave was good. The role plays about the difficult customer had proved to be very interesting and all the trainees had taken on the role of one of the

harried customer service assistants. All the trainees had said that they had learned something. From what Niki could remember, the role players had done a fairly good job. 'Perhaps I should have made some record of what they had done well', Niki thought. 'For that matter, where they could have improved would have been useful too, I suppose.'

When Niki had asked the marketing manager why she thought the program was ineffectual, the marketing manager had replied, 'Well, I do conduct performance appraisals, you know'.

Discussion questions

1. What actions could Niki have taken before and during the training course to ensure that appropriate learning would occur?

2. What questions about the development of the learners should Niki have asked the marketing manager?

The management of knowledge

CHAPTER OBJECTIVES

At the end of this chapter you should be able to:

1 differentiate between explicit knowledge and tacit knowledge

2 describe the knowledge creation processes of externalisation, combination, internalisation and socialisation

3 discuss the four stages of HRD

4 describe how the legitimate system can be managed

5 describe how the shadow system can be managed

6 describe how the interaction between the legitimate system and the shadow system can be managed

7 discuss the role of the HR developer.

The chapter begins by emphasising the importance of organisations creating new knowledge so that they can survive their dynamic and turbulent environment. Nonaka and Takeuchi (1995) have suggested a model of knowledge creation by differentiating between explicit and tacit knowledge. **Explicit knowledge** can be expressed in words while **tacit knowledge** is highly personalised, is held within the subconscious mind and is hard to formalise. From this differentiation four knowledge creation processes can be identified. **Externalisation** occurs when tacit knowledge is translated and expressed into forms that are comprehensible to the conscious mind, often in the form of a metaphor, an analogy or a model. **Internalisation** is the reverse process — converting explicit knowledge into tacit knowledge, usually by using logical or critical reflection. **Combination** is a process of systematising concepts into a knowledge system by combining old and new explicit knowledge. Finally, **socialisation** involves the sharing of tacit knowledge between two parties without the use of language. The strength of socialisation is that the shared experience is accompanied by the associated emotions and the specific contexts in which the shared experience is embedded.

As with any resource, current knowledge needs to be maintained and nurtured. The four stages of HRD — investigation, design, implementation and evaluation — are the primary processes that organisations use to maintain their current knowledge. These four stages have been a major component of this textbook.

To create and maintain knowledge capital, CEOs and managers must recognise the existence of the two basic systems that comprise the organisation — the legitimate system and the shadow system. This means that the CEO or manager has to manage the legitimate system, manage the shadow system and also manage the tension between the two systems. The **legitimate system** is administered through ordinary management. **Ordinary management** is based on the precepts of Newtonian thinking that all processes can be examined and implemented in a rational, logical and linear sequence — and for the legitimate system this is correct. The legitimate system manages the everyday activities of the organisation, operates in an environment of close-to-certainty and is committed to the efficient use of its resources. The legitimate system uses negative feedback and single-loop learning. **Negative feedback** dampens any aberrant behaviour and brings this behaviour back to a predetermined standard. **Single-loop learning** maintains the 'status quo' by not challenging basic values and beliefs. The **shadow system** is administered through extraordinary management. **Extraordinary management** is based on the precepts of positive feedback and double-loop learning. **Positive feedback** has an amplifying effect which escalates small changes. In **double-loop learning**, basic values and beliefs are challenged. The shadow system has three roles — to identify, import and create new knowledge; to challenge the fundamental values of the legitimate system; and to ease the journey of new ideas into the legitimate system. To govern the shadow system the manager needs to undertake a number of activities, including establishing **shadow networks** and communities of practice, using the invisible forces, building shared visions, creating and testing mental models and using systems thinking. In managing the tension and interactions of the legitimate and shadow systems, the CEO or manager has to aim for a state of balanced instability. This is achieved by ensuring that the legitimate system does not have too much power but that the new ideas of the shadow system are not incorporated without due thought.

The role of the HR developer in the organisation of the new millennium is one of being the steward of knowledge capital. The HR developer carries out this role by helping the organisation to create new knowledge, identifying and importing relevant explicit knowledge, arranging for the new knowledge to be disseminated throughout the organisation, maintaining the knowledge resource by using the **four stages of HRD** and assisting managers to manage the two basic systems in the organisation — the legitimate system and the shadow system.

THE IMPORTANCE OF KNOWLEDGE

It was once held that the two most basic resources available to an organisation were money and time and that one could be exchanged for the other. So, for example, if a project was falling behind schedule it was just a matter of buying more equipment or hiring more staff and thus catching up on time. This old dictum is no longer true.

Knowledge has now become an equally critical resource. Unfortunately, though, there is no simple exchange equation between money and time, on the one hand, and knowledge, on the other. Knowledge has to be created, learned and maintained, not simply purchased and maintained. Further, while a certain type of knowledge may be appropriate today, there is no guarantee of its relevance in the future. So knowledge may even have to be unlearned. This means that, while creating and acquiring knowledge may indeed cost money and take time, simply investing money and time does not guarantee useful knowledge.

Knowledge is a different resource (Sveiby 1997). Consider most resources that are available to an organisation; the more they are used, the quicker they are depleted. This is true of raw materials or capital equipment. However, knowledge does not decrease with use; in fact, the more it is used the more it expands. Try to hold onto knowledge and the world passes you by. Someone else (often several someone else's!) will discover or create the same or even more advanced knowledge. Conversely, spread your knowledge around and it comes back multiplied ten-fold.

Knowledge is a complex resource that needs careful management. Knowledge may be held in organisational systems, such as the computer systems and the manuals of procedures, but it also resides within the minds of individual staff members. Such repositories of knowledge are often termed knowledge reservoirs or silos. Knowledge, of itself, can be quite ephemeral as often the only physical evidence of its presence is the successful or unsuccessful use of the knowledge. Finally, it is often difficult to predict what future problems will occur let alone what knowledge will be needed to overcome those problems. As a commodity, then, organisations have to treat knowledge as the critical and valuable resource that it is — and this means *creating* and *maintaining* knowledge.

CREATING KNOWLEDGE

To survive in the dynamic and turbulent environment that is the commercial world of the new millennium, all organisations have to create new knowledge. This is the most basic function of businesses today. Without new knowledge the organisation will starve and die. Creating knowledge must become a strategic imperative for any organisation and this imperative has two thrusts. The first strategic thrust for the organisation must be the positive management of diversity (see chapter 3). The diverse characteristics of every staff member must be seen as a creative form of energy that needs to be mobilised, celebrated and harnessed.

The second strategic thrust is the actual knowledge creation process itself. Nonaka (1991) and others have provided an important and valuable insight into knowledge creation. Firstly, they differentiate between two types of knowledge. *Explicit knowledge* is held in the conscious mind and can be expressed in words and shared in the form of data, written ideas, specifications and manuals, for example. *Tacit knowledge* is held in the subconscious mind and is highly personal and hard to formalise — for example, subjective insights, intuition and hunches. Tacit knowledge is encompassed in the saying, 'We can know more than we can tell' (Polanyi 1997). While explicit knowledge can be transmitted easily between individuals, tacit knowledge is not easily expressible and is difficult to share with others. Tacit knowledge has two dimensions (Nonaka and Konno 1998). One component is the personal skills and abilities, the results of which are most readily seen in the master craftsperson. The second dimension is cognitive and consists of the individual's frames of reference (see chapter 2) as well as schemata and mental models. Therefore, tacit knowledge links, and also overlaps, with the individual's frames of reference. Surprisingly, tacit knowledge is seen as the foundation and catalyst to the majority of decisions that the individual makes.

Using this difference between tacit and explicit knowledge, a paradigm of four knowledge-creation processes has been proposed (Nonaka 1991; Nonaka and Takeuchi 1995; Nonaka, Takeuchi and Umemoto 1996; Nonaka and Konno 1998).

Externalisation occurs when tacit knowledge is translated and expressed into forms that are comprehensible to the conscious mind of the individual and to others. The articulation of tacit knowledge involves techniques that help express one's ideas or images, such as words, concepts, hypotheses, figurative language (metaphors, analogies or narratives), models and visuals. It is believed that externalisation holds the key to knowledge creation, as it generates new, explicit ideas from tacit knowledge. Externalisation is most often seen as, although not limited to, a sequential process of:

- *a metaphor*, where one thing is intuitively understood by imagining another symbolically. For example, one could say that the shadow system of a business organisation acts like an amoeba, in that part of the amoeba reaches out, latches on to an anchor and pulls the rest of the organism forward. The association of two things in a metaphor (i.e. an amoeba and an organisation) is driven by intuition and does not aim to find differences between them. A metaphor is useful in externalisation as it creates a network by relating abstract concepts with concrete ones.
- *an analogy*, which harmonises the contradictions inherent in metaphors. It does this by rationally focusing on structural/functional similarities between the two

concepts and thus on their differences. So, an amoeba is a non-thinking entity and searches for an anchor aimlessly. An organisation (or an individual, for that matter) should be more discriminatory in its search for future anchors by bringing problem-solving intelligence to bear on the selection process.

- *a model*, where the clearer aspects of the concept that are being derived from the tacit knowledge can be depicted in a pictorial or verbal form. Models often start out as rough descriptions or drawings which are then clarified, modified and extended as the externalisation process continues to surmount the gaps and inconsistencies.

Combination is a process of systematising concepts into a knowledge system — whether that knowledge system be within an individual or an organisation. It involves the conversion of explicit knowledge into more complex sets of explicit knowledge. Thus, existing knowledge is reconfigured through sorting, adding and combining old explicit knowledge with new explicit knowledge. At the organisational level, the combination process relies on three processes. Firstly, the process captures new explicit knowledge (for example, from journal articles or at conferences or from competitors) and combines this new information with present explicit knowledge. Next, this new combined explicit knowledge needs to be transferred and disseminated throughout the organisation. Thirdly, the new combined explicit knowledge needs to be recorded, usually in a more succinct and usable form (for example, in plans or reports or as procedures). The strategic planning procedure for the legitimate system, as discussed in chapter 4, is a good example of the combination process. Interestingly, much of the literature on the *learning organisation* emphasises this combination process — especially learning from competitors and other organisations — as if it is the sole process for bringing new information into the organisation. As Nonaka et al. emphasise, however, combination is but one of the knowledge creating processes.

Internalisation converts explicit knowledge into tacit knowledge. There are at least two procedures that are of crucial importance to internalisation. The first is the use of *whole body experience*. For example, when conducting Train the Trainer workshops, the HR developer stands in front of the class and delivers information — on learning objectives, questioning, the use of visual aids, the structured learning strategies, and so on. This delivery is the combination process. However, the trainees find a big difference between listening to the HR developer's explanations and actually conducting a 20-minute theory session in front of the class. It is this 'whole body experience' of conducting the session in front of a class which converts their new, combined explicit knowledge into tacit knowledge. Thus explicit knowledge becomes imbedded into values and actions by being merged with, or perhaps even replacing, current frames of reference, mental models and personal skills. The second crucial procedure is the use of *reflection*. Figure 2.1 shows the wholistic learning process and identifies two reflective procedures that are useful to internalisation. The first is logical reflection where the individual contemplates the content of the knowledge. The second is critical reflection where the individual examines his or her personal frames of reference. The *learning cycle*, as discussed in chapter 9, provides a solid foundation for the internalisation process because of its emphasis on reflection.

Socialisation involves the sharing of tacit knowledge between individuals without the use of language. Exchanging tacit knowledge relies on four components:

1. at least *two individuals*
2. spending *time* together

3. being in close *physical proximity*.
4. each willingly being involved in *self-transcendence* — moving beyond ego-centricity to genuinely empathise with others.

Interacting face to face with another and being non-defensive allow an individual to open up and accept the possibilities of acknowledging, and possibly accepting, another's tacit knowledge. The classic example of socialisation occurs with a master and apprentice. Much more passes between the two besides verbalised explicit knowledge as socialisation allows a deeper understanding of the other's ways of thinking and feeling. The strength of socialisation is that the sharing of experience is accompanied by associated emotions and specific contexts in which the shared experience is embedded. Another good example of socialisation occurs when the needs investigator visits the work area. While explicit knowledge is accessed via the needs investigation techniques (for example, interviewing), the investigator is also exposed to a host of other inputs — implications from interviewees' nonverbal behaviour, sensing the culture, impressions gained from the work area layout and decor, to name a few. It is because of this socialisation process that the strong recommendation was made in chapter 5 for the needs investigator to always visit the worksite.

This four-phase paradigm of knowledge creation — externalisation, combination, internalisation and socialisation — can be viewed as relevant to organisations (as originally intended by Nonaka and Takeuchi) or as applicable to individuals (as proposed by Andrews and Delahaye 1998).

In creating new knowledge, every effort should be made to ensure that the four processes of externalisation, combination, internalisation and socialisation operate as a total package, rather than as four separate actions. Nonaka and Takeuchi (1995, p. 71) suggest that there is a spiral of knowledge creation, as depicted in figure 14.1.

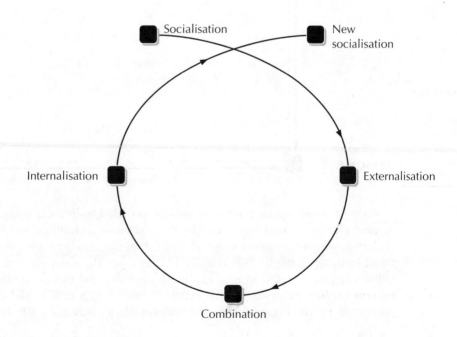

FIGURE 14.1
The spiral of knowledge creation

Although this figure indicates that knowledge creation starts with socialisation, the process could feasibly commence with any of the four. For example, while extroverts may indeed start with socialisation, an argument could be mounted that introverts are more likely to begin with externalisation. The use of the four processes is also likely to be quite complex. Figure 14.2 shows the interaction between two people. Person A retrieves a concept from her or his tacit knowledge and externalises it. This new knowledge is now explicit and is transmitted to person B who combines it with her or his current explicit knowledge, thus creating new knowledge. Person B may choose to transmit this new explicit knowledge back to person A (as indicated by the dotted line) or may choose to reflect and/or experiment to internalise and create more new knowledge (as indicated by the solid line). Person B may then choose to externalise this new tacit knowledge back into new and more complex explicit knowledge and (following the dotted line) pass this on to person A who combines this new and more complex explicit knowledge with current explicit knowledge and then (still following the dotted line) internalises this new and even more complex explicit knowledge into tacit knowledge, thus creating even more new knowledge. While this interaction is going on, the two actors are sharing socialisation, thereby creating more tacit knowledge between them. Considering that figure 14.2 is depicting just one original thought that is shared and which could possibly occur within seconds, the dynamic capacity of knowledge creation is an awesome form of energy. If only organisations would unleash it!

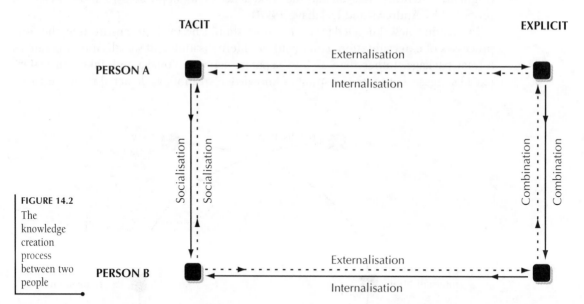

FIGURE 14.2
The knowledge creation process between two people

Ways of assisting the four processes of knowledge creation have been discussed extensively throughout this text. The most obvious techniques have been discussed under the implementation stage of HRD. For the combination process, the structured learning strategies (see chapter 11) are often the most efficient methods. Individuals can be exposed to new explicit knowledge and can combine this with their current explicit knowledge. This often occurs when a new model of equipment is purchased by the organisation. The individuals already have the basic operational knowledge but can readily assimilate the new requirements of the operating procedures of the new model. The organisation can often import new explicit knowledge from competitors by, for example, slightly changing manufacturing procedures, which can lead to cost savings, or using a new marketing approach to sell products that competitors have found to be more dynamic. However, for both externalisation and internalisation, the unstructured learning strategies (see chapter 12) are usually more efficacious. For both the individual and the organisation the unstructured approaches encourage the reflection and critical thinking that are the basis for constructive and challenging thought. These dynamic approaches allow people to be creative and share feelings without the underlying and inhibiting expectations, such as having perfect knowledge, contaminating the process. Indeed, the unstructured learning strategies encourage story telling through the use of metaphors and analogies which are the basic catalysts for externalisation. The unstructured approaches also induce the reflective thought process that is the lynch pin of internalisation. Finally, mentoring (see chapter 12) is the most recognised support system for socialisation.

However, knowledge creation also occurs at the other three stages of HRD. Certainly, during the needs investigation stage (see chapters 5 to 8), the investigator is attempting to uncover not only the explicit knowledge of the staff but also to extricate their tacit knowledge. Indeed the interaction between, for example, the needs investigator and an interviewee is very similar to that depicted in figure 14.2, although much more complicated and detailed. So even at this early stage of the HRD process, knowledge is being created. This is an important point often missed by CEOs and managers. During the design stage (see chapters 9 and 10), the designer is frequently involved in externalisation as he or she is developing a program that will satisfy the defined need. Even the evaluation stage (see chapter 13) is a learning experience as new insights are achieved, either by contemplating new data or by interacting with staff and managers. So, at every stage of the HRD process, new knowledge is generated and this underlines the importance of an organisation effectively and professionally utilising the four stages of investigation, design, implementation and evaluation.

MAINTAINING KNOWLEDGE

Creating new knowledge is only half the story. As with any resource, knowledge needs nurturing — a process that, for physical resources such as money and equipment, is called 'maintenance'. The maintenance of the knowledge resource means that knowledge has to be disseminated throughout the organisation — not in a haphazard fashion but in such a way that the appropriate knowledge is available to the appropriate area at the appropriate time. There are three important facets to the maintenance of knowledge:

1. *New knowledge has to be proselytised.* When new knowledge that is critical to the future viability of the organisation is identified, then this new knowledge has to be promulgated astutely, being targeted at the most fertile and needy parts of the organisation. This dissemination has to be completed carefully yet energetically.

2. As people depart from the organisation (or move from one part of the organisation to another) *current useful knowledge has to be replaced.* While some knowledge (mainly explicit) is stored in organisational systems (for example, in manuals of procedures), most of the operational knowledge, especially the tacit knowledge, is retained by people. If a person moves, the knowledge goes with that person. The area losing the person needs that knowledge replaced. Further, if the person is moving to another part of the organisation then that person needs knowledge appropriate to that location.

3. *Useless knowledge has to be unlearned.* In chapter 2, we discussed the concept of unlearning. It is most likely that old knowledge is retained, for a certain period, alongside the new. If the old knowledge is not rewarded then it will gradually atrophy. This is a natural process and, in times gone by, was sufficiently efficient. However, knowledge is now increasing at an exponential rate. This means that organisations and individuals have to become actively engaged in jettisoning old knowledge, before memory is clogged or before it interferes with the use of new knowledge.

How can organisations deal with these twin imperatives — not only creating but also maintaining knowledge? Firstly, organisations must ensure that their most fundamental developmental process is operating consistently and effectively. This fundamental process has been referred to in this text as the four stages of HRD. Unless these four stages — investigation, design, implementation and evaluation — are managed realistically and competently and also given due deference (with, for example, sufficient financial backing) then the knowledge resource cannot be managed effectively or efficiently. Limiting the energy and investment in the four stages of HRD is not only a false economy, but frequently a fatal error.

The efficient and effective management of the four stages is the first step in creating and maintaining knowledge. The second step is the wise, proficient and masterful management of the two basic systems of the organisation — the legitimate system and the shadow system. The adept execution of the four stages of HRD and the management of the two basic systems, together, lead to that modern Holy Grail — the learning organisation.

THE FOUR STAGES OF HRD

The four stages of HRD — the needs investigation, design, implementation and evaluation — are the founding processes for managing the knowledge resource. Unless these four stages are implemented according to the accepted principles and practices as discussed in this text, little headway will be made in managing knowledge in a concerted, coordinated and productive manner. Knowing what knowledge is required by which centres and individuals within the organisation and ensuring that these centres and individuals acquire the appropriate knowledge has two critical outcomes.

Firstly, the appropriate use of appropriate knowledge contained within appropriate knowledge reservoirs in the organisation (for example, staff who use the knowledge for the benefit of the organisation, or the manuals of procedures) ensures the current and short-term viability of the organisation. This, of course, comes under the jurisdiction of the legitimate system. Accordingly, the legitimate system must investigate the needs (see chapters 5 to 8) suggested by its strategic planning process (see chapter 4) and as suggested by the activities of the shadow system. Identified needs have to be designed (see chapters 9 and 10) to ensure the most efficient and effective implementation of the required learning. The implementation must be efficient so the money is not wasted but it also has to be effective to ensure that the strategic plans are successful. The designed learning programs have to be conducted and managed by HR developers who have the required competence and professional ability (see chapters 11 and 12). Finally, to ensure that the designed learning program has delivered the learning outcomes that will contribute to the continued viability of the organisation, the legitimate system must institute an evaluation process (see chapter 13). Properly managed, the four stages of HRD interact as a dynamic and relatively pro-active process that imports, disseminates and maintains the knowledge required by the legitimate system to survive the current and immediate future. Improper, lazy or negligent management of the four stages leaves the current viability of the organisation to the whim of chance — and without current viability, there is no future viability.

The second critical outcome has to do with the shadow system and has two parts. Firstly, appropriate knowledge used appropriately in the legitimate system provides a firm and steadfast foundation as an operating base for the shadow system. A solid operating base allows the shadow system to see more clearly into the future (for example, by providing sufficient resources, such as time and money). Further, it is difficult to know what to change if an operating base is ill-defined. Secondly, the operating knowledge of the shadow system is not pro-grammed knowledge. Rather, it is the knowledge of the learning processes that is paramount. In learning new knowledge, the processes needed are precisely those that have been discussed under the four stages of HRD. Actors in the shadow system must be highly competent in the processes of needs investigation (for example, interviewing and questionnaire design), design (for example, selecting appropriate strategies for their own learning), implementation (for example, being self-directed learners or even developing key stakeholders in the legitimate system) and evaluation (for example, being able to assess the appropriateness of new knowledge). However, rather than using the four stages in a linear fashion as occurs in the legitimate system, the actors in the shadow system have to use them when and where, and in whatever order, is appropriate. Further, the speed at which the search for new knowledge takes place is often so fast that the overlaps between the four stages are magnified greatly.

The four stages of HRD, then, provide a foundation-stone in the quest of managing knowledge. For the legitimate system, the four stages are essential for the immediate viability of the organisation. In the shadow system, the techniques used in the four stages become critical processes that the actors need to use, automatically and competently.

A learning strategy for the shadow system

One common and easily managed knowledge-creating strategy for the shadow system is to bring together a group of young first-line managers as a project team. Rather than implementing some specific project, these 'young guns', as they are sometimes called, are charged with a general objective — to identify future organisational responses if some basic assumption on which the organisation operates is suddenly altered. For example, take a manufacturing organisation which has had a competitive edge based on an exclusive agreement with a government department for the long-term supply of a particular product. The 'young guns' may be given an objective such as 'Suppose the Department of Works and Machinery advised us that we would have to competitively bid for the supply of the (particular product) every 3 months —

what changes would we have make to our organisation?'

The underlying objective of this strategy is two-fold. Firstly, the 'young guns' are being developed and, accordingly, the learning strategy (and incidently the control strategy) used is usually action learning. Secondly, the shadow system is given an opportunity to analyse and challenge the assumptions of the legitimate system and to ponder, analyse and dissect a possible future scenario. The 'young guns' will be operating on two levels — their own development and identifying new knowledge for the organisation. When operating on these two levels, they will be conducting several needs investigations (as the objective is multifaceted) at once. As they investigate they will be learning new information. At the same time they will have to consider how the organisation will be

changed to accept the new scenario. While doing this they will have to evaluate each new idea and proposed strategy for change. As they could be operating on several new possibilities, some of which will need to be integrated and some of which will be 'stand alone', each possibility could be at a different stage of investigation, design, implementation and evaluation. To further complicate the issue, they will be operating at two levels — personal and organisational development — and in two different directions — the assumptions of the legitimate system that need to be challenged and the future external environment of the organisation.

Before they start, the 'young guns' will need to be competent at the various practices and have a thorough understanding of the principles of the four stages of investigation, design, implementation and evaluation.

MANAGING THE TWO BASIC SYSTEMS

Management is about the care of the resources in the organisation. For some organisations, for example in the manufacturing industry, the primary resources are the capital equipment and the raw material being converted by the capital equipment. For this type of organisation what is produced by the capital equipment is sold and the resultant revenue is fed back into the organisation to continue its viability. Money is the exchange mechanism in this interaction and money also becomes a measure of the success of the organisation. However, by and of itself the capital equipment does nothing. People are essential to the operation of capital equipment, either directly or indirectly. Hence, even the most simple of business functions, the manufacturing organisation, needs four obvious resources — time, raw materials, capital equipment and people, the latter usually referred to as the human resource. However, as discussed throughout this text, the critical constituent of the human resource is people's knowledge. During the industrial revolution, and as exemplified by the scientific management theories of Taylor, organisations could once survive on the detailed and complex knowledge of a few people — usually the owners and key specialists — and have the majority of staff receive limited training.

Now, of course, life is nowhere near as simple. The capital equipment has become more complex, usually replacing the more mundane tasks. Strangely enough, it was these mundane tasks which once made training so simple and knowledge such a cheap commodity. In the coming years complex equipment may mean fewer staff, but these fewer staff have to have high levels of tacit and explicit knowledge. Further, these days, organisations have gone beyond converting raw materials, with service industries increasing at an exponential rate. Indeed, some organisations exist only by selling knowledge. Alas, management theory has had difficulty in keeping up with these changes. It is not so much that management theory is wrong, just that management now has additional complexities to consider and the older management paradigms cannot cope.

Ralph Stacey (1996) has been one of the key writers for this new perception of management theory. Using complexity theory, he points out that any organism has two main systems — the *legitimate system* and the *shadow system*. These two terms have been used frequently throughout this text, so we will just review briefly the underlying theory. The legitimate system is attracted to the state of 'stable equilibrium' where the future can be predicted with certainty. The aim of the legitimate system is to keep the status quo. However, the shadow system is attracted to the state of 'explosive instability' where the future is uncertain but where creativity reigns supreme. Over the last two millennia there has been an acceptance that stable equilibrium is good and explosive instability is bad. Indeed, until now, this has been so. Change was very slow so stable equilibrium could cope easily. Rampant creativity caused unwanted changes for change's sake and ultimately led to anarchy. Intuitively, throughout history, kingdoms and organisations such as the Church eschewed instability and pursued stability.

Now, though, we live in an age where the only constant *is* change. The amount of information is doubling every few years. Technology is old after three years. Competitors appear out of nowhere. If an organisation operates under the assumptions of stable equilibrium, then the organisation will be by-passed and left behind. However, rampant creativity is still not an option as this path still leads to anarchy. In this new age, such a simple solution as choosing one or the other is no longer feasible. For the long-term viability of the organisation, it is essential that the legitimate system and the shadow system be kept in a state of **bounded instability**. Bounded instability is a state of paradox in which the two contradictory forces of stability and instability are operating simultaneously, pulling the system in opposing directions. This means that the shadow system is pulling the organisation towards creativity but this force is balanced by the legitimate system being attracted towards stable equilibrium.

The role of the modern manager is to maintain this exquisite tension so that the organisation is kept in a state of productive bounded instability. This means that neither the shadow system nor the legitimate system should become too powerful because one leads towards anarchy and the other towards a slow but sure death.

Rather, each system should be invested with sufficient resources and power to maintain the appropriate state of bounded instability. In some organisations the legitimate system will be comparatively larger with a smaller shadow system. A good example of this is McDonald's. One of the competitive strengths of McDonald's is the manufacture of a product that is similar the world over. To achieve this they have a superb legitimate system where all critical knowledge is well documented and all staff are given the appropriate development. Judged on resource allocation and power, McDonald's has a smaller but still very effective shadow system which explores the future and identifies changes that can be instituted with limited negative effects on the organisation. Research and development companies, however, will have large shadow systems with a legitimate system resourced just sufficiently to keep the organisation on track in the immediate future. However, as a general observation, it would be true to say that most organisations have the ratio skewed too far in favour of the legitimate system. The results of this imbalance can be seen in massive industrial disputes, savage shifts in market share, traumatic staff redundancies and sudden closures of whole departments or centres.

To achieve a productive state of balanced instability the leader needs to effectively manage:

* the legitimate system
* the shadow system and
* the interaction between the legitimate system and the shadow system.

MANAGING THE LEGITIMATE SYSTEM

The legitimate system is administered through what Stacey (1996) refers to as ordinary management. No organisation can carry out its day-to-day tasks or build on its existing strengths unless it practises ordinary management with a high degree of skill. Ordinary management is the stuff of the Master of Business (MBA) degrees. The rational and linear conventional strategic management planning process for the legitimate system (chapter 4) that is linked with the operational planning (see figure 4.1) is the heart of ordinary management. Operational planning is the first of the classic managerial functions, the other three being organising, leading and controlling. Both conventional strategic planning and the four managerial functions are based on the Newtonian paradigm which assumes that an entity can be broken down into its component parts, examined, measured and then be reconstructed into a new and possibly better entity. This assumption is quite correct for a physical entity such as a motor vehicle and approximately correct for the legitimate system of an organisation which is facing an external environment that is close to certainty. Hence all the theories that undergird the conventional strategic planning and the four managerial functions operate quite successfully while retained in the legitimate system and when they are used only to ensure the immediate viability of the organisation into the near future — from a few months to about two years, at the most. Beyond this time frame, the future is too murky and too far-from-certainty for the Newtonian paradigm to be of any assistance in the management of an organisation.

The basic administrative assumptions of management in the legitimate system stem from negative feedback and single-loop learning. *Negative feedback* processes (Stacey 1996) come from the engineering professions. Such feedback has a dampening effect and is designed to bring differing behaviours back to a prescribed norm or standard. So, in an airconditioned room when the temperature rises above a set temperature, the airconditioning unit pumps in more cold air, bringing the temperature back to the pre-set standard. Thus, negative feedback has a dampening effect. *Single-loop learning* (Argyris 1992) was discussed in chapter 2. Single-loop learning does not question or challenge the underlying values or beliefs of the organisation. Accordingly, the organisation decides what will be learned by the participants and when this learning will be made available. Again, the assumptions of negative feedback and single-loop learning are quite appropriate for the legitimate system.

Based on these two assumptions — negative feedback and single-loop learning — the predominant knowledge creation approach used by the legitimate system is the combination process. Typically, the conventional strategic planning process identifies new explicit knowledge that is needed by the organisation and the staff and this explicit knowledge is then imported, usually in the form of training courses and workshops. Accordingly, the legitimate system is the predominant user of the formal expressions of the four stages of HRD — investigation, design, implementation and evaluation. By concentrating on explicit knowledge, the legitimate system feels that it can still remain in control and that no unpredictable issues will be raised that may 'rock the boat'. Explicit knowledge can also be managed efficiently and effectively. The danger, of course, is that the organisational culture and the strategic mission of the legitimate system may have become obsolete and explicit knowledge presented as single-loop learning will never challenge the fundamental underlying values.

Beside ensuring the immediate viability of the organisation and tending to the day-to-day organisational processes, the legitimate system has three other roles:

1. It ensures that the efforts of the organisation are coordinated so that the desired outcome is achieved. This is known as *effectiveness* and can be measured by the extent to which the organisation achieves its strategic and operational objectives. Effectiveness is usually measured by a financial standard such as profit before tax or the return on investment to shareholders, with other non-financial measures such a market share also being useful.
2. It ensures that the desired outcome is produced with the least cost. This is known as *efficiency* and is usually measured by financial indicators such as capital value to income generation ratios and quality benchmarks such as wastage of raw materials.
3. It *audits* the new ideas of the shadow system. As the shadow system identifies new strategies for the future survival of the organisation, these new ideas have to then survive the gauntlet of the decision processes of the legitimate system. This gauntlet is an auditing process and is a very complex and dynamic mixture of rational logic, the organisational culture and organisational politics. Specifically, the legitimate system will make sure of at least the following:
   - The new product/service/value is not so alien that it could confuse the customer.
   - The new product/service/value does not use a disproportionate ration of the organisation's resources.
   - The legitimate system is not facing 'new product overload' that will confuse or tire the workforce.

- Appropriate standing plans are promulgated so that the new product/service/value can be adopted easily.
- Appropriate single-use plans, including formal HRD programs, are designed, implemented and evaluated to ensure both the smooth entry of the new product/service/value and also that high quality is maintained.

For the chief executive officer (CEO), supervising and regulating this auditing process is by far the most difficult role in managing the legitimate system. All the other tasks in managing the legitimate system — strategic planning, the day-to-day activities, ensuring effectiveness and efficiency — have relatively clear guidelines defined by Newtonian-paradigm-based management theories. These theories are comparatively easy to follow. However, managing the auditing role of the legitimate system requires much more finesse and there are no linear rules to follow. The CEO has to consider the appropriate mix of resources and power that will be allocated to the legitimate system to judge the new idea compared to the amount of resources and power that the shadow system should be given to proselytise their new idea. On the one hand, the legitimate system has to have sufficient resources and power to ensure that useless and potentially damaging ideas are not absorbed by the organisation. Such inappropriate ideas will endanger the effectiveness and efficiency of the organisation. On the other hand, the legitimate system is naturally committed to stability and any new change threatens this supposedly ideal state. Blind adherence to stability will result eventually in severe damage or even death for the organisation. So balancing the comparative resources and power available to the legitimate and shadow systems is one of the most important functions of the CEO.

MANAGING THE SHADOW SYSTEM

As Stacey (1996) points out, the problem with an omnipotent legitimate system is that it traps the organisation into an endless repetition of its past. Such omnipotence quashes creativity because negative feedback dampens any variation in behaviour and single-loop learning continually reinforces current values and behaviour. However, the closer an organisation is pushed towards chaos the more the organisation is likely to generate new and more complex forms of behaviour based on more robust and realistic values. Thus, the only way that an organisation can avoid the trap of obsolescence is to allow the shadow system to search for the new ideas that will ensure the future viability of the organisation. The shadow system is governed best by extraordinary management.

The essence of the shadow system is embodied in a conversation I had recently with the CEO of a government department. I was making the point that, back in the 1960s when NASA was initially charged with the responsibility of landing a human on the moon, there was no inkling of the wonderful products such as Teflon that would be discovered during the quest. The CEO said that the issue was much deeper than that. It wasn't just that new products were discovered but that these new unforeseen products solved unforeseen problems that had arisen between the 1960s and the 1980s. This, then, is the role of the shadow system — not just to identify new products or new values for the organisation, but to arm the organisation with sufficient options that will help it combat any unforeseen problems or allow the organisation to take advantage of any new opportunities that may arise.

Of course, based on the Newtonian paradigm of thinking, it is tempting to view the legitimate system and the shadow system as just two separate sections of the organisation. Again, this perception is too simple. Indeed, sometimes staff do work separately in the shadow system, as suggested by 'a closer look 14.1'. In this example, there are a group of 'young guns' who are working 100% of their time on a developmental project. The segment 'a closer look 14.2' provides some more techniques that have been used to operate in the shadow system. The examples described in the 'a closer look' segments are often raised when the discussion turns to the shadow system, most probably because they provide a readily identifiable picture of what is possible.

a closer look 14.2

More learning strategies for the shadow system

Some typical examples of ventures that managers can use in the shadow system include projects, matrix teams and the meeting place.

1. Projects
Similar to the 'young guns' example, projects are often the venture of choice by managers — most probably because the investment can be justified to the legitimate system. There are a number of variations but typically each project has three objectives:

(a) There must be an improvement to a product or service.
(b) There must be a financial return on the project.
(c) The project must be a learning experience for the staff involved.

2. Matrix teams
Matrix teams work well where the organisation is divided into product or service departments. For example, an organisation servicing rural industries may be divided into the departments of Intensive Crops, Organic Crops, Animal Husbandry and Native Fauna. These four departments represent one arm of the matrix. Members from each department are then asked to form teams, with each team having at least one representative from each department. These teams are often given creative names — The Constructing Larger Emus team and The Environmentally Friendly Crops and Animals team — to emphasise the alternative thinking that is needed. The objectives of the teams are to:

(a) identify knowledge from the other departments that may be useful in the team member's department
(b) identify new products or services or different future

organisational values and culture from combining the knowledge from each department.

3. The meeting place
Staff tend to meet naturally in places around the organisation. This may be at the store room while they are waiting for equipment and materials, at the Records Department while waiting for a file or even outside the elevators. Now the legitimate system would regard these waiting periods as a waste of time. For the shadow system these periods are fertile times where knowledge can be exchanged. For the shadow system, these sites are worthy of development so that the staff can exchange ideas and knowledge. The development may be simply the provision of some comfortable chairs or even a coffee station.

The examples in 'a closer look', though, are really just special cases, albeit they are more visible than most. More commonly, staff move in and out of the shadow system several times a day. As Andrews (1999) comments, the knowledge generation in an organisation is more about the everyday actions of many rather than the plans of a few. For example, the manager of the Registry and Records Branch of an organisation may be driving to work one morning listening to the radio. The DJ on the radio may make some comment that triggers an idea in the mind of the manager. On thinking about this idea the manager may see an improved way of managing the records of the organisation. Once at work, but over a period of several months, the manager then works steadily towards introducing the change. The manager would not spend this period of months working solely on the new idea. Rather, a few minutes one day, an hour the next, 10 minutes the next may be invested in the idea. The majority of the manager's time would still be spent in the legitimate system. However, the times the manager is thinking about the new idea, and working to introduce it, represent the time the manager is spending in the shadow system.

This view of staff moving in and out of the shadow system several times a day most probably represents the majority of the activity in the shadow system. If we use the metaphor (after all, we are involved in externalisation!) of large and small business, it is reported that over 60% of business in Australia is conducted within the small business stream. Similarly, it is likely that over 60% of the activity in the shadow system is conducted by the staffs' frequent daily visits. The more overt examples given in 'a closer look' most probably represent only 30% to 40% of the activities in the shadow system. For the CEO, managing the special projects in the shadow system is relatively straightforward. However, supporting the frequent visits of staff to the shadow system requires discrimination, and subtlety; discrimination in that the intention of some staff (albeit a minority) may not be the welfare of the organisation; and subtlety, in that heavy-handed support of the well-intentioned can in fact kill off the creative endeavour.

The processes of extraordinary management can be examined by discussing the three roles of the shadow system and the role of the manager in the shadow system.

The first role of the shadow system

The primary responsibility of the shadow system is to identify new knowledge for the organisation. There are two basic sources for this new organisational knowledge. One option is to *import the new knowledge* from another system (for example, from another organisation or from some new research finding by a university or professional body). In this case the knowledge may not be new to the world at large but it is 'new' to the organisation. The second option is for the organisation to *create the new knowledge* through the processes of externalisation, combination, internalisation and socialisation.

While the literature in the area of managing the shadow system is in its infancy and still growing, there is considerable agreement that the shadow system cannot be managed by the mechanistic processes of ordinary management. Rather, the shadow system is managed by establishing a value system that reveres and celebrates learning. Wheatley (1994) suggests that leaders need to harness the **invisible forces** that can be used by the organisation for direction and self-renewal. The main invisible force to be harnessed to manage the shadow system, then, is a culture and value system that cherishes and honours learning. If such a culture and value system is endemic throughout the organisation, then opportunities to discover new knowledge, and efforts to disseminate the new knowledge, are encouraged and rewarded. As discussed earlier, knowledge creation depends on the everyday efforts of the many rather than the plans of a few (Andrews 1999). Individual staff members need to know that they will be encouraged to create new knowledge and pursue such opportunities. The supervisory and management team need to know that they have to encourage such pursuits so the 'many' do visit the shadow system for short periods every day.

An organisational culture that reveres and honours learning will exhibit the following characteristics:

- Accepting **failure** as a natural process in learning. The actors in the shadow system need to know that failure is not a dire consequence but an opportunity to examine information as a feedback process and to reflect on different options.
- Using *positive feedback* which has an amplifying effect which escalates small changes (Stacey 1996). For the legitimate system with its high needs for control, the thought of positive feedback generates high levels of anxiety. Indeed, there is some basis for this fear. After all, continuous positive feedback will push the organisation into anarchy. However, without positive feedback creativity is lost and creativity is the name of the game in the shadow system.
- Recognising the importance of **loose links**, sometimes referred to as weak ties (Granovetter 1973). The impetus for most new knowledge comes, not from familiar networks, but from unusual sources. So, for example, significant new insight into customer needs comes not from current customers but from that part of the population who have nothing to do with the organisation. Therefore, the actors in the shadow system need to interact with sources that are not frequented by the organisation — for example, attending a conference that has nothing to do with the organisation's usual activities.
- Acknowledging the powerful bonds of the **six degrees of separation** (Paulos 1990). It can be shown that any person can be linked to any other person in the world within six steps. This has powerful consequences for the shadow system in locating new information and in communicating new information to the legitimate system in the organisation. In searching for new information, the actors in the shadow system must move beyond the first contact to discover the other contacts in the link of the six degrees of separation. In communicating the new information, the shadow system must recognise and encourage the ongoing effects of the six degrees of separation.
- Using the **theory-in-use model II** (Argyris 1992) where any interaction is based on valid information, the participants have free and informed choice and the participants keep testing the validity of the choices, especially as the choices are being implemented.
- Accepting that the shadow system is the realm of *double-loop learning* (Argyris 1992). The actors in the shadow system must be always questioning the underlying values of current decisions, activities and even the culture of the legitimate system.

Based on these activities, the predominant knowledge creation approaches used by the shadow system are the externalisation, internalisation and socialisation processes. Of course, as the actors in the shadow system interact with others, both within and outside of the organisation, they also use the combination process to interact. However, the other three processes are certainly the prime generators. In the shadow system there is a continuing thirst for new knowledge and the actors will use a variety of techniques from the four stages of HRD to continue the learning process. Interviewing, focus groups, action learning, discussions, designing and experimenting with learning strategies follow each other in a continuous blur. So, with positive feedback, double-loop learning and the four processes of knowledge creation, the shadow system is an exciting, creative, scary and exhausting place to operate. Simply because of this intensity, most staff have to return to the legitimate system, firstly for a period of recovery. However, a second benefit of this return is that the staff can reflect on their shadow system activities and review them in the rigorous reality of the legitimate system.

The second role of the shadow system

As well as creating new knowledge, the shadow system is continually challenging the fundamental values of the legitimate system. The fundamental values of the legitimate system are encapsulated in the strategic mission statement of the organisation (see chapter 4) and the organisational culture (see chapter 10). These fundamental values allow the legitimate system to make decisions efficiently and often automatically.

However, these fundamental values may be effective only in the present time. There is no guarantee that they will continue to serve the organisation successfully in the future. The role of the shadow system, therefore, is to continually test and challenge these fundamental values. Whereas the legitimate system attempts to maintain the values through single-loop learning, the shadow system uses double-loop learning to challenge the fundamental values.

This challenging process, of course, can be seen by the legitimate system as threatening and this perception gives rise to organisational defence mechanisms and **theory-in-use model I** actions (see chapter 2). A frequent ploy of the legitimate system is to create a committee to review the 'new idea' (or 'threat', as the legitimate system may view the innovation). The problem with committees, as far as the shadow system is concerned, is taht they are predicated on negative feedback loops — and this negative process has a distinct dampening effect. So, a significant challenge for a manager is to allow the legitimate system to use its auditing responsibilities without having that process become too defensive.

The third role of the shadow system

Strongly connected to its challenging responsibility, the shadow system has another, frequently overlooked role. It is of little use identifying a wonderful, new idea if it will not be accepted by the legitimate system. So, once a new idea has been identified and defined, the shadow system must then bend its energies to formulating a package that will ease the journey of the new idea into the legitimate system. Frequently, this package will be based on the unstructured learning strategies discussed in chapter 12 as these strategies are ideal for developing the deeper levels of the HLO (see chapter 9) — and it is these deeper competencies that are needed for the introduction of new and even challenging ideas.

The role of the manager

How, then, can this shadow system be managed? Not surprisingly, and unlike the case of the legitimate system, there is no simple, linear-logic answer to this question. However, various authors have suggested several insights. Stacey (1996) includes the following:

- *shadow networks* are self-organising groups who have similar experiences, interests and expectations. They often form to offset the alienating and deskilling consequences of the legitimate system. These are informal groups that may be long lasting or short lived. They explore opportunities on how to deal with the conflicting, the ambiguous, the frustrating and the alienating. Such shadow networks form naturally but are usually ignored by the legitimate system until they are perceived as too disruptive. Unless restrained, the legitimate system will use negative feedback in an attempt to control the perceived irresponsible behaviour. However, many of these shadow networks are potential sources of creative energy and the manager does have the choice of harnessing this energy.
- a **community of practice** is a group of people who carry out similar tasks. People who carry out similar tasks always tend to form natural groups. The typical example given of communities of practice are the various professional bodies, such as the Australian Human Resources Institute. However, informal communities of practice can also be found within any organisation. From the point of view of the shadow system, such bodies are hotbeds of learning as the members recount difficulties experienced and challenges overcome. Providing unobtrusive support for these groups can pay handsome dividends for the organisation.
- the **law of requisite variety** is based on the cybernetic assumption that an organisation must achieve the goal of continuing adaption to its environment if it is to survive and succeed. The external environment will continually deliver a number of changes or shocks and the organisational regulator or adaptor (i.e. the conventional strategic planning process and the shadow system) must deliver at least an equal number of responses. By itself the conventional strategic planning process is too reactive and, as discussed under 'the creation of knowledge', the organisation needs a stock of pro-active solutions from the shadow system.

Peter Senge's (1990) highly innovative and original work has also provided some insights into the way the shadow system can be managed. He suggests that managers need new disciplines, including:

- *building shared visions*, which is made up of four skills. The majority of staff do personally care about the organisation, so the leader needs to encourage the personal visions of staff about the organisation and build these personal visions into a composite whole. Leaders need to continually communicate and seek support for their own vision by asking 'Is this vision worthy of your support?'. 'Visioning' is an ongoing process. While at any one point there will be a particular image of the future, this image will be ever-changing. The shadow system is at the heart of this ongoing challenge. Visions need to be a blend of the extrinsic and the intrinsic. Visions which concentrate only on the external world of the organisation — for example, beating a competitor — can quickly become a defensive posture rather than the pro-active stance that is needed. Visions should also have an intrinsic component — for example creating a new product or a better customer service standard — and defining this component demands higher levels of creativity and innovation. As discussed previously, Wheatley (1994) suggests that these visions become one of the main invisible forces that can be used by the organisation for direction and self-renewal.

- *creating and testing mental models*, which is the whole reason for the existence of the shadow system. This discipline needs high levels of reflection and inquiry skills to avoid invoking defensive routines (see chapter 2). Because our minds move so fast, we often move too quickly from some observable data to generalisations without testing the underlying fundamentals or searching for other possible explanations. The leader needs to challenge these leaps of abstraction. Leaders need to balance advocacy (persuasively presenting their own views) with inquiry (having the underlying assumptions of their own and others' views examined). As discussed in chapter 2, leaders need to differentiate between espoused theory and theory-in-action so that underlying values can be examined clearly. Of course, while this is occurring the leader will have to recognise and defuse any defensive routines.

- *systems thinking*, which includes five skills. By seeing interrelationships, not snapshots of events, the leader will not focus on static images and linear explanations but rather will concentrate on the dynamic complexity of the event. One of the hallmarks of the shadow system, and thus the learning organisation, is the ability to move beyond blame. Mistakes are seen as what they really are — merely learning experiences. A good leader should be able to distinguish between detailed complexity and dynamic complexity. Detailed complexity occurs when a number of variables have to be considered. Dynamic complexity occurs when cause and effect are distant in time and space and when consequences are subtle and not always obvious. By focusing on areas of high leverage, the leader can use small, well-focused actions to produce significant, enduring improvements. Finally, the leader must focus on causes, not symptoms, to ensure long term benefits. Overcoming symptoms is temporary and merely guarantees that the leader will have to intervene at an ever-escalating rate.

Control — to be or not to be?

Managing the shadow system is not an easy process. The natural inclination, to increase controls when faced with an unpredictable climate, is overwhelming but must be avoided. Direct control, with its emphasis on negative feedback, is the very antithesis of the management skills needed in the shadow system.

Of course, allowing open slather is also an invitation to disaster. The manager, then, needs to use more indirect controls. For the special cases and projects there are several options available — carefully selecting staff who will be given significant resources to operate in the shadow system and providing 'sunset' clauses in any projects, to name two. However, to manage the other, major part of the shadow system — the day-to-day forays of staff into creating new knowledge — is much more subtle and difficult. The only enduring answer is to rely on the 'invisible force' of organisational culture — building a climate that encourages and celebrates the individual victories that occur every day. For this we need to examine how good leaders manage the interaction between the legitimate system and the shadow system.

MANAGING THE INTERACTION

To lead and govern the shadow system, Stacey (1996) suggests that extraordinary management approaches are needed. Therefore, the activities in the shadow system are predicated on positive feedback and double-loop learning. However, this activity is very threatening to the legitimate system. It is this very tension that needs such sensitive, confident yet directive leadership from the manager. On the one hand, it is important that the results of the shadow system are never applied blindly but that such results run the gauntlet of the auditing process of the legitimate system. On the other hand the shadow system must be protected from the predatory defences of the legitimate system so that the shadow system does have the time, energy and creativity to explore the external environment, continually examine the core values of the organisation and test possible alternative options.

Managing the interaction between the legitimate system and the shadow system is about managing the tension between them — keeping the organisation in a state of balanced instability. An appropriate level of balanced instability is achieved by the judicious investing of resources and power in each of the systems. This judgement can come only from experience — experience as a CEO combined with experience within the particular organisation.

Fear of failure is one of the most pernicious threats to maintaining a balanced instability within an organisation. Unfortunately, this fear often means the CEO or manager becomes too conservative and gives too much power to the legitimate system. Just as detrimental is the existence in the legitimate system of theory-in-use model I (see chapter 2). Model I is based on the assumptions of:

- striving to be in unilateral control
- minimising losing and maximising winning
- minimising the expression of negative feelings
- appearing to remain rational throughout the interaction.

When managing the interaction between the legitimate system and the shadow system, the CEO or manager has to actively combat any recession into fear of failure and the use of model I.

Just as dangerous is the CEO or manager who reacts too quickly and violently and leans too far in the direction of change — especially change that has been unplanned. Such over-reaction is usually due to the long-term existence of an insufficiently powerful shadow system. An insufficiently powerful shadow system leads to a paucity of future options — and new ideas in the organisation and future options are the defence that an organisation needs to combat the unexpected vastness of the future.

Managing the interaction between the two systems is also a political feat. Organisational politics occur naturally and can be a positive or negative influence, depending on how the energy is managed. A lot of organisational politics goes back to the fundamentals of adult learning — people defending their frames of reference. One way a manager can influence the positive use of organisational politics is to provide appropriate arenas and expert management of process to ensure that the energy, and the associated generation of ideas, can be brought to the surface. The unstructured learning strategies (chapter 12) provide the means for managing the process and all the manager has to do is select the appropriate forum — and this can be a delicate task guided by the exigencies of the current issue, the organisational climate and the objective to be attained.

Pedler, Burgoyne and Boydell (1997) suggest a very innovative and unusual analysis of an organisation, an analysis which provides a useful and practical approach to managing the learning organisation. Rather than using the traditional hierarchical chart to examine an organisation, they suggest that the energy flows of an organisation should be mapped. These energy flows move around four key activities in the organisation (where energy may be information, resources, consciousness, attention and so on):

1. *Policy*, which is at the organisational level. Policy incorporates all the planning that goes on in the organisation.
2. *Operations*, which is also in at the organisational level. 'Operations' covers the productive capacity of the organisation.
3. *Ideas*, which is at the individual level. Only individuals have ideas and this resource is critical to the ongoing life of the organisation.
4. *Action*, which is also at the individual level. Only individuals can take action and this energy is the basis of any productive effort.

Each of these four key activities interact and depend on each other. The authors suggest that an e-flow (energy flow) analysis can be conducted to identify bottlenecks and gaps in the energy circulation. For example, if the analysis indicates that there is little attention being paid to the policies of the organisation then the CEO needs to allow each of the two basic organisational systems to investigate. The legitimate system is best situated to examine the policy-operations link as this is to do with the day-to-day operations. The shadow system needs to examine the ideas-policy link, as this has to do with knowledge generation.

Senge (1990) provides an overview of the responsibilities of the CEO or manager in bringing together the seemingly disparate efforts of the legitimate system and the shadow system. He suggests that the true leader has three basic roles:

1. As a *designer*, which includes three responsibilities. Firstly, the leader needs to identify the governing ideas — the purpose and core values — of the organisation. Secondly, the leader should foster strategic thinking. Thirdly, the leader needs to create learning processes. These three responsibilities cannot be assembled immediately but can only be instituted over time. However, it is these fundamental assumptions that underpin the design of any organisation and which have the most lasting impact.
2. As a *teacher*, where the leader helps people achieve more accurate, more insightful and more empowering views of reality. This places the leader in the role of a facilitator, rather than as an 'expert', and locates the HR developer as a direct extension of the leader.
3. As a *steward*, which is almost solely a matter of attitude. This stewardship operates on two levels. The first is stewardship of the people in the organisation, which stems from the keen realisation of the impact that one's leadership can have on others. This is particularly so for those actors in the shadow system as they are not protected by the accepted behavioural traditions of the legitimate system. The second is stewardship of the larger purpose that underlies the organisation. This goes beyond the mission statement generated by the conventional strategic planning process (see chapter 4) which may, for example, suggest increasing the organisation's profits by 10%. This has limited motivational value for the average staff member. The leader needs to tap into the fundamental purpose of the organisation's being, its larger purpose — changing the way businesses operate, how the organisation helps society, the personal satisfactions that staff can gain from being associated with the organisation.

RECOGNISING THE TWO SYSTEMS

Recognition of the existence of the two basic systems unlocks a number of insights into the appropriate management of an organisation. Firstly, it explains why traditional management theories do not always work. The traditional management theories are useful only for that part of the organisation that is operating close to certainty — i.e. the legitimate system. Secondly, a well-managed legitimate system is the only component of the organisation that can handle the day-to-day activities and guide the organisation through the immediate future. Thirdly, an all-powerful legitimate system will lead the organisation to a relatively slow but sure death. Fourthly, the shadow system is the only component of the organisation that can handle an external environment that is far from certain. Fifthly, the shadow system is a delicate form but has the potential to be malignant. It is delicate in that, if not appropriately resourced with assets and power, it will not produce the desperately needed future options for the organisation. It is malignant because, when managed inappropriately, it can lead the organisation to disaster. Sixthly, the shadow system is heavily dependent on the creativity and goodwill of the people in it, so it has to be managed with care and subtlety but with an overall sense of control.

THE ROLE OF THE HR DEVELOPER

The human resources literature began to expand in 1990 with a rapidly escalating interest in the concept of the learning organisation. Some of the writings were very intuitive and powerful, while others were more suited to the pop art industry. One of the best definitions of a learning organisation is as follows:

> A Learning Company is an organisation that facilitates the learning of all its members and *consciously* transforms itself *and its context*.

(Pedler, Burgoyne and Boydell 1997, p. 3)

This definition provides the life objective for the HR developer. The HR developer continually explores and implements options that will not only develop the organisation but also its surrounding environment.

If the modern leader is the steward of the organisation, then the HR developer is the steward of the knowledge resource of the organisation. This stewardship comes to the HR developer as a direct delegation of the modern leader's other major role — the teacher. The HR developer accepts and operationalises this stewardship role by:

- creating new knowledge by managing the knowledge-creating processes of externalisation, combination, internalisation and socialisation;
- identifying and importing relevant explicit knowledge from outside the organisation;
- disseminating knowledge throughout the organisation. This dissemination process is most often achieved by the four stages of HRD — needs investigation, design, implementation and evaluation — that have been the main emphasis of this text.

However, assisting the shadow system to inculcate new knowledge into the legitimate system, via the unstructured learning strategies, is a growing responsibility;
- maintaining the knowledge resource through the four stages of HRD;
- recognising the difference between the two basic systems of the organisation — the legitimate and shadow systems — and assisting the managers to manage these two systems.

And the successful implementation of this role is what helps the organisation to become that most robust and viable of entities, the learning organisation.

GLOSSARY

bounded instability — balancing the tensions between the legitimate system and the shadow system so that the organisation remains viable

combination — systematising concepts into a knowledge system by combining old and new explicit knowledge

community of practice — a group of people who carry out similar tasks

double-loop learning — where basic values and beliefs are challenged

explicit knowledge — knowledge held in the conscious mind and can be expressed in words

externalisation — when tacit knowledge is transformed into comprehensible forms using metaphors, analogies and models

extraordinary management — the processes used to manage the shadow system

failure — seen by the legitimate system as a bad outcome but seen by the shadow system as a positive feedback process that enhances learning

four stages of HRD — investigation, design, implementation and evaluation

internalisation — converting explicit knowledge into tacit knowledge by using 'whole body experiences' and reflection

invisible forces — mainly used in the shadow system, one of the most prevalent is a culture that embraces learning

law of requisite variety — the organisation must provide responses which number more than, or at least equal to, the number of changes delivered by the environment

legitimate system — one of the two basic systems that comprise an organisation, governs the day-to-day activities of the organisation (see shadow system)

loose links — having connections with unusual sources so that new knowledge can be created

negative feedback — has a dampening effect and is used in the legitimate system to bring aberrant behaviour back to a prescribed norm

ordinary management — the processes used to manage the legitimate system

positive feedback — has an amplifying effect and is used by the shadow system to escalate small changes

shadow networks — self-organising groups who have similar experiences, interests and expectations

shadow system — one of the two basic systems that comprise an organisation, searches the external environment for new knowledge and also creates new knowledge (see legitimate system)

single-loop learning — learning that does not challenge values and beliefs

six degrees of separation — everyone is separated from everyone else by a maximum of six human contacts socialisation — sharing tacit knowledge directly

tacit knowledge — knowledge that is highly personal, held in the subconscious and hard to formalise

theory-in-use model I — where interaction is based on striving to be in unilateral control; minimising losing and maximising winning; minimising the expression of negative feelings; and appearing to remain rational throughout the interaction

theory-in-use model II — where interaction is based on valid information, free and informed choice and participants keep testing the validity of choices

QUESTIONS

For review

1. Differentiate between explicit knowledge and tacit knowledge.
2. Describe the three important facets to the maintenance of knowledge.
3. Describe how the four stages of HRD help an organisation to maintain its knowledge capital.
4. Discuss the three roles of the shadow system.
5. Describe the activities a manager should encourage in the shadow system.
6. Discuss the three basic roles a manager should undertake when managing the interactions between the legitimate system and the shadow system.
7. Discuss the role of the HR developer in the organisation for the new millennium.

For analysis

8. Compare and contrast the knowledge-creation processes of externalisation and internalisation.
9. Explain how the learning strategies discussed in chapters 11 and 12 can be used in the four knowledge-creating processes.
10. How does extraordinary management differ from ordinary management?

For application

11. Examine *Gas Blast Esso's Fault* in a closer look 1.1 (see pages 4 and 5). As a HR developer, what suggestion would you now make to the management of Esso so that they can improve their operations?

REFERENCES

Andrews, K. (1999). *Knowing, Learning and Unlearning in a Knowledge Creating Company: An Inductive, Theory-building Case Study*. Unpublished doctoral thesis, Centre for Professional Practice in Education and Training, Queensland University of Technology, Brisbane.

Andrews, K. and Delahaye, B. L. (1998). *Tacit Knowledge and Psychosocial Filters: The Knowledge Creation Process in Australia*. The Knowledge Creation Management in Asia Conference, Singapore, March 6–7.

Argyris, C. (1992). *On Organizational Learning*. Cambridge, Mass.: Blackwell.

Granovetter, M. S. (1973). 'The strength of weak ties.' *American Journal of Sociology*, 78, 1360–1380.

Nonaka, I. (1991). 'The knowledge creating company.' *Harvard Business Review*, November–December, 96–104.

Nonaka, I. and Konno, N. (1998). 'The concept of 'Ba': Building a foundation for knowledge creation.' *California Management Review*, 40(3), Spring, 1–15.

Nonaka, I. and Takeuchi, H. (1995). *The Knowledge Creating Company: How Japanese Companies Create the Dynamics of Innovation*. New York: Oxford.

Nonaka, I., Takeuchi, H. and Umemoto, K. (1996). 'A theory of organisational knowledge creation.' *International Journal of Technology Management*, 11(7/8), 833–845.

Paulos, J. A. (1990). *Innumeracy: Mathematical Illiteracy and Its Consequence*. Vancouver, WA: Vintage Books.

Pedler, M., Burgoyne, J. and Boydell, T. (1997). *The Learning Company: A Strategy for Sustainable Development*. London: McGraw-Hill.

Polanyi, M. (1997). 'The tacit dimension.' In L. Prusak (Ed.), *Knowledge in Organizations*. Boston: Butterworth-Heinemann.

Senge, P. M. (1990). 'The leader's new work: Building learning organizations.' *MIT Sloane Management Review*, Fall, 112–128.

Stacey, R. D. (1996). *Strategic Management and Organisational Dynamics*. London: Pitman.

Sveiby, K. E. (1997). *The New Organizational Wealth: Managing and Measuring Knowledge-Based Assets*. San Francisco: Berrett-Koehler.

Wheatley, M. J. (1994). *Leadership and the New Science: Learning about Organization from an Orderly Universe*. San Francisco: Berrett-Koehler.

INDEX